# The Moon Princess
*Memories of the Shan States*

# The Moon Princess
## *Memories of the Shan States*

*Sao Sanda*

RIVER

BOOKS

This book is dedicated to my husband Peter Simms in loving memory.

First published and distributed in Thailand in 2008 by
River Books Co., Ltd
396/1 Maharaj Road, Tatien, Bangkok 10200
Tel: (66) 2 225-4963, 2 225-0139, 2 622-1900
Fax: (66) 2 225-3861
Email: riverps@ksc.th.com
www.riverbooksbk.com

Editor: Narisa Chakrabongse
Design: Narisa Chakrabongse and Reutairat Nanta
Production: Paisarn Piammattawat

ISBN 978-974-9863-37-4

Cover: *The author in Shan traditional dress, taken in London, November, 1947*
    *to commemorate the royal wedding of Princess Elizabeth and Prince Phillip.*
Frontispiece: *The author in ceremonial dress, ear-boring ceremony, standing looking disgruntled.*
Back cover: *Saohpa of Kengtung, Sao Kwang Tai and family, c. 1930s, Sao Sai Long*
    *his young son standing behind him later became the Saohpa.*

Printed and bound in Thailand by Bangkok Printing Company Limited

# Contents

# *Preface*

My original plan was to write an biography of my father, but without the necessary papers and records for research it was not possible. I have written instead a personal account of my family and my life. It is neither a political nor a scholarly book. However, in order to put things into perspective and to understand the present complicated political situation, I have gone back several decades to try to illustrate how and why there is such a wide gap between the thinking of the Shan and the Burman.

My father and other princely rulers were cautious, loyal and law-abiding, never doubting British assurances of their protection. Unlike the Burman, the Shan and other ethnic leaders had no major grievances against the British, considering their rule benign. Therefore, when Independence came they put their trust in the Union, being prepared to see the Burmans as brothers with whom they could live on equal terms, working together towards peace and progress.

The Burmans, on the other hand, did not want to be slaves under the British and were bitter at the loss of their monarchy. They wanted to rid themselves of colonial rule and by any means to become supreme rulers themselves. One cannot blame them for having such an attitude. However, the Shans had joined them to gain freedom from the British and once independent did not wish to have a new master lording it over them.

Such being the case, the scenario of a happy family of federated states within the Union did not materialize after Independence in 1948. Then from 1962 onwards under a military regime, the situation has only worsened.

I hope my book will explain why for the last four decades the Shans have been struggling for equal opportunities and responsibilities within the country's government as their constitutional right. The ruling military regime, however, have been unwilling so far to accept such requests, deeming any opposing views as unconstitutional.

The problems are complex, as recent events involving the Sangha have shown and careful contemplation will be necessary if they are to be solved in earnest and in sincerity. Although there seems to be no viable answer, continuous dialogue is the only way.

Dr Susan Conway's book, *The Shan* has reminded people of the existence of the Shan, their art, culture and customs. Her conscientious work has given the Shans a boost to their morale and a pride in their heritage.

I have many people to thank including my family and friends, for making this book possible. Of those who extended help, I would like to mention especially John Okell and Martin Smith, who kindly read my first draft and gave me invaluable suggestions and advice. Martin's periodic contacts, provided me with much needed encouragement as I continued writing.

To David Greenway, Sumet Jumsai, Charles Letts, and Martin Morland my gratitude in providing without hesitation names and addresses of those in the publishing world they knew, who might have share similar interests to me and would be willing to publish my book.

I would like to express my gratitude to family and friends who have not all been acknowledged individually for obvious reasons, or who have allowed their treasured photographs to be used in the book. Special mention though must go to Dale and Nadine Flinders, David and JB Greenway, Joan Plaisted and Bill Sharpe who generously sent me photographs of Yawnghwe taken on their visits. Happily some of these appear in the book and only they will know which of the photographs are theirs.

I owe a great deal to those who made suggestions and criticisms, but the views and opinions expressed in the book are my own, and, ultimately, I alone must be responsible for any affront caused and errors that occur in the text. The transliteration of Shan names is difficult and frequently inconsistent. In this book, I have endeavoured to use the most commonly found version for proper names of Shan rulers and their States.

It has been my good fortune in finding Mom Rajawongse Narisa Chakrabongse, my sympathetic and understanding publisher. Her enthusiasm and interest in the culture and history of the Tai peoples has been of great advantage in making this book feasible. To her, I owe my utmost thanks and indebtedness.

Finally, I am deeply appreciative of all the help provided by Khun Paisarn Piammattawat, Chris Shelley and others of River Books, both in Bangkok and London.

Sao Sanda Simms
Isle of Wight
2007

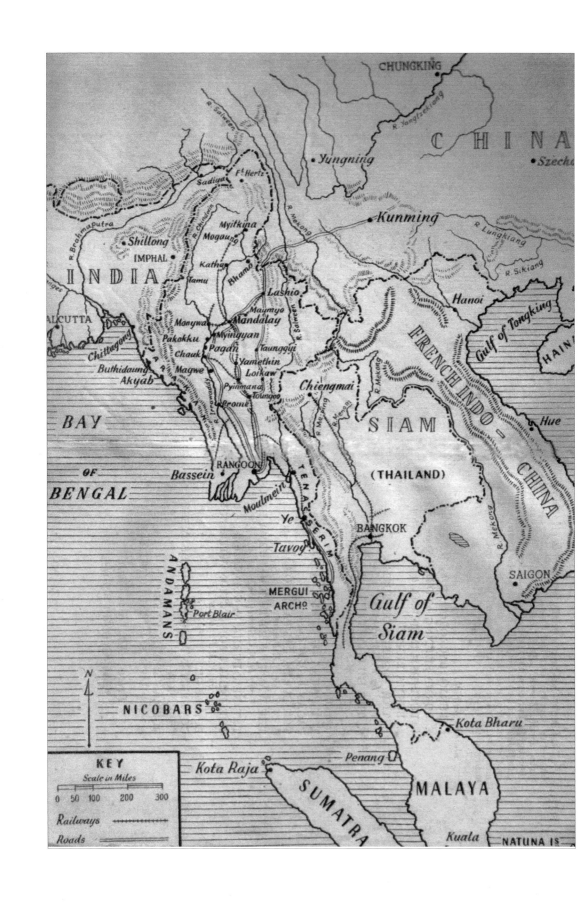

# I

## *From Early Times*

### *Beginnings*

"It's a royal daughter, my lord," reported the *hsala* gravely. My father gave a sigh of relief. It was the eighth day of the new moon in the eighth month of the lunar calendar, the year was 1290 of the Buddhist Era, but most important of all, it was a Saturday. It was the day attributed to the *naga*, a mythical half-serpent and half-dragon. To be born under the sign of the *naga* was not always considered good. For like the great creature one was liable to have a fiery temper, be swift and treacherous in action.

Although my father had hoped for a son he was relieved as a Saturday-born daughter was more controllable and for him, would be less of a nuisance.

The old *hsala*, who was the Court medicine man, thought otherwise. A slight, bony man with a serious countenance, who hardly smiled, he not only cured all our ailments with his powdered herbs, bits of bark and strong potions, some sweet and some bitter, but also read the stars. The twinkling stars and constellations were like an open book to him, as he noted their various positions with care. He would interpret any changes and tell us what lay ahead for each of us. It was astrology, in its simplest form. Horoscopes were written on palm leaves and from what he read in the stars he could foretell what the future held.

To him, a Saturday-born was still a Saturday-born, whether a boy or a girl. He had, of course, seen many born under the sign of the *naga*. For them he could never predict goodness. It was also a general belief held by most of our people that a Saturday-born was to be watched, and to ward off evil many meritorious deeds had to be performed.

On the evening of that day, a distant headman from one of the villages on the Inle Lake came and presented my father with a rare lotus. From a single stem blossomed five snow white lotuses

The *hsala* was called in, and his usually stern countenance broke into a smile. He at once pronounced it a good omen, and said it would bring my father good fortune and greatness.

It was a gift from the *phii*, the guardian spirit no less, the *hsala* announced. My unfortunate birth on this day of the *naga* was thereby transformed into an auspicious event and I had been redeemed. It appeared that having a Saturday-born daughter was not going to be so unfortunate as it was first thought. The *hsala* was satisfied. All was now well, and one need no longer worry. Heads nodded all round, yes, the lotuses would bring good fortune.

*Map of Southeast Asia.*
*(Longman's Burma Pamphlets 1944)*

My father Sao U Hpa had become the ruling prince, or Saohpa of Yawnghwe, a year before I was born. So these new predictions were for some future good fortune. His official title Saohpa in Shan or Tai, means the Lord of the Sky. Yawnghwe is one of the Shan States which is a part of Burma. I grew up in Yawnghwe and lived in the *haw* or palace, until 1947. To understand who I am, who my father was, where Yawnghwe lies, and who the Shan are, we must first look at a little history. Gradually, the story will unfold of how our family, having lived in Yawnghwe and the Shan States for most of our lives, came finally to be living in exile, in different parts of the world.

After the military coup in 1962, I felt an urgency to record my father's life, my childhood and how we had all lived happily together. With my husband Peter's encouragement, I started writing an earlier version of this book, in which I wanted to express my bitterness and anger at the uncivil manner in which General Ne Win and the army had treated my father.

I felt I had a duty to document the disrespect that had been shown to a principled man who was no longer alive to defend himself, as they continued to besmirch my father's name and what he had stood for – unity and equality through federalism.

At first it was to have been a biography of my father, but that was not feasible, as all the necessary papers were in Yawnghwe or Taunggyi in the hands of the military regime, and they were impossible to get hold of. I decided I would have to be content with recounting our personal family life.

However, that book remained unfinished as my husband and I were once more on the move. During the intervening years there was never enough time to continue on the book, whilst I was working and co-writing with Peter on our other projects.

When Peter passed away in 2002 I was left with an emptiness of mind and spirit. It seemed I would never be able to go on with the things we had planned to do together, least of all to continue with our writing. As months passed, while gradually going through our papers, I once again found my unfinished book. I knew then that this would be a way to keep busy and to pull together the pieces of my shattered life. Thus, I begun revising and rewriting, reassembling the fragments of our lives.

The book ends in 1962, a date which was a turning point for our family and the Shan States. But one cannot help observing or hearing what life is like in today's Burma and it is difficult not to comment. Accordingly, I have added a paragraph here and there concerning the conditions to be found in the two level society that exists in Burma today. Nevertheless the main focus remains an account of how our family was caught up in political events which swept through their lives to culminate in death and disaster.

Much has already been written by people who hold different views and opinions on the events of the coup and the years that have followed. I feel I do not need to add to them. Neither do I have the heart nor do I feel it appropriate for me to delve back into the last forty or more heart-rending years. Peter and I were no longer living in the country and did not experience with our family, the sadness and fearful days that they encountered.

I hope, however, that my siblings will continue the story of our family. Each will have a narrative of their own on how they grew up and what they experienced during the period from November 1947 to 1957 when I was away from the family. They will also be better qualified to record the events of the post-coup years through which they lived until they were forced to leave the country of their birth. Those members of our family who stayed on, despite the hardships, I am afraid will never have a chance to voice their experiences.

One brother, Tzang[1] has done so. His book relates why he felt it was necessary for him to go underground to fight for the rights of the Shan against the military regime. About a year or so later after the coup, Sao Mye, the Mahadevi with her children Ying and Leun, and Harn, managed to escape from the claustrophobic and oppressive atmosphere in Burma. Living in Thailand, in 1964, she became head of the Shan State Army. Much, however, still needs to be told and it is for the other brothers and sisters to fill in the missing gaps.

A few years ago a friend said that I had taken things philosophically. He had expected me to be bitter and resentful after all that had happened to us personally and to the country. What he said was true. It did not seem right to be bitter or angry, since holding such sentiments could not lessen our suffering nor our unhappiness. It did not mean however that we did not feel our lives had been shattered.

At that point in 1962, the mere fact that we were Shan and were children of Sao U Hpa had some unfortunate consequences. It was not only Peter and I who had to leave, but also Sai Hseng who lost his job at ICI because of such prejudice. Other members of the family gradually became unwelcome in the progressively Burman society and had to leave. It was not easy for any of us to adapt to strange surroundings and start new lives, but it had to be done. Unless one has gone through such experiences, one cannot imagine the anguish and pain each of us felt or feel still. Today our family live in different corners of the world which gives us little opportunity for us all to be together. We can only hope that given time things will change, and hope that the change will be for the better.

## Mong Tai

Our family history stretches back over six hundred years. How our forefathers lived and what they did were revealed largely through orally transmitted accounts from generation to generation. It would seem that our ancestors lived very much in a world of their own, contained within themselves.

Later from our annals and history books I was to learn that we, the Tai people, had come from Nanchao, an ancient kingdom in China.

The Shan States is a remote corner of what used to be part of the British Empire in Southeast Asia. We Tai call it Mong Tai. It was little known to the West before the Second World War except to the British administrators who governed us and the missionaries of various denominations, who wanted to convert us to Christianity. One could say that in those distant days, there was no reason for anyone to know anything about the Shan States nor the people who lived there.

During the time of British colonial rule, our country was called the Shan States by the administrators. It covered an area greater than England and Wales[2], and

**UNION OF BURMA**
POLITICAL DIVISIONS

0          MILES          150

Demorcation
not agreed

INDIA

Singkaling Hkamti

KACHIN STATE

MYITKYINA

CHINA

Chindwin R.

Katha

7

Bhamo

Mawlaik

Namwan Assigned Tract
on perpetual lease from
China

Nam Ting

EAST PAKISTAN

FALAM

Irrawaddy R.

NORTHERN
SHAN STATES

Lashio

Demorcation
not agreed

Shwebo

Mogok

N.E. SPECIAL DISTRICT

Nam Hka

Monywa

SAGAING

MANDALAY

SPECIAL
DIVISION OF
THE CHINS

Myingyary

Pakakku

6

Kyaukse

SHAN    STATE

SOUTHERN
SHAN STATES

Kengtung

INDO
CHINA

Mektilla

Minbu

Yamethin

MAGWE

TAUNGGYI

EASTERN
SHAN STATES

AKYAB

3

5

Thayetmyo

Salween R.

Kyaukpyu

LOI-KAW

Sandoway

Toungoo

KAYAH
STATE

1955, Not yet transferred
by Union Govt to karen
State administration

BAY OF
BENGAL

1

Prome

Papun

KAREN
STATE

Henzada

Tharrawaddy

2

Maubin

Insein

Pegu

Thaton

PA-AN

THAILAND

BASSEIN

RANGOON
Syriam

Myaungmya

MOULMEIN

Pyapon

4

Irrawaddy R.

ANDAMAN    SEA

Coco Is.
(Burma)

Tavoy

BANGKOK

Andaman Is.
(India)

----- International boundary
-·-·- State boundary
- - - Division boundary
......... District boundary

DIVISIONS OF BURMA PROPER
1   Pegu
2   Irrawaddy
3   Arakan
4   Tenasserim
5   Magwe
6   Mandalay
7   Sagaing

Mergui

GULF
OF
SIAM

*Map of Burma, from
Hugh Tinker.
(The Union of Burma,
1957)*

lay on a fertile plateau between Burma to the west, and China, Laos and Thailand on the east. Ever since the late 1960s, the eastern part of this region has become known as the Golden Triangle, where hilltops are ablaze with colourful poppies that are harvested for grade one opium. It was then a much fought over area between the nationalist armies of non-Burman groups and the Burman army. The region, later became infamous with drug barons, warlords and the remnants of the KMT, all fighting each other for the control of the drug trade.

The KMT were the Kuomintang, which was the nationalist army of Chiang Kai-Shek. After the end of the Japanese war in 1945, these remnant groups fleeing from the Mao Communists stayed on in the area, creating quite a problem for the newly independent country from 1948 onwards.

Perhaps some clarification is necessary here to explain who the Shans are. In the past and even now, whenever anything is written about the Shan by westerners, they tend to describe us as being one of the numerous tribes who live in Burma. In fact, historians have recognized that Upper Burma, as we know it today, was under Shan or Tai rule from 1287-1555. The first rulers were known as the Three Shan Princes. They and their descendants ruled for over two hundred and fifty years.

When the kingdom of Pagan was attacked by the Mongols in around 1287, the Shans together with other groups took the opportunity to come down to settle in the fertile lands along the banks of the Irrawaddy and other rivers which ran through the country.

Of the three kingdoms founded by the three Shan brothers, the Ava dynasty was the longest and most distinguished. There were nineteen reigning kings over a period of nearly two hundred years from 1364-1555. They had their own administration and ruled their kingdoms according to their laws. However, before long, with frequent social and commercial contacts between the Burmans of the Pagan kingdom and themselves, the culture and language of their neighbours were soon assimilated by the Shan people. Buddhism, undoubtedly played a major role in cementing these relations.

Before the Burman-Shan encounter, the Burmans had already subdued the Mon, who were in the country before them and had absorbed much of the Mon culture and tradition. In turn, the etiquette and tradition of the Pagan Court, so clearly a mixture of Burman and Mon cultures, were closely copied by the Shan courts. Later, the Shan Court of Ava began to consider these customs, albeit adopted ones, as their very own. Brahmins officiated in the functions of the Shan Courts, together with the *hsala*, the medicine man cum astrologer, choosing propitious days for ceremonies and officiating at them. Some of the regalia and paraphernalia were duplicated in the Shan princely courts and, in administrative matters as well, several procedures were taken from Pagan.

So close were the similarities between the Shan Courts and those of the Burman kings, that in later times it led to some confusion. The two famous Burman kings, Tabinshwehti and Bayinnaung, were from the Toungoo dynasty which reigned from 1486-1752. Their first capital was at Pegu, and later during the Alaungpaya or Konbaung dynasty, the capital was moved to Shwebo.

The first Europeans who came, visited the Court of Toungoo at Pegu, which was situated in what came to be known as Lower Burma. But westerners who came later, began referring to the court of the Burman kings as the Court of Ava, although it was not until 1765 that Ava became the capital of the Burman kings.

During that period of Shan rule, there was a great deal of intermingling between the two races through intermarriage, wars and occupations. There were also intrigues and in-fighting at the different Courts which often led to internecine wars. Soon Shan who had become influenced by the Burmans of Upper Burma, were fighting Shan from the south. The latter were allied to the Mon and also to Siamese royalty. There were also wars with the Shan Saohpas from the present-day Shan plateau. Often there were cross-border alliances, so that when one king needed help, another went to his rescue. This usually happened when their kingdoms were in danger of being attacked by superior forces.

In many ways, the constant switching of loyalties must have created instability for the ordinary people, who appear to have been long suffering with little recourse. Many, though, did flee from one kingdom to the next, hoping to find a better life somewhere new. But times were hard for them, when all that the ruling monarch wanted was power and glory. Greed and continual lust for war to achieve control over vast lands and peoples, eventually led to the downfall of the Shan dynasty of Ava.

As the power of the Burman kings grew, so did their influence increase. Over time the three races of Shan, Burman and Mon became more and more intermixed. Much of the Shan and Mon cultures were absorbed, leaving that of the Burman trait dominant.

There was, however, little cultural assimilation and impact on the Shan people who lived in the hills and plateau to the east of them. These Shan had migrated south together with the three brothers, but had opted to remain in the highlands. They remained aloof and considered themselves a race apart, settling themselves into different *mongs*. They also maintained close relations with the other Tai peoples, the Siamese and the Lao. To the former, we were always referred to as the Tai Yai, meaning the Great Tai. Like us, the neighbouring Tais lived in *mongs* ruled by a *Chaopha* or prince.

*Mong* is a Tai or Shan word, which can be translated to mean a kingdom, a principality, or a state. The names of these *mongs* can be confusing since Mong is used as a prefix in some names such as Mong Yai or Mong Nai, but not in others, as for instance with Yawnghwe or Hsenwi. That is why I suppose, the British opted to call the various *mongs*, states, hence the Shan States. On the whole, I have used state instead of *mong*, although *mong* is used for the period before British colonisation.

The Shan who came to live on the Shan plateau were independent and valued their own freedom. As far as the ruling princes were concerned, they were content with their states. Even though some may have been fairly small, none of them wanted to be subject to another larger one. Unlike a Burman king or ruler, they had no real concept of unity, nor did they want to form one large Shan kingdom.

This was unfortunate, for as a united group they could have had a better chance when facing an adversary. Regrettably, there was no one Shan prince militarily astute or strong enough in the fifteenth or seventeenth centuries to take overall charge as had the Laotian warrior king, Fa Ngum, who united the different *mongs* and created the Kingdom of Laos.

The desire of the highland Shan to be left to themselves, did not mean that they were isolated. Wars and intermarriage brought Shan princes and princesses into contact with the Court of Mandalay and other neighbouring courts. Thus began the gradual assimilation of the etiquette and code of behaviour of the royal courts.

The Burman kings had always been eager to be supreme rulers of large territories, and by 1752, there was a loose union of Upper and Lower Burma, within the horse-shoe of the surrounding hills and plateaux. This territory was later to become known as Burma Proper.

Before annexation, of course, there were no pictorial accounts to show us how our ancestors lived, what they looked like or what they wore. It is thanks to the British administrators such as Sir George Scott, Sir Charles Crosthwaite and others, that we have written accounts and photographs of the Shan Saohpas and their people.

Some such as those of my grand-uncle, Sir Sao Mawng (also Maung) and his Mahadevi, show them in their full regalia attired similarly to King Thibaw and his Queen, Supayalat. Such ceremonial attire, with its heavy headdresses and richly ornamented garments, must have weighed a few kilos. Other photographs of Sir Sao Mawng show him in different outfits, one a sumptuous rich, patterned Chinese silk cut in the style of a Mandarin coat, indicating that there was wide contact as well with the Chinese court.

*Sir Sao Mawng, the Saohpalong of Yawnghwe and his Mahadevi. (The Pacification of Burma, Sir Charles Crosthwaite)*

*Sir Sao Mawng, Saohpalong of
Yawnghwe, c. 1920s.*

*Sao Nang Ya, Mahadevi of
Yawnghwe, c. 1920s.*

*Sir Sao Mawng with British officials and wives: Standing L to R:
Miss McCallum, Vernon Donnison, Mr Brown and unknown person
Sitting L to R: Mrs Donnison, Mrs McCallum, Sir Sao Mawng,
Mrs Donnison, elder, and Miss Brown. (Donnison Collction)*

There are also photographs of a Saohpa's high throne with opened white umbrellas above it. His ministers and officials are seen sitting on the floor, facing the aisle down which the prince is expected to walk. In front of each of the men are token offerings. The scene is not unlike that encountered by a British envoy when seeking an audience with King Mindon or Thibaw at the Court of Mandalay. A similar high throne sits in the front Royal Throne Audience Hall of our Yawnghwe Haw.

These photographs faithfully record how our grand uncles and aunts lived a hundred years or more ago. Quite often their mode of dress was influenced by their neighbours. For instance, the Kengtung Saohpas wore the court attire that resembled those of the Siamese and the Laotian courts, whereas Hsipaw and Yawnghwe kept close to the Court of Mandalay. The earlier ruling princes in Mong Tai were autocratic with full powers, administering their *mongs* as they wished. Considered to be great warriors they made war at the slightest provocation. Although untouched by western influences, they had extensive connections with other eastern kingdoms.

Thousands of photographs taken in those early days and even those taken today, invariably show Shan men and women living in simple, wooden and bamboo houses, tilling their land, or herding their buffalos. The men are typically shown wearing the basic Shan costume of baggy trousers, Chinese in origin, modern Mao jackets without a collar, and a turban, sitting on the wooden floor or on the ground on mats of woven bamboo. Some are not so neatly attired, wearing large floppy hats on their heads over turbans as they stand outside their houses on stilts. There are also pictures of the foot soldiers who are not in uniforms, but are tattooed freely over the body, with animals and Shan characters which were spells to protect them from their enemies. They carried long swords and lances, and looked pretty tough.

The women were usually photographed wearing long sarongs or *sin*, and a jacket with fastenings on the right side of the breast. Sometimes, the *sin* was extra long, trailing slightly on the ground. These ceremonial sarongs, worn for weddings and very special occasions, were woven from silk into beautiful patterns, again adapted from the court of Mandalay. The everyday attire in the Shan States has hardly changed through the centuries, men still wear their baggy trousers and the women their *sin*.

Interestingly enough, although fashions in clothes for Shan women continued to be copied from Mandalay, Shan men did not adopt the sarong or *phasoe* worn by Burmans but kept to their baggy trousers. We hardly ever saw Burmans in those early days. It was only during and after the Japanese occupation, when Burmans came up to the Shan States that we became accustomed to seeing men in checked sarongs. Since until then they had only been worn by women, we found it effeminate and bizarre on men.

The numerous photographs taken between 1886 and 1920, capture a time when our ancestors had their first encounters with the British. They had never seen a white face until then, and it probably amused them as much as it amused those who were the writers and the photographers. Each must have wondered about the other, not quite certain what kind of relationships they would have with each other.

Early European travellers considered the Shan tribal and primitive chiefly because they did not inhabit a materialistic world like the West nor did they conform to their idea of sophisticated society. The photos of people in wooden or bamboo huts walking barefoot confirmed their assumptions. The British, however, were soon to realise that despite the simplicity of their lives, the Shan were "... in many ways a civilized people, unwarlike, and given to agriculture and commerce ..." wrote Sir Charles Crosthwaite, Chief Commissioner of Burma in 1912.[3]

When talking about Burma, many people think immediately that it is a country inhabited by one race, the Burman, and thus is a homogeneous whole. Even though there has been an absorption of cultures, as explained earlier, the peoples of the country are not one ethnic group. The other major races who live within the country are the Arakanese, the Chin, the Kachin, the Karen, the Karenni, the Mon, and the Shan. We have seen how the Burman have always lived in the plains and along the valley of the Irrawaddy River, while the Shan together with the other minorities live in surrounding hills and the Shan plateau.

Within these regions there also live numerous groups of people with their own cultures and customs, notably the Intha, Padaung, Palaung, Pa-O, and Wa. Most are subsistence farmers, living in villages or in small groups scattered over their territory.

These ethnic groups in their colourful costumes were, and still are, an ethnologist's delight. Nearly all of them are also to be found across the borders; to the east in Laos and to the southeast in Thailand. The name of each group varies slightly from country to country but their costumes identify them. Thus to name a few that I remember from Laos, there are the Meo, now called Hmong, the Yao, the Akha, the Kwii, the Kha Kaw, Kwen, Lamit and Kamu.

Generally, it is the women who wear brightly woven material, though some like the Pa-O are more subdued. Some groups are identified by their jewellery. In particular, are the Padaung women who wore a number of brass rings around their necks and became known as 'giraffe-necked' women. Bertram Mills showed a few in his circus in London in the Thirties.

The Burmans are classified as Tibeto-Burmans and originally came from eastern Tibet. They form the most populous of all those who live and share the country. Today with increasing intermarriage between the Burman and others, often encouraged by the authorities, they are likely to continue growing in numbers and in cultural dominance.

The Shan people, as mentioned earlier, belong to the Tai race. They are the same peoples as the Lao and Thai, the Dai from Yunnan in China and the Ahom who live in Assam, India. The closeness of the Shan to the Lao and the Thai is not a mere fact of history. Living first in Thailand and then in Laos, I began to notice how similar we were culturally and linguistically. Anyone speaking a basic vocabulary of twenty of thirty words of either of the three languages can travel quite happily in the Tai countries without being lost or hungry. For example, the words for 'to eat, to sleep, water, rice' and other essential words are the same. Although there are slight differences, in very little time I found that I could make myself understood in Laos and in Thailand. People would always say to me, "If you are a Tai then you are my sister. We Tai are all brothers and sisters." The remark was comforting and always made me feel at home.

Of course, we Tai look very much alike with our Mongoloid features of straight black hair, slanting eyes, round faces and light brown skin. Most of the women are slight in stature and not much taller than 5 ft 2 ins. Many Shan men are perhaps taller, with a heavier build. To many westerners, we Orientals tend to look the same. One of the first questions I have been asked throughout my life has been, "Are you Chinese?" Upon answering 'no', I would then be asked again, if I was Japanese? I suppose it is only natural, and non-Orientals are right about our looking Chinese, since they were our ancestors. After all, if one were walking down Piccadilly or Oxford Street in London, it would be difficult for anyone to guess what Asian nationality one might be, least of all to guess that one was a Shan.

Anyway, to find our beginnings, we have to look back to China in the ninth century BC. At that time, the Chinese culture was spreading and by the third century the Chinese had annexed the two southernmost provinces of Kwangsi and Kweichow.[4] The original inhabitants of these two provinces were Tai and cognate to the Chinese. This, however, did not stop the Chinese branding both the Vietnamese and the Tai as barbarians south of the Yangtze River.

There is no doubt that the birthplace of the Tai was in China. Some believe that it was in the region around Kwangtung, near present day Hong Kong, others that the Tai were forced to leave northern China and, moving southwards, settled around Tali Lake, where they formed the largest group in the kingdom of Nanchao, now Yunnan. Although they formed by far the greater part of the population, they do not seem to have been the rulers, since the kings and nobles had names that cannot be related to the Tai language.

In earlier times, the Shan kingdoms of Mong Nai and Kengtung nearest to the Lao and Siamese borders were well known in the Tai world. So were Hsipaw and Yawnghwe that shared their western borders with ancient Burma, and Hsenwi was renowned for making frequent attacks against its neighbours. Despite these battles, there was constant travelling between the Tai families, and borders were not demarcated until after the British had annexed Upper Burma and the French had established a protectorate over Laos.

There have always been many dynastic marriages between ruling Shan Houses and nearly all the princely families are related to each other. In spite of these close ties, there was much fighting between the different ruling princes in the early days, each jealously guarding their kingdoms, but inevitably losing out to the more powerful.

It seems that the Shan kingdoms continued to exist only at the price of constant armed defence against their larger neighbours. In this way, by the time the British arrived many of the states were considerably reduced in size. When the Shan States were annexed under the British Indian Empire, the British decided to let the princes alone and allow them to continue ruling their states. Administratively after the annexation, the Shan States came directly under the general control and supervision of the Governor of Burma, while Burma Proper had its own government. This dual control by the British meant that at no time did the government of Burma Proper rule over the Shan States.

The Shan States that existed in the early days were varied in population and size. There were different levels of rulers and not all were recognised as full

Saohpas. Before annexation, there were forty-three states in the South, and five in the North. After annexation several states were amalgamated. Later by 1959, they were reduced to thirty-four. Kengtung State, bordering Thailand and Laos was the richest and retained much of its land covering an area of 12,000 square miles. According to the 1957 census it had a population of nearly 400,000. The smallest State, Kyon, with an area of twenty-four square miles, only had a population of 2,500 people. But the total population of the Shan States then was well over three million, with Yawnghwe, Hsenwi and Hsipaw being the most populous States.

## *Yawnghwe*

In area Yawnghwe is one of the larger of the Shan states and its position has made it important. It is situated in the central and southern region of the Shan States and stands south-east of the old Burmese capital, Mandalay. One of the main routes leading to Taunggyi and beyond into central Shan States passes through Yawnghwe. Today, the route is a key highway for the military government, with its garrisons in Taunggyi.

Taunggyi, meaning Big Mountain in Burmese, lies fourteen miles to the north-east of Yawnghwe, the capital of Mong Yawnghwe. This well-known hill station has an altitude of 3,000 feet. During the time of the British, it was much liked by the officers of the Frontier Service for its cool, refreshing air. Although it belonged to Yawnghwe, it soon became the administrative centre for the Southern Shan States, and it was here that the British Commissioner had his office. The Residence, an imposing colonial style building was situated at the foothills of the Taunggyi Crag.

It was then a quiet little town with hundreds of cherry trees lining the roads. In the spring, white and purple crocus flowered under these blossom trees and were a beautiful sight, similar as might be seen along the Backs of Cambridge Colleges or on the lawns of St James's Park in London. Sadly, that tranquil town of 50 years ago is no longer recognisable in modern-day Taunggyi.

Very few visitors in modern times will know that Yawnghwe town, the place where they board their fish-tail motor boats to take off for the Inle Lake, was at one time the busy capital of Mong Yawnghwe. An eastern city gate and part of the walls of this ancient capital were still standing when I was young, but I understand that they have now been pulled down. What the tourists will also not have realized, nor noticed, is that to the northeast of the town stands a palace, where once the ruling prince and his family lived.

The *Haw*, our palace, is still standing, though no members of the family live there any more. It has been turned into a museum by the present government and is called the Museum of the Shan Chiefs. Tour groups are now taken round the large rambling palace, with its numerous halls and rooms, in which I grew up and which I loved so much. I am naturally delighted that the authorities are taking such care of this hundred-year old building, since there are not many *haws* left. Some of them were burnt down by the Japanese or bombed during the Japanese occupation. Those that were left standing have variously been turned into museums, or are being run as schools or hotels.

Although I knew that the Inle had become a tourist attraction with motorised boats flashing across the lake, I had not realized the extent to which it had been transformed. That was why I was utterly amazed to learn from Andrew Marshall's book, *The Trouser People*, that though people may know nothing of Yawnghwe's history, in 2002 they did know it as a tourist town where there were hotels, restaurants and peep-shows.[5]

Four years on, a click on the Internet shows that it has truly been discovered, with quite a few hotels advertising themselves as places of beauty and tranquillity, a veritable Shangri-la. Despite the flow of tourists, certain parts of Yawnghwe town still seem relatively quiet. Its rows of wooden houses with corrugated iron roofs stand along dusty roads uncluttered by cars or bicycles, looking pretty much as they did when I was young. I imagine that unless one is connected with the tourist trade, life continues pretty much as before.

According to tradition, the Tai of Yawnghwe had earlier lived in the oldest of the Burmese capitals, Tagaung, near the Irrawaddy River before they moved to the Shan plateau. At some time before 800 CE, an army from China or Tibet captured and totally destroyed the city. Those who survived split into three groups, one of whom migrated to the area around Yawnghwe. The *mong* they founded was called Khambojarattha with boundaries that were much larger than those of Yawnghwe today.

One of my early recollections is going with the family one March to a *poy*, which was the annual festival at the Bawrithat Pagoda. The pagoda still stands today on the road that runs between Yawnghwe and the railway terminal. A special *tawmaw* or pavilion of bamboo, had been built for my father, the family and his ministers to preside over the three-day celebrations. All I can remember is that on all sides the wind swept down from the flat plains, creating miniature whirlpools of dust and loose papers. It rattled the walls so much that I thought the pavilion would come down.

The *poy* was held to celebrate the foundation of the original capital. After the fall of Tagaung and flight to the Shan plateau, the first ruler of Yawnghwe had built his new capital, Kawthambi (Kosambi) on the site where the Bawrithat Pagoda was built.

At a later date, two new capitals were built on the eastern shores of the Inle Lake, because the prince felt that the flat plains made it impossible to put up an effective defence. The first of the new capitals was built near the village of Mongsawk, later to be called Fort Stedman. It was named after Colonel E. Stedman who led the British column that came to the relief of Yawnghwe in 1887. The other was at Thale-U also near Mongsawk. Unfortunately, the sweeping flood waters of the Heho Mawnang plain broke through the hills on the west swamping these last two capitals and completely destroying them. Through the clear waters of the lake, one could still see pillars that people believed were part of the ancient palace at Thale-U. These were treated with great respect and unless it was absolutely necessary, no one would row near the site for fear of disturbing the *phii*, or guardian spirits of the palace.

## Sao Si Hseng Hpa

It is here that the history of our ancestors begin. The annals tell us that in 1359, Sao Si Hseng Hpa built his capital, Yawnghwe, where it stands today. *Yawng* means highland and *Hwe* valley, translated from Shan it becomes, Valley among the Hills.

Legend has it, and it is generally believed, that during the ancient times a *bodhi* tree, golden in colour, grew in the centre of the town and brought prosperity to its inhabitants. The capital was then called Nyaungshwe meaning 'golden bodhi tree' in Burmese. It also has been suggested that perhaps the Burmans could not pronounce Yawnghwe, so that was why they called it Nyaungshwe.

What I find confusing is why the British adopted the name Yawnghwe which was Shan, but not Saohpa, the Shan title for a ruling prince. Translated from the Shan, Saohpa means the Lord of the Sky, or Lord of the Heavens. The Burman kings were wont to refer to the Saohpas as Lords of the Sunset, which was not very complimentary. The author Maurice Collis met a few princes as he travelled around parts of the Shan States and also decided unfortunately, to call them 'the Lords of the Sunset', which did not augur well for their future.

The Burmans preferred to address the Saohpa as *Sawbwa* in their language and the British adopted this usage I suppose because administratively they had a better knowledge of Burmese than of Shan. Therefore, my father was referred to as Sawbwa of Yawnghwe, a title that combined Burmese and Shan. The Burmans, generally used only their Burmese version and called him the Sawbwa of Nyaung-shwe. So I was surprised to read "The Sawbwa of Nyaungshwe" (official British name was Yawnghwe)[6], used by a Burman in writing about my father.

As a child I used to be told stories and legends about our forefathers and the origins behind the festivals which were held annually. However, when I grew up I began to realize that many were not mythical tales at all, but real historical accounts which had been passed on orally from generation to generation.

Over the six hundred years since the time of Sao Si Hseng Hpa, the history of Yawnghwe seems to have been remarkably tranquil, at least compared with most Asian nations. Of the twenty-eight Saohpas before my father, only one dynastic murder was recorded and that was in comparatively recent times. Before that, Yawnghwe's only anomaly was a female ruler, Princess Nang Nung Pe, the wife of Hkun Hom Hpa who was the Saohpa from 1574 to 1608. Her name in Shan literally means the Lady who wore Brocades. One imagines that these rich materials must have come from India and China, showing how much trading there was between these territories in those days.

Their son, Sao Htoi Hkam became ruler and their daughter became *Mahadevi* of the Mong Mit Saohpa. Unfortunately, the son died in 1615 without an heir. Thus Nang Nung Pe became the ruler for about three years. Administrators then took care of the state until Sao Awng Hkam, her grandson, returned from Mong Mit in 1630. He ruled until 1658.

It appears that the extent of the states varied from time to time depending on their neighbours and the state of warfare between them. Much depended too on how the Shan princes were treated by the powerful Alaungpaya or Konbaung dynasty, whose realm lay towards the western plains. When there was internal strife and disarray within the kingdoms of the Konbaung dynasty, which was often, the Shan princes were left alone. Then in their eagerness to conquer other Tai states, the warring kings left Yawnghwe free for a while and gave it time to prosper.

Interestingly enough, when these Burman kings went marching into battle against other Tai neighbours such as Lanna, Lang Xang and Ayutthya, large contingents of men were recruited from the different Shan states. Shans were considered good soldiers and expert in elephant warfare. It was the king or the Saohpa who rode the elephants and led them into battle with their long swords and lances.

During such periods, Mong Yawnghwe was able to extend its territory westward into Burma Proper[7]. The twenty-first Saohpa, Sao Yun who ruled from 1762 to 1818, was able to issue a royal order in 1808 declaring authority over thirty-nine lesser *mongs*, making Yawnghwe one of the largest of the Shan States. Proof of these claims can be found in the Shan families who still lived near Toungoo. It must have been quite a feat to have conquered such a vast area. But, after Sao Yun, successive rulers apparently were unable to control so large a kingdom. They made new treaties and agreements with subordinate states and the territory of Yawnghwe gradually decreased. Today, the state covers only the central area of this large kingdom.

Worthy of note is that one of Pagan Min's queens, was a Yawnghwe princess who through her influence at court, was able to help her half-brother to usurp the Yawnghwe throne in 1852, after the murder of the rightful ruling prince.

At that time, Pagan Min was one of the most blood-thirsty kings in the history of Burma, and his half-brother Mindon fearing for his life, had fled from Mandalay to Shwebo. During that time, Sao Nang Hkin, the widow of the murdered Yawnghwe prince, went to Mindon with her four year old son and asked for his protection.

In February 1853, when Pagan Min was deposed by his Chief Minister, Mindon became king and ruled from 1853 to 1878. The young Yawnghwe prince, Sao Mawng, was adopted by him and was brought up at the Court of Mandalay, while the rest of the brothers and sisters remained in Yawnghwe.

It is from this date onwards that Yawnghwe became more closely linked to the Court of Mandalay. These close associations naturally led to the assimilation of language and customs as it had in earlier times. The Burmese language was used for administrative purposes, and was taught in schools. It was spoken in a Shan dialect as it is today. Often it is a mixture of Shan, Intha and Burmese and being a melange of the three languages, it was not always easy for a Burman to recognise it as his own mother tongue. It must, therefore, have fallen short of the classical language that was spoken at the courts of the Burman kings, and of that spoken now in the modern cities of Rangoon and Mandalay.

Later on at Cambridge, when I tried speaking the little Burmese I knew to one or two of the Burman undergraduates, they could never understand me. Instead, they would laugh at me and say I had an atrocious accent.

Despite the mingling of languages and close contact through the centuries, each culture has assimilated only what it has wanted from the other. Thus, the two races still remain separate with a dividing line between the people of Yawnghwe and Burma Proper. They know that even though they speak Burmese, they are not Burmans, and as Shan, Intha or Pa-O their own language and culture is maintained.

Even before my grand-uncle's close ties with the Mandalay Court, the Burman-

Shan relationship was already in existence as explained earlier. Burman kings of different dynasties and the Shan princes had always maintained mutual respect for each other. In the reign of King Bayinnaung, for example, although he subdued the Shan, and tribute had to be paid, he left the Shan rulers in place recognising that they were different from the people he ruled. Other subsequent kings soon realized, that they could never administer a land of forests, hills and plateaux that was so ideally suited to guerrilla action. Thus even the most bellicose of the Burman kings exercised only a limited control through their own administrators and a scattering of Burmese garrison troops.

The main form of control they did exert was by taking members of the ruling princely families as hostages, and forcing them to live at their courts. Whether they liked it or not, the prettier of the Shan princesses would be taken into the king's household as one of his wives. This was usually welcomed by some of the Saohpas, as it gave them a more favoured position. But there was no mercy given if her father failed to offer the annual gifts, or was foolhardy enough to rebel. The alliance could not save a hapless princess from torture, imprisonment, or even execution, when such an occasion arose.

It so happened, that while Sao Mawng was growing up in Mandalay, the usurper died and his brother, Sao Naw Hpa ruled Yawnghwe. Six years after his accession he became involved in a conspiracy with one of the Mandalay princes, and King Mindon sent a force of a thousand men to subdue the rebels. After a few month's fighting Sao Naw Hpa was defeated, but escaped to Toungoo. He then fled to Rangoon and to Karenni, in the eastern hills. Later, Sao Naw Hpa went on to Siam where he is believed to have died.

In 1864, King Mindon arranged for his adopted son Sao Mawng who was then about sixteen years old to accede as Saohpa of Yawnghwe. Sao Mawng ruled peacefully without any problems for twenty-one years. In 1878, King Mindon who was a devout Buddhist and much respected monarch died. After his death, there was much in-fighting and a palace coup, and he was succeeded by King Thibaw. His sadism and irrational behaviour towards the Shan convinced a group of Saohpas that they could no longer accept him and had to find an alternative. His Queen, Supayalat, was an ambitious and blood-thirsty woman and had had all the members of the royal family killed in fear of competition. She was a strong influence behind the throne and wielded a great deal of power.

Some of the Shan princes decided to rebel and to set up a rival prince to help in dethroning Thibaw. Their choice fell on Prince Limbin, a minor Burmese prince who had taken refuge in Rangoon, which was already in British hands. He had been allowed to live there and was being given a small pension by the British. About 1885, he accepted the Shan offer and moved to Kengtung. Here the so-called Limbin Confederacy, also known as the League of Shan Princes[8], was declared. Other Saohpas were invited to join in the overthrow of Thibaw.

While these schemes and military manoeuvres were being put forward in the Shan States, the British had occupied Mandalay by the end of 1885 and had sent King Thibaw and his Queens into exile to India.

About the same time, Sao Mawng decided to make a trip to Mandalay but had to return in a hurry as his cousin Sao Chit Su had staged a palace coup, with the help of the supporters of the Limbin League. He is reported to have brought back with him the Legya Queen and her son. Flying King Mindon's standard, Sao Mawng thought that after he had settled the Yawnghwe affair, he could muster enough support to fight the British. In the ensuing battle to the east of Yawnghwe, Sao Mawng was wounded in both legs. He, therefore, decided to go to Mandalay and to return when his wounds were healed.

Leaving some soldiers behind, he entrusted the recapture of the *mong* to his half brother, Sao On. Obviously in those days a ruling prince was always accompanied by his fighting men, since it was unsafe travelling any great distance without them. One could easily be attacked by a rival prince who had ideas of taking a slice of one's territory or by robbers and dacoits.

The situation in Yawnghwe did not appear at all good. Sao On was strong enough to defeat the small neighbouring states, who supported the League. He eventually managed to overthrow the usurper Sao Chit Su, who had the full support of the Limbin Confederacy. In doing so, he naturally became the enemy of the Limbin League. Thus, before long, the whole force of the Confederacy banded together against Sao On.

In the meantime, having established his authority as Saohpa of Yawnghwe, he told Sao Mawng quite plainly that there was no need for him to return, as he was ruling satisfactorily and would continue doing so.

Sao On was obviously an astute and shrewd person. Finding himself under extreme pressure from the Confederacy and without enough men to defend Yawnghwe, he declared himself an adherent of the British Government, and sought

*Saohpas with Sir George Scott.*
*(Courtesy of the Oriental and India Office*
*Collection, The British Library, London (163/1/155)*

*Sao On, shaded by gold umbrellas on an elephant.*
*(Burma Handbook, Sir J. G. Scott)*

aid from them in his fight against the superior forces of the Limbin Confederacy.[9] He sent a few messages and one of these is given in Sao Saimong Mangrai's book, *The Shan States and the British Annexation*.

Sao On's messages that he was being threatened by the main army of the Limbin Confederacy had an immediate effect. Although they were short of troops, the British decided they could not afford to allow an acknowledged ally to be overthrown. It was felt there was an urgent need to establish British ascendancy over the Shan States, and a force was therefore quickly assembled under Colonel E. Stedman of the 3rd Gurkha Regiment.

What is not known for certain is whether Sao On was conscious that his cry for help from the British, would serve as an invitation for the British to enter Shan territory and to annex the Shan States earlier than might otherwise have happened. Certainly, once the forces of the British had a foothold in the territory and were seen to be strong and powerful, the princes of the League and other Saohpas submitted without further resistance.

### British Forces to the rescue

Here is an account of how Yawnghwe became involved with the British military and how Mongsawk became Fort Stedman.

It appears that the column started off from Mandalay in December 1886 and met with little armed opposition, but quickly found that all law and order had ceased to exist. To protect themselves against the roving brigands and outlaws, the villagers had destroyed the roads, which were probably only dust roads, wherever possible. They had felled trees or dug ditches across them in an attempt to make them impassable. Although the British did not know it at the time, this was the situation throughout the whole of the Shan States. It was February 1887 when the column finally arrived near Yawnghwe, a distance of about 100 miles as the crow flies. It had taken them almost two whole months to reach there.

Colonel Stedman was in charge of the troops, while a Mr. A. H. Hildebrand, who was at that time Deputy Commissioner of Tharrawaddy, was chosen as leader and was to be responsible for political affairs. His instructions were clear, no offence or trouble was to be caused to the people, and the goodwill of rulers was to be sought. As his deputy he was given Mr J. G. Scott, later Sir George Scott, who had already shown an intimate knowledge of Burma. He and Hildebrand did not get on well together.

By February 10th, the column had reached Bawrithat Pagoda and there they were told that the Yawnghwe Saohpa, Sao On, was coming to make his submission. He is described as arriving on an elephant shaded by five gold umbrellas, with his son following behind on a second elephant with four gold umbrellas, and a photograph shows them approaching the camp. Scott took an instant dislike to the Saohpa and described him as a: "Thick-set short man with a freckled face. Small half-closed bright eyes, but unpleasant looking... about 45. Plumes himself on being the first Sawbwa to accept British suzerainty, but his submission was due to a just conviction that it was his only chance of safety."[10]

Earlier, letters had been sent to various rulers giving them assurances that the British had no intention of interfering in the internal affairs of their States, so long as British supremacy was recognised. The British policy being to reward anyone prepared to offer his submission, they did not look too closely at the legitimacy of any self-declared ruler. In this instance, as Sao On was in possession of Yawnghwe, Hildebrand was happy to recognise him as Saohpa. Back in Mandalay, Sao Mawng was granted a pension as compensation for relinquishing his titles. My grand-uncle appears to have accepted the loss with equanimity.

There were no proper roads then, so elephants were used by the princes to get around, as well as for warfare, with horses widely used for transporting goods. Once roads were built after annexation, the mode of transport became horse and carriage or bullock carts. By the middle of 1887, the British strategy of leaving the ruling princes alone had paid off, and the Superintendent of the Shan States was able to report that the Southern Shan States were at peace.

Reunited with their families, men were at last able to create a life for themselves. They began to have time to cultivate their land instead of having to march off as foot-soldiers for their princes. Traders, too, with their animals, were able to move around their areas with complete confidence.

Under the British administration, the Shan princes also began to learn to live with each other in peace, thereby bringing prosperity to their people. There was no need for them to quarrel so much amongst themselves, seeing that many of the princely families had married amongst themselves and were all related to each other.

By 1888, the major Saohpas had been persuaded to accept the simple form of *sanad* which included the acknowledgement and guidance of a Superintendent. In fact from that time on to 1897, they were left with virtually all their powers, including the collection of revenue. Only in criminal cases involving a European or an American did the Superintendent have charge of the case. In civil cases the Saohpa had jurisdiction even over British people. Yawnghwe and Hsipaw were to be the first of the Saohpas to have British advisers attached to their courts.

Most importantly from the British viewpoint, the pacification of the Shan States created a buffer zone along the west bank of the Mekong River that put a stop to any French plans to advance into the lowlands of Burma. It is interesting to ponder, however, whether if the British had not annexed the country of the Shan for this reason, our political status might have been different? We might then not have been considered a part of Burma and left alone.

Times change and it is difficult to imagine that Yawnghwe at that time had become a focal point for the British in the southern Shan States. Fort Stedman developed into an important headquarters for the army and the civilian officials started to create an administrative centre in nearby Taunggyi, which was then under the control of Yawnghwe.

It is such a great pity that I never had the occasion to visit Fort Stedman again and to savour its importance in those early days. On 19th March 1890, the Indian Viceroy's representative, Sir Charles Crosthwaite, held his first Durbar in the Shan States at Fort Stedman. He noted in his diary that many of the Shan rulers had never met before and that the British administration was creating a united country. Both the Saohpa of Yawnghwe and the Saohpa of Mong Nai each received a decoration and a gold chain of honour from the Viceroy for the services rendered. Towards the end of his rule, the British had lost patience with Sao On, considering him a born intriguer, but despite that they gave him a KSM. He died in 1897.

The KSM was the highest of the Burmese titles of honour created in those early days by the British. It was known as *Kyat thaye zaung shwe Salwe ya Min*. The insignia consisted of a chain of nine gold strands connected by patterned gold discs and was worn over the shoulder like a bandolier. The Governor had the prerogative of conferring the honour on behalf of His Majesty the King. Later the chain was turned into a medal and became known as the King's Service Medal.

Sao Mawng, who had waited for twelve years in the wings until Sao On's death, was at last recognised by the British. Despite his earlier feelings against the British, he did not bear any resentment towards them and ruled Yawnghwe with great skill, bringing prosperity and stability for nearly thirty years. The British were pleased and, recognising his worth, allowed him to maintain the traditional signs of Tai royalty with the right to nine white umbrellas. As well, he received a KSM (1901) and a KCIE, Knight Commander of the Indian Empire (1908). He had a distinguished career both within and outside his State and was granted a nine-gun salute in 1906.

In 1903 and in 1911, he attended two of the Durbars held in Delhi. Then when their Majesties, King George V and Queen Mary visited Burma, he was in attendance in Rangoon with his Mahadevi. One can imagine them in their heavy shimmering ceremonial dress all waiting in line patiently, with the other Saohpas and their consorts, in the uncomfortable heat of Rangoon.

In 1909 when the Burma Legislative Council was formed, Sao Mawng was appointed a member, a position he held until 1922 when the Federation of the Shan States came into being. He then became a member of the Federal Council of Shan Chiefs, which gave them the right to express their ideas on federal affairs,

*A group of Saohpas at the Delhi Durbar 1902.*
*Sitting: Mongpawn, Kengtung, Mong Nai and Yawnghwe.*
*Standing: Karen chiefs, Gantarawadi with Bawlake and Kye-bogyi*
*on either side of him. (Courtesy of the Oriental and India Office Collection,*
*The British Library, London (430/78/73)*

including the budget, and on more general matters of concern to the new Federation. This Federal Council of Saohpas, headed by a British Commissioner as President, worked well, though it was not devoid of problems.

For the first time in history the northern and southern Shan States were joined into a single body. Peace was a new experience for the Saohpas and British administrators had to work hard to maintain unity within the Shan States. At the beginning, it must have been quite a challenge and often exasperating for the colonial officials.

A decade or so later, progress came to the Shan States. There were tarmac roads, with four-wheeled vehicles driving along them. With post and telegraph also established, there was communication throughout the States. In the villages, there were only dust roads, but they were roads. Most people still travelled in bullock carts, on horse back or just walked. As I recall, bicycles had not even been introduced, but it did not bother the villagers. What was important was that they could live a normal life, cultivating their fields and selling their produce at the five-day bazaar, instead of being levied to fight inter-state battles.

Apart from the foreign administrators, missionaries also established themselves in the various states. They undoubtedly helped the rulers and his people understand western ways. Since they were no longer fighting with each other, the princes soon found themselves with riches to build new palaces of brick and mortar, and to acquire motor cars. Their children were now being educated in convents and

*HRH The Prince of Wales visited Mandalay in 1922, when some*
*of the Saohpas were presented. Sitting L to R: Mong Yai, Hsipaw,*
*Yawnghwe, HRH The Prince of Wales, Governor*
*Sir Reginald Craddock, Kengtung, Mongnai and Tawnpeng.*

missionary schools. Many of the princes' sons were recruited into the British
Indian Army or were sent off to England to study. The Hsipaw Saohpa was so
enlightened that by 1917, his eldest son had already graduated from Oxford.

These changes delighted the younger rulers, while the older ones naturally
found it difficult to adapt to the modern world of the twentieth century and preferred to observe from the sidelines. Those princes who were genuinely interested
in the people they ruled, began to work with the colonial officials. Each state had
its own problems and much depended on the Saohpa himself and the British
Superintendent or Administrator, as to how these were solved. I assume, that a
great deal rested on how willing a Saohpa was to listen to the adviser, who was
there to give him guidance; and for the administrator, whether he had a genuine
interest in the prince and his people.

It must have been very difficult for some of the young and inexperienced
administrators to be faced with such great responsibilities. Typically for Imperial
British officials, many took these problems in their stride. Some of them managed
to make friends with the princes and their families, introducing them to a wider
outlook on life.

A major problem was language. Although most Saohpas knew English and
Burmese, only a few spoke either language well. Business had to be carried out
through an interpreter, which I am sure was not always satisfactory. Even when
people speak the same language, misunderstandings arise, so how much more
difficult it must be when there is no common language between the two.

Since the British administration had a longer experience with Burmans,
Burmese became a common language used administratively to communicate with
the Shans and other ethnic nationalities. Unfortunately, very few colonial officials
made attempts to learn the languages of other ethnic peoples and those who
wanted to had to do so in their own time and at their own cost.

It was a great pity that more emphasis was not laid on the teaching of the mother tongue, such as the Shan language in the Shan States, and Kachin, Chin and Karen in their own states. Though local schools were allowed to teach the mother tongue in the lower grades, it was discontinued when the country became independent. Had an interest been taken in our languages and cultures, it may have simplified matters for both educational and administrative purposes: thus providing a better relationship all around, not only between the British administrators and the Saohpas, but with other ethnic leaders. It would also have helped in the preservation of ethnic languages and literature, encouraging literacy and the publication of newspapers and books.

Some educated Shans realising that the educational system was inadequate, began to form Shan Literary Societies in order to preserve and strengthen Shan literature and language. In addition, they felt it their duty to encourage the young to be conscious of their own culture and heritage.

Later, with Independence, Burmese became the official language in the administration and in Parliament and English was dropped. Although it may have been a good concept to have a common language, it was eventually to be used as a tool for Burmanization.

Having to use Burmese officially meant that all non-Burmans had to learn the language to communicate with the Central and State governments. It was a significant step which affected the lives of all residents who did not have Burmese as their mother tongue. Unless one was proficient in the language one could not advance. Numerous British, Eurasians, Indians and Chinese with only a smattering of the language had to leave since they could not longer earn their livelihood. Similarly, Burmans who were western educated found it extremely hard to adjust in the newly independent Burma. For many, it became a nightmare.

Yet Burmese had to be learnt and I wonder what the Burmans thought of Shan and other ethnic politicians, when they had to give speeches or present Bills in Parliament. Were they able to make themselves understood?

*Shan State Council of March 1934 of Saohpas from both*
*Northern and Southern Shan States. (From left-right)*
*My father, fifth from the left in the second row,*
*sits between the Kengtung and Lawksawk Saohpas.*

# III

## *1896-1930s*

### *Lord of the Sky*

My father was the apex of our society and we were taught to respect and obey him. Indeed, our lives revolved around him and the Court of Yawnghwe. My father was Sao Shwe Thaike, the Saohpa of Yawnghwe. He was born in 1896, eight years after the British annexation of Upper Burma and the Shan States. He was a nephew of Sir Sao Mawng, the former Saohpa and no one could have foreseen at his birth, that he would one day become the Saohpa Long of Yawnghwe. In Shan, *long* means great. So his title was the Great Lord of the Sky.

My father was a typical Shan of medium height at about 5 ft 6 in, with fair skin and a rather round face that seemed to project a feeling of being completely at peace with himself. He had a certain presence which made people respect him. He was the sixth child in a family of nine. His father, Sao Chon, was a younger brother of the then Saohpa, and held the post of *Myosa*, or governor, of one of the administrative divisions of Yawnghwe State. Indein division which he administered was composed of two hundred villages on and around the Inle Lake. One of the major villages of the Inle, Indein was well known for its large complex of ancient pagodas. It was here that my father spent his early childhood.

When he was old enough he went to the Shan Chiefs School at Taunggyi which was especially designed by the British as a training ground for young boys who were expected one day to become either a Saohpa or a minister of state. The school was run rigorously on the lines of an English public school, with an English headmaster and Anglo-Indian teachers.

When the First World War broke out, my father who was then about eighteen was recruited into the British Indian Army. One of the over eight million men enlisted from the British Empire for the Asiatic and Egyptian theatres during 1914-1918, he was sent to Mesopotamia to fight the Turks. He was later promoted to Subedar. Before the Second World War, colonial subjects were not permitted to hold the King's Commission but instead the Viceroy's Commission in the Indian Army. There were three ranks for the VCOs (Viceroy Commissioned Officers): Jemadar, Subedar and Subedar Major. The Jemadar was the equivalent of a lieutenant, a Subedar a captain and the senior Subedar-Major, almost the equal of the colonel.

I am not sure how many people still know where ancient Mesopotamia was. The 'Land between the Rivers' as it was known locally, was an area that lay along

*Sao Shwe Thaike, the Saohpa of Yawnghwe.*
*(Reproduction with permission of the James*
*Green Centre for World Art, Brighton & Hove*
*Museums)*

*Sao Shwe Thaike in uniform, during service in Mesopotamia, 1914-1918.*

the rivers of the Tigrus and Euphrates. During World War I and after in 1918, the region came under British control. Later Mosul, Baghdad and Basra were formed into one political block and it became known as Iraq. It was only in 1932, that modern Iraq, as it is recognized today came into being, and as we all know only too well today, it is hemmed in by many neighbours: Turkey to the north, Iran to the east, Syria and Jordan to the west and Saudi Arabia and Kuwait to the south.

My father rather enjoyed military life and I am sure he would have liked to continue as a soldier, but in 1924 he had to resign his commission and take up state administrative duties. He was given the post of *Myosa*, a title for a lesser ruling prince of the Heho Subdivision of Yawnghwe. There were three grades of Shan rulers recognised by the British administration – *Saohpa*, *Myosa* and *Ngwegunhmu*. *Myosa* is a Burmese word literally meaning Eater of Towns and was widely used by the Court of Mandalay, as in the olden days the *Myosa's* main function was to collect taxes.

It was not unusual in those days for Asian men, in particular kings and princes to be married to several wives. Following the custom of the Mandalay and other neighbouring courts, Sao Mawng married ten wives, though some say he even had twenty. None of them produced any offspring and, as was the accepted custom, he decided to adopt one of his nephews as his heir. His choice fell on one of my father's half-brothers who was eleven years older than he.

Sir Sao Mawng had found a young British officer, Mr. F. S. V. Donnison[11] of the Indian Civil Service (ICS), to be a pleasing and an efficient person. Thus when he became ill, he requested that Mr Donnison became Yawnghwe's administrator to help in governing the state. After Sao Mawng's death in 1926, the British decided that his adopted son did not have the necessary qualities to succeed him, neither were the other princes who contested the throne considered suitable. Accordingly, after much deliberation by the British administration, in October of 1927, my father, who was thirty-one years old, was chosen to become Saohpa of Yawnghwe. By the time I was born he had become the ruler of Mong Yawnghwe. I am his third child, and eldest daughter.

*The Saohpa and Mahadevi of Yawnghwe arriving
for his inauguration 1927. (Donnison Collection)*

Vernon Donnison and his wife Ruth were special and unusual for British officials of that time. They made an effort to gain my parents' confidence and to become friends with them. My mother, with hardly any English at all, seemed to have had a wonderful time *en famille*, as many of the Donnison photographs show. I remember very little of that time. Many years later, Peter and I managed to see them once in Didcot in the 1960s. Since we led a peripatetic life, we sadly didn't meet them again. I was, however, fortunate enough to meet up with David and Annis, their children, some fifty years later.

## Round Table Conference

Since the early 1930s in Burma Proper, there had been unrest and a growing anti-British feeling amongst the Burman politicians and university students. With the rising tide of nationalism the status of Burma as a province of India became an emotional rallying point that united all classes of Burmans against the British. It appeared that there were those who were in support of separation, and others who were against. The latter called themselves the anti-separatists, and took a firm stand. In addition, there were other groups such as the Anglo-Burmans, the Indians and Chinese who had been born and bred in Burma, but who did not

*Sao Shwe Thaike, Yawnghwe Saohpa, at the Round Table Conference 1931.*
*(Courtesy of the Oriental and India Office Collection, The British*
*Library, London (784/1/77)*

always join the Burmans in their demands, as they usually had a different outlook. They were quite content as things were and did not want change.

Early colonial officials and traders usually had to come alone to take up their posts. As a result they mixed freely with the society they were in, with many becoming attached to the local women. This was easily understandable as most of the British wives seldom came out to what they felt were outposts of disease with an unbearable climate. The many children of these liaisons were unaware as they grew up of who their fathers were. Later, things changed and inter-marriage was allowed and accepted. The offspring were known as Eurasians, Anglo-Indians, or Anglo-Burmans. They kept very much to themselves, and subsequently inter-marriage between them created a class of their own. Most, quite naturally, looked towards Britain as their motherland, and, although not considered truly British, they did have a certain position in the fabric of Burmese society.

During that period within Burma Proper there tended to be a wide social gap between the British and the people they ruled. It was taken for granted, though not stated, that the existing social strata was graded. The British civil servants formed the top echelon, followed by the Indian Civil Service (ICS) which was mostly composed of Eurasians and a few Burmans. The British mercantile community came next, and formed a strong group. Other nationalities, including the Burman, followed behind. Not surprisingly, such hierarchical concepts offended the Burmans, who questioned why they were considered inferior to the white faces.

As a result, the time before the Second World War was a somewhat uneasy one and relations between the British and the Burmans were not always smooth. This was the period portrayed by George Orwell in *Burmese Days* and Maurice Collis in *Trials in Burma*. It was perhaps the social conditions that these authors describe that the Burmans were fighting against. However, over the years, the

Administration gradually began to accept more young educated Burmans into the exalted ICS, and some British commercial firms also recruited them. The numbers grew in the late 1930s, but then came the Japanese war.

(The professional class had made a break through, however, and there was no turning back. Burman men and women were accepted into the social hierarchy. Many of the British who came to the country after the Second World War found it difficult to believe what they heard about the behaviour and attitudes of their predecessors. But the diplomats and business people who came to Asia after the Second World War were almost like a different breed of British. They took an interest in the people they met and tried to assess and understand the local situations of their host countries.)

In an endeavour to resolve the many problems which were continually facing the colonial administration, a decision was made to convene a meeting in London, with representatives from all the important sectors of the community within Burma. Its aim was to discuss the issue of the separation of Burma from India. The meeting, known as the Burma Round Table Conference, lasted for over six weeks from 27 November 1931 to 12 January 1932.

The British government was already committed to giving both Burma and India some form of independence within the Commonwealth at an unspecified date in the future. The question of separating the two countries was not, therefore, a simple administrative reorganisation. There was a great deal to be worked out by the Burma Office. Also, when the separation was effected, it had to be so designed that it led towards self-rule for each.

My father, who had only been a Saohpa for a few years, was selected as observer together with the Saohpa of Mong Mit, Sao Khin Maung, for an earlier conference, when they discussed the outline of a Constitution for a separated Burma. But when the big conference took place, my father and the Saohpa of Hsipaw, Sao Ohn Kya, were selected by the Federated Shan State Council to be full members representing the Shan. They were accompanied by the Saohpa of North Hsenwi, Sao Hom Hpa, and the Kyemmong of Kengtung, Sao Kawng Tai, who attended the meeting as Advisors.

It was my father's first visit to England and he was very impressed by what he saw, admiring the senior politicians and civil servants he met. As a ruler, he was particularly interested in seeing what a democracy, especially that of a colonial power, really meant. He left for England convinced that the British government would be acting in good faith.

All four of the young Shan rulers had either been educated abroad or had served in the British Indian Army and therefore had some experience of the outside world. Sao Ohn Kya, as mentioned before, had been to Rugby School then Brasenose College, Oxford, before working in England for another two years after taking his degree. On his return, he helped in the administration of Hsipaw State and became Saohpa in 1928 when his father died. He was about three years older than my father, so I imagine Sao Ohn Kya was able to show him around London. Sao Hom Hpa had served in the army like my father, and had been appointed Saohpa in 1925. The youngest of them all was Sao Kawng Tai, who had travelled widely around Europe for two years in the early 1920s. He was to become Saohpa in May 1937, but was regrettably assassinated in October of the same year by one of his nephews, who felt that his branch of the family had greater right to the title.

The Prince of Wales opened the meeting with encouraging words. Later, Lord Peel, the Chairman, pointed out that Britain recognised that there were difficulties ahead since Burma was made up of "majority and minority"[12] communities with different interests, and with differing degrees of political development. However, despite being aware of the disparity between the different groups, it appears that the British did little to seriously resolve this problem.

During the meeting, it was soon discovered that a chasm existed between the Burmans on one side and the Shans and other members of the Frontier Areas on the other. The division became wider when one of the Burmese delegates stated in his speech: "We wish to protest against the unfair and unjust selection of delegates to the conference. My friends the Sawbwas are Burmans, but they have been made to identify themselves as a minority party. They claim their own rights...The Burmans have lost their country and now they are threatened with minority rule..."

The Burman delegate had not been telling the truth when he said the Shans were Burmans. True, we all lived in one country but we were all different peoples with our own languages, customs and culture, as is found in Great Britain, with the Irish, Welsh and Scots. It seems that he would have preferred for only Burmans to be at the Conference rather than the other ethnic nationalities representing themselves. The Round Table Conference confirmed the differences which had been observed by Lord Peel.

Despite these problems, the princes seemed quite content with assurances given by the Secretary of State that any decisions regarding a new constitution concerned with the separation of Burma from India, "would not be determined without an opportunity given to the Shan Chiefs to state their view on the matter."

The  Round Table Conference revealed the depth of feeling the Burmans felt towards the Shan and created a most unpleasant atmosphere of political bitterness. It probably came as a complete surprise to my father to learn how the Burman politicians actually felt, for he had a number of good Burman friends who had seemed to understand the subtleties of the Burman-Shan question.

Little wonder that when the time came for discussions on the advent of independence for Burma, the non-Burman people felt they were right to request continued British protection in the face of such an unfriendly stance by the Burman politicians. It was not only the Shan, but other groups such as the Eurasians, the Indians and others, who had also requested that some thought be given for Burma to be accorded Dominion Status.

Following the London Round Table Conference my father's interest in politics grew and, always with an eye on the welfare of the Shan people, he fought with enthusiasm and eagerness for the retention of their autonomy. He realized some change had to take place, but he believed it had to be gradual, rather than a rushed response to emotional calls for reforms. Time was needed for adjustment if there was to be a change in the system. Time, however, was not on our side.

Once more back in the Shan States, there was much for the young princes to do. They needed all their wits about them to protect their people and to try to bring them into the modern era. Already in the major towns of the different states, there were schools and clinics, but there was never enough money in their Treasuries for development on a large scale. A generation had now been sent to Rangoon and Mandalay for further education at the respective universities. But there was still a lack of manpower and importing educated men from the Indian and Burman Civil Services was not the answer. Rather the Shan themselves had to be educated to develop their own country.

In the past, there had never been problems living with other ethnic peoples, including the Burmans, as each went about their own way. However, politicians in Burma Proper were greatly influenced by western socialist and communist ideology thus generating a rise in nationalism. Indian politics and the demands for independence also had an impact on the young politicians whose nationalist sentiments produced such slogans as 'Burma for the Burmans' and 'This is our land', indicating they no longer wanted to be ruled by the British.

At that time, the British felt that the increase in this form of political agitation within Burma Proper might easily influence certain elements in the Shan States, especially university-educated students. So political agitators from "the plains" were not allowed to come to the Shan States, for fear of their creating trouble and possible disturbances. Burman politicians were outraged by this prohibition.

Nevertheless, Shan students returning from Burma Proper did bring back various slogans such as 'Down with the Saohpas' and 'Down with feudalism'. Ironically, these were shouted loudest by students who had been educated on grants from the their very own states.

Certainly, the Round Table Conference had shown my father the bitterness of Burman feelings towards the Shans. The Saohpas were in a difficult position and realized they had to find strategies to deal with these unfriendly politicians. How could they make them understand that they knew their people were backward, that they were doing what they could to alleviate these conditions and therefore there was no need for Burmans to interfere in Shan affairs.

The result of the Round Table Conference was the 1935 Government of Burma Act, which came into force in 1937. There was no change in the administration of the Shan States and the Saohpas continued ruling as they had done centuries before under the control of the Governor of Burma. This naturally did not please the Burmans and a large number of political activities began throughout Burma Proper.

## Sao U Hpa

My granduncle, Sir Sao Mawng, had left Mong Yawnghwe running efficiently and smoothly helped with the advice of the British Commissioner and the Administrator. It was now my father's responsibility as ruler of Yawnghwe to continue the status quo. After his return from England he found much to do. He was always busy, travelling to Taunggyi for the quarterly Federal Council meetings, visiting other princes in their states and making tours of his domain. In a few years' time, he was to find the peace and tranquillity of the previous reign unexpectedly disrupted. Politics would come to paradise to disturb the peace and soon there would be the Japanese invasion.

My father had married four sisters who were his cousins on his mother's side. Their father, U Hla Bu, was the Revenue Minister of Yawnghwe, a Shan from the neighbouring state of Nam Kok. The eldest sister, Sao Nang Yi had two sons, Sao Hseng Hpa (whom we called Sao Sai) and Sao Hseng Ong (known as Sai Hseng). As the senior wife she held the title of Mahadevi, a Sanskrit word meaning Great Goddess. She was usually referred to in the family and in the Yawnghwe Court as Sao Mye Mong, translated from Shan it meant Princess Mother of the Mong,

My mother, Sao Nang Sanda, was the second sister. I was born in 1928 and when I was under three years old, my mother died. She was only twenty-one. Quite naturally, and as was the custom, the Mahadevi adopted me and brought me up as her own.

My memories of the Mahadevi though vague, are clearer than those of my own mother. Indeed, until I was in my thirties, I had no idea that Sao Mye Mong was not my real mother. Perhaps this was because she treated me just as she did her own sons; nor had anyone ever told me otherwise. I remember her as being gentle and soft-spoken. A complete contrast to my father, she made an ideal wife for him. My father had a short temper and when he shouted and raved in anger, she just sat and listened attentively. Often she found herself intervening for others upon whom my father's wrath had fallen, and managed somehow to calm him down and to be sensible. She complemented my father and she coped with him in her own quiet way.

Sao Mye Mong, must have been an extraordinary woman for her time. When there were few cars, let alone women drivers, she used to drive a little green Austin Seven with a canvas hood, taking my brothers to Taunggyi. Sai Hseng, my second elder brother remembers what a good driver she was. I, unfortunately, only saw

*Sao U Hpa, Sao Mye and Sao Sai.*

*Sao U Hpa and Sao Nang Sanda, my mother. (Reproduction with permission of the James Green Centre for World Art, Brighton & Hove Museums)*

*Sao Nang Yi's inauguration as Mahadevi, surrounded by white umbrellas with officiating Brahmans standing in the foreground.*

*Sao Ah Sit, father's younger sister, with her husband.*

*Family group – Sao U Hpa, Sao Mye, Sao Sai, Sai Hseng and Sanda, c. 1934. (Donnison Collection)*

*Sao Mye in her Austin 7.*

the little car sitting for many years in one of our garages after her death. Being a soldier's wife, she had been taught by her husband to handle a gun. She soon became adept at using a firearm and in her target practices seldom missed hitting the bull's eye.

She carried out her duties with tact and care, never turning anyone away who wanted to tell her their worries and misfortunes. In those days, the afternoons were entirely devoted to those who wished to call on her. They would be served 'English tea' – tea with milk and sugar, cakes and sandwiches. If they preferred, they could drink the fragrant Shan green tea and nibble such savoury Yawnghwe specialities as an onion and pork bagi, or specially prepared fish dumplings wrapped in banana leaf.

If there was to be a big alms offering of food to the monks, which took place on days of the full and waning moon, our Buddhist holy days, women callers would help by peeling garlic and onions, cutting vegetables and generally assisting in the preparation of the food. Alms offerings for the Buddha images at the Central pagoda of Yawnghwe were usually of glutinous rice, pieces of different fruit and sweetmeats. These were served in emerald green banana leaf cups made by the visitors, and neatly arranged in the big gilded lacquer bowls.

On other days a card game or two might be played. But at most times, the women were always busy preparing for one festival or the other. There were silk robes for the Buddha images which had to be hand sewn with great reverence, embroidered with sequins and gold thread. The robes for the Phaung Daw U Buddha images, were changed when they were brought to the palace during the festival, while other robes for Buddha images in the Haw and in pagodas in town, were changed at Thingyan, the Buddhist New Year, after the images had their annual wash and polish.

It was during the months before winter, when there was time away from religious duties, that the women who came to the Haw settled down to knitting and crocheting cardigans and shawls under the supervision of Sao Mye Mong. One would see them engrossed in the complicated patterns, each trying to outdo the other in the number of days it took to finish one of the garments.

The cold season in the Shan States was brief, but it could be really cold with heavy mists and frost. Often we sat around charcoal braziers to keep warm, wearing hand-knitted sweaters and cardigans. It was then that we had the luxury of making ice to serve to our visitors. A tray with a layer of water about half an inch deep would be left out on the veranda during the night to freeze. In the morning, we would break the ice into pieces and crunch them with great enjoyment.

It was in the southern wing of the palace where Sao Mye Mong would install herself in the afternoons that these activities were carried out, and the Back

Hall was also used when there was a great deal to be done. I suppose that these get-togethers were really a sort a women's club or organization, only that no one had thought of calling it as such. Although each of the women had genuinely come to help, they also wanted to pick up snippets of the latest gossip which were going around. They seemed to have a marvellous time joking with each other, and at times singing and laughing.

I grew up amongst people who seemed always to be smiling and laughing. I feel sure that my childhood must have been blissfully happy, if bliss means being surrounded by people, being pampered and spoilt, never having to lift a finger, and never bothering

*Sanda and Sai Hseng.*

or wanting to find out how others lived. It is true that growing up in a princely family and being treated as a princess, meant there was little I saw of life outside our Yawnghwe court. There seemed not a care in the world as I had whatever I wanted.

There was, however, much to learn as one grew up since we all had to live by certain norms. At least in our family I was to discover that my father did not tolerate 'folies de grandeur' – a lesson I learnt at an early age.

When I was not yet four my father sent me to a local school which was not very far from our palace. Not wanting to walk even a short distance, I used to be carried to school astride my maid's hips or rode piggy-back on a bodyguard's back. I was obviously very spoilt by them. The school was run by a prim, but pleasant spinster wearing gold-rimmed spectacles below a thin fringe of jet black hair. There were about twenty of us altogether, the pupils being mainly composed of cousins and children of the Yawnghwe officials. We were taught arithmetic and Burmese and I remember having to learn the alphabet by rote. We would all shout at the top of our voices and I am sure the noise must have been deafening. Everything was memorised by repeating aloud after the teacher. The lessons were written on a blackboard and we copied these onto a black slate, which we carried home for home-work. I can't recall having any books at that little school.

The mistress was patient and hardly scolded me. But one day I must have been inattentive, so she gave me a tap on my knuckles. My reaction was quick, picking up a ruler I hit her back, before grabbing the inkpot from her desk and throwing it at her. I then ran home thinking I had done the proper thing. Young as I was, I must have thought the mistress had no right to strike me, a princess. However, what I thought proved to be completely wrong. My father was furious when he heard about the incident. He knew many Saohpas' children behaved badly, but he did not think a child of his should be one of them. Instead of beating me, he made me sit in a corner where I was ignored. It could have been only for an hour, but it seemed an eternity. Somehow it was a punishment I have vividly remembered and it taught me never to strike anyone in anger. It also made me realize that one had to respect one's elders and that nothing was lost by being polite to others.

My father was always stern and strict with his children. He considered us his soldiers and, applying military discipline, would command "come here" or "go there"; and, "do this" or "do that". He did not believe in disobedience and had no time for arguments. Whatever he said we had to do. I regarded my father with great awe and always tried to be obedient.

I was allowed to appear in my father's presence twice a day – once in the morning to bid him good morning and once at night, generally my bedtime, to pay my respects and ask for his blessing. Sometimes my brothers were with me and we showed our respects with a *wai*. Putting our palms together, we lifted them to our forehead and, with our feet firmly tucked under us, we touched the floor three times. This *wai*, as we say in Tai, is always used when we say our prayers and pay homage to the *mon sao*, the monks. As a sign of respect and humility the young usually *wai* their elders and teachers. In Thailand and in Laos the *wai* remains prevalent.

In Burma too, there is a polite form of greeting – the *shi-koe* – which is like a *wai* and is often used by the young when they visit their elderly relatives. The usual form of address for an employer was often *thakin*, meaning master in Burmese, an honorific title similar to 'sahib' in India. When British administrators and traders arrived, they were addressed in the same way. Just as servants and office boys address their bosses as *thakin*, the wife is addressed as *thakin-ma*, or mistress. Although high-ranking Burmans enjoyed being addressed as such and still do, many disassociate themselves from a term which they see as having been introduced by the British to emphasize their superiority.

On rare occasions when it was bedtime for me but dinner time for my father, I would be allowed to stay up late and have an English dinner with him. In his wing of the palace, we sat on chairs at a long table with my father at the head. The table, covered with a white tablecloth, would be laid with knives and forks with white napkins shaped into boats sitting on the side plates. A tall Aladdin lamp sat in the middle of the table casting a soft bluish light. I don't remember what the first courses were, but it was the desert I used to wait up for, even though I could hardly keep my eyes open. Boy, our white-haired Indian cook who did the English cooking, used to make wonderful desserts. One was an orange filled with delicious ice-cream and another fresh home-grown strawberries crushed with cream making lovely pink and white streaky patterns.

Children were really the responsibility of the women; it was in their domain that we grew up. Though my father was strict with us, we tended to be pampered and spoilt by the various relations. Each of us had our own nannies, whose entire time was devoted to looking after us. My nanny was a very young country girl who more or less grew up with me. It was only when I was five or six years old, that I was allowed to wander around the Haw at will and it was then that I saw my father a little more. But I kept my distance, and unless he called for me I hardly went to the north wing, which was where he was installed.

## Seeking an audience

His early army days had given my father a wider view of life and a broader basis from which to carry out new ideas and reforms for his state. He was always conscious that as Saohpa and ruler of his state, he had a duty towards his subjects. He never turned anyone away who came to seek an audience.

The villagers often came very early even before our breakfast had ended. But my father would never see anyone until he had smoked his cheroot after the meal. I can still see him sitting cross-legged on a red velvet cushion beside his throne, where we had our meals at a round, low table. At first his face looked serious behind a pair of horn rimmed spectacles, but soon he would break into a smile as he took his first puff of the cheroot. Then holding it between his thumb and forefinger, he would roll it slightly and put it up to his ear to hear the crackle of the crisp *thanaphet* leaf in which the cheroot had been rolled. A silver spittoon was always at hand to catch any falling tobacco ash, to avoid burning holes in his clothes. These cheroots in diameter were equal to a shilling, or a modern ten pence piece, and about eight inches long. They were specially rolled for my father by an aunt. As he puffed, there would be a fragrance of burning bark and jaggery. It was a treat to see him puffing away at his long cheroot with such satisfaction. Having smoked for about five minutes or so and enjoying every minute, my father was ready to face the world.

Many of the villagers came on a bazaar or market day, which took place every five days. So when they came to see my father they did not mind waiting. Most of the villagers came in family groups and sat in the inner audience hall. They knew that whatever problems they brought with them their ruler would try to find some solution. Usually, he simply directed them to the correct departments or ministries. In fact, many of the people came just to *kandaw*, to pay him their respects, bringing with them their first fruit and vegetables of the season.

These villagers may have come from as far away as a day's walk or more from the surrounding hills, their journeys starting the night before in order to arrive as early as possible at dawn. Others, bringing firewood and charcoal, came in bullock carts driving along narrow, bumpy dirt tracks. The ringing of the shrill metal bells in harmony with the deep staccato sound of the wooden bells of the bullocks, would herald their arrival in town. Some who came on foot, carried full woven bamboo baskets on their backs supported by a strap from the forehead, like the Gurkhas in Nepal. Among the produce they brought for sale were dried chillies, tobacco, tea, and *thanapet* leaves. There were as well bales of strong, soft Shan paper made from the green weeds of mountain streams, or at least so I was told as a child. I understand that the paper is actually made from the bark of a small Asian mulberry tree (*Broussonetia papyriera*). The mulberry leaves fed to silk worms are from another tree of the same family. The bark undergoes a laborious process to reduce it to a pulp. It is then thinly spread on to a tray with wood frames and left to dry in the sun to become a sheet of Shan paper. Nowadays Pindaya, which lies west of Inle, seems to be the main centre for its production. We found the same kind of paper being made by the Lanteng people in northern Laos, while a similar paper was widely used in Nepal.

Those families travelling to the market from Inle, came in either flat-bottomed sampans, or long dug-out boats which they rowed standing on one leg, while the other, hooked around a long oar, made the strokes through the water. Imagine my surprise when I bought a Penguin copy of George Orwell's *Burmese Days* recently to re-read, to see a leg-rower of the Inle Lake on the cover.

Fresh vegetables, fresh and salted fish, rice both white and red, lengths of cotton and silk materials, gold and silverware and lastly, cheroots both long and fat or short and thin, the produce of the Inle Lake were all transported in these dug-out boats. In those days, it was only the very rich merchants who used the one or two outboard motor boats that existed.

Equally, fifty or sixty years ago, there were hardly any motor vehicles on the roads; perhaps only two or three lorries which came to the market, carrying Indian or Pakistani traders with goods such as soaps, candles, torches, and tins of condensed milk and sardines. Sometimes people living on the flat plains of Mye-lat, known as the Pa-O, brought potatoes, their cash-crop, grown on fertile soil of a rich, orange colour. It was too far for them to walk and they usually came in one of these overloaded, decrepit lorries.

Bazaar days were a social event. No one was ever in a hurry. People sat around in groups, chatting about their families and their crops. Everyone moved in a leisurely manner taking their time, slowly getting their business done. All the time in the world seemed to be at their disposal. So when they came to see my father, they did not mind waiting. They had a whole day ahead.

It was appropriate for the villagers to be received in the inner audience hall, as here stood the gilded throne on a raised platform. Above it hung a silken canopy. The heavy teak throne, which was the size of a large bed, had ornate carvings of thousands of flowers and leaves all studded with semi-precious stones. On top of the couch lay a thick red velvet cushion, and a triangular pillow placed at the head. The facings of the pillow had a tiger, my father's insignia, embroidered on either side with gold and silver thread.

The villagers sat in awe looking at the royal regalia on this raised dais and all around them. A tall gilded chair stood behind the throne, and hanging on the surrounding pillars were faded and unsmiling portraits of my grand uncle, Sir Sao

*Empty lower level of the Royal Throne Audience Hall.*

*Exterior of the Shan Palace Museum, Yawnghwe, formerly the royal palace.*

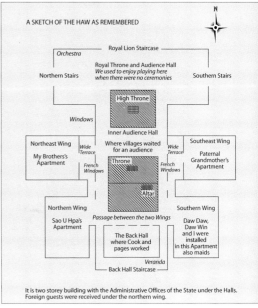

Mawng and his Mahadevi, as well as other relatives, creating a family portrait gallery. The white and yellow ceremonial umbrellas were tied to these thick teak pillars, white for the Saohpa and yellow for his Mahadevi. A gilded rack supported the jewelled encrusted swords and sheaths of the Saohpa, and on a table lay the bejewelled betel box and golden spittoon. Gold and silver bowls of different sizes with decorated bands around the rims all formed part of the regalia. These were usually carried in procession on ceremonial occasions by the bodyguards.

After Sir George Scott called on my grand-uncle, Sir Sao Mawng, he wrote in his diary that he had been shown around 'his magnificent new Haw' where he had seen some brightly coloured chromolithographies hanging in the audience hall. I believe they were of the German Emperor, the King of Italy and Abdul the Damned, although who he was I do not know. Other pictures he saw were of King Mindon and Queen Victoria hanging behind the throne.[13] Since I had no idea who the pictures represented, I suppose I took little notice and I cannot recall them accurately.

This palace, of course, was the one we were living in. It certainly was a grand structure built of stone and wood. The roof was surmounted by a tall spire, or *htee*, of seven-tiered roofs, called *pyathat,* and was in the architectural style of the palace of Mandalay. The red-painted *htee*, trimmed with gold, glittered in the sunshine as it tapered up into the blue sky.

## The Haw

The Haw, now a museum as mentioned before, is a two-storey building with four large halls, one behind the other forming the centre. The front hall, known as the Royal Throne Audience Hall, extends across the whole length of the building. On either side of the inner halls are four wings. The two on the northern side

*Southern wing of Haw, my room at the
top is marked with an arrow.*

were occupied by my brothers who had the eastern wing and my father the wing
behind theirs. On the southern side, the eastern wing was where my paternal
grandmother, whom we called Sao Nai, lived with her youngest daughter,
Sao Mya Sit, and her family. They occupied both the two floors of that wing.
At that time, Nang Nyunt Mae, who was my father's third wife and my third
aunt, also mother number three, occupied the wing behind. This southern wing
was the women's domain, so it was here that I also lived. Both my brothers'
and grandmother's wings could only be reached by crossing an open terrace
from the Inner Audience Hall and from our wings, by wide verandas.

Fragrant flowers such as Queen of the Night, honeysuckle, white jasmine and
a creeper whose name I did not know, climbed abundantly up the southern wall
and trailing along the railings of the veranda. The heavy clusters of the orange
trumpet-like creeper and the soft yellow of the honeysuckle, made striking Impres-
sionist patterns of orange, yellow and green against the white-washed walls. At
night the air used to be filled with the sweet, pungent fragrance of the Queen of
the Night and jasmine, each vying with the other for attention.

When my elder brother, Sai Hseng and I visited the Botanical Gardens at
Gibraltar recently, we were greeted by a mass of brilliant, orange blossoms. We
were told they were the Cape honeysuckle and that late summer was their season.
It was a splendid display with splashes of orange and green, which so reminded
me of our Haw, and I wondered when those plants had been taken and planted
in Yawnghwe. At last, I was to learn their name. The exquisite fragrance of the
jasmine followed us as we walked around the Spanish villages. Memories crowded
in and I felt a longing for those far gone days of my childhood.

The northern side of the palace had less light and much of the walls were
covered with deep, green ivy. Here grew a large sapodilla tree and a Chinese plum
tree, their branches extending upwards. When they were in fruit, we could pick
them either from the veranda or the garden below. It was always cool on this side.

A veranda stretched along the three sides of the Back Hall. On the southern end by our wing we had large earthen water containers standing to catch the rain-water. When we had a really heavy shower the containers would fill up with fresh, clear water which we used for washing our hair. There were no modern shampoos then. Instead we used the bark of a certain tree, called *thayaw*, that was soaked-with sweet smelling herbs to produce a slimy jelly-like mixture. It was rubbed thoroughly into the scalp and our long hair, until a soft foam formed. It was then washed away with the rain water leaving the hair beautifully clean and soft. This herbal shampoo was the only thing we used at home and I was not introduced to western shampoos until I came abroad.

The ground floor of my father's wing was used as a guest apartment and it was here that many Saohpas, British officials and later Japanese officers were enter-tained. It was furnished in western style with sofas, tables and chairs. Our foreign guests hardly ever came upstairs into our private domain, unless they were making a tour of the palace. Maybe it was a year or two before the war, that modern con-veniences were installed down here and possibly at about the same time electric lights. The generator came on as soon as it was dusk and went off around nine, after the orchestra had played its masterpiece for the evening.

## *Bodyguards and* phii

When the villagers arrived they were led into the inner audience hall where they sat on the cool polished wooden floors waiting to see Sao U Hpa. On occasion, if there was a single person or a small family who were known to my father, they would be taken to his wing. Sai Hseng remembers making sketches of these villagers when he was home from school, which he was encouraged to do by his father. He was the budding artist in our family.

The bodyguards were a friendly group, who used to make pots of green tea and provide betel for the visitors, or sometimes our relatives. Betel is chewed all over Asia. Generally, the green betel leaf is used to wrap a dab of white lime, a piece of betel or areca nut, as well as cardamom, cumin or even tobacco. The bulging packet is chewed with great pleasure producing a bright red liquid that is spat out. Although betel chewing blackens the teeth no one seems to worry. It is still common to see hill tribe peoples and Vietnamese with black decaying teeth.

*View of the Back Hall with its twin stairways.*

I cannot recollect how many guards there were, but the chief one directly responsible to my father was a fat and opulent-looking man. He wore a big ruby ring on his finger, and a revolver on his hip. He and his men enjoyed playing football, which I imagine the British troops at Fort Stedman had taught their fathers. They took part in annual competitions against the police and other teams made up of teachers and civil servants. Sao U Hpa presented the winning team with a large silver bowl, and often it went to the bodyguards.

While the villagers waited, they chatted with the bodyguards, exchanging stories. Their favourites concerned the guardian spirits of the Haw. The belief in spirits, *phii* in Shan or *nat* in Burmese, is common amongst the people of Southeast Asia; they are to be found guarding rivers and mountains, houses and villages, gate posts and trees. It is not animism. As Buddhists, these spirits are not worshiped but are appeased as a reassurance for the smoother running of one's life. Since they are generally believed to be found everywhere, one feels it is better to be on the right side of the guardian spirit rather than on the wrong side, which could bring about disaster.

People who have visited Thailand will have noticed little miniature houses that are to be found in all house compounds for the guardian of the house. Sitting on pedestals, they are elaborately decorated and often garlanded with necklaces of white, sweet smelling jasmine flowers. They can also be seen in the compounds of hotels and business buildings. The one near the Erawan Hotel in Bangkok some twenty or thirty years ago was considered to bring good luck and prosperity to anyone asking for its blessing. It become so popular that the shrine had to be enlarged and made grander.

Similarly, on entering a Shan village one will see a little wooden house which has been built for the village guardian. In it will be found a glass of water, a bunch of flowers and a lit candle, and sometimes even offerings of fruits and sweet cakes. Also at the base of the largest tree in the village, often a banyan tree, offerings of water and flowers will be found. Weary travellers seeking shade and rest make these offerings, asking for a safe journey or giving thanks for its protection. When motor cars became the mode of travel, the guardian spirits of special banyan trees were asked to protect cars and give their owners safe passage, avoiding accident or death on the road. At the same time, the white *chedi* or pagoda found standing in the middle of the village is not forgotten. Devotees can also be seen here paying their homage.

An annual festival is held at Mount Popa to propitiate the thirty-seven *nats* revered by the Burmans and people come from all over the country to take part in these celebrations. *Nats* are legendary figures, who in Burmese history have died glorious and heroic deaths. There are many contradictory stories about these carved and painted figures, both as to their origin and their date. Mount Popa, some miles southeast of Pagan, is where two heroic brothers and a brother and sister personified as *nats*, are believed to live. They are considered to be very powerful and are held in great esteem. Other revered *nats* are those who are said to have met their death in chilling circumstances such as being buried alive or burnt at the stake on the order of tyrant kings.

I have never been to this great festival but I have witnessed a few *nat poys* at which the *nats* are invoked and propitiated. The mediums are known as the *nat kadaw*, which translated from Burmese means the *nat's* consort. It is she, who foretells the future for the individual or can forecast events for the country as a whole. The *nats* have to be appeased with esteem and respect, for if they feel they might have been slighted in any way, there is no knowing what the consequences could be.

During the performance, every detail is watched carefully – how the *nat kadaw* moves her hand or her head, her facial expressions and the manner in which she speaks, as, once she is possessed these actions form part of the interpretation. The colour of the garments the medium has chosen, and the way she walks, also give the believers a precise indication of the message being sent by the *nat* invoked. There is, indeed, something uncanny about *nat pwes* for when the beat of the special *nat* music, *nat hsein*, is played to invoke the spirits, one becomes irresistibly attracted to the rhythmic tempo, whose beat is reminiscent of the voodoo drums seen in Hollywood films.

Apart from this annual festival, people in general, when faced with a major quandary in their lives, will invoke help from the *nats*. I am told that the former Prime Minister of Burma, U Nu, just before the General Elections of 1960, met a terrifying storm on his return flight from a trip abroad. He immediately ordered a *nat pwe* to be held as soon as he landed for he felt that unless he appeased the *nats*, he would not win the elections. The storm, he considered, was a bad omen. Thus even U Nu, a most devout Buddhist, believed very strongly in the powers of *nats* and always looked to them for guidance. On that occasion, however, it seems, there was little help given in solving his problems.

It is not surprising, then, to find that for ordinary Shan people, the *nats* or *phii* were part of their lives. They believe that the guardians of the house, the village, the forests and rivers are there to give protection. Their existence is real and they can be invoked for assistance, such as at times of uncertain harvests and droughts.

*The eastern staircase, guarded by two* nagas.

Here at the Haw, I learnt that there was one important *phii* that guarded the eastern stairway, which no one but my father and his family could use. It led into the front Royal Throne Audience Hall and only on ceremonial occasions were other people allowed to climb up the stairs after asking the *phii's* permission. It was said that if a person climbed up the stairs, without asking first, he would be lifted up by the *phii* and thrown down. Two *nagas*, mythical serpents, also guarded the staircase. Their heads stood about five foot high on either side of the lowest step and their bodies formed a stone balustrade to the top of the stairway.

The other powerful spirit was the guardian of the high throne in the front audience hall. It was sacrilege for anyone to sit upon it, except for the Saohpa. If anybody else did so, they vomited blood and died. There were apparently many other *phii* and the Haw was full of them and their protective power.

I forget which month it was when we had to appease them all by placing a banana leaf bowl, filled with glutinous rice, sweetmeats, a sprig of flowers and a lighted candle, near every pillar in the palace. We children had a wonderful time running from the Back Hall where the offerings were being prepared to the many pillars throughout the palace.

The story I liked best about the *phii* and had heard a number of times, concerned the spirit who lived in one of the large banyan trees outside our compound. None of the bodyguards went under that tree after dark and if they had to pass it on their way home, they went in pairs singing at the top of their voices to scare the *phii*. He was a playful spirit and used to pull the ears of passers-by or tug at their clothes. So one had to run as fast as one could to escape him.

Since these guardian spirits were to be found everywhere living in trees and rivers, guarding houses and villages, it was difficult to ignore them. There were both good and bad *phii*. The good were usually guardian spirits, while the bad caused harm to human beings, as did the witches. I was told that some witches turned themselves into fiery balls and flew around. We often saw these bright orange-tinged balls, in twos and threes, gliding above the marshy fields along the flat road leading out of Yawnghwe to the north. Much later in life, I learnt there was a meteorological explanation for what are known in Europe as will-o'-the-wisps – flickering phosphorescent lights at night found over marshy ground said

to be caused by methane combustion. When approached, the mysterious light advances, but remains always out of reach, leading to supernatural beliefs. Nevertheless, in Yawnghwe, to the superstitious and the ignorant, it was easy to believe that these were witches flying around, plotting whom to harm next.

So when night fell and all was dark, I imagined all kinds of spirits everywhere. To make matters worse we had no electricity in those days and we went around the Haw with a candle or a paraffin lamp. The shadows cast from these dim lights used to frighten me and I generally clutched on to my young maid, Nang Muon, hiding my face in case we met a *phii* as we went from one wing to another.

## Afternoon tea

My father really didn't have a daily routine when he was in residence. There were days when he had to go to Taunggyi, to see the Commissioner or to attend a meeting of Saohpas. If the day was spent in Yawnghwe he never missed going down to his office which was below the inner audience hall. It was down here, that many of the Yawnghwe State administrative offices were and where the villagers who needed help came to see the officials. If there was a court case to be tried, my father had to go across town to the judicial offices. It was his duty to be there for most of the serious cases.

On some afternoons, Sao U Hpa would come and grace us with his presence in the southern wing. Those occasions I remember must have been before I was sent off to the boarding school at Kalaw. When he came over from the northern wing through the second inner audience hall there would be a sudden hush as soon as his footsteps could be heard. As he walked towards his throne, we would all *wai* and pay our respects. No one spoke until he broke the silence by asking one of our visitors how she was and news of her family.

Sometimes Sao Nai, my paternal grandmother mentioned earlier, would be calling at the same time, or a tall, thin great-aunt who was the Mahadevi of the former Saohpa, my father's uncle. I was a tomboy and used to run around in

*Sanda, 3 or 4 years old, sitting in Royal Throne Audience Hall.*

*Left: Family in 1933, entertaining a foreign guest, in the Inner Audience Hall.*

dresses and pinafores, playing hide and seek, or football with my cousins in the front audience hall. But when word came around that my father might call, I had to stop playing and get myself dressed up. I had to wear a *hseu* (*ingyi* in Burmese, a short blouse which was usually of transparent white lawn with a flap either to the right or left which was fastened by five buttons. The *sin* (*longyi* in Burmese) was firmly wound around my waist reaching to my ankles.

While my father conversed with the guests, a tray containing a cup of tea and a plate of Huntley and Palmer biscuits would be thrust into my hands and I would carry it until a few steps from my father, then dropping on my knees negotiate those last few feet on my knees. On those occasions, a beaming father would pat me on the head for managing to balance the tray without upsetting it.

In a society such as ours there was a strict protocol, which was especially observed in my father's presence. He was our lord and master. We sat facing him on the floor with our feet firmly covered with our *sin*. If he was sitting, one was not allowed to stand near him. One always occupied a position further down the room from him. One had always to face him and never turn one's back on him. One did not speak until one was spoken to. One never pointed a finger, nor one's feet towards him. One never touched him, nor mentioned him by name. I had no idea what his name was until I was quite grown up. My father was always Sao U Hpa, the Lord Father of the Sky, to all of us.

It was the same for us, too – nobody called us by our names. We were always addressed as *Sao*, meaning either Prince or Princess, in Shan. In the family we generally used pet names or filial terms with each other, such as elder brother or sister, so an outsider would not necessarily know our names. We didn't have the system of surnames, but children of Saohpas were generally known as Sao from Yawnghwe or Hsenwi, depending on which state they belonged to.

Since we expected to be respected by our fathers' subjects, it was important that we were just as respectful to them. We were taught to be courteous and polite to our elders and I would never have called out to an elder person by his or her name. They were always addressed as uncle or aunt, brother or sister, a custom I found common in most Asian societies.

Sao U Hpa did not stay very long at tea, but came only because he had probably not seen his mother for a few days and, knowing she would be visiting us, made the effort to come and pay her his respects. Often, he left us when the gong had just struck four. It signalled the end of office hours too, and sometimes he would call for his two private secretaries to come and have a game of tennis with him. The tennis courts lay in front of the Haw on the southern side between the two drives that led into the compound, from the east and the south. I am not too sure, but perhaps from time to time there was a fourth player. At any rate, Ko Lat who was a smallish man and the other Ko Kyaw, tall and thin, enjoyed these games despite the occasional swearing from my father.

When my father was away in Rangoon from 1948 to 1962, his eldest son, Sao Hseng Hpa, who had been made the *Kyemmong* in 1939, was left to administer Yawnghwe State. Then Ko Lat as Chief Minister, was able to offer his help and guidance to my brother.

Just behind these courts stood a small *wat* or temple housing a number of Buddha images connected to our family. An old aunt looked after the place and she came daily to change the flowers and water offerings, light candles and joss sticks.

Occasionally I would accompany her but I had an ulterior motive. This was to watch the peacocks that lived under the temple. They were dignified looking birds with beautiful blue-green plumes. It was a wonderful sight to see them with their tail feathers in full display, each iridescent eyespot gleaming in the light. Handsome though they were, they had a loud, ugly call.

Exactly opposite the tennis courts, on the northern side was a paddock for schooling horses. In the mornings I used to go riding round and round the ring on a pony. I was somewhat timid with the horses, and later, when as an older child I might have gained confidence, the horses were taken away by the Japanese army. Anyhow, my morning rides were quite gentle and sometimes I rode out into the country to the east of the Haw, to where the Gurkha milkmen lived with their families. At other times, I rode out with a bodyguard and Nang Muon following on foot, to the sugar cane fields which lay a little further east on the road to Fort Stedman. As we went along the road we would get whiffs of the syrupy jaggery cooking. On our arrival, the owner of the cane field would cut lengths of sugar cane, dip them into the jaggery he was cooking and give these to us. I would chew off the thin layer of the crackling, transparent jaggery, then peel the sugar cane and chew that. It was a delightful treat and very thirst quenching after a hot ride.

I was never allowed to go too far or to stray away from the road, as tigers were known to roam the eastern hills, and they sometimes came down to the valley. Thickets grew just beyond the bund on the north-eastern limit of our compound with the dense jungle beginning only a kilometre or so away. The bund was a high embankment where people would walk of an evening, as did our maids and back-hall pages. From time to time, they reported hearing the roar of a tiger after they had kept their trysts by the bund.

There was no hunting allowed to the east of the bund where the marshes began and where water fowl and wild ducks lived. My brother, Sai Hseng, remembers an incident when two foreigners were caught shooting ducks in the marshes. They were brought before Sao U Hpa who told them that the area where they were shooting was protected, but since they did not know that they would not be charged. He advised them, if they really wanted a good day's shooting, to go to Inle where they would find snipe and other water fowl.

## Telling the time

Once Sao U Hpa had left us, our other guests also made their departures, as the gong struck the hour of four. In those days few people wore watches and there were not many clocks. Most village people had no need to worry about the exact time, as they simply rose at sunrise and went to bed at sunset, with noon dividing the day in two. For the townspeople it was different and many relied on the strokes of the gong to tell them the time. The hours throughout the day and night were struck out on a flat gong, hanging in the front audience hall of the palace, by the bodyguard on duty.

In addition, every evening at six as dusk fell, a small orchestra installed in the northern corner of the front audience hall would play a long piece of music. The orchestra consisted of a number of gongs, drums, cymbals and a trumpet-like wind instrument which sounded like a bagpipe. When it was nine o'clock, they played again as eloquently as they could. By midnight and at three in the morning, however, sleep had overcome the players and one could hear only a few bars of music. Six in the morning brought new life and vigour. The sound of the music woke us all up to see the sun rising in a clear blue sky, far over the eastern hills.

When my husband and I were both working in Rangoon, we went back to Yawnghwe for a holiday. Peter could never get used to the orchestra striking up in the middle of the night, and it kept him awake most nights. The shrill notes of the wind instrument and the beating of the drums were indeed strange sounds to hear when waking from a deep sleep.

The Royal Throne Audience Hall was very spacious and could easily hold four to five hundred people sitting on the floor. Towards the middle of the hall on a raised level stood the high throne. On the throne stood a bowl of sacred leaves which were an offering to the guardian *phii* of the Haw. People took their slippers and shoes off when they came into the audience hall as a sign of respect for both the *phii* and the Saohpa. It has always been an Asian custom to take off shoes and slippers in a temple or monastery, or in the presence of someone who is revered, such as the monarch. But this custom did not come easy to the westerners who felt it was servile to remove footwear, and from time to time this caused a contretemps at the Burman courts.

I wonder what happens today at the Haw. A friend has told me that although it is now a museum, this important point of Shan etiquette is still enforced. In front of the dais on either side stood two large gongs. These were only sounded when there was a royal death to be announced, or if a disaster had taken place. During the time of my grand-uncle, the deep booming sound meant that the city was being attacked and it was a 'call to arms'. All available and able men were expected to report for battle immediately.

When there was a large number of monks to be offered alms food or when the Phaung Daw U images were brought to Yawnghwe, it was this large hall which was used for the ceremonies. It was also in this hall that the annual allegiance ceremony took place at Thingyan, the Buddhist New Year, when all the Yawnghwe State officials came to pledge their loyalty, followed a month or so later by school children coming to pay their respects to their Saohpalong.

I don't remember how many schools participated in this latter ceremony, but they were mainly from primary schools. The students were on their best behaviour and in their best clothes, but it was the young girls who always stole the show, with their brightly coloured Inle silk *sins*, or sarongs, with white transparent jackets and flowers in their hair. The boys and girls would first receive their blessing from their prince, then they would walk from the front hall into the inner hall where my brothers and I would be waiting for them. They came in long lines and each was handed a small packet wrapped in Shan paper that contained a coin, which probably was the equivalent of a sixpence. There was silence as the children filed past us to collect their pocket money, then as soon as they reached the stairs, there was a great clatter as they departed.

## *A glimpse of the outside world*

When Sao Mye Mong passed away everything came to a halt in the court of Yawnghwe. Like her sister, she had succumbed to the dreaded tuberculosis which was a common disease in those days with apparently no cure. Rumour had it, and it was incredulously believed, that they had both died young because as commoners, it was not in their destinies to attain such high positions in the Shan hierarchy. It is incredible that people should have dreamt up such a story, since not all Mahadevis were from princely families, nor were other wives princesses.

My father was devastated by our mother's death. To help lessen his grief, it was decided that he should take a sea voyage. His good friend, Taik Or, a Chinese millionaire arranged that they should go from Malaysia (Malaya then,) to Canton and Hong Kong. He owned a large establishment called the Ching Chong Palace then in Rangoon. After Independence the Shan State Government bought the place and called it the Kambawza Palace. Unfortunately, this large complex no longer belongs to the Shans, since it has now been taken over by army officers and families. Sao U Hpa made the cruise, accompanied by his friends and my two elder brothers, Sao Sai and Sai Hseng. His friends gave him a good time, and my brothers remember being left on board each night with my father's butler cum batman, with little to do.

Much later, my elder brother was told by one of the friends who accompanied them, that one night my father had thrown overboard all his wife's jewels, saying he didn't want to see them anymore and that he did not want anyone else to wear them. In his own way, my father must have loved this wife very much and his action showed the extent of his loss and his deep feelings. Perhaps it was a fitting tribute to someone who was kind and understanding and who had helped him through his early life, first as a soldier, then as Saohpa.

Her two younger sisters, the third and fourth wives, Nang Nyunt May and Nang Mya Win, were at school in Taunggyi and were brought home to look after

*Family group, Sao U Hpa, Sao Mye and the three older children, c. 1934.*

us children. The first we called Daw Daw, meaning aunt in Burmese, though she was number three mother. She was always cheerful, a plump and cuddly person with a big heart. Never to have a child of her own, we became her children. Number four mother, was much younger. After her schooling in Taunggyi, she was expected to go to university in Rangoon. We called her Daw Win, Aunt Win.

It was arranged that the two sisters should take me to Bassein to stay with a Karen school friend of Daw Daw's to help get over Sao Mye Mong's death. The Thein family were Christians. They were a practical group of people, who did everything for themselves and did not depend on servants. The daughters in the family all took turns to cook and to go to the market. The mother, who was about sixty and whom I called *phwa phwa* meaning grandmother in Burmese, was a small person. She was not unlike my own paternal grandmother – forthright in speech and energetic. The daughters and the only son, Ko Ko Wilson, had all been to Rangoon University and were working as nurses and teachers. The eldest daughter, Aunty Kitty, was Headmistress at the Baptist School in Taunggyi and that was how we came to know her. What a complete contrast to our Shan families who always found an excuse to keep their daughters at home.

The stay in the delta brought one new experience after another. What fascinated me in the household, was the chickens kept in pens under their tall, stilted wooden house. As a Buddhist, even at that age, it had been instilled in me that to keep livestock for slaughter as food was sinful. Accordingly, one tended to look down on people who were fishermen or butchers, believing that they were a debased class of people who when they died, would certainly go to hell. There, they would suffer the indignity of dying like the animals they had killed, a thousand times over.

Much later, when we were in Laos, we often found temple murals depicting hell – men were tied to trees and some were being boiled in a pot over a fierce burning fire. These were not unlike the murals I had seen on the walls of the Yawnghwe pagoda as a child. In my childhood naivety, I wondered if *phwa phwa* would go to hell for keeping those chickens.

I remember *phwa phwa* as an avid reader – if she was not with her chickens, she was in her favourite deck chair reading the newspapers. With her spectacles perched low on the bridge of her nose, she would read the paper from cover to cover. Coming from Rangoon, they must have been two or three days old. With no wireless or radios in those days, these Burmese papers were the only means of keeping abreast with news of what was happening in the rest of the country.

It was at Chaung Tha that I saw the sea for the first time – the coconut palms, the golden sands, the waves rolling and beating against the grey rocks and the collection of beautiful shells on the beach, were a wonderful sight. A small seaside village then, it has today become one of the main holiday resorts for tourists. When we made the trip from Bassein we walked all the way, although I was carried piggy back for most of the time. When we were thirsty someone would climb a coconut palm and we would drink the refreshing, cool coconut water.

I remember hosts of green parakeets flying overheard returning from their day's search for food. Once they were settled you could see them high above on the boughs of the trees sitting side by side to pass the night together. Then in the morning with a great chatter and flapping of wings, they would fly off forming a patch of green against the sky. Karen men believed that to drink the blood of a monkey gave them strength and agility, so when they saw a monkey it would be shot. I thought it was a horrible thing to do and I was glad they only managed to shoot two during our whole trip.

I have no memory of Bassein itself, but when my husband and I visited it over twenty years later I was told that it had changed very little. They still made the hand-painted sunshades in beautiful colours for which the town was famous, before imported black cloth umbrellas came and spoilt their market. Peter and I, must have travelled on the same kind of steamer on which my aunts and I had made the trip so many years ago. We went through the Twante Canal and a network of rivers with banks on either side interspersed with mangroves, green paddy fields and small villages of bamboo and thatched houses. Usually a white pagoda crowned the highest point in the village and nearby grew mango and banana trees. Sometimes, a tall spreading banyan tree was seen growing in the middle of the village to offer shade from the hot sun. It was a lovely sight, so peaceful and calm. Certainly, there had not been many changes since my last visit in the mid-1930s.

We met my father and brothers in Rangoon at the end of our holiday. I think we must have stayed there few days, for I recall sitting in the car outside the Sun Cafe in the afternoons. We didn't go in as it was considered improper for women to go into public places such as cafes and tea-rooms. So the driver took our order and came out carrying a large tray with curry puffs and glass bowls of vanilla ice-cream, which we solemnly ate in the car. When families went out to eat in the evenings, as in Chinatown or to the Indian section of town in Mogul Street, men usually sat at tables on the sidewalk, but women were served their food in the car.

My aunts and I stayed with some Burmese friends who worked in the railways and lived near the railway line. My father and brothers stayed at the Minto Mansion Hotel, which sounded romantic and mysterious to my ears. It was destroyed during the war for we never heard of it again. Soon our holidays were over. My brothers were to go back to their school in Taunggyi, while I was to be sent to a Methodist boarding school called Kingswood in Kalaw, another hill station.

Back at Yawnghwe, the tasks before Daw Daw were many and there was little time for her to try to adjust herself to her new duties. Apart from running the family and the house, looking after our own guests and my father's State guests, she had to attend to hundreds of other problems much as a lady of the manor in 19th century England would have done. Certainly the events of each day kept her well occupied and there probably never was enough time for husband and wife to spend time together as in a normal marriage. There was little time to consolidate their marriage, while any minor disagreements which they might have had could not easily be ironed out and had to remain unsolved.

As well, it was one thing being a younger wife who had specific duties and who kept her distance from her lord, but it was something else to be suddenly brought into close contact with a husband she hardly knew. Though she was a dutiful and faithful wife and fond of my father as he was of her, I wonder what their real feelings were for each other. I have often wondered how when a man has many wives he can be in love with all of them. Conversely, it can hardly be expected that all of them could be in love with the one man. I imagine that there had to be a favourite wife on his side, but what were the feelings of the chosen one? Would she learn to love him one day or would she feel that being his wife was merely another duty she had to perform?

*Yadana Mawng Aung pagoda, in the centre
of Yawnghwe town.*

# IIII

# *Growing up*

## *Thingyan – Buddhist New Year*

Our day-to-day lives in Yawnghwe varied little from year to year, punctuated by the festivals which occurred in eight months of the year. These were either held in honour of a certain pagoda or to celebrate a particular Buddhist event. Some months, two pagoda festivals would clash in the Inle villages. National festivals such as Thingyan, Buddhist New Year in April, and Tazaungbon, the festival of lights in November, were held all over the state and the country as a whole. Our Easter holidays generally coincided with *pii mai* or Thingyan and the annual State allegiance ceremony. There was no fixed day for Thingyan as the dates were determined by the lunar calendar, but usually the three days fell around 12th and 13th of April.

As a young child I was told I had to be a good girl during Thingyan as on the first day the Thagya Min, king of the *Devas* (the heavenly gods), descended to earth to assess who had been good and who had been bad. Three cannon shots heralded both his arrival and departure.

It was on the second day that he made his decision. The good had their names written down in the Golden Book, while the bad had theirs recorded in a dog-skin book. On the third day, having accomplished his mission, he left for his heavenly home. But he habitually left his pipe behind and would come back to fetch it the following day. So it was only on the fourth day, the first day of the Buddhist New Year, that we were free from his scrutiny.

During these three holy days people went to pagodas and monasteries and observed the Eight Precepts. Ordinarily, lay people took the Five Precepts, known as the *Pancasila*. These undertakings are not to take life, not to steal, not to commit adultery, not to tell lies and not to drink in excess. The additional three are not to eat after noon, to refrain from using perfumes and jewellery and to refrain from singing and dancing.

Like other families, we got up at dawn as the sun rose over the eastern mountains, and made our way to the pagoda in the centre of town, walking in procession, as we normally did on other Buddhist holy days. The bodyguards, in their black baggy trousers, red trimmed khaki jackets, and red turbans led the way. They carried our alms offerings of flowers and candles, water and food arranged in silver and golden lacquer bowls. My father, usually dressed in a silk Shan suit with a pastel pink turban, came next and we walked a few paces behind. The maids and pages followed with our sunshades, in case the sun got too hot before we returned home.

We would perhaps number some ten or fifteen people by the time other relations joined us, and in a long line we walked leisurely along. Fortunately there was little traffic then and if there did happen to be a lorry or a bullock-cart, they very kindly pulled over to the side of the road to let us pass, before once again stirring up clouds of dust from their whirling wheels. If we happened to pass other townspeople walking along, they would sit down on the road to make their *wai*, paying homage to their Saohpalong and letting us pass.

Arriving at the pagoda, we took off our shoes and slippers and entered by the eastern entrance. A covered passageway led into a square room and facing us in an alcove was a large sculpture of a seated Buddha. The sculptor had made the corners of the mouth turn up slightly, and as I sat with my palms together looking up in prayer, there seemed to be a faint smile on the gentle and benign face.

A pungent smell of joss sticks, burning wax and a fragrant scent from jasmine and frangipani flower offerings already on the altar assailed our nostrils. We spent about ten minutes saying our prayers and making our main offerings, before proceeding on a tour of the pagoda, stopping at the other altars on the northern, western and southern sides.

The walls of the wide passages which connected the different altar rooms were covered with provincial-style, brightly coloured murals depicting the life of the Buddha. The local artist had painted his women with great sweeping curves, giving them voluptuous looks. These pictures showed the ladies-in-waiting to the queen of Prince Siddhartha – some lying in sweet slumber, others snoring, some curled up tightly, others sleeping with their arms and legs in all directions displaying their breasts. They lay spread out on the floor, as the prince is shown tip-toeing and picking his way towards the inner chamber, where his wife lies asleep with a smile on her face clasping their little son to her bosom.

This was the scene prior to the departure of Prince Siddhartha, when he renounced all worldly things to go in search of Truth and Enlightenment. Most children, myself included, learnt about Buddhism through our elders. We said our prayers in Pali which we memorised, but did not understand. Later one began to learn about the Buddha, the Dhamma (His teaching) and the Sangha (the monkhood) by listening to the *Jataka* tales (relating his former incarnations) and looking at murals in pagodas. We were also taught what was right and wrong, good and bad, and to behave towards our elders with respect.

Before reaching the eastern side of the pagoda once more, we would stop beside the tombs of my great uncle, the Saohpa and his Mahadevi. These two gilded tombs lay in a courtyard of the pagoda where we placed flowers and lit a few candles, asking them to share in our merit. Neither the dead nor the many *phii* were ever forgotten when we went to pagodas. And nearly every *wan phra* or holy day, such as when there was a full moon, we would go to our mother's tomb which lay behind the pagoda. Here we lit candles and offered fresh flowers leaving with her our many thoughts. Now, beside her lies another tomb, that of Sao U Hpa.

It is forty years since his passing and I wonder if a time will ever come, when I will be able to go and pay my respects to him once more.

Having been to the pagoda we would carry on to the other monasteries, of which there were seven in Yawnghwe. Usually we did not go to all of them, but went to three one week and four the next. However during Thingyan we had to go to the pagoda and all the monasteries for three days running. While my father talked on Buddhist scriptures and philosophy to the different abbots at the monasteries, other people would arrive. Then together with three or four other families we would take the Eight Precepts in Pali, followed by a sermon, at each of the monasteries.

By the time we reached home we would all be pretty exhausted. The children, in particular, felt tired not from walking to one monastery after another, but from the boredom of sitting quietly with feet tucked under, listening to what was being discussed between our elders and the abbot of the monastery, but understanding little, since the conversation was peppered with Pali words.

On these holy days, my father generally retired to his little room on the top floor of his wing. Here he would spend the day in meditation and prayer. At other times too when he had a problem, it was to this room that he retreated.

I would do the same and climb up to a similar room at the top of our southern wing. It was cool up there as a gentle breeze floated through the open doors. Instead of meditating, I sat day-dreaming looking out at the magnificent view: on one side I could see right across town and on the other, the road leading out of Yawnghwe for miles on end. The houses were mainly of wood and bamboo and stood in square compounds where mango, banana and guava trees grew. In some compounds tall, proud palms with clusters of coconuts grew along the edge of their gardens.

Beyond the immediate circle of houses and tree tops could be seen the spire of the Yadana Mawng Aung pagoda at the centre of the town where we had just been. The spire or *htee* of semi-precious gems shimmered and sparkled in the sun throughout the day. Against the dark green of the banyan trees and the red flowers of the flame of the forest trees which lined the roads in twos and threes, the gold of the pagoda shone all the brighter. Looking towards the other side, it was fascinating trying to guess what was coming along that road. Tiny dots in the distance would gradually begin to take shape – lorries overloaded with goods half falling off, or a long line of bullock carts their wheels grinding eek-eek-eek monotonously along the road as they came into view.

I loved my room because from high above it was possible to look down on the people below going about their daily business. In one sense I was completely remote and detached, yet in another way I became attached, as I spent many an hour wondering about their individual lives.

On the second afternoon of Thingyan, we made the round of the seven monasteries to witness all the Buddha images being washed. Women fetched hundreds of pots of water from the wells of the different monasteries and took them, balanced elegantly on their heads, to tables laden with Buddha figures large and small. Sandalwood and other flowers, that had been collected a few days before from the forests nearby were crushed, and, together with rose water and eau de cologne, were mixed into the water we carried. The men then gently washed the Buddha images. New robes, some of silk and embroidered with gold thread and sequins, were then put on. Women were never allowed to touch the images, so once we had fetched enough water for one monastery and said our short prayers, we would make our way to the next. It was hot and we were grateful for a moment of res-pite under the shade of banyan trees by the wells, waiting for the men to arrive.

By the time we came to the last monastery, a mischievous cousin, helping to draw water from the well, would throw water all over us instead of filling our water chatties. Amid much laughing and giggling we would all join in splashing water over each other. One of our elders would cry out "Children, remember you are meant to be fasting, don't play around". She was right, of course. We had taken the Eight Precepts and should have been observing the day with solemnity and meditation. The day after to-morrow was really the day to start our fun.

At the end of the third evening, I generally failed to keep the fast. So defying the elders, a maid was often bullied into going down to the kitchen to cook some rice. Before long, a fragrant, appetising smell would come wafting up as she carried in a plateful of steaming white rice. It was garnished with salt, sesamum oil and *hto nau*. Nothing else was needed to complete this feast. *Hto nau*, made from soya beans is very much an acquired taste like the Burmese *nga pi*, or the Thai *khapi*, which is fermented fish paste. It is a favourite Shan food.

*Hto nau*, which literally means fermented beans, is nothing like the white tofu, which is made in a different way and can be bought in supermarkets in England and France. *Hto nau* is black or dark brown in colour, having been fermented, made into flat cakes, and dried in the sun. There are a number of different ways of using it to make tasty dishes. In this instance, the flat cake was toasted and pounded into a powder then sprinkled over the hot rice. Even now it is always a treat to receive a packet of *hto nau* from the Shan States.

Great attention was given to the *Thagyan sa*, a broadsheet issued on the eve of Thingyan in which the arrival and departure of the Thagya min is announced. Each year, astrologers worked out the exact time and what he was carrying in his hands. Water augured a cool, prosperous and peaceful year, anything else meant uncertain times. If a bad year was predicted, then an extra number of charitable works and good deeds were performed to gain merit and to avert, if possible, the misfortunes predicted.

In cities such as Rangoon and Mandalay, water throwing starts on the very first day of Thingyan and few people think of fasting. Hose pipes and trucks filled with drums of water are a regular feature, and water play gets very rough. When my husband and I lived in Rangoon, we joined a group of merrymakers and got completely soaked as we called on our various friends, before having a wonderful lunch at one of the houses.

*A Shan band with long drum.*

It was different in Yawnghwe. Water throwing only started on New Year's day after the annual audience at the Haw. This was held so that the ministers and secretaries of Yawnghwe State, together with the three Myosas of the three districts, village headmen and all other officials assembled in the Royal Throne Audience Hall could renew their allegiance to their Saohpalong. On this occasion my father sat by the high throne on the raised dais with the officials sitting below, facing him.

After some official business had been discussed, and my father had spoken to a few of them, they took their oath of allegiance.

I can picture quite clearly in my mind the rows of men sitting on the floor with serious faces, holding between their folded palms conical, banana-leaf tubes, each containing a flower and a sprig of *tha pye* leaf, sacred leaves known in English as Eugenia. Just as clearly I can hear the voice of Sao U Hpa giving them his blessing.

"For the homage and respect you bring me, may you and your families be free from all evil and harm, may both your mind and body be tranquil and at peace; and may you be free from all illness. May your life be long and one of good health, good fortune and prosperity".

When the audience came to an end and my father descended from the dais, we, together with my cousins, would ask his permission to sprinkle water on him. From silver bowls filled with rose-scented water and with flower petals floating on the surface, we would gently sprinkle him. We would then walk down the rows of officials asking their permission to do the same. This was carried out with politeness and courtesy, as it was a symbolic gesture of washing away all sins and evils.

However once my father had gone through to the inner audience hall, we began splashing the water much more freely. Unless they were quick on their feet, the beautifully silk-suited, pink turbaned officials soon found themselves thoroughly drenched. Sometimes, a brave and young official would ask permission to pour water over us and we, too, would be completely soaked.

It is sad to think that this age-old ceremony no longer has any meaning in the modern world. Without a Saopha, the moving experience of this ceremony can never be repeated, and remains only a memory.

In Laos, on our first visit in 1955 we were fortunate enough to witness such a ritual, where officials of the kingdom had come to make their oath of allegiance to the king. I was amazed at the similarity of the two ceremonies. Alas, the Lao tradition has also been abandoned as there is no longer the Kingdom of Laos, nor a King.

## Kam sang

In 1936, my eldest brother was due to go to England to further his education so my father decided that he should hold a *kam sang* for my brothers and at the same time, I should have my ears bored. Naturally, the *hsala* and the brahmin who officiated at the court had first to work out the most auspicious day for the event to take place, as was done for weddings and other important occasions. The *kam sang* is the ceremony when young boys in a Buddhist family enter the monkhood as novices for a week or ten days. It is generally a great occasion for any family concerned and each will strive to make it as successful as possible. Certainly for

*Shwe Yan Pye monastery, outside Yawnghwe.*

us, it was to be a grand affair, with male cousins joining in to become novices and female cousins joining to have their ears pierced.

The front grounds of our palace, where the tennis court and the riding ring were, were transformed into gilded pavilions, used for feeding the monks and guests, as well as providing shelter for those who had come from all over Yawnghwe state. The festivities were to last for seven days.

The series of rituals began with a long procession through the capital. My two brothers, riding on elephants and shaded by gold umbrellas, led the way while the cousins and others followed on horses and ponies with new bridles and decorated saddles. The howdahs on the elephants were also decorated and the elephants themselves were draped with gold and silver cloths. The boys were all dressed up and bejewelled, apparently in the manner of princes at the Mandalay Court.

Female relatives, all in their best silks with beautiful flowers in their hair, carried offerings for the Sangha and shaded themselves with Bassein parasols that added an even greater richness of colour to the procession.

Musical bands with young men and women dancing happily walked behind. This long line halted at our grandmother's apartment, then at the houses of our eldest uncles and aunts, where my brothers and cousins stopped to ask for their blessings. The ceremonial procession supposedly symbolized the last appearance made by Prince Siddhartha before he abandoned his family, his throne, his kingdom and his riches to become a recluse in search of Truth and Enlightenment.

The next day my brothers and the other boys with shaven heads, but still in their lay dress, came before the assembly of abbots and elderly monks. The Sangha sat in a row and in front of them were placed the various offerings which the women had carried the day before. Our family and guests sat some distance away facing the Sangha.

The ceremony began with the young initiates requesting permission to enter the monkhood. When permission was granted each abbot gave to a particular novice, the yellow robe. Once the robes had been put on, the novices joined the holy assembly of the Sangha.

After a long sermon by the chief abbot, the ceremony ended and the monks departed for their various monasteries, accompanied by the young novices. As they passed before us we made a *wai* of obeisance and paid homage to the newest members of the Sangha.

During the seven days of festivities, monks from all the monasteries in town and other abbots who attended from Inle Lake, were fed and offered alms. Apart from relatives, which ranged from the grandparents of each novice to fifth and sixth cousins, friends and villagers who had come from near and far were also fed and given gifts. One can imagine the large number of people fed, and the great pride Sao U Hpa took in seeing the ceremony come to such a triumphant end. This was his first *kam sang*, but he was later to hold two more for his other sons. My father was deemed to have been most fortunate in being able to hold three such ceremonies, and to have been blessed with so many sons.

In general, every Buddhist father and mother prays that they may have the good fortune to hold an ordination ceremony for their son before their deaths. So strong is the belief that such ceremonies would bring them merit, that parents would spend hundreds and thousands of *kyats*. Even if they did not have the money, they would beg or borrow it from somewhere, however high the interest.

My brothers stayed at the monastery for a week. During this time, they were taught the Buddhist Scriptures from the Pali Canon, the *Tripitaka*. Also they performed certain duties and ran errands for the abbot and elder monks. In additon, they had also to fast, as Buddhist monks eat only before midday, their early first meal being the *manet-sun* at dawn, and *ne-sun* at about 11 o'clock.

Every morning while my brothers were at the monastery, they, together with with other young monks, made their rounds through certain areas of the town with their black begging bowls for alms food. They started out from the monastery at around five-thirty when the newly-risen sun was less hot. They walked past us, their eyes firmly on the ground as we dropped our offering of rice and a piece of fried fish or pork into their bowls. No monk is allowed ever to look up and take notice of things happening around him, for as a member of the Sangha, he is expected to be above secular life, and only to concentrate on the Buddhist scriptures and meditation.

Anyone visiting Thailand and Laos will have seen this early morning ritual, which is a sight not easily forgotten: the pale yellow of the rising sun beaming on the long line of saffron-robed Sangha, as they make their way down a street with their heads bowed. Sitting in front of each house, a member of that family will first make her obeisance, then place the offering into the begging bowls of the ten or fifteen monks as they pass, before waiting for the next group until all the offerings are finished.

I am not certain whether the *kam sang* took place first, but it was during one of these seven days that the ear-boring ceremony was held. This ritual is usually performed at puberty when a young girl turns eleven or twelve years old. It is not a religious ceremony in contrast to the ordination of young boys, but a social one

*Sanda sitting in ceremonial dress for the ear-boring ceremony.*

proclaiming that the young girl has come of age. Although I was much younger, for convenience sake, it was decided to hold the ceremony at the same time.

I can remember Daw Daw and other aunts fussing over me and dressing me up in court dress worn by the ladies at the Court of Mandalay. In modern times this form of dress is usually worn by brides, or for very formal occasions and by athe *min-thami*, a female Burmese dancer. The *sin* or *longyi*, was extra long as it trailed behind and I had to walk very slowly with small mincing steps. My *sin* was claret-coloured, embroidered with gold and silver thread with thousands of sequins forming little circular patterns. My jacket was white, worn over a silk bodice, of matching colour to the *sin* but in a lighter colour. A bare U-shaped neckline was left, since the bodice only came above the breasts. Numerous strings of gold and jewelled necklaces were worn to fill the bare space. Since I did not possess any of them, I imagine they were borrowed jewellery from rich friends.

On my head I wore a headdress which was conical in shape and heavily decorated with gold and semi-precious stones. You can imagine what a weight it was. In the olden days it was worn by my grand-aunt, Sir Sao Mawng's Mahadevi for formal occasions, and also by our mother when she became Mahadevi. The headdress worn by Thai and Cambodian classical dancers was similar to these. No wonder these classical dances were slow, with little movement.

The ceremony began with a long recitation by the *pon na* or brahmin, which seemed endless. It was hot in the pavilion and I felt stifled in all the heavy clothes. Then suddenly there was silence and I felt a sharp prick on one ear, then on the next. I remember feeling a burning sensation all over after my ears had been pierced. A gold needle with a diamond stud at the end had been left in each of my ear lobes. As far as I can recall that was the end of the ear-boring ceremony and I was very glad to take off the headdress. It must have been boring to say the least, as a photograph shows me pouting and quite disgruntled.

*Sao Sai and Sai Hseng with Uncle San Lin, the school monitor.*

*Sanda in long* sin, *about 9 or 10 years old, dressed to take part in a school concert.*

## Taunggyi

While the years after the passing of the 1935 Burma Act were an explosive time in Burma Proper, things were quieter in the Shan States and the tempo of life was slow and gentle. Taunggyi, the administrative centre was one of the hill stations where colonial officials could enjoy a more relaxed atmosphere. Officials living and working there benefitted too. By becoming less formal, they no longer treated the Saopha with indifference, and their relationships improved. Official visits made to the various states became less awkward as they tried to adjust to local customs. However, I was too young then to understand what was going on, and saw the Superintendants or Assistant Superintendenst who came to see my father as tall, white, shadowy figures.

My two brothers were still at Taunggyi, attending the Shan Chiefs School. It was always a wonderful occasion when my aunts and I could go and see them. The school seemed to me a friendly place. The buildings were scattered around a rectangular piece of ground, with the dormitories ranged along one side of the rectangle and the classrooms on the other. I loved seeing my brothers in their uniform of white Shan trousers, dark jackets and pastel pink Shan turbans. They looked very smart, as, indeed, they had to be for they were under tight discipline.

Sai Hseng remembers the early morning roll calls at six every morning, with each student struggling to get dressed, trailing their long turbans of six or seven feet as each rapidly wound it around their heads. What a scramble it must have been. They were not spared the rituals of the English Public school for there was serious sports such as cricket and football. In their lessons, they were expected to be proficient in English, Shan and Burmese, while mathematics also played an important part. The town of Taunggyi was strictly out of bounds.

There were some exciting times too at the school, and Sai Hseng recounted one such event that happened in the early 1930s. At only seven years old, he was the youngest student at that time, but recalled that: "During the uprising in Burma Proper of the Galon rebellion, we at Shan Chiefs School had a strike and all the boys, except one, walked out and we barricaded ourselves in the pagoda at the top of the hill, south of Taunggyi.

"Uncle San Lin, who was our mother's brother and the Senior Monitor at the school, came to negotiate on behalf of the school authority which was, of course, the Saohpas on the school board."

The Galon uprising, actually began as a purely domestic issue concerning taxes imposed by the colonial government, but it soon gained momentum and grew into a national issue. Due to the timing of the school walk-out, it was at first feared that it might have had some political connotations.

Both the authorities and the British officials expected long, tiresome negotiations, but what an anti-climax it was when they finally found out the student demands. It appeared that all they wanted was to be allowed to go once a month to the cinema in town. I believe that everyone was so relieved that the demand was met without a murmur.

At holiday times, life was less formal and we used to drive up to see my brothers. Our visits to Taunggyi usually began early in the morning, in order to get to the school in time to have mid-morning snacks of Yawnghwe goodies. The stretch of road from Yawnghwe to the Bawrithat Pagoda was flat, with paddy fields on either side. A common sight were water buffaloes standing on the edge of the paddy field, their young owners perched on their broad shoulders. There were also egrets standing on one leg waiting patiently to catch the fish swimming in the flooded fields.

We soon came to Shwenyaung, where the railway terminus is situated, and it was here that we joined the highway leading to Taunggyi and on into the interior of the Shan States. Back in the early years of annexation, when the site for the railway terminal was decided, Sir Sao Mawng was invited to view the place and to give it a name. He chose what he felt was an auspicious name, and called it Shwenyaung, the reverse of Nyaungshwe, the name of his capital. The names in Burmese mean the Golden Bodhi Tree and Bodhi Tree Golden respectively.

Gradually we began climbing, but before that, we would pass an avenue of flame of the forest trees, their bright, red flowers forming a canopy overhead. As the road wound up the green forested hills, the air became cooler, then on a bend we would suddenly see the White Crow Lake. It was so called both because of its shape which resembled the two wings of a crow spread out in flight, and because a white crow was found here many years ago. It was presented to the then Saohpa, as it was considered highly auspicious to own an albino animal. Similarly revered were white elephants. Indeed, they have been the cause of at least one war among the Asian kingdoms such as when Ayutthya was attacked, because the Siamese king refused to give the Burman king a white elephant he had requested.

We continued climbing up the winding road, passing hills covered by a mass

*Bawrithat Pagoda on the road to Shwenyaung the
railway terminus.*

of differing shades of green where tropical trees and clusters of bamboo grew.
Around another bend, and soon we could see the Taunggyi Crag jutting up high
into the sky, just behind the town, dominating our view. It was a favourite picnic
spot, where an abundance of wild orchids could be found. Looking up from the
Yawnghwe valley the houses could be seen perched together in groups at the foot
of the Crag.

Sometimes on our visits we would see Sao Kya Zone of Hsipaw State. He was
a senior boy, who used to play football and the banjo. He knew all the latest songs
from the films and would entertain us. If Daw Daw knew some of the songs, they
sang together and it was fun.

Sao Kya Saing, his younger brother, was educated in the United States, and
became Saopha in the 1950s. When the 1962 coup took place he disappeared after
being arrested by the army. No one really knows what happened. He was married
to Inge Sargent, an Austrian lady who has written about the anxiety and agony of
that time in her book *Twilight Over Burma: My Life as a Shan Princess*.[14]

On one of the visits when the newly-released *Wizard of Oz* was on at the only
cinema in Taunggyi, we all went to see the much-talked-of film. It was my first
ever English picture so I did not really understand it. Although thrilled to be taken
to the cinema, I was frightened. I did not know who the strange characters were,
nor could I follow what they were doing. Nevertheless, I found myself thinking
about the film for a long time afterwards.

At the end of the Japanese occupation, the Shan Chiefs School was renamed
the Kambawza College. It was run by Sao Sai Mong, one of the many uncles
from the Kengtung family, and his Burmese wife, Mi Mi Khaing. They were both
scholarly people and wrote several books between them. Although there are no
longer Saohpa sons to be educated and trained, the buildings are still being used as
a state school.

One of the great festivities in those days was when all the Saohpas came to Taunggyi, to attend the annual Durbar. It was an occasion when the Governor generally came up from Rangoon to preside. It also provided an opportunity for the various Saohpas to discuss the problems of their states with the Governor. They must have hoped that he would listen and dutifully pass their concerns to the British government. But did that happen, I wonder? Undoubtedly, it was also a time when the princes themselves could unite to speak with one voice, but this rarely happened.

Although Taunggyi was a quiet hill station, it came alive when there was a Durbar or a major conference of the princes. On such occasions all the Saohpas and Mahadevis would be splendidly dressed. In the 1920s and 1930s, women wore their hair in high buns on top of their heads, which were decorated with flowers or glittering hair pins. It was also a wonderful opportunity for the women to show off their jewellery of sapphires and rubies, and was clearly a day in the year, which was greatly looked forward to, in a similar manner to those attending a Garden Party at Buckingham Palace. Everyone was determined to look their best and to show off their riches.

The town would suddenly come alive, bustling with people and noise while an influx of motor cars created traffic jams. Taunggyi filled up not only with the Saohpas and their families, but also with their retinues. It was a complete move from their various capitals to their Taunggyi palaces. There would be many gatherings of relatives and friends, and official parties given by the Commissioner.

Nearly all the Saohpas had their palaces along the foothills of the Taunggyi Crag, giving them a wonderful view of the town. Having a residence made life easier for the Saohpas if they had business at the administrative capital and needed to stay a few days, as a number of them lived many miles away. We too had a palace in Taunggyi, although Yawnghwe was only twenty miles away. However, the palace was convenient for my father when he had meetings which went on late into the night.

As can be imagined, it was a profitable time for the Indian and Chinese shopkeepers and other merchants alike. They never missed a trick, flattering and beguiling their customers, and there would be a constant flow of women buying clothes and textiles to take back home. The provision stores, likewise usually run by Indian merchants, made their profits at this time of year, providing Becks beer and Johnny Walker Red Label or Vat 69 whiskeys for the cellars of the Saohpas. The princes took the opportunity to stock up for the next few months, so they could entertain proudly any visiting British officials or other Saohpas.

As I grew up I soon began to learn some of the norms of our Shan society. When my father went to see other Saohpas who were also in town, he would take me along with him. As the Saohpa was my elder, I had to *wai*, and if we were sitting on the floor I had to firmly tuck my feet under me and sit facing him. As mentioned before, one never knew their names and they were all addressed as uncles and aunts.

One of the princes, now long dead, was a good friend of my father's. He was Sao Hkun Kyi of Hsahtung. My father and he shared similar views and ideas concerning the Shan States. His Mahadevi was slim and elegant with a beautiful smile, whom I called Sao Ah, meaning aunty. She was a kindly person and I loved going to visit them in their Haw in Taunggyi.

Hsahtung state lay south of Taunggyi and east of Yawnghwe and the people he ruled were chiefly Pa-O. He was a good ruler with an understanding of his people. He worked hard and encouraged these semi-nomads to settle down in villages and to become agriculturists. The Saohpa himself paid for young men to go away to school and a few to Rangoon university, because he believed they had something to contribute towards the progress of their State.

However, although he was well liked by many of his subjects, he could not satisfy all of them. Many of the up-and-coming young Pa-O politicians were not only anti British, but rejected the Shan feudal system, saying the Shans discriminated against them. Their feeling of neglect and anger against Saohpas was fuelled by activists of the AFPFL (Anti-Fascist People's Freedom League), who perhaps did not foresee the chaos an uprising would create. It was not a good time for the prince nor was it easy trying to pacify these young hot-heads.

Another family we used to call on was the Tawngpeng Saohpa, Hkun Pan Sing, whose state was mainly populated by the Palaung. It is a Northern Shan State and in those days it was a tea-producing *mong*. My father and he got on well, and shared common ideas on progress for the Shan. He had travelled in Europe and had sent his sons to be educated in England. One of them became a pilot and was killed in active service during World War II. Uncle Tawngpeng had several beautiful daughters, and it was said that he had a large number of children from his many wives.

They were incredible years – if only time could have stood still, or at least gone more slowly. In retrospect, the Saohpas certainly had a great deal to do if they were to achieve their ideals, but sadly they had neither the knowledge nor the time to do so.

## Sao Sai goes to England

On the 8th August 1936, my eldest brother Sao Hseng Hpa (Sao Sai), set sail from Rangoon on the S.S. *Yoma*, an eight thousand ton ship of the Henderson Shipping Line for England. Sao Sai recounted how my father was so keen to have him well prepared for King's School in Canterbury, that he sent him when he was five years old to learn English at a small private school in Kalaw. It was only when he was about eight or nine years old that he went to the Shan Chief's School at Taunggyi. To further improve his English, the Headmaster's wife gave him private tuition. He enjoyed these sessions as he was always given tea and cakes. He was also coached on how to behave once he got to school, but I'm sure it was probably very different, when he found himself at Canterbury.

It must have been quite a daunting experience for Sao Sai who was only about twelve or thirteen to leave for England alone. My father and all the family went on board the ship to see him off. When it was time for us to leave and we had all wished him bon voyage he put on a brave face and waved to us as the launch departed. He then ran to the other side of the ship hoping to catch a last glimpse of us only to find that the sides were all boarded up and he could no longer see out. He later told me he was so disappointed that he broke down and sobbed, "I think it was the only time that I ever felt so disheartened and sad."

What a voyage it must have been for such a young boy to make on his own. It seemed that no one bothered very much in those days about any trauma he could have suffered. Admittedly, young children of the colonial officials were also sent back at an early age for their education, but at least they had the consolation of returning to their own country, with their grandparents and family to befriend them. As for Sao Sai, although he was curious and willing to learn, it must have been difficult for him to adjust to foreign life. The King's School at Canterbury, was one of the smaller public schools recommended by Sir John Claque, a friend of my father's. I am not sure whether he realised that his son was attending a school claiming to have been founded in 597, making it the oldest school in England, although its recorded history only starts from the sixteenth century. However, by 1936 when Sao Sai arrived, the ancient school had recently been redeveloped and he found himself in one of the newer boarding houses, Walpole House with Ronald Groves as the Housemaster. My brother was known as Sao Sao I and his younger brother who joined him in the same house two years later, as Sao Sao II. Later, they both became prefects.

Little did we think when we waved him goodbye that it would be ten whole years before we would see him again. It was only after the end of World War II and the end of the Japanese occupation, when he came home.

## Kingswood School

It was now my turn to be sent to a boarding school. Sao U Hpa was set on sending me to Kingswood, as he felt I would learn English quicker being the only Shan girl there amongst English and Eurasian girls. Most of the other Saohpas' daughters went to St Agnes Convent in Kalaw or St Anne's in Taunggyi. It was really very daring of him to consider sending me to this American Methodist school which was a co-educational establishment. It was run by the same organisation as that of the Methodist High School in Rangoon and its pupils came from families working for such companies as Bombay Burma, Burmah Oil Company and Shell.

It was typical of my father that he was determined to get all the details correct. I hold two notes written by him, one to the abbot of a monastery in Yawnghwe and the other to an official, giving my birth date according to the lunar calendar and asking them to confirm the equivalent date in the Gregorian calendar which he had meticulously worked out. The date was confirmed as 20th October 1928.

*A deserted Kingswood School, Kalaw front view, c. 1960.*

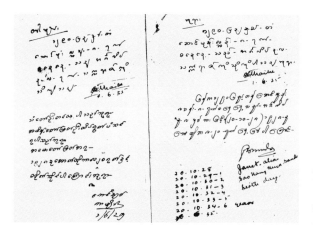

*Sao U Hpa's note verifying the date of my birthday and checking my name for entrance to Kingswood School.*

Armed with this information which he had checked from these two sources he was able to enrol me at Kingswood as Sao Nang Mya Sanda. All was well except for the fact that the Principal, Miss Mellinger, thought the Shan name which translated as Princess Lady Emerald Moon was too long for use at school. Instead, she renamed me Janet (the name of her niece in Ohio) with the surname Thaike, my father's last name.

It was in this way that many of the Saohpas' daughters and sons became known by the English names given to them at these schools. My eldest brother's wife, Sao Shwe Ohn was called Pat, my second brother's wife, Sao Hom Noan, became Audrey and other cousins were known as Victoria and Nancy, or Ivan and Vincent.

It is a pity in a way that we all adopted English names, as the Shan names for women are pretty and gentle. Both the Shan and the Lao have names with similar meanings such as Kham (gold), Nam (water), Hom (fragrant), Noom (tender, young), Hseng (jewelled) and so on. A large number of names are taken from Pali like those in our family. My three sisters are Sita (water), Hayma (forest), Ratana (gem), and myself Sanda (the moon). Men are usually named after great warriors, fierce animals and things pertaining to might and power.

Sao U Hpa decided to take me to Kingswood himself. What an honour this was! Miss Mellinger introduced my father to the teachers and then took us on a tour of the school. Quite a stir was created, as none of the European children had ever seen a Shan Saohpa at such close quarters, dressed in his Shan suit with a large turban on his head.

The formalities were soon over, and after giving me a gentle pat on my head and some words of encouragement, Sao U Hpa and his retinue of aunts and uncles, secretaries, bodyguards and maids made their departure. With a loudly beating heart and choking as I desperately tried to suppress my sobs, I waved until I could no longer see the cars. I was now quite alone in my new and strange surroundings.

Though Kalaw was only about forty-five miles, or a two-hour drive, from Yawnghwe, I was utterly desolate. One would have thought it was the end of the world. Gone was the confidence and defiance I had had at the little primary school. I couldn't help thinking that perhaps had I behaved a little better I wouldn't have been sent to this alien place.

However, my future stepmother's niece, Evelyn, one of the senior girls, re-members that I didn't seem to have entirely lost my fighting spirit. She recounted that on the first day I was at school, though I was pretty miserable, I had said to her and the other senior girls who were trying to comfort me, "I am not going to stay here. I am going to the station, and I will get a taxi and go home". On being asked, how would I go without any money, my reply was, "I shall tell them that I am the daughter of the Saohpa of Yawnghwe". How insufferable I must have been. I do not recall this incident at all, but I am sure it was true.

School proved to be much more fun than I had expected, but I lived only for the weekends when parents were allowed to come and see their children. Daw Daw was the faithful one who used to turn up nearly every weekend in my first year. On these days, we would drive out into the countryside and sitting beneath towering pines, my aunt would unwrap little packages containing delicious Shan food which I missed so much in school. Each week there was something differ-ent. I loved the fragrant purple glutinous rice which was eaten with fried fish, or with little lumps of palm sugar, if one preferred it that way. Fish rice and pork rice wrapped in banana leaves, a speciality of Yawnghwe and the Inle Lake, were also favourites. There were countless sweetmeats flavoured with coconut and sweet-ened with palm sugar all so delicious and mouth watering, too many to remember.

Sometimes, my aunt arrived early and we would drive to Aungban, near Heho where a good friend of her's was the Mahadevi of Hsamongkham. She was the daughter of the Saohpa of Samka, the state which lies to the south of the Inle Lake. She was tall and slim with a long slender neck and she always wore a three-strand pearl necklace. In contrast, her husband the Saohpa was small in stature with a smiling face.

Hsamongkham was one of the Myelat states where many of the Pa-O, Danu and Taungyo peoples lived. The soil, almost red in colour, is rich and fertile and in those days vegetables such as potatoes, onions, and garlic were grown here, while the fruits included oranges and pineapples. Most of the produce was sent to Burma Proper.

Kalaw, I learnt to love. As a hill station it was perfect. Pine trees covered the hilltops and being some 3,000 ft high, it had a temperate climate. The main rail-way line from Rangoon and the plains came through the little town. Snake-like, the railway line slithered round hillsides and through tunnels, gradually descending to Heho, a tiny market village in those days. Today, it is a busy airport both for civilians and the military. Leaving Heho, the railway line comes through the wide, flat Yawnghwe valley stopping abruptly at Shwenyaung, the terminus.

There was something special about Kalaw. Except for its altitude, it was quite unlike Taunggyi. It was a quiet, primly laid out town. Here old British government servants, colonels and judges came to retire. Each had built their own house as they might have done in Cheltenham or Bournemouth nestled among the forest of pine. In their beautifully-kept gardens grew temperate flowers as roses, gladioli, chrysanthemums, iris, and pansies, together with gorgeous tropical flowering trees such as jacaranda and acacias. The orchards were filled with wonderfully flavoured ripe, red strawberries, peaches and plums. There was a profusion of colour in these gardens. Surrounded by pine trees, the air smelt fresh and clean.

The long drive which led to the school was lined with acacia trees and when they were in bloom, a canopy of pink and white blossoms formed above the road. There were pine trees growing everywhere, and on one side of the drive were tennis courts where passion fruit climbed in abundance over the slopes. The drive ended beside a large basket-ball field.

Kingswood stood on one of the main hills that made up Kalaw. It was neatly built with two large buildings on either side of a covered play shed. The first floor of one of the buildings housed the girls in dormitories with rooms for the live-in teachers. The Principal had a suite of rooms below, together with the large dining room and school offices. The other building consisted of an Assembly Hall and classrooms.

The boys were accommodated in a large house further up another hill. We had mixed classes and played games together, but had our meals at different tables. At study hour, we could sit where we wanted and the older students would sit together in mixed groups. A teacher on duty kept watch to see that we were really doing our home work and not playing around.

I was surprised that we learnt our lessons quietly. We were taught not only to read and write, but also to draw. I was very excited to find that by putting two circles one on top of the other, adding whiskers, two up-right ears and a tail curling upward, you had created a pussy cat sitting with his back to you. Then came the crayons. With these I never tired of drawing rainbows. I was obsessed with trying to create masterpieces with these rainbows, splashing the colours over mountain tops, acres of paddy fields and isolated bamboo houses.

When after a heavy rainfall, a real rainbow appeared across the sky seemingly just in front of the school, we younger girls would rush out and run after the dazzling colours trying to find the end of the rainbow and buried treasures. It was all great fun.

After rainbows came the fairies. We read stories about fairies and elves. To my mind, fairies were English and they lived only in the world of my school, while the *phii* or spirits were from the world of my home. Fairies were dainty and tiny, light-hearted and happy, and one did not have to fear them as one did the *phii*. I loved peering into the little hollows of tree trunks across which a spider had spun his web, imagining the fairies living there. Through the lacy curtains I could see the banqueting hall. To me, the little beads of crystallized gum were fairy lights and drops of dew sparkling in the sunlight, were glittering gems. What a fantasy world I lived in! But it was not a world I thought of taking home.

Perhaps even at that age, I was beginning to see the difference between school and home. They were two distinct worlds in my mind. There was a western way which did not fit with our strict, ancestral customs, nor did our eastern way of life fit into that of the west. Of course these differences have become somewhat reconciled today, but I doubt that they will ever be so completely.

One of the things which troubled me was that neither the older girls nor the teachers minded that their protruding breasts showed under their dresses. At home, breasts were bound tightly under bodices to make them flat, and in fact, it was thought shameful to show any part of your body to anyone other than to your husband. Somewhat incongruously, however, Shan mothers suckling their babies never minded in the slightest showing off their naked breasts, while in the west, until recently, mothers did not breast feed their babies in public.

Having learnt some English and hearing the other girls talk about their 'Daddy and Mummy', I became braver towards my father. When for the first time I went home for my holidays and saw him walking in some procession or other, I impatiently asked the car to be stopped and, crying out 'Daddy, Daddy', ran and jumped up into his arms. He was both taken by surprise and pleased at the same time that I had began to speak English. He felt I was making progress. From that time onwards, I was less afraid of my father and as he liked talking to me in English, our relationship became less formal. Our family now became trilingual, speaking Shan, English and Burmese.

## Sai Hseng goes to England

It was soon the turn of my elder brother, Sai Hseng, to be sent to England, where he was to join our eldest brother, Sao Sai, at King's School. Once again, aged only twelve or thirteen, he had to make the voyage alone. I suppose he was in the care of the ship's Captain, who during the voyage told him that there was likely to be a World War, and that he would have to leave the ship at Marseilles. A Thomas Cook representative met him there and he continued his journey by train to Canterbury. The reason for the diversion soon became clear for it was September 1938 and an important time for England. As Sai Hseng later wrote in his memoirs, "I learnt later that it was during the Munich Crisis when Neville Chamberlain was trying to appease Hitler."

On arriving at the school he was to find gas masks on all the boys' beds and windows blacked out; with such precautions being taken he realized that war was undoubtedly imminent. However it was not until 3rd September 1939, a year later, that war was to be declared.

Despite the doom and gloom of that time, one can imagine the joyful reunion that the two brothers must have had. What a great deal they had to tell each other, for it was a good two years since they had been separated and much had happened during that time. Sao Sai had many things to recount about the school and the English people he had an opportunity to meet, while Sai Hseng was able to give news of our father, the new stepmother, other members of the family and

Yawnghwe, with all the detail which letters can never convey. Then, there was his sea voyage and the train journey from France, all new and exciting experiences to relate to his brother.

Little by little Sao Sai was able to guide his younger brother through school life, so full of "dos and don'ts". When war broke out the school was evacuated to Cornwall near St. Austell. Sai Hseng recounts how the boys were given the task of removing the beds and luxurious furniture from the hotel they were to occupy in favour of their school beds and furniture. All the fine linen also had to be taken away and replaced with those from the school. Despite turning the hotel into a Spartan public school, the place maintained its charm. The swimming pool still existed, as did the beautiful grounds. All in all, the move to this temporary abode turned out to be a pleasant change for the boys.

While the other Houses were installed in the hotel, Walpole House was allotted a lovely country house in its own woods not far from the hotel and Sai Hseng remembers having to walk through a wood to go for his piano lessons. He enjoyed playing the piano and he was proud to have won a prize for his House when there was a competition. The boys continued with their lessons and with biology came dissecting which he didn't much enjoy. The war continued and together with the older boys, he joined the Cadet Corps. As Prefects, they were given guard duty down on Carlyon Bay. On occasions, the boys used to stop fishermen coming along the beach and ask them what they were doing. The men would often take umbrage and thoroughly enjoyed cursing the boys. However, on the whole the Cornish villagers good-naturedly tolerated the newcomers.

During parade in the Officers Training Corps (OTC), Sao Sao I, who was slight in build, is remembered as being smaller than the rifle he carried. Appparently the rifles dated back to the Boer War! He left in July 1942 to go up to St John's at Cambridge to read engineering, so was spared having to carry the heavy rifle for too long.

The war seemed endless and, with bombs falling on St Austell and along the coast right up to Plymouth, it felt near to home. One exciting occasion was in March 1944 when Field Marshall Montgomery, an old King's pupil, came to visit the school in Cornwall, perhaps when he was inspecting the troops preparing for the D Day landings. Soon after D Day, Sai Hseng left King's for Cambridge to read agriculture at Pembroke College. Once again, his elder brother was to show him the ropes. A year later Sao Sai came home to Yawnghwe. Being ten years away, he found a great many changes.

## Colonel and Mrs Jimmy Green

It must have been some time in 1936, that Jimmy and Dorothy Green came to see us in Yawnghwe. Jimmy was a Colonel in the Burma Rifles when I met him. It was in his battalion that my father served, so they became friends. He had first come to Burma from the Indian Army way back in 1918. As a recruiting officer, he travelled widely in the Frontier Areas taking numerous photographs of the various peoples he came across. He was an amiable person with a kind manner and people took a liking to him.

*Daw Daw and self in a boat 1936.*

*Sitting L to R: Aunty Marie, my stepmother's half-sister and Pat; Standing L to R: Daw Daw and Nang Ngwe Kyi, one of Hsenwi Saohpa's wives.*

On this visit, my father decided that we should go out to the Bungalow on Inle Lake for a picnic. In those days motor boats were not widely used and we were rowed there by eight men. The long dug out had a bamboo matting cover in the middle to shade us from the sun. Four men stood at the prow and four at the stern and in unison, they rowed with their legs, practising a form of rowing which, I believe, is unique to Inle. The boat moved smoothly and swiftly, and we did not have to endure the noise of the outboard engine.

They were the first English visitors who made an impression on me, perhaps because Jimmy showed me a trick in which he made his thumb disappear. I don't remember how it was done, but it certainly kept me wondering and I am sure he had to perform his magic a number of times for me that day. Dorothy was a striking beauty with a charming smile and I became immediately attached to her. It was also the first time that I had met an English couple, who happily talked and joked with us. I hadn't been at Kingswood for long and my English was still faulty, but their informality made our family forget our shyness and timidity.

I was glad that on this visit the Greens had come only to pay a social call and not to go on a shoot. I am sure that like other English friends, Jimmy had on occasion accompanied my father on shoots, for the Inle was full of wild ducks and snipe. Much later, when I met them again in England they felt like family. Jimmy was one of my father's oldest English friends and had known our mother, the first Mahadevi. I used to go and see them during my school holidays, and they were kind and hospitable.

Jimmy like Major Enriquez, developed a keen interest not only in the Chin and Kachin peoples, but also in other ethnic groups who lived in the hills and the hinterlands, inhabited by a diversity of tribes.

The Padaung live mostly in and around Kayah, Southern Shan State. The majority of them are Christians. Their custom of wearing brass rings around their neck is still maintained, but may slowly disappear as young women of future generations leave their villages to go elsewhere to be educated and to work. I have heard that today some hoteliers and those in the tourism industry are exploiting the ethnic Padaung. It seems totally unacceptable that one's compatriots could be put into compounds for tourists to gape at. It was bad enough for the few who were shown in Bertram Mills' circus some sixty or seventy years ago when Burma was still under colonial rule, but to organize such shows for tourists today is incredible and positively inhuman. Of course, it is possible that those participating have been enticed by the money they can earn for their hard-up families back in their villages.

Surely, if the organizers genuinely wanted to show Padaung culture, it would be better for the hardier tourists to seek them out in their own environment, where they could see the villages and their surroundings to learn first-hand how the Padaung actually live.

The Palaung from the Northern Shan State of Tawngpeng grew tea, while others also live in the Southern Shan State. The women wear colourful jackets, broad bands or torques around their heads and hoops over their stripped red skirts – a costume similar to those of the Kachin women.

The Wa were often known in those early days as 'head-hunters'. They live on the north-eastern border of the Shan States, just north of Kengtung and east of Hsenwi states respectively, falling within the Golden Triangle. Originally animists, many have been converted to Christianity, although today opium seems to have become their major pre-occupation.

When Jimmy died, Dorothy turned their house in Surrey into a museum. It was full of Shan and Kachin artefacts and there were thousands of photographs that Jimmy had taken of his favourite ethnic peoples. Included in these were those of my family in earlier days. Soon everything in the little museum was donated to The Royal Pavilion, Libraries and Museums in Brighton. A special centre was then set up in memory of Colonel Jimmy Green in 1998. It is currently known as the James Green Centre of World Art, which is supported by the James Henry Green Charitable Trust.

As an anthropologist, Jimmy took a special interest in the customs and beliefs, habitat and way of living of the peoples he photographed. His pictures also capture the beauty of massive hills and rivers, and the thick, wooded valleys of these territories. Some of these many photographs have now been published by the Green Centre in a beautifully laid out book. It is a fitting memorial illustrating his love for the people of the Highlands of Burma. Apart from leaving behind this fine collection of extraordinary photographs for us, he also gave us an understanding of how others saw us in those days. Since then, of course, much has happened and the young are no longer found in these remote hills. Many have joined nationalist groups fighting for equality, while others have gone to major international cities to find their niche in the modern world.

As Elizabeth Dell has written "The 1,600 photographs of the Green Collection provide a valuable and very specific record of Burma between the First and Second World Wars, when the British and Indian military had a profound impact on its peoples and territories."[15]

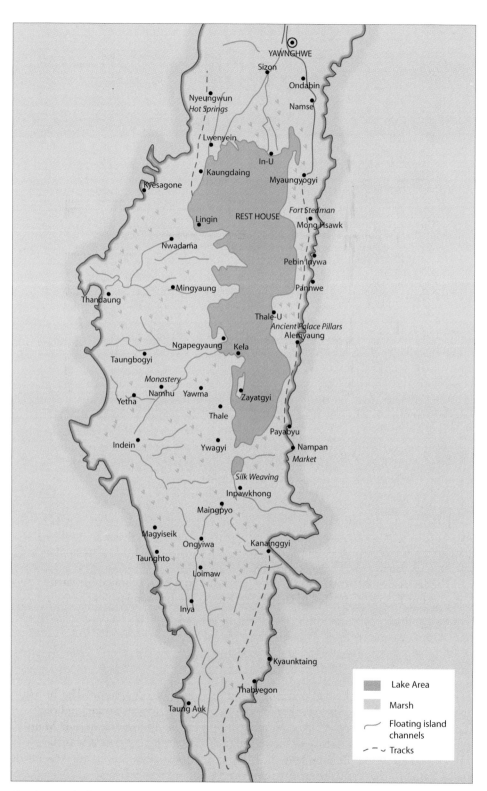

YAWNGHWE
Sizon
Ondabin
Nyeungwun
Hot Springs
Namse
Lwenyein
In-U
Kaungdaing
Myaungyogyi
Kyesagone
Fort Stedman
Lingin
REST HOUSE
Mong Hsawk
Nwadama
Pebin Inywa
Mingyaung
Pannwe
Thandaung
Thale-U
Ancient Palace Pillars
Alemyaung
Ngapegyaung
Kela
Taungbogyi
Monastery
Yetha
Namhu
Yawma
Zayatgyi
Thale
Payabyu
Indein
Ywagyi
Nampan
Market
Silk Weaving
Inpawkhong
Maingpyo
Magyiseik
Ongyiwa
Kanaïnggyi
Taunghto
Loimaw
Inya
Kyaunktaing
Thabyegon
Taung Auk

Lake Area

Marsh

Floating island
channels

Tracks

*Sketch map of Inle.*

# IV

## Inle and Intha

*Phaung Daw U Buddha images.*

### The Phaung Daw U Festival

The annual event which takes place on Inle Lake has now become internationally renowned. A few years ago the *Geographical Magazine* published a detailed and explanatory article with beautiful pictures and tourists today seem to travel from all over the world to attend this six hundred year-old celebration. It usually takes place in the lunar month of Thadingyut, which falls sometimes in late September or early October.

The festival was a favourite of mine, and one to which I looked forward throughout the year. It was sad that even though my husband and I spent four years in Rangoon, we never once managed to make the trip back to Yawnghwe to attend this event. As many as sixty years have passed since I last participated in the Phaung Daw U festival, and I envy those friends who have managed to do so in recent years.

October 1945 must have been one of the largest and most crowded, with everyone celebrating the end of the war and the Japanese occupation. The British had returned and, with peace, there was a new lease of life for young and old. There was a general feeling of relief and there was much to rejoice about. Many who had fled from the Japanese to the villages of the Inle, felt that it was the sacred powers of the Phaung Daw U Buddhas that had protected them. As a result many came to the festival to show their reverence and respect.

The Yawnghwe valley runs north to south with the Inle Lake stretching south-wards to Samka State. The lake gradually becomes a river and the waters of the Nam Philu, meaning an ogre, drain the lake and wind their way through Samka State. Further south the river flows through Kayah State and eventually joins the Salween river. To the east and west the lake is enclosed by hills which rise on each side to some 5,000 ft.

Little did we realize, when Peter bought a Kha drum in northern Laos that it was a product from our own backdoor. It came from a Shan village known as Ngwe Daung, the Silver Hill, near Loikaw, in Kayah State. Apparently, it was in the late 1890s that the last genuine bronze Kha drum was made. Many people travelling in Thailand and Laos will have seen these drums, but today it is only in museums that one is likely to find the original, ancient drums which were crafted by hand. The drums, with one, two and three frogs sitting around the rim, became popular in the 1960s and 1970s, with a number of them being displayed in hotels in Bangkok. However, most were, I believe, manufactured in bulk and faked to look antique.

Inle Lake was one of the three administrative regions of Yawnghwe State. In those days, the area of the lake was seven miles across from east to west and about fourteen miles from north to south. The numerous small rivers and channels lead-ing into the lake tend to become silted or blocked by water hyacinths and water weeds unless cleared annually. All these years on, the habitual silting will have undoubtedly lessened the area of the lake.

Long channels led to villages built in the interior of the lake. A tall bamboo pole with an old tin can on top would be the only sign showing the entrance to a village. Other times a bunch of knotted reeds indicated which channel to follow. It can be incredibly difficult to enter a village when the lovely mauve hyacinths blocked the entrance. In fact, unless one was an inhabitant of the lake, it was

*Girl in a sampan with sun shade.*

*Reflections.*

almost impossible to find one's way around. Once a channel has been cleared, the boat eventually emerges into open space revealing a village, often a cluster of houses seemingly suspended in mid-air. As the village houses are built on long bamboo or wooden stilts, from a distance all one can see is the expanse of the water below and the blue sky above.

From the time of Saohpa Sao Si Hseng Hpa, through twenty-nine successive reigns until the time of my father, it has been the custom to take the Buddha images from the monastery at Namhu in a procession of boats through various towns and villages. In my father's day, this event took over a fortnight, covering some twenty different localities. At some places, it was a one-night stop, at others a brief few hours in the morning so that alms-food might be offered.

There was a belief when I was young that should the tour of the Phaung Daw U Buddhas not take place, the State of Yawnghwe and particularly the Inle, would suffer disasters and epidemics, causing a large number of people to die. I cannot remember whether this has actually happened, but certainly the period of the Japanese occupation was not a good time for the state.

The other tradition is that only four of the images can be taken on procession, with the fifth, aptly named 'the royal guardian of the monastery', always remaining at the Namhu monastery.

Apparently, very many years ago the fifth Buddha was taken on tour. No sooner had they left the village, than a great and fearsome storm arose. There were flashes of lightning and loud claps of thunder, and the entire sky was dark with thick black clouds hanging low. It was morning and everything had been fine when they had started out. The boatmen made their way towards the nearest floating islands for shelter and managed to get the royal barge carrying the images anchored safely.

*The Karaweik barge surounded by small boats of worshippers.*

The storm abated as suddenly as it had arisen. Once again the sky was blue and the sun shone brightly. When the men were ready to start off on their journey again, they could not find the fifth Buddha *rupa*. The attendants were in great fear and trembling and had no idea what to do. Then from a distance shouts were heard and there appeared in view a messenger from the Namhu monastery. "The Buddha, the Dharma, the Sangha. What holy wonder. The fifth Buddha image is back in the golden casket at the monastery", he cried.

Everyone was awestruck. A miracle they could not have imagined experiencing in their life time had occurred. Thus for many years since then, the fifth Buddha image has never been taken out of the monastery whether on tour or elsewhere. Then in 1965, for whatever reason it is not known, the fifth Buddha image was taken out once more and the royal barge overturned. Once again only four of the images were recovered, but the fifth, like before, was found back on its golden throne at the Namhu monastery. To commemorate this incident, a golden Hintha (a mythical bird) was erected, rising high into the sky to mark the place.

Since the lake is not very deep, when there are strong winds, the waves can be very high. Both my brother, Sai Hseng, and Daw Daw experienced the storms. During the Japanese occupation, when she was on her way back to Yawnghwe to see my father from our Inle village, Daw Daw was caught in a storm. She had to spend several uncomfortable hours anchored on one of the floating islands. She told us that it was very frightening and she was terrified that she might drown. So accounts about storms on the lake shouldn't be taken too lightly.

*The Karaweik
close-up.*

## Karaweik Phaung

The day for the arrival of the Phaung Daw U Buddha images at Yawnghwe was always one of great excitement and activity for everyone in the capital. As a young child, I remember being awakened at dawn and dressed quickly. Suddenly I would hear my father's voice shouting "Hurry, hurry, we'll be late." We were bundled into cars and taken to the landing stage where a special boat was waiting for my father. We then sped through the canal and across the water to the bungalow that stood in the middle of Inle.

After an early breakfast, my father changed into his long, shimmering, golden embroidered coat, which is worn only for very special ceremonial occasions. My two brothers were dressed similarly to my father, wearing pastel coloured silk turbans and matching coats. After a while my father with my two brothers were taken to the magnificent Karaweik Phaung to await the Phaung Daw U images.

A '*karaweik*' is a mythical bird, and '*phaung*' means barge. In those days, the *phaung* was constructed on a wooden platform covering the widths and length of three long, large dugout boats. In the middle of the platform stood a golden throne on which the royal images were placed. The bow carried the head and the stern the tail, the whole structure representing the form of the mythical bird. In the middle, the roof of the pavilion supported three separate multi-tiered *htees* of glittering colours, which tapered up into the sky. The barge was so intricately made that I wondered at the time and labour that must have gone into building it. The *karaweik* was decorated in diverse colours and was a stunning sight, sitting serenely on the clear blue waters with a red crystal ball in its beak.

*Bodyguards following the procession.*          *Below: Teams of leg rowers in long, thin boats.*

My father did not have to wait too long, for suddenly the sound of gongs across the waters gave warning of the arrival of the Phaung Daw U Buddhas. Necks would be craned and, catching sight of a dot on the horizon, one kept one's eyes fixed on it. Then suddenly, two or three racing boats appeared towing the small royal barge, shining and glittering in the sunshine. It is this barge which takes the Buddha images around the villages of the lake, while the larger Karaweik *phaung* is used when the Saohpa goes to fetch them to his capital. It is used again three days later, when he takes them to Linkin village on the next stage of the tour.

When the two barges were abreast of each other the Buddha images were transferred from one to the other. Then, as if at a given signal, all the gongs would be sounded and with loud cries from the men in their racing boats, the larger barge moved forward. The special orchestra which had accompanied the Buddha images in the smaller barge began playing regal music as it followed behind. Sometimes another small barge followed, like a floating stage, on which young girls from different villages danced to the music of their own orchestras.

On the royal barge, white and gold ceremonial umbrellas unfurled and my father could be seen making his obeisance in front of the highly decorated throne on which the four golden Buddhas were placed. This is the particular moment of

the entire festival which I always remember with an ache in my heart. It is something which I cannot explain, but whenever I think of the Phaung Daw U festival, it is this picture that I see before me. My father sitting with his feet tucked under him, the palms of his hands placed together touching his forehead with a look of serenity on his face, a solitary figure in the midst of the rousing cries and cheers. The glittering Karaweik in the bright sunlight, the blue waters and the cloudless sky above created for me, an unforgettable picture. It barely lasted a moment. The gongs soon reach a crescendo, and the royal barge slid forward again, as the waters lapped gently at its sides.

The procession on the water was most spectacular. Hundreds of leg-rowers in long dugout boats strung together stern to prow and numbering some ten or twelve boats in a single line, would tow this golden barge to Yawnghwe. Each of these racing boats carried twenty to thirty men from the different villages of the lake. Standing in equal numbers on either side of the waist-high rail running down the middle of the boat, the men held on to it with one hand. Then, balancing himself on one leg with the other leg wrapped around the long oar, the rower pushed himself forward, dipped the oar in the water and made a swift stroke. All rowed in unison to the beat of the gong. The cox, with gong in hand, could be seen first at the head of the boat, next at the rail dancing and shouting encouragement to the men. The strokes these boats kept were as exciting to watch as those of the Oxford and Cambridge racing crews.

The participating villages were distinguished by a flag flown by each boat or by the same colour outfits in which each had chosen to dress their men, creating in effect a kind of uniform. Baggy Shan trousers, Chinese-style jackets and turbans were the usual dress. Sometimes one or two boats of young novice monks in their saffron robes would join the long line.

As soon as the racing boats flashed past with the golden barge gently floating behind, followed by the State barge, there was a mad scramble to be first to reach the channel which led back to town. Our State barge, a wooden house boat of the type one might see on the Thames at Chelsea or any English canal, had been anchored a little distance away from the Karaweik. As the barge was engineless it needed a tow from at least two racing boats to keep it moving at a good steady pace. Invited State guests such as other princes, the Commissioner and some other government officials were on board. After the war, apart from Saohpas, most of the invited guests were largely those from the diplomatic corps and Burmese government officials. Numbering about twenty, they were entertained with food and drink during the morning's festivities. Soon after my father and brothers departed from the bungalow, we, the women of the family made our way towards the State barge and joined our guests.

Growing all around us in large clumps were an abundance of water lilies in a variety of colours – a lovely deep red, pure white and white with purple tinted petals. There were also the beautiful, tall lotuses of white and pink, standing proud of the water and forming another pattern above the ripples of the lake. Further on were the water hyacinths which formed carpets of mauve and green. At that time of year, the patches of different colours formed by these flowers were an artist's dream.

When the royal barge at last reached Yawnghwe, the images were placed onto the waiting gilded chariot. My father would be handed his special Buddha, the roundest in shape, and almost staggering under its weight, he carried it slowly to the chariot. Over the years, all five Phaung Daw U images have lost their original form, gradually become spherical, due to the countless sheets of gold leaf that have been rubbed on, adding yet a little more weight in gold each year.

From the landing stage, known as the arrival stage, the chariot was slowly pulled across the town by people on foot to the Haw, with my father following behind shaded by white umbrellas. All along this route were carpets of silks, velvet and flowers. Women and children who had been up since dawn created a carpet on the road patterned with roses, jasmine flowers, sandalwood blossoms and frangipani. In addition, either side of the road was decorated with woven bamboo screens to which were tied banana leaves and green branches.

At special points gilded pavilions were erected and at these the chariot would make a momentary stop. Immediately a great murmur would rise up as people in the packed pavilion paid homage to the golden images.

Once at the Haw, the Buddha images were carried up the eastern stairway into the front Royal Throne Audience hall and placed on the high throne. The hall was filled with people of different ethnic groups from near and far. Offerings of flowers and water were made, and gold leaf was patted on the images before they were given new robes. The discarded robes, taking pride of place, were put on our family altar. Because of the great powers of the Phaung Daw U images, it was

*Applying gold leaf to the
Phaung Daw U Buddha images.*

believed that if a piece of the old robe is carried in a locket around one's neck, it will protect the wearer from all harm. Similarly, the Siamese and the Lao also wear pieces of robes and small gold or bronze Buddha amulets around their necks.

After an hour or so, the Buddha images were taken to the Royal monastery in the middle of the town, which is just behind the main Yawnghwe pagoda. Once the chariot arrived and the Buddha images had been carried into the monastery, a rhythmic chanting of prayers resounded through the whole building and one could smell the sweet flagrance of flowers and joss sticks floating up above the dense crowd, before vaporising in the open air.

Here the images rested for three days, whilst celebrations were held in their honour. The festivities included gambling, drama and dance shows, as well as side-shows, similar to those found at summer fair grounds in Europe, with hundreds of stalls selling food and colourful goods in the area around the monastery.

People who had crowded into Yawnghwe for the celebrations, generally went first to the Royal monastery to pay their homage to the Buddhas. In the mornings before noon, the area around the throne was covered with gold and silver trays, containing bowls with alms offerings of food. In fact for twenty-four hours of the day, the monastery was usually full of worshippers offering water, bunches of flowers, joss sticks and candles. A line of men, holding small squares of gold leaf, awaited their turn to put the gold on to the images. So throughout the three days the monastery was never empty.

## Origins of the *Phaung Daw U Buddhas*

The origin of the festival and that of the Phaung Daw U Buddha images is fascinating. According to popular belief, the Buddha images had been presented to King Alaungsithu of Pagan (CE. 1113). His greatest possession was apparently a magic barge, which floated through the air like a magic carpet. In this he travelled extensively all over the eastern world. On one of his trips to Madras he stopped at the island of Mallayu, where a holy man, thought by some to be the god Indra himself, gave him the five Buddha figures. Carved from sandalwood, they were said to hold supernatural powers.

Since he placed these in the prow of his barge, they came to be known as the Phaung Daw U Phaya, meaning in Burmese, 'The prow of the Royal Barge Buddhas'. Alaungsithu then returned to Pagan. On one of his magical journeys, coming to the Inle Lake, he accidentally drove his barge into the side of the

*Phaung Daw U Buddha images.*

*The Phaung Daw U monastery at Namhu.*

mountain range along the western shore. The barge, descending through the huge gap it had created, came to rest at Than-htaung village. A cave was found nearby, and the five Buddha images were put there for safety.

It was, however, not until the reign of the first Yawnghwe Saohpa in 1359, that they were discovered. Local people, noticing supernatural waves of light emanating from a cave in the midst of the jungle, bravely went in to investigate. When they found the five Buddha statues they were at a loss, not knowing what to do. Eventually, the villagers went to their ruler to report the extraordinary phenomena. Believing that it was his destiny to take care of the Buddha images, he and his ministers sailed down the Lake to Than-htaung. Then, in formal procession they walked through the jungle to the cave. The Saohpa and his entourage paid their respects and hoping they were not committing a sacrilege, reverently requested permission to carry the images back to the capital.

They must have done the right thing as nothing untoward happened, and the Buddha images remained in Yawnghwe for a number of years, until wars and invasions threatened their safety. It was around 1615, during the reign of Nang Nung Pe, our female ruler, that they were removed to a distant part of the Inle Lake to Indein. Much later, they were moved once more to the monastery at Namhu, which became their permanent home and is where they reside to this day.

Namhu village is believed to have been founded by two brothers from Tavoy, named Nga Taung and Nga Naung, who were in service with Saohpa Sao Si Hseng Hpa. One day, they asked if they might go back to Tavoy and bring back their families. The request was granted and they returned with thirty-six families. The families first settled in Nan The, a village near Yawnghwe, but eventually they spread out creating new villages as they expanded.

The descendants of the Namhu villagers were given the responsibility of looking after the Phaung Daw U Buddha images forever, and they were known as guardians or temple-slaves. For the services they had to perform, the prince awarded them a number of privileges. Chief amongst these was being exempt from military service. In addition, they were given a certain amount of money to maintain the special position which they held in the Intha community.

Over many decades, the original thirty-six families have expanded greatly. Twenty years ago, the census figures for the lake dwellers showed them numbering some 70,000, some forty per cent of the whole population of Yawnghwe State. These villagers call themselves Intha, meaning lake dwellers, or sons of the lake.

The Intha speak a dialect of Burmese, which is not very easy for many of us to understand, but the language has some similarities with that which is spoken by those who live in Tavoy. The town of Tavoy, situated in the extreme south of Burma, was Mon country in centuries past. Nakhon Pathom, which lies thirty-five miles west of modern Bangkok used to be their capital. The Mon are the oldest inhabitants of both Burma and Thailand, and on the maps one can see that Tavoy lies in a straight line from Bangkok. Perhaps the two brothers were of Mon origin. Many of the villagers of Namhu also speak Tai, and it is reasonable to think that some of the families who migrated to Inle might have been early Tai. It would be interesting to trace their origins and Thai scholars may already be engaged in this research.

Most of the villages are built completely in the water, so boats have to be used for getting around. Ywama, one of the larger villages was where there was a daily market, similar to the Floating Market in Bangkok. All the wares such as vegetables and fruit, wet and dried fish were piled in boats and sold by the viss, roughly equivalent to a kilogram. Fish and pork were weighed and strung together by skeins of bamboo. We knew when the floating cafes serving rice and curry or noodle soups were approaching as an appetising aroma wafted towards us. People rowed between these boats paddling expertly so to avoid hitting each other. There was usually a crush and when we went there, we had to manoeuvre quickly so we wouldn't be pushed aside and suddenly find ourselves outside the market area. It used to be a pleasant market without any outboard motors when I was young, but now it has become noisy and crowded.

There was another much larger market at Nampan, which took place every five days. Most of this village was built on land. Here one found a greater variety of goods. Vegetables came from the gardens around Nampan or from floating gardens, which were plots of floating islands composed of water hyacinths, weeds and reeds. Many were fenced around and staked firmly together into a large plot to prevent it from floating away. Most village houses were also built on floating islands staked together in a similar manner.

It is difficult to ascertain the pattern of the Inle economy today. Some sixty years ago, groups of villages carried on a particular trade with each group complimenting the other. For instance, those villages in the middle of the lake around Kayla village were fishermen and kept livestock such as chickens and ducks. Those living on the eastern shores near Thale U grew bananas and water melons.

Thale U was particularly known for its different varieties of bananas, popularly referred to as 'golden', 'red' and 'sweet-fragrant'. A big bunch of bananas which was usually bought on a bazaar day would hang in our southern wing. I remember how inviting they were, and I especially loved the small yellow bananas that were

*Lone fisherman.*                    *A single sail boat.*

deliciously ripened and sweet. Until I was tall enough, I had to jump up to reach the bottom tier to pull off a banana as the branch swung from side to side above my head.

Farmers from the western shores provided rice, and betel leaves, while those from the eastern shores produced mustard, sesamum and peanut oil.

Silk came from Inpawkhone and cotton material from surrounding villages. The cotton woven in Inle was called '*pin-ni*' and Thalay produced most of it. The material was a light sandalwood colour, the dye for which came from a special bark. Most Intha men wore suits made from this durable material. Ywama produced the famous and most useful Shan bags which most of the male population of Inle wore slung over their shoulders. In these brightly coloured bags were carried their tobacco pouch and betel nut boxes, and probably their money. They were also a favourite of the hill people who lived in the mountains around Inle.

Naturally, the silk weavers and merchants were wealthier than most, living in wooden houses of two storeys. A few even owned property in Taunggyi and Rangoon, and were a prosperous group.

Large ornamental silver bowls moulded with figures often depicting the life of the Lord Buddha were made at Nampan. These bowls are generally used for carrying flowers and candles when going to the pagoda, and the smaller ones for drinking water instead of glasses. Nearly every household possesses them and at the Haw, we had a whole selection of Nampan silverware. In addition, it was here that the finest scissors, the ceremonial *dahs* or the swords, and pots and pans were all made.

On the whole, except for salt which the hill people brought down to the market, villages in Inle were self-sufficient. The Intha are by nature both thrifty and diligent, bringing prosperity not only for Inle, but for Yawnghwe state as well. Times have changed of course and tourism thrives, but I wonder whether this change has brought them overall the same prosperity as they had in the past.

## At the Festival

The two hundred villages of Inle, large and small, are situated either along the shores, some by the main channel leading towards the capital, or in the middle of the lake. Wherever they lived, and whatever their trade, the Phaung Daw U festival for the villagers was an annual affair which no one wanted to miss. During the three days they would first go to the Royal monastery to perform their devotions and pay reverence to the Buddha images. Then their duty done, they were free for the rest of each day to wander around at leisure, seeking out family and friends, determined to enjoy themselves.

For some, it was to the gambling tables that they would wind their way. Rich and poor alike could not resist the temptation to win or lose their fortunes. The stakes could run into thousands of *kyats*, but compared to the famous casino tables of Europe, it was child's play. There were a number of different gambling games to choose from, but not roulette which was unknown in those days. Serious gamblers who wanted to break the bank played only the Four Animal game.

The four animals in question consisted of an eel, a cockerel, a frog and a pig, which were painted on a rectangular oil cloth. The cloth is diagonally divided with the pig sitting at the top, the cockerel on his right and the eel on his left. Below him lies the frog, his legs outspread. The pig and the frog are black, the eel and the cockerel red. I do not remember what the odds were, but in the 1950s in Rangoon, we used to play this game at parties. Not unlike sitting at the gambling tables, there would be loud shouts of eel or frog, red or black, as the four-sided top, with the animals painted on its faces, was spun around.

It was at the far end of the festival grounds that the two or three long bamboo gaming huts stood, each with four to six betting tables lining the walls. As it got late into the night, the tables filled up and the stakes got higher and higher. It was then that the Johnny Walker Red Label would appear and tins of Players 555

*The banker at the four animals gambling table, the eel and frog are clearly seen.*

cigarettes were passed around. The higher the stake, the more lavish the entertainment provided by the gambling house. One could be sure that for both gamblers and croupiers alike, they were settling in for a long night.

For the more imaginative, there was another gambling game based on thirty-six animals. In a separate hut, a large picture of an old Chinese mandarin, with thirty-six animals distributed over his body, hung over the table on which bets were placed. I do not recall how they were all distributed, although I can remember the positions of some: a white horse on top of his head, a *naga* (the snake) by his right ear, while a butterfly was by his left ear. In his right palm he held an elephant and a tiger sat on his chest. The chart was considered to be sacred and it was treated with great respect.

To play this game, one had to be highly inventive or superstitious, or good at riddles and puns. A riddle is set, and the answer is put into a little box, which is pulled to the top of a tall bamboo pole standing just outside the hut. When the time for the answer comes, there is a great deal of noise from firecrackers and beating of gongs, as with great excitement crowds gather to hear the result.

Those with a good imagination can turn any little incident into an omen sent by a *phii*. Dreams or events became omens related to one of these animals. Thus, if one dreamt of an enemy, it signified a snake. Conversely if one met someone noble in a dream, or dreamt of doing a good deed, it could be interpreted as a horse or a white elephant. Though none of these related to the riddles, people betted on a hunch. In fact, although some old people may have remembered the riddles and the answers, no-one could be sure that the answers would be the same.

I think it was during a Phaung Daw U festival when I was about twelve, that I thought I would try my luck. It so happened that on a certain day, I had been in the garden and a beautiful, pale, yellow butterfly alighted on my arm. This must be a sign, I thought. I didn't know what the riddle for the day was and even if I had been told, I doubt I would have understood its meaning. Still, I thought I should ask around as a cousin or an uncle might know. In the end, although uncertain, I decided to bet on the butterfly as an omen which could not be ignored. I sent a *kyat* of my pocket money down to the betting table and waited anxiously to hear the gongs and the firecrackers announcing the answer. To my utter amazement I had won! But my joy was short-lived for when my father, who was never fond of gambling, heard about it, he forbade me to ever gamble again.

Though he was strict in this way, he did not mind us going to the *poy* and playing the six animal game. This was really a children's game and we played with one *pya* or two, probably equivalent to one pence. Later, I began to see why he had chided me, because he was afraid that I might go further without realising the consequences of becoming addicted to gambling. After all I had been lucky enough to win thirty-six *kyats*, which was a fortune for a girl of twelve. Indeed, I might have been tempted to try my luck again and then lost everything.

The money the contractor gained from the gaming tables were taxed by the state and created revenue for the state treasuries. I assume the more *poys* there were each year, the more the coffers were filled. The contractor had to be an enterprising and efficient businessman to cover his costs. In spite of the many festivals we had and talk of large sums of money, I understand there were never sufficient funds in the treasury to carry out the many development plans my father desired.

## *Theatrical Performances*

There were so many things to do and see at the *poy*. With aunts and cousins, maids and bodyguards, we wandered around the side-shows and saw things like a calf with two heads, or a boy of six or seven playing with a python. The magicians were fun and I well remembered the pleasure of seeing a magician pull a rabbit or eggs out of handkerchiefs. Other attractions were a man who swallowed fire, or juggled with six plates.

We took our time as we strolled past the stalls. Wooden puppets depicted princes handsomely dressed in long *pasoes* sitting on white horses, with decorated stirrups and saddles. By pulling the right strings they seemed to gallop. In the semi-darkness of another stall a line of round, black eyes belonging to papier mache owls stared at us – the lucky *dee dot*. There were also medicine men, sitting behind jars of powdered herbs, rhinoceros and stag horns, tiger teeth and claws, elephant and peacock tails, each said to have some medicinal or magical property.

Until I went to boarding school, I used to wear a tiger's claw set in gold as a pendant and on my little finger I wore a ring made from strands of elephants' tail. Both were supposed to act sympathetically on my character, giving me the strength of a tiger and the long life of an elephant. Such beliefs are found not only in Burma, but all over Asia and Africa, which is one reason why controlling poachers is extremely difficult for the Wildlife Conservation organizations.

Having inspected the side shows, we would then peruse the various food stalls. Here smoke from numerous wood fires and the petrol lanterns hanging in the stalls made our eyes water, but the delicious smell of Shan delicacies tempted us further into the smoky haze. Having selected our favourite snacks, we made our way towards the *zat*, the stage where dance and drama were performed. The shows went on all night, commencing about nine and finishing only at dawn, with a triumphant beat of a drum.

The evening's performance normally began to the beats of the *nat-hsein*, the special *nat* music. The first dance, dedicated to the *nat* of dancing was performed by a female medium with flowing hair tied with a red band around her head. It ensured that nothing went wrong during the evening's performance. Although these are childhood memories I feel sure the medium's dance continues as before.

Next followed a collection of solo and chorus dances mainly performed by young women. They were a lovely sight, their richly embroidered skirts of gold and sequins glittering under the bright lights and their jewels flashing with the slightest movements. Then came the comedians, the *lu pyet*. Most of their puns and stories were bawdy in nature. Many of the better known comedians often turned to satire, criticising the political situation or joking about well-known personalities. Their scope was endless and similar to what we see on television shows in Europe. Though people took these criticisms as jokes and purely fun, the *lu pyet* are now heavily censored by the present government.

After the comedians, came two men dressed as Ministers of the Royal Court of Mandalay to give the plot of the play to follow. This part I found extremely boring, as did all those who did not understand the nuances of the Burmese language. Many of the stories enacted were taken from the *Jataka* Tales which relate the former incarnations of the Lord Buddha. A few favourite stories were repeated

*A min-thami in solo dance.*

over and over every year at different *poys*, but the audience never complained. The only complaint might be if the *min-tha* (male actor) and *min-thami* (female actor) failed to make the more romantic members of the audience cry in their love duet.

This duet is the most representative of all Burmese dances. It is quite similar to Siamese dancing, as both originated in India. The hand gestures, eye and head movements, and the various postures all have specific meanings. The *min-tha* with swift hand movements, will in the course of the duet move around the stage a number of times, with a jump here and a prance there. The *min-thami*, wearing a very long *longyi* (sarong), uses deft foot movements to flick up the end of the skirt. Then, holding a fan in one hand and her skirt in the other, she dances in a half-sitting, half-crouching position.

The music is boisterous and lively, and the dancers reflect the mood. A clash of cymbals will bring the *min-thami* down on her haunches and up again, repeated several times. I imagine that only trained dancers have the energy to jump up and down, while moving across the stage with such grace, that she seems to float.

The performers were all Burmese, generally from Mandalay, and the troupes were contracted for the duration of the *poy*. All the songs, both popular and classical, were sung in Burmese. Even if the audience could not understand the words, the catchy tunes were learnt through repetition. The classical plays were better understood, as everyone being Buddhist was well versed in the *Jataka* stories. Most of the scenes are known by heart, since most were performed over and over again. While people living in the capital spoke more Burmese and understood more than those from outlying regions, lack of understanding did not hamper them as they were at the *zat* mainly to watch the dancing and to listen to the songs.

The stage was covered and raised some five feet off the ground on stilts, with the orchestra on the ground sandwiched between the stage and the audience. The centre piece of the orchestra is the *saing-waing*, a circular wooden frame supporting graduated gongs. A man sits in the middle of the circle and hits the instrument with two padded, knobbly sticks. I believe one often judged the quality of a dance troupe by the size of the *saing-waing* – the more famous the performers, the bigger the *saing-waing*. I loved watching the musician as he twisted and turned, playing one set of gongs on one side, then switching to the other in quick succession.

In the open space in front of our pavilion and the orchestra, sat the happy chattering audience in family groups. People generally arrived at dusk, armed with blankets and pillows, to stake their places. There was no charge for the performance as the players were paid by the contractor. Having reserved their places, people came and went as they liked during the performance, getting up to wander around the food stalls, have fun at the side-shows, or lose money at the gambling tables.

However as soon as the duet music started, there was generally a mad rush to get back to see the elaborately dressed *min-tha* and *min-thami* sing and dance.

When the play commenced at about two o'clock, many of the children in the audience, like myself, found it hard to keep awake. I would make myself comfortable on the carpet, or with my head on the lap of one of my aunts, and fall asleep. Occasionally, I awoke to the loud beat of a drum or cymbal, or a lamenting voice of the princess and sit up to see what it was all about. The plays were a favourite with the older generation, and on some nights my aunts stayed up till dawn.

My description of the *zat* will bring back memories for many old Burma hands. Since it is an all-night affair, unless one really loved listening to the over-loud music and energetic dancing, it could have been quite an annoyance. Still, I am sure many tourists have seen the dancers' duets and admired their graceful movements.

After three days of the festival, the Phaung Daw U images sailed once more in the golden barge, to one of the villages on the western side of the lake. My father, and his entourage went in the State barge as far as Linkin village. Here the Buddha images spent the night, before continuing on their tour of the other Inle villages.

Returning to the capital in the evening, we would pass through the *poy* area, and find half the stalls stripped and a vast empty space where only a few hours ago people were jostling around. I was always sad to see the Phaung Daw U *poy* at an end, but I needn't have worried, for in a month, there would be another one.

The festival of lights, Tazaungbon, usually took place in November. Delicate, Chinese laterns in various sizes were either home made or bought. Little oil lamps or small candles were used to light them. All the houses in town, including our own, would be decorated with a large number of these flickering lights. The best decorated house was given a prize by my father, who used to walk around Yawng-hwe judging which displays were the finest. We children followed behind enjoying the display of twinkling lights.

In Thailand, the same festival is called Loy Kratong, and I remember floating the little banana leaf boats filled with flowers and a lit candle down the Chao Phraya river in front of our house in 1954. It was an enchanting sight to see hundreds of glimmering lights drifting down the river at night.

A min-tha *and* min-thami *dancing a duet.*

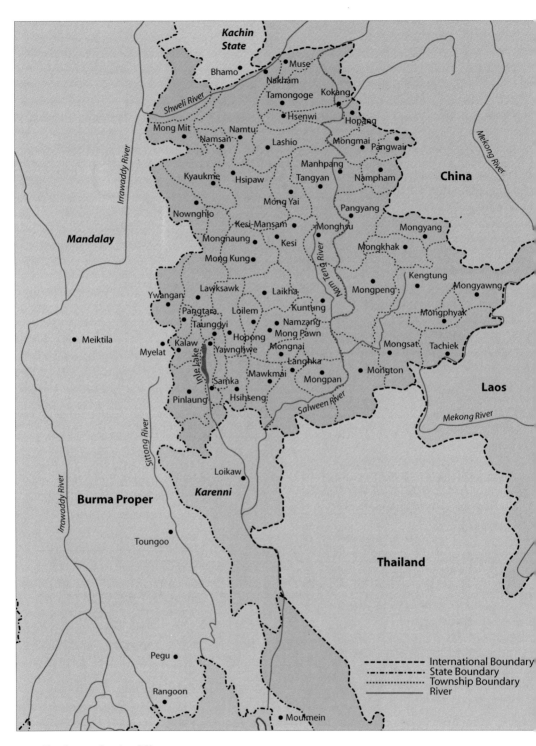

*Sketch map showing different
States and major towns.*

# V

## *Duties of a Saohpa*

### *On Tour*

In Burma Proper, the political unrest which had been growing for many years, became more serious when a group of Rangoon university students, including Aung San and U Nu, joined the elite Thakin movement in 1936. Thakin, as has been mentioned earlier, means 'master or lord', and the name showed that they wished to be master of their own country. The Thakin movement was vehemently anti-British and a private army was soon formed. In 1937, when the first ever election was held for Burma Proper, stipulated by the 1935 Act, Dr Ba Maw, an eloquent speaker and a shrewd politician, was elected as its first prime minister. Two years later at the next election, he lost out to U Saw, another clever politician.

It appeared that the young politicians were still not content, even though much of the government by now was already in Burman hands. They wanted more – freedom from British colonial rule.

It was into this unfriendly atmosphere that Reginald Dorman-Smith arrived as Governor of Burma. He was unfortunately to see this outpost of the British Empire crumble and eventually to be lost to the Japanese. Any ideas he may have had for Burma's future never became realities.

Things were somewhat different in the Shan States. Although the implementation of the 1935 Act had diminished some of their power, the Saohpas began to believe that the Shan States had a chance of attaining Dominion Status within the British Empire.

The Federal Council meetings of the Shan Saohpas continued until the Japanese war and it appeared that there might have been a certain understanding of the Shan position. The meetings were held quarterly either in Maymyo, Rangoon or Taunggyi. Sometimes the Governor himself chaired the meeting and at other times, the Commissioner of Federated Shan States, who was also the

*Sir Dorman-Smith, the Governor, visits the Shan States with the Laikha Saohpa, 1941.*

President of the Federal Council. The gatherings were described as interviews with the Shan princes and I suppose they were so termed, because the Saohpas were reporting on what was happening in their respective states to the Chairman.

Most of the princes attended when finance, defence, education, agriculture and medical matters were the main subjects discussed. From all accounts there was an exchange of ideas, but the discussions did not seem to be totally frank. When questions were asked regarding the aforementioned subjects, there was often not a direct reply, and the the Saohpas were told the question would have to be referred back to His Majesty's Government.

At each meeting my father always had questions to ask. He was not afraid to speak his mind and it appeared that at times other princes did not agree with him on particular issues. There were always inadequate funds alloted to each state for medical facilities, education and public works and he was concerned that not enough Shans were being employed in these services. He felt that if they were not qualified they had to be trained, instead of bringing in people from the outside who were neither sympathetic nor caring.

Public expenditure for each of the states and the Federal Shan State was always a concern. For example, when a medical handbook in Lahu was published, he questioned the fairness of providing Rs. 500 for its publication, while no corresponding books had been published for the Shan or Taung thu peoples. Surely if there were funds for one there should be for the others as well.

At one of the meetings held in February 1940, my father had asked for the formation of a second territorial Battalion, expressing his anxiety over the advancing Japanese and his fear that Chinese army deserters were crossing into the Shan States to seek refuge. The reply he received was that the Japanese were still a long way from the Burma frontier and that it was doubtful whether they would be able to continue their campaign in China much longer. As history soon showed, the Japanese occupying forces arrived sooner than was expected.

Later in 1941, the Governor told the Saohpas that an assurance had been given by the Secretary of State to the effect that "the position of the Shan States would be taken into consideration whatever the proposals for the modification of the existing system of constitutional government on Burma is taken up, and that the Federation of Shan States would be consulted in respect of any change that might affect their interests."[16]

The princes listened and hoped that these assurances could be accepted wholeheartedly. My father was quoted as saying that he "wished to emphasize that Burman ministers must not interfere with Shan State affairs – the Chiefs liked the Burmans as friends but not as masters." He had not forgotten the animosity and superiority that the Burmans had shown towards the Saohpas at the Round Table Conference of 1931. Sadly, these feelings have not abated and continue uncurbed into the 21st century.

Meeting other princes, exchanging views and discussing the future of their individual states gave the Saohpas some form of cohesion. In spite of this, the threatening war and the slow progress attained for the Shan States, was an anxiety.

In one of the reports he presented to U Nu in late 1959-60, my father wrote, "the Shan Administration knowing that there was not enough teachers, doctors or nurses and there were difficulties: set to work on education, health, public works,

*Sai Hseng at the ancient pagoda complex of Kuk Ku with bodyguards and regalia. It is now a tourist attraction.*

construction and giving these items priority. The Shan people are very devout Buddhists, and are contented people: and because of this attitude, the country was unable to become as prosperous and progressive as it was hoped."

Knowing how difficult it was dealing with his subjects, my father was ever conscious of his duties as a Saohpa. Apart from the audiences at his palace, Sao U Hpa made tours through his states to establish further contact with his people, going to distant villages to gather first-hand information. I don't think my father at any time made any distinction between his subjects of varied ethnic groups: the Taung thu meaning hill people in Burmese, who today prefer to be known as the Pa-O, Danu, Intha, Taung Yo, red Karens and others.

Much of the hills and mountains surrounding Inle and the Yawnghwe valley were inhabited by such minority groups who looked very much like the Gurkhas of Nepal. They are strong, sturdy people, used to carrying heavy loads on their backs up and down mountains. They spoke their own language and only a few were Shan or Burmese speakers. Some of these mountain people are still nomads, and even those who have settled in villages, build their bamboo and thatched houses precariously at an angle on mountain sides. Having to make a subsistence living off small holdings must have been difficult, and they considered themselves hard done by compared to the Shan and Intha villagers living in and around the Inle, who had an easier way of life.

My father's aim was to keep as closely in touch as he could with his people, and that was why whenever anyone came to see him, he always granted them an audience. He knew that as a ruling prince he had an obligation towards his subjects. He was responsible for law and order, for the effective administration of his state, and for overseeing the general well-being of his subjects.

Sao U Hpa took his second son, Sai Hseng, on several of these tours, before he left to go to school in England. They also toured the Inle villages, going in the State barge. It was probably on one such occasion, when a photograph of my brother with some of the bodyguards carrying the royal regalia, was taken at the ruins of the Kuk Ku pagoda complex which lies to the east of Fort Stedman.

I, too, was fortunate to go with my father on one of his regular horseback tours to the eastern hills, which took several days. The State of Yawnghwe, as mentioned before, was divided into three districts for administrative purposes: Inle, the eastern hills and the western hills west of Inle Lake. In those days, there were no proper roads only dirt tracks and mule paths, and the only means of transport was the bullock cart. Those who could afford it, rode on their mules or ponies, but many just walked from village to village. It was dangerous in the thick jungles and lofty mountains of the western and eastern districts where tigers and panthers roamed. There were also barking deer, samba and wild fowl which were hunted.

The Pa-O were hospitable and at every village, we stopped and were offered water in a silver cup, taken out of a cool earthenware water pot. The women wore black knee-length shift-like dresses with a V-shaped neckline both front and back, turbans, colourful leggings and heavy chunky silver jewellery. Some of the younger ones wore their hair in a bob with a thick fringe. One of these women walking down Knightsbridge on a summer's day with a pair of high heel shoes, could easily be considered quite chic. As we rode along our route, they watched us shyly from the edge of the road. Young children hung to their mothers' skirts afraid of the intrusion into their village by strangers. Some mothers held their babies to their breasts suckling them heedless of inquisitive eyes. Pye-dogs or mongrels ran here and there barking, which made our horses irritated and uncomfortable.

For the long trip, both Daw Daw and I wore breeches and topees, since it was more comfortable to ride horses in trousers, than in a *sin*. We created much amusement for the Pa-O women, as it wasn't common then to see women in trousers. In the evenings, when they saw my aunt dressed once more in a *sin* and jacket with her long hair knotted into a bun, they would gasp, for they had not believed her to be a woman until then. I think it was the only occasion I can ever remember Daw Daw in trousers.

Around sunset, we generally reached our destination, which was often a major village of the area where there was a *htamong*, the civic headman of about ten villages. As soon as we came to the entrance of a village, the reception committee headed by the headman, would pay homage to my father with a goblet of water and a bunch of flowers or *tha pye*, sacred leaves, whenever it was available. He would then take the reins of Sao U Hpa's horse to lead him to the rest-house with us following. Three or four men would open up gold ceremonial umbrellas and falling into step would shade their prince from the red, sinking sun.

If the inhabitants of the village were Buddhist, we would find a small pagoda and a *wat* or a monastery. There would also be a cluster of small sheds which served as market stalls for the five-day market. Bamboo and thatched houses stood on stilts scattered over the cleared patch of ground. Sometimes a pavilion was specially built to accommodate us, but in this village, whose name I have forgotten, we stayed for the night in the monastery rest house or *salop* in Shan.

We found the wooden floors covered with carpets. These carpets with blue or red backgrounds and a floral design in the middle, I discovered later, were manufactured in Birmingham and are to be found in many houses all over Southeast Asia. Dark hand-embroidered velvet curtains were hung to partition the room.

The scenes depicted the many lives of the Lord Buddha and featured figures of princes and princesses, ministers of court, soldiers with swords and lances, some on horseback and others on foot, and kings riding on elephants. It was a marvellous sight. At the slightest movement, the figures, richly embroidered in gold and silver thread seemed to come suddenly alive. How painstakingly each curtain must have been made. The little figures were cut and sewn on individually, with every sequin and gold thread balanced to give the correct effect of the attire of the different personalities being represented.

I don't think many of these curtains, which are about eight to ten feet in length, are made today, since only a few may still have the skill or the patience to carry out such a lengthy and laborious task. In the 1960s when we were in Bangkok, we saw many of these curtains that had been smuggled out across the border being sold in antique shops. They were fetching four figure sums, which made me realise how valuable and scarce they had become. Nowadays, instead of such long curtains, embroidered squares are made as decorative wall hangings and have become a cross-culture, cross-border cottage industry which is popular with the tourists.

Once installed in the rest house, visitors came to pay their respects to my father. The men would be dressed in baggy Shan trousers, and jackets without collars which fastened down the front. They seldom used the long silk turbans – instead towels were wrapped around their heads. Here they would sit on the floor in a line. Placed in front of them or still slung over their shoulders were the veritable Shan bags, a square woven bag of different patterns and colours, with a broad strap. Behind them sat the women and children in groups, chatting and giggling amongst themselves. When small babies cried the mothers would quickly put them to their breasts and suckle them.

## Common Problems

Looking back to those years, it would seem that the economic and social problems encountered by the Pa-O were no different to those found in other Shan villages, or indeed in most underdeveloped countries of Southeast Asia. One of the major problems was the lack of roads and means of transport. Footpaths and dust roads did not provide easy or fast access. It often took two to three days for the sick to get to a hospital in a major town. That is if they believed in western medicines or had been coaxed into seeing a doctor. Many relied on herbal medicines given to them by the *hsala*, their village medicine man. Children would have to walk for two or three hours to get to school and often they did not go to school at all. There were, of course, the monastery schools where young boys had a rudimentary education, but this was not enough.

Vast amounts of money were needed to provide schools and clinics, but even if there had been money for such facilities, it would not have been easy persuading young trained men and women to go and work in these remote villages. This was a major problem, and when the Shan politicians began shouting for progress and down with the Saohpas, they had forgotten these difficult situations. I am sure other Saohpas did what they could, for they would have met similar problems.

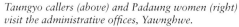
*Taungyo callers (above) and Padaung women (right)
visit the administrative offices, Yawnghwe.*

I suspect there was very little my father could do, except to promise that he would try to make their lives a little better by providing a travelling midwife or a teacher for some of the larger villages. Even those commitments were not easy to arrange: no townsperson ever wanted to go into villages in remote areas. Yawnghwe State revenues were such that there was little possibility of it stretching to include schools and clinics for all the major villages. There was probably an overall plan for the State, but without sufficient funds its implementation was impossible.

These tours undoubtedly were invaluable to my father, as he was able to see for himself how badly off, or how prosperous, the villagers really were. And from his observations he was able to assess their various needs. He was a conscientious ruler who tried very hard to help alleviate the hardship the people in the hills endured, but it was a slow process. Though most of what he saw was nothing to rejoice at, he had hopes that something could be done to remedy the problems during his years of rule. He was perhaps an optimist. Although there was little he could do for the moment, I am sure he felt that these tours gave him a basis upon which he could plan the annual State budget, if the funds were there. Such matters he would then discuss with the Commissioner or the Administrators, but again it all depended on the British policy of the time.

The number of British administrators allotted to a Saohpa and his state largely depended upon its size and location, as well as on the hierarchy of the Saohpas. There was also the matter of language. In those days, not all rulers were proficient in English or in Burmese, as mentioned before. I understand that many of the British officers also used to tour the state for which he was responsible to see what was needed. I wonder though if they were ever able to do anything independently. Or were their hands tied, since available funds were small and they had to wait for instructions from higher up. What was considered a priority? Transport and communication, or education and health? It could not have been a simple decision for these administrators.

The rulers obviously needed understanding, caring and dedicated officials to assist them. Many of the British officials were young men who had no previous experience. Though they had come through the Indian Civil Service system, they were often not sufficiently equipped to deal with the princes who were often older and very different in outlook. There was certainly a gap in thinking and moral values between the older princes and those who became Saohpas just before and after the Japanese occupation. The former had absolute powers, had fought in battles and perhaps had little consideration for the common people.

There were complaints that some of these administrators were not "thoroughly acquainted with the customs of the Shan States" and that the service was "burdened with Officers whose experience previous to their services in the Shan States has been spent in Burma or elsewhere, and who came to the States with pre-conceived ideas that render it difficult for them to appreciate our system of Government."[17]

Some officials tended to overstep the mark and it was a joke amongst the princes, that Saohpas generally wined and dined with the Governor in Rangoon, but at home "they had to obey the orders of the Governor's most junior officers." As a result the administrator had a difficult task in dealing with the princes or gaining their confidence.

It may have been different, however, with the younger princes who had taken over from their aged fathers. Many were either educated abroad or had had a university education and were unbiased, so there was less ambiguity and confusion in dealing with them. Unfortunately for these princes, due to the rush for independence and demands for the renunciation of their powers, there was no real time to judge or value the work they had accomplished for the Shan States.

My father was considered one of the enlightened rulers, but even he, I am sure, had difficulty in getting his views across to his British administrator since they probably did not share a similar outlook.

A lasting picture I have of Sao U Hpa is as a silhouette sitting bent over his work with the bright sunlight streaming through the open windows from behind. I remember him at his desk in his wing, early in the mornings working out to the smallest detail certain projects he had in hand. He would write and re-write memoranda and minutes. He would add and subtract long columns of figures, checking and re-checking the amounts as he went along. He always wrote very slowly and formed each letter carefully. And when he was signing an important document, it would take long seconds to complete his signature, which was strangely enough always in English. He liked to be precise and meticulous, and wanted other people about him to be the same.

My father was enthusiastic and worked hard. Though susceptible to new ideas, he took his time in coming to terms with them. I think that had the Japanese war not taken place nor the post-war years of political unrest occurred, he might have realized some of his ambitions. It must nevertheless have been an up-hill task for him, never knowing in which direction he could move.

The tour with my father was an experience to treasure, althouth I was too young to appreciate its full significance. To me it was simply a wonderful outing in the hills, going from village to village and seeing the different peoples.

I loved the long rides and hearing the incessant shrill chirping of the crickets, which made me feel the forest was alive with thousands of little creatures, even though we hardly ever saw them. I also loved the times when I was hot and thirsty, and finding a bale tree someone would pick a fruit. Cracking it open I ate its soft flesh quickly, before it got too bitter from being exposed to the air. Nevertheless, the trip had also been tiring with the constant climbing of one hill, only to descend into the valley and start climbing again.

Very many years later, when my husband and I walked and rode through northern Laos in 1955, it was the same kind of terrain. The Meo (Hmong) and Kha (Lao Theung) porters took us through the hills, and these trips reminded me of the tour I had made with my father.

I began to realize our tour was coming to a close when we came down towards the foothills. It became cooler under the clusters of feathery bamboo groves and occasionally a brightly coloured jungle fowl would rush out of the undergrowth. Once we came to the paddy fields, it was worth halting for a while to look at the elegant egrets and cranes standing motionless as if asleep, but striking like lightning when a fish swam by. The rice farmers here lived in a little more comfort and had an easier life than those villagers living on the hilltops. Roads were more accessible and it took them only half a day's walk to get to the five-day bazaar at the capital.

## Exams for the Sangha

Buddhist examinations known as *Sa pyan pwe*, inaugurated by my father many decades ago, were held every July. It was a three or four day annual event, when the younger members of the Sangha took examinations on their knowledge of the *Tripitaka*, the scriptures taught by the Lord Buddha and referred to as the three baskets of the Pali Canon. As a devout Buddhist, Sao U Hpa felt that all the monks should be fully versed in the teachings of the Buddha and well disciplined. He hoped that these exams would in due course help to make them learned and wise monks, worthy of the devotion and respect lay people accorded them. I was happy to learn that despite what has happened in the country, this festival still continues so many years later.

For administrative purposes, Yawnghwe town was divided into eight sectors, each headed by a senior civil servant or trader who was responsible for the moral

*Yawnghwe's central monastery where the Phaung Daw U Buddhas rest for three days, and where other important ceremonies take place.*

and social welfare of its inhabitants. Generally, a team from each group would undertake to help organise these religious affairs, including cooking and feeding the Sangha and their followers. Sometimes, they also had to find accommodation for the followers who had come from afar.

Everyone was happy to give up their time, be it to help in the make-shift kitchens or buying goods and preparing alms offerings for the monks. Men were usually the cooks each with his own favourite recipe. But the standard fare on these occasions was a five-dish meal which varied each day. The dishes consisted of curried pork with mango-pickle, or pork with pickled bamboo shoots, fried fish, and a tasty somewhat bitter kidney bean soup of Inle origin called *se kha*. As side dishes, there was a fresh hot chilli sauce, fresh leaf vegetables and crispy, fried buffalo hide with plain hot rice. For desert, there was *letpet-thok*, which was fermented tea-leaf sprinkled with oil and sesamum seeds, eaten with fried peanuts and garlic. Incidentally, this delicacy can now be bought in packets in most Thai and Chinese supermarkets in the UK and in Canada. Green tea and lumps of palm sugar then followed, rounding up the meal.

To have all these dishes ready by 11 o'clock for offering to the Sangha before noon, meant that the cooks and helpers had to begin very early in the morning, well before sunrise.

It was always a pleasure to see the young monks enjoying their meal, sitting four to a table on the floor. Second helpings were never refused and they ate heartily. The elder monks, however, ate with dignity, and in less of a hurry.

On these mornings, my young cousins and I used to go and lay jasmine, frangipani, sandalwood blossoms, rose and lotus petals on the red roll of material, which covered the footpath leading up to the Royal monastery. When the Sangha walked over the elaborate patterns that we had made, the flowers were crushed by their bare feet and sent up a strong fragrance filling our nostrils as we sat beside the path with folded palms.

Sao U Hpa came to attend these proceedings every day. Part of the exams involved recitations of *Sutras* and scriptures. Although my cousins and I scarcely understood a word of what was being said in Pali, we had to be as good as gold as we sat listening each day. At the end of these examinations, prizes were given and young promising Sangha were selected for further studies, some going to Mandalay or even to Ceylon. These exams became quite famous and many monks came from all over the Shan States and Mandalay to participate. The visiting Sangha were amazed to find the examinations of such a high standard and so well organised. They told my father it was a great achievement for him to have created such a Buddhist event. My father must have been proud to see each year an increase in the numbers of Sangha attending the *Sa pyan pwe*.

Life in Yawnghwe in those times, seemed to go from one festival to the next. In between were *kam san*g the ordination ceremony for young boys, births, weddings and funerals of family and friends, which we all had to attend. Visitors came and went. So there was never a dull moment. But at the same time, there was no rush and bustle, as things happened at a slower tempo. Although outwardly the life at the Yawnghwe court might seem simple, it was in fact quite complex with rules of behaviour that had to be observed diligently, with little or no change over the years. To the outside world, I suspect our customs and traditions might have seemed somewhat strange and behind the times. However, over the centuries Tai culture has taught us to have reverence and respect for our elders, to show politeness to those around us and to learn to be devout Buddhists.

Perhaps we did then live in a restricted society of 'do's' and 'don'ts', but there seems to be no reason why one cannot be modern, yet still maintain the courtesy of Tai ways. The modern material world offers us far too great a range of things and ideas to choose from and we are easily sucked into a whirlwind of consumerism. Life becomes fast and furious with little time for reflection. New ideas are adopted without thinking, while our culture is relegated to history. Yet there is much for us to learn from and preserve in our Shan heritage.

I have lived several decades away from Yawnghwe, and I find it refreshing to see how innocent we were then to the ways of the modern world. It was not an ideal life, but at least time was our own and we were our own masters.

## Remarriage

My father's remarriage did not surprise me. I had been told by many that it was certain that he would remarry, and that this time it would be to a Saohpa's daughter. I believe he had a choice of one or two other princesses, but chose the youngest one. I cannot recollect what actually happened, how quickly it had all been arranged, when the wedding was and when my father and his bride returned to Yawnghwe. I believe that the wedding was in June 1937, and the ceremony had been held in Hsenwi. Nor do I remember what the immediate changes were in the family, except that she lived in my father's wing.

Daw Daw, I am told, went away for a while. Later, when she returned she continued living in the southern wing, which was where Daw Win and I also lived, when we came back for our holidays.

My stepmother was a half-sister of Sao Hom Hpa, the Saopha of North Hsenwi State. Her mother, who was one of the many wives of the old Saohpa of

*Sao Hearn Hkam with her brother, Sao Hom Hpa, the Hsenwi Saohpa.*

*My new stepmother with her convent friends and nieces, 1938.*

*Sao U Hpa and Sao Hearn Hkam, on their wedding day in 1937.*

*Sao Hearn Hkam, my new stepmother in Tai Neua dress, 1939.*

Hsenwi, came from Mong Yaw, a place some fifty miles to the east of Hsenwi near to the mighty Salween River. The marriage to my father had been arranged by her half-brother. Sao Hearn Hkam, as she was known, was twenty years younger than her husband to be. Her princely brother having decided that she was old enough, and of an age ripe for marriage, had taken her out of the convent where she had been studying. He felt it was no longer necessary for her to continue with her schooling. This was not unusual behaviour since a good marriage was thought to be better than an education for women.

When he proposed that she was to marry my father, a man twice her age, she was probably in despair, as it was an open secret that she was madly in love with a young prince from Kengtung. But as so often happens in these old families, no one would listen, least of all her brother, who wanted to see her marry well. To be fair to her brother, I understand he had asked her if she had anyone else in mind she wanted to marry, but, presumably out of fear, she had answered in the negative, not wanting to confess to her understanding.

One can imagine how unhappy she must have been with the arranged marriage. Nevertheless, although she felt no emotions towards her future husband, I am sure she must have been attracted to the fact that he was a senior and important Saohpa, rather than a mere prince or a minister of Hsenwi State. In fact, he was quite a catch, and certainly she would be doing far better than her other half-sisters if she did decide to marry him. Sao Hom Hpa may have first met my father at the Shan Chiefs School, and later they were in the army together. They had gone to London in 1931 to attend the Round Table Conference and must have met at other Saohpa meetings, so they were not strangers to each other.

If she had been brave or modern enough to resist an order from her Saohpa brother, the only option would have been to run away with her young prince. But it would have been unbelievably painful if she had done so, since it would have brought disgrace and dishonour to the Hsenwi House.

In many ways, there was little choice in those days – as a younger half-sister, it was a duty she owed to her brother. He had brought her up, clothed and fed her and given her an education. Besides, he was also feeding and housing her aged mother, so she had a debt towards him. I often wonder, how she must have felt having to throw away her youth to marry and care for a man she hardly knew, or could hardly have been in love with.

But it just shows how strong the ties of obligation were in those days. Even in the late thirties, a girl had to do what her family wished. I am truly grateful that I was never put into such a position of being forced against my will to marry some man my family wanted, nor have I had to suffer the anguish and pain that both my aunts and my stepmother must have had to go through, each in their own different ways.

Arriving in Yawnghwe must have been rather daunting, a young woman having to meet so many potentially hostile strangers. For although it had not been her choice to become the wife of a widower with three children, and two other wives, she had to accept them, since they were there before her.

She faced no easy task as there was a great deal to learn. A convent schooling and knowledge of English were not sufficient preparation for dealing with the many human problems which existed in the court of Yawnghwe.

Our mother, the late Mahadevi, may not have had a western education and spoke only a few words of English, but she had learnt through experience her various duties and responsibilities. She attended functions and entertained the Commissioner and other government officials as easily as one who spoke their language. She capably carried out her duties as Mahadevi with tact, both in State affairs and within her own family.

When my stepmother entered our family, she must have been aware that things were not going to be smooth and simple for her. She had to show in Court that she was capable of replacing the late Sao Mye Mong, not only in her activities and responsibilities, but in the way she handled those who were both friendly and unfriendly towards her.

Once she had decided to marry my father, she must have realized that there was much to be gained by being a Saohpa's wife. Being a princess she had an advantage over others. Thus, after the birth of her first son Hso, meaning Tiger, she was proclaimed the Mahadevi of Yawnghwe. Her ambition had been fulfilled. There was naturally ill-feeling, some resistance and heartache within the Yawnghwe Court, but it was inevitable. As a princess, she was in a favourable position to be chosen as Mahadevi and to receive the blessings of the British administration. In the family and the Court, we began calling her Sao Mye Mong, but to the outside world she was usually addressed as Mahadevi.

The fact that we, my two brothers and I, were away at school I am sure helped to make things easier for my stepmother. She was able to begin her life without the usual distress and bitterness which so often arises in such step-mother step-children relationships. There was only Daw Daw at that time in the palace for her to confront. My stepmother was also fortunate as it gave her time as well to get to know my father, whom she had not known until her engagement and marriage.

## *Living in a polygamous family*

Her western education had probably given my stepmother to understand that monogamy was the only desirable form of marriage. At the same time she must have realised that having accepted an arranged marriage she had inevitably to cross the threshhold into a polygamous family. Daw Daw who carried the title of Taung-saung thakin ma – 'Lady of the south wing' in Burmese – never posed a threat. Not having children of her own, she took over as a foster mother, caring for my half brothers and sisters as her own. Soon she was looking after not only the children, but most of the affairs of the family at the Court of Yawnghwe as the new Mahadevi found it dull merely being a mother and a housewife. She began taking an interest in state affairs and politics, and was the only person the British officials saw at parties and state functions. She was young and ambitious, determined to achieve what she wanted.

Though Daw Daw didn't play a part in the social whirl, she acted as a rampart at home upon which my stepmother could lean. As can be imagined, on occasions the usual arguments and fights between husband and wife got out of control, and it was Daw Daw who became the mediator and peace-maker, restoring tranquillity within the family. Such a relationship, might seem strange from a western outlook, but for us it was a means of keeping the family together.

At that time Daw Daw Win, the fourth sister and fourth wife, was at Rangoon University where she had gone after her schooling at the Baptist Girls' School in Taunggyi. An attractive and lively person, she made many friends at the university and her women friends made her conscious of the possibility of having a career, of being independent and marrying someone of her choice. Of course, it was unfair – she was still young and being in Rangoon had given her a certain freedom. How could she reconcile herself to returning to the life she was destined to lead in our polygamous family? Perhaps she could have made a break, but unfortunately the coming of the Japanese war dashed her dreams of freedom. Once back home with us in Yawnghwe, there was no escape, and she had to perform her duty towards my father as his wife. I can well imagine the anguish and the frustration she must have felt. At that time, I was too young to ask her questions and too young to understand. I expect that, not unlike my stepmother, once she had made up her mind she too had to carry on as best she could.

Whatever her inner turmoil, Daw Win brought back exciting things from Rangoon. They included jars of Pond's cold and vanishing creams, 'Evening in Paris' perfume and the strains of 'Red Sails in the Sunset', that she occasionally sang or hummed. I had never seen face cream before so it was a novelty, replacing the *thanakha* which until then was the only thing I had used. This was a pale cream substance obtained by rubbing the *thanat*, *Limonia acidissima* bark, on a flat stone surface with splashes of water. The texture depended on how much water was used. This smooth paste was used either thinly all over one's face or applied as a circular daub on one's cheeks. Instead of perfume, we used sandalwood paste made in the same way. It kept us cool and smelling fragrant.

As a small child who was thoroughly spoilt, I took things for granted and didn't have a care in the world. Little did I realize the distress and the unhappiness which must have existed within the family in those days. Living in a polygamous family, and seeing only the outwardly smiling faces, I never once stopped to question the feelings of those involved. Nor did I ever once detect or think of the pain and bitterness that must have existed.

Those English women, wives of Assistant Superintendents and other British officials, can be forgiven for being shocked at finding such polygamous families. With their very different moral outlook, it must have been bewildering to associate with us and to tolerate our behaviour. They probably found it difficult to comprehend, and questioned how these wives could accept their situation, or live together under one roof with their different children? Many questions must have remained unanswered. However, modern Western eyes are seeing things only from one side, when they conclude that an arranged marriage is like a slave being sold into marriage. How little understanding they have of a world they do not know.

It is only when one has lived and grown up in such a family, that one can understand the norms that governed our lives. In those days, the family was a powerful unit which controlled one's action. Obedience, duty and courtesy were our guidelines. It was impossible to step out of line unless one wanted to disgrace and dishonour the family. To do so would be a major step and it was usually extremely rare for young women to take such action.

For economic reasons and status in society, families with daughters generally wished to have a wealthy or powerful son-in-law. Thus, regardless of how many wives a man might have and with no consideration given to the young woman's feelings, the daughter would be made to marry him. As already seen, she may have been in-love with someone else, but that would be of no consequence. Certainly, she would be cajoled and threatened in one way or another, leaving her no option but to give in. If she did resist and eloped, she could well be ostracized. In such a tightly-knit society it would be an impossible situation with the parents losing face.

It is never easy to generalise, but, despite what I have said, many arranged marriages such as these in Saohpa families and elsewhere have tended to work out well. Mainly, I imagine, this was because no romance was involved. The role of the first wife was to condone her husband's many liaisons. In our family, it was the chief wife's duty to take care of all the Saohpa's children, giving them her attention and affection. In any case, as mentioned before, in Shan, the Mahadevi was known as Sao Mye Mong, which meant Princess Mother of the Mong. So, she was effectively mother to all, both within her family and without.

At that time, the relationship between my stepmother and her husband's three children was cordial and polite. Sao Sai, my eldest brother was in England. Sai Hseng, who had a year to wait before going abroad, used to come home for his holidays and found her quite communicative. As a boarder at Kingswood, I too came home only at holidays. I did not, therefore, get to know her until the Japanese war and the occupation. My eldest brother from time to time wrote home. He was told his father was too busy to read his letters, so he had to write to her instead. "Dear Aunty" he began his letters.

My first recollection of my stepmother was of a young, attractive woman sitting on the floor in the front room of my father's wing. Her long hair was flowing down her back, kept out of her face by a white hairband. She held a book in one hand and with the other, she picked up slices of green mango from a plate in front of her, dipping each slice into chilli powder and salt. As she read she munched on her slice of mango.

This was how I often found her, for she loved washing her hair, was an avid reader, and was very fond of munching on acid and sour fruits. I wasn't sure what books she read, but when I was older, I found out that she was a great fan of historical romances. We didn't talk to each other very much and when we did, it was in English. I expect since I was still learning English at school I didn't have much to say.

One time when I came home for the holidays my stepmother had just given birth to one of her sons. She had been installed in a pavilion especially built in the northern garden for such occasions. She lay beside a large fire place looking tired and small under the pile of quilts and blankets. The baby was all swathed in a very large piece of white cloth with only his little face visible. This was the manner in which all of us, as babies, were wrapped up for about a week or so, before we were allowed to have freedom of movement. I think there was a fear that if baby were left unbound, they might easily twist their neck or do some other harm to themselves – an old wives' tales, no doubt.

It was also in this pavilion that my father carried out his hobby. When I was on holiday, my father would sometimes send for me to work the bellows for the fire. He took an interest from time to time in alchemy, but never revealed what he was hoping to achieve – was it to walk on air, or merely to make gold and amass a fortune? Not knowing much about alchemy myself, I didn't ask any questions.

From time to time, Sao U Hpa's face would light up and a little smile would appear as he examined the tiny capsule of mercury, encased in an egg-shaped container. I have no idea what he was thinking but once it was put back into the container, I continued with the bellows. After an hour's session or so, it became quite tiring working the bellows and we'd stop. Since he was a busy man, I don't think he had a great deal of time to spend on this hobby.

## *Travel before the War*

When school closed for the winter holidays, the family generally drove across the Shan States to Hsenwi to spend part of the holidays there. This was a good arrangement, for it gave my stepmother a chance to see her family and relations, and for my father, provided continuing contact with the other Saohpas.

The drive to Hsenwi took us two or three days passing through a number of southern States with mountains and valleys. If we did not stop to pay respect to the princes through whose States we had to pass the journey was quicker. Once or twice, my stepmother's nieces, who went to the convents of St Agnes in Kalaw and St Anne's in Taunggyi, would return to Hsenwi with us. Though there were no harsh feelings or a difficult stepmother-step daughter relationship, I did not call

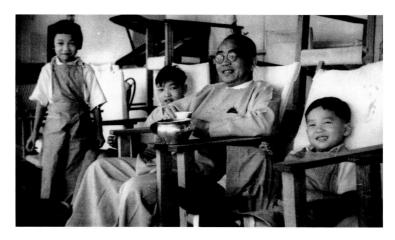

*Sao U Hpa with his younger children,*
*Ying (standing) Hso and Tzang.*

her mother, but conveniently followed what her nieces and nephews called her, which was Aunty Agnes, Agnes being her convent name.

Our journeys invariably started at the crack of dawn. We were all woken up at four-thirty or so, and however well we had packed the previous night, there were always a mass of things we had forgotten.

From my room, on top of the south wing, I would hear the sounds of cocks crowing and dogs barking. The creaking of bullock carts could be heard quite clearly, as could the steady ringing of bullock bells as they came into town or made their way out towards the paddy fields. Soon blurred, shadowy figures became people and, quite suddenly, the first rays of the sun would brighten the skies, piercing through the mists which hung low in the valley. It was on winter mornings like these that one did not mind having to get up early. The air was crisp and fresh, though a little chilly. We huddled over a small charcoal fire toasting sticks of glutinous rice, *khao lam*, which had previously been cooked in short lengths of bamboo. We ate it with *neua yong*, strips of dried meat which were then fried.

Five-thirty would be the time of departure, and we would all pray that my father would be in a good mood. Amidst our chatter, we would keep an ear open to catch the slightest shout or yell from the wing opposite. Once any little thing went wrong, such as a piece of paper of some importance being mislaid, there would be an uneasiness. A typical scene would entail a search by my stepmother through all her things, while Daw Daw went through my father's clothes. I, and any cousins who were around, would be made to look through my father's desk drawers and to go through things on his table. The head page would be sent down to look in my father's office, which lay immediately beneath the inner hall. While all this was going on, one of the maids or boys would do something absolutely stupid, like spilling tea all over the table or producing the wrong shoe for the wrong foot, while my father was dressing. This would be the final straw and Sao U Hpa would explode with rage – shoes would be thrown or there would be a box on the ear for the nearest culprit. This performance was almost a ritual, for we could not go anywhere without a crisis of some sort.

Eventually after a tense five or ten minutes, which always seemed hours, the shouting and mutterings would cease, and the paper would have been found in his own writing case, which no one was allowed to touch. A peal of laughter would come from my father and he would say how silly he was not to have thought of the writing case. After this charade he would be in good humour.

All of us, in the meantime, would have seated ourselves with blank looks on our faces, not daring to smile, or say a word, pretending that we had not heard what my father had said about himself. For who would have dared to have agreed with him that he had been rather silly! In later years he began to have a sense of humour and we could tease him and laugh with him when such a crisis arose.

Our journey at last began. We left in a convoy of two or three cars. I cannot remember how we all split up, but there was usually a bodyguard in each of the cars. There was also a lorry for the cook with all his pots and pans and provisions for the journey. The maids and the pages went with the cook in the lorry to look after us at the rest houses, when we did not stay with one of the Saohpas.

I remember that one rest house had a ghost. Most of the night was spent asking each other, "who was that?", "did you hear?" when we heard footsteps or a creaking board. Eventually about three o'clock, there was a terrible noise in the kitchen of pots and pans being thrown around. Groping around in the dark for candles and matches and peering at each other in the dim light, we decided it had to be a ghost. Then, lighting more candles with prayers and incantations, the bungalow was exorcised. It stopped the noise but I have no idea whether it continued haunting the place. Of course, we did not have much sleep that night.

Hopong, which was some ten miles to the north-west of Taunggyi was generally our first stop. We were given another breakfast with hot coffee and sweet, vanilla sponge cake when we arrived. The Saohpa had three daughters, Lena, Thelma and Noreen who went to the convent in Taunggyi. Thelma, who was about my age, grew to be very pretty. When we saw her again after the Japanese war some four or five years later, she was tall and looked like a Tahitian beauty.

Not many miles outside of Hopong, beside some caves, was a beautiful green, green pool we used to go to when staying in Taunggyi. A stream ran down the side of the mountain into a deep pool before it meandered off into the valley. Tall trees with spreading branches provided the necessary shade. It was a wonderful place for picnics and I loved going there.

Sometimes we would stop at Mong Pawn which was only twenty-seven miles from Hopong, as Sao Sam Htun and his family were always very pleasant and hospitable. His wife, a princess from Mong Mit, was full of life and energy. She was a sister of Sao Hkun Hkio, the Saohpa who became the Head of State for Shan State in the Union of Burma, and later, Burma's Foreign Minister. The Mahadevi of Mong Pawn, Sao Hkin Thaung was popular amongst the British government officers and, having had a good convent education in Maymyo, she got on very well with everyone. Unfortunately like her husband she died young. Their eldest daughter Peggy became the fourth Shan girl to come to Kingswood when I was there.

Sao Sam Htun was one of the Saohpas whom Maurice Collis visited on his trip to Kengtung and the northern Shan States and he is mentioned in his book *The Lords of the Sunset*. There is also a lovely picture of the Mahadevi in the book.

By great misfortune the Saohpa of Mong Pawn was assassinated with General Aung San and his Cabinet in July 1947. Sao Sam Htun was a brilliant man. He did not go to Cambridge, as his brother-in-law had, but had a natural feeling for what was needed for the Shan States. He was a few years younger than my father, but they saw eye to eye on several points concerning the country. When he was killed he left a vacuum which was impossible to fill. He was a great loss to the Shan States. He was quiet, unassuming and hard working. He was, I believe, remembered mainly for his simplicity, his kindness and friendliness to his people.

A story is lovingly told of him in which he was mistaken for a villager by one of his subjects. One evening before the Japanese occupation, he had been walking on the outskirts of Mong Pawn dressed casually only in a pair of old, baggy Shan trousers and an open-necked shirt. He was hailed by a villager driving a bullock cart which had unfortunately got stuck in a deep, muddy pothole in the road. The villager asked if *ai sai*, young brother, would help to push the cart out of the mud. The Saopha was quite happy to help, and together they managed to push the cart clear onto the hardened surface of the road. After acknowledging the help given, the villager drove away into town.

A few days later, the same villager had to go to the State administrative offices on some business. Imagine his surprise, kneeling to let the approaching Saohpa pass, to recognise him as his helper. He threw himself on the ground asking for

*Sao Hkun Hkio, Saohpa of Mong Mit and his English wife, Mabel.*

*Mahadevi of Mong Mit, Sao Hkun Hkio's mother.*

pardon, which the Saohpa, who had enjoyed his little incognito adventure, was only too pleased to do so.

The journey from Mong Pawn onwards consisted of wonderful forests and mountains. The altitude on average was about 3,000 ft above sea level, and traversing the plateau we would at times suddenly come across open savanna land with the tall grass swaying in the slightest breeze. Suddenly a narrow gorge would appear as the road twisted and turned through the mountain side. Sometimes, rolling hills stretched before us, seeming to go on forever. Clusters of feathery bamboos stood out against the dark, tall trees on the mountain side. Driving along at a speed of around thirty miles an hour, through the open windows would sometimes waft an almost over-powering scent of an unknown jungle flower.

The forests were full of the chirping of crickets and with the drone of the car most of us nodded off to sleep. Daw Daw in a soft but strong voice, would help to keep us awake, as she sang popular Burmese songs. Her favourite, a classical song, was of a young queen, who sits looking out of her window at a beautiful moon. With sadness in her heart she sits and waits, keeping count of each hour being struck, but still her lord does not come. With an aching heart, she realizes he will not be coming that night and wonders where he might be?

There were two routes out of Loilem, one leading north towards Laikha, and the other south towards Mongnai. Sometimes we went to visit the old Saohpalong of Mongnai, who was a contemporary of my granduncle, Sir Sao Mawng. His state was one of the oldest of the Shan States. A large state, it was once prosperous and populous. The Mongnai family in earlier days had extensive relationships and was connected by marriage to the Mong Pawn, Mong Mit, Maukmai, Mong Nong, Wan Yin and Nawng Mawng ruling families. In the 16th century, Mongnai also had close connections with the Kingdom of Lan Na, present-day Northern Thailand.

Taking the northern route, we would eventually come to Laikha and by evening we would be in Mong Kung. As these two capitals lay on the main road we would stop briefly to greet the Saohpas. The Saohpa of Laikha, Sao Num was younger than my father. At that time, he had little interest in politics, and loved being surrounded by lots of friends and relations. He had an easy manner and a happy smile. He seemed to be a contented man who lived by the maxim that it was best to live for today, for tomorrow is another day. He had, it was rumoured, more than twenty-seven wives. He generally wore his turban at a rakish angle, and he used to be teased about his wives mercilessly. Unfortunately, as with other Saohpas, he too was taken into detention when the 1962 coup took place.

The Saohpa of Mong Kung was completely different – very solemn and serious and very slow to make up his mind about anything. Unlike most of the Saohpas, he was very badly treated by the Japanese when they were retreating, being taken as hostage to Kayah State. His eldest son, Richard, the Kyemmong, was sent to England for his education. Before he could help his father with affairs of State, he died of cancer at an early age of thirty-four. He was married to Nancy, my sister-in-law Pat's younger sister. They were both my stepmother's nieces.

## Shan hospitality

There was an informality between the Saohpa families and if we were getting late with all the social calls we had made during the day's travel, we would be persuaded to spend the night at either of the two states. It was marvellous that we could turn up as a party of about ten or twelve and be told that once our luggage had been unloaded, we could wash, change and soon have dinner. Everything was taken care of – not only were we fed dinner but food was provided for our next day's journey. As it was with us in Yawnghwe, there was never any fuss when visitors arrived. Whatever the time of day, a meal and refreshments were always served. This was Shan hospitality.

This was the reason why Saohpas or Shan officials were taken aback if they happened to call on British officials at meal times. They were never invited in but were often sent away, or told to come back at another time or wait until the meal was finished. In those days the British were more formal, and maintained the usual British reserve, so we always thought them unfriendly and aloof, without thinking that there might have been an explanation for such behaviour.

Whilst living in England, I gradually began to learn why the British always seemed so unwelcoming. I put it down to the fact that an English meal required a degree of etiquette and formality because it was usually eaten at a set time. In addition, the meal was generally cooked only for those who were eating it – four steaks for four people with nothing to spare. In contrast, we were less formal and had our meals at any time. Also an extra person or two made no difference at the table, since there was always enough rice and other dishes to go around. One had to accept that it was a completely different way of life. Of course, things have changed, and with frequent travel to foreign lands one finds fewer British people standing on ceremony.

To continue with our journey we sometimes drove at night since it was not considered dangerous, for there were no insurgents or bandits then. But there were tigers and panthers that came out at night in search of prey. I never saw one, though sometimes I remember being woken up by the car coming to a grinding halt, throwing us forward in our seats. The driver would whisper "That was a tiger crossing the road". However, by the time we clambered to look out of the car windows, the animal would have disappeared amongst the trees.

In the days before the Japanese occupation, a fairly good network of roads had been left behind by the public works division of the British administration. In addition, we had other efficient services, such as railways and postal systems to be grateful for. Recently, some correspondence of my father's, written on his voyages to England towards the end of 1930 and 1931 to attend the Round Table Conference, was discovered. It showed how reliable the postal system was in those days although ships were the only mail carriers.

He wrote to his eldest son, Sao Hseng Hpa, from Kensington Palace Mansions, London in October 1930. Another of the long letters written on board the M. S. *Johan van Oldenbarnevelt*, on 3rd November 1931 was to our mother, in which he said he was to disembark the next day in England. In his letter he described staying at the Mena Hotel in Cairo and seeing the Pyramids. On the envelope he had written only "The Mahadevi of Yawnghwe State, Yawnghwe

(Southern Shan States), Burma". Also, an earlier postcard written from Colombo to her second sister and my mother, was posted on 19th October 1931 and addressed simply, "Sao Nang Sanda, Hawdawgyi, Yawnghwe (Southern Shan States) Burma". It was received nine days later, franked Yawnghwe, 28th October 1931.

Yawnghwe, seemed to have been well known and a long address was not necessary for a letter to reach its destination. Nowadays, despite letters being sent by airmail, they never seem to get there as quickly as they did in the old colonial days. I don't intend to get involved in debating whether they were 'the good old colonial days' as one hears from time to time, but it does illustrate how in earlier times certain things worked. We did not have to be anxious wondering whether letters or trains got to their destinations, for we knew they would.

## Hsenwi, our destination

From Laikha and Mong Kung we had a choice of routes going to the Northern Shan States; a longer route was via Mong Yai but unless my father had business we generally took the shorter route to Lashio.

Lashio, long a trading centre, became prosperous and important when the Burma-China Road was routed through it just before the Japanese war. Numerous convoys of food and building materials were carried to the frontier and into China from here. The change in the town's financial status was immediately apparent, for unlike the Shan towns we had passed through, which were mostly a long main street of small bamboo and thatched houses on stilts, here there were more wooden houses and instead of thatch and bamboo for roofing, corrugated iron sheets had taken their place.

The narrow streets and lanes in the market area were filled with busy Chinese and Shan-Tayok (Shan-Chinese) people. There were rows of little shops selling imported goods such as textiles, shoes and tinned food. Indian shopkeepers stood in front of their stores inviting people to come in and inspect their wares in fierce competition with the Chinese. Small tea shops and cafes were everywhere, not only one or two, as in the towns we had passed.

Then as now, lorries and trucks lined the streets laden with goods on their way to China. Nowadays, there is a thriving black market along the border area. Even then, the town itself looked as if it were peopled only by the Chinese and not Shan. Though Hsenwi and its neighbouring towns were still inhabited by Shans and Kachins, Lashio was already an administrative centre as it is today.

The main part of Hsenwi lay in the valley but the Saohpa's Haw and those of his relations were built on the side of a hill. Higher up and almost on top of the hill, stood a small pagoda, which the Saohpa had built as his private place of worship. Driving up the short steep hill, we suddenly came upon the large, imposing stone building. Unlike our own palace, it was architecture in the colonial style, neat and compact, decorated with European furnishings and furniture. As far as I can remember, I recall feeling that this new Haw was a complete contrast to our rambling home. There was also an old Haw which I do not remember at all. The new Haw and many of the other houses were completely destroyed during the war, and, in fact very little of old Hsenwi remains today.

The Saohpa, Sao Hom Hpa, was a tall and distinguished looking man, whom we addressed as Sao Long Hpa, meaning elder uncle. He had a handsome, oval face and was greying at the temples. His booming voice made all his wives and servants shudder when he called out for one of his needs, such as a glass of water or a cheroot. He was also boisterous and, like my father, short tempered. Whenever an argument arose between them, which was not unusual, and as neither would give in to the other, it was only solved by their walking away from each other. When they met again, they would have either forgotten their argument or decided to ignore it. My uncle had little interest in politics then, but was a strict and severe ruler, who did not like anyone raising an objection or contradicting him. It was even rumoured that he did not think twice of sending such people to jail for a short spell to make them change their minds.

The Saohpa had six wives. Two were princesses from Hsipaw and Kengtung respectively and had been Mahadevis one after the other. As neither of the princesses could make their marriages work, after a long and complicated process the Saohpa agreed to a divorce, allowing them to return to their respective States. He had no children of his own so adopted the only son of his younger brother, Sao Hman Hpa, the Kyemmong. Wanting to have a son and daughter, he also adopted one of the daughters of his elder half-sister, married to a Frenchman. Their school names were Ivan and Victoria. Later, Victoria returned to using the name she had been christened with – Elaine. People in Hsenwi generally referred to them as *Sao Hsa taw* and *Sao Sami taw*, meaning royal son and royal daughter respectively.

Sao Long Hpa's true passion in those days was playing mahjong. This was the only thing for which he had infinite patience, and the only time he was jovial was when he had won a game. In order to be at the mahjong table as early as possible

*Saohpa of Kengtung, Sao Kawng Tai and family, 1930s. Sao Sai Long, his young son standing beside him, later became the Saohpa.*

*Sao Hman Hpa, Kyemmong of Hsenwi and family. Pat, my sister-in-law, stands behind her father c. 1940's.*

*My father, stepmother and the Saohpa of Hsenwi.*

after breakfast, he habitually got up at 5.30am to take a long walk. By 9 o'clock, he would be sitting at the mahjong table. I suppose this early morning exercise enabled him to sit and play for as long as he wanted. So when other players were shifting uneasily in their seats, he could quite happily sit on, continuing all through the night if necessary.

Our arrival being a special occasion, Sao Long Hpa stopped playing to talk to my father and to acknowledge our homage. However, after only a few minutes, he would go back to his game. This obsession with mahjong not only annoyed my father who never gambled nor knew the first thing about cards, but also the government and State officials, who used to have business to discuss and papers for him to sign. Nevertheless, whatever the business was, everything had to wait until the game was finished.

Though originally his only passion was mahjong, after several years of the country's independence, he decided to take an interest in politics. During the troubled times from 1958, he became Head of State for Shan States. When the elections came in 1960, my stepmother lost her seat as he was not prepared to support her. Instead, he made his own brother, Sao Hman Hpa, the new Hsenwi member of parliament, to her great disappointment.

Later, when my father and other Saohpas were detained during the 1962 coup, he, Sao Hom Hpa was not. It made us all wonder what inducement he had offered General Ne Win so that the military would leave him free. Perhaps being a master at mahjong had taught him how to manage his adversaries to his own advantage.

The Kyemmong, Sao Hman Hpa, his brother was a man of humility with an honest outlook. He was certainly not a grabbing politician. In fact, he was a brave man who underwent a harrowing experience during the Japanese period. He had been parachuted down behind enemy lines in General Wingate's campaign for the reoccupation of Burma, but was unfortunately captured by the Japanese and sentenced to death. Through the offices and goodwill of one of the Japanese officers stationed in Lashio, it was possible to negotiate and save him. The negotiations came just in time, for he was about to finish digging his own grave when he was released.

Although I do not recall, Elaine, who has an excellent memory, talks of lavish English breakfasts being served on silver platters at the Hsenwi Haw. Since my father was down to earth, we in Yawnghwe never enjoyed such luxury. The only food of Hsenwi I remember clearly was the warm *to-fu*, a kind of a very thick pea-soup, which the Tai Neua or Shan Tayok vender used to bring in the early misty mornings. It was mouth-wateringly delicious, eaten with fried crushed garlic, a touch of soya sauce and chilly oil, sprinkled with coriander and spring onions.

## Dr Gordon Seagrave

On one of our trips to Hsenwi it was planned that I should have my tonsils out. It was to be done by Dr Gordon Seagrave, an American doctor who worked in the remote frontier town of Namkham at the American Baptist Hospital. Dr Seagrave ran a nursing school to which many girls from different Shan States were sent for training. Also young enthusiastic men and women who were Kachin, Indian and Chinese came to join the hospital.

Namkham hospital became famous for its surgical and humanitarian work. Many mountain people who had no faith in western medicine in the early 1930s, came in large numbers when they found that there was a cure for goitre. This affliction, caused by an iodine deficiency in the salt they used, was fairly common in the region. Since he had to deal with so many different people, Dr Seagrave first began learning Shan and Kachin. Soon he was multilingual and was able to gain the confidence of those who came to seek his help. It was also the missionary spirit and the commitment to their humanitarian work of both Dr Seagrave and his staff, which made the hospital so successful.

The war brought him and his nurses further fame, for he attended to the British soldiers as they retreated into India, marching out with them. When the British re-occupied Burma, he returned with the troops. But when independence came, he was in disgrace with the then AFPFL government. His crime was that he had helped the wounded and sick alike, making no distinction between those who were insurgents and those who were not. When he was released he carried on his work in Namkham, with devotion and a passion for those mountain people who needed him so much until his death in 1964. His book *The Life of a Burma Surgeon* [18] tells of his life's achievements in the Shan hills.

The only thing I remember about the operation was just before going under the anaesthetic. I looked up into Dr Seagrave's kindly face, "Don't be frightened, it will be all right", he said gently. He then said a prayer, which seemed to go on for ages. The next thing I knew I was back in my room. The best part of my stay at the hospital was the wonderful room I had overlooking the Shweli river. On this side of the river lay rice fields and Burma, on the other, mountains and China.

Namkham meaning golden waters is a town inhabited by a mixture of Shan and Chinese people. They are usually referred to as the Tai Neua in Shan and Shan Tayok in Burmese, meaning Shan-Chinese. They are similar to the Tai Dam who live in Laos near the Shan-Laos border at Namtha. The houses and temples in this town have tiled roofs, many with two or three tiers, and show architectural influences from their neighbours across the border. Except for the dress of the women who are distinguished by their tall, cylindrical shaped-turbans, there are perhaps few other difference between the two banks of the Shweli.

It is over the bridge to the north of Namkham and Muse that the Chinese Shan States of Mong Mao Chefung lies and to the east, the State of Kokang. Apart from the many Chinese and Shan-Chinese within the Hsenwi State, there are also the Kachins, mostly in the area between Namkham and Kutkai. There are five main groups of Kachin, the Jingpaw sub-group being the largest. They are said to be of Tibeto-Burman stock, one of the latest immigrant groups to enter the country.

To the north of Hsenwi State lies the Kachin State itself which covers the northernmost region of Burma. The sources of the Chindwin and Irrawaddy rivers are to be found here. The latter is longer and runs the entire length of the country. During the colonial times, the British army recruited large numbers of young Kachin, who later fought valiantly against the Japanese. Although they were animists in the olden days, most now follow the Christian faith.

The women's costumes are striking, showing a love of vivid reds and silver ornaments. The beautifully designed silver mantles which are worn over the shoulders like a shawl, indicate the family's wealth. The chunky discs and different silver shapes that make up the decoration must weigh many kilograms.

Today, young Kachin men and women who have opted to live abroad in exile have found jobs as engineers and scientists, holding down responsible posts. Unfortunately not many of the elderly Kachin leaders, who had high hopes for their young, are still alive to see their achievements.

*Sao U Hpa in uniform 1942.*

# VI

# *War Years*

## *War approaches*

Despite the onset of the war in Europe, our lives in the Shan States continued without much change. However, we were beginning to worry about my two brothers in England since we had not heard from them for many months.

Then as the Second World War spread further, the Shan States Treasury contributed towards military expenses in forming Territorial Forces 13 and 14 and the MT section (1-16). My father rejoined the army on 1st January 1940, as Captain. He served with the 13th (Shan State) Territorial Battalion of the Burma Rifles in Taunggyi. A year later, he was promoted to Major.

At that time the four battalions of the Burma Rifles were chiefly composed of Chin, Kachin and Karen soldiers stationed in Mingaladon, Mandalay and Maymyo. It was the six battalions of the Burma Frontier Force, originally made up of Indians and Gurkhas, who were stationed in the Shan States, the Chin Hills and Kachin State. Their duties were similar to those of the Military Police, namely to keep an eye on the border areas. With the approach of the Japanese, the Burma Frontier Force was expanded to include Chin, Kachin, Karen and Shan. At the same time in preparation for the war, a special reconnaissance battalion was formed. Its role was concerned with internal security, mostly involved in noting and reporting on any enemy movements along the Burma-Thai-Lao frontier. In fact, they were intelligence units, who travelled widely in the remote border areas, making contact and gathering information from local hill peoples.

My father was posted away to a camp at Takaw on the road to Kengtung. Takaw lies on the banks of the swift flowing Salween river. Like the Mekong River, its source is to be found in the high mountains of the Himalayas. It flows through numerous deep gorges down the length of the Shan States to the Andaman Sea. Takaw sits some 800 feet above sea-level in a gorge. Since it is strategically placed, it was obviously a good listening post.

What is now known as the Golden Triangle had once again become as important politically and militarily as it was in the early days of annexation. In the 1940s it became a buffer against the menacing Japanese, then later it became a no-man's land against the invisible but perceived threat of Communist encroachment in the '60s and '70s, from Cambodia, Laos and Vietnam.

When we went to visit my father at his camp, he took us on a brief outing to Kengtung. There is little I can remember of the trip. What I do recall is seeing a large emerald, green frog on the dinner table. I wondered what a live frog was doing in a dish. I was soon, however, to find out that frogs were a delicacy and we were to eat it. I have a feeling that I left the table without any dinner that night. Later I was to learn that it wasn't only the Kengtung people who ate frogs, but that it was a popular dish to be found in France and elsewhere.

I am not sure how long my father was at Takaw. He was later moved back to Taunggyi where he remained in the army until the Shan State Government was dissolved on 20th April 1942. It was also the first day that the Japanese bombed Taunggyi and Heho.

## Advance and Retreat

When we broke up for our Christmas holidays at Kingswood in 1941, none of us had the slightest idea that for many it would be the very last time we were ever to see each other. The war in Europe had hardly affected us, but it was the Japanese bombing of Pearl Harbour on 7th December, which brought the war nearer to home. Once the Japanese had started on their warpath, there was nothing that could stop them. Within the following week, they had sank the *Prince of Wales* and the *Repulse* of the British Fleet at Singapore. Then having landed troops in Siam, they had marched into Burma at its southernmost tip. Despite the rapidity of the Japanese attack, neither the British administration in Rangoon nor the British government thought Burma could be taken so easily.

On 23rd December, Rangoon was bombed for the first time. People watched in the streets as the first bombs fell on Mingaladon airport, and later the air battles above them. Many were killed and wounded on that day. Up in the Shan States there were hundreds of rumours and no real news, but talk of the Japanese advance were persistent.

About the middle of January 1942, the Japanese marched through from Siam, and by the end of the month Moulmein had fallen. At that time, it was estimated that there were more Japanese forces on the ground than the British. Although there was some air defence, it was not sufficient.

In early March the Japanese arrived in Rangoon, as they simultaneously carried out a three-pronged attack on Upper Burma. The march eastward was towards the Shan plateau coming up to Taunggyi and northward to Lashio. By the end of April, Lashio had fallen, thus cutting off the Burma Road for the retreat of the Chinese and allied troops. It became apparent that Burma could no longer be defended and what had begun as a gradual retreat of the British forces and evacuation of civilians, took on a more urgent tempo.

As Mandalay and other northern towns were being bombed and occupied, the speed of retreat and evacuation increased. Mandalay fell to the Japanese at the beginning of May. By now, thousands of civilians were trying to escape, making for the shorter route out of Burma from Kalewa on the Chindwin river to Tamu and Imphal. Others walked up to Myitkyina hoping to be airlifted out, only to find that the Japanese were a step ahead. Guessing that this was what was intended, they had kept up a constant attack on the airfield until it was completely destroyed. People still kept arriving hoping to find a plane that could fly them out. But there was little hope of escape that way. Thus began the great trek northward into the Hukawng valley, along the Ledo road and into Assam and India.

Homes and possessions had to be left behind. Joining the long march out of the country, each person carried only what he or she could. Many books have been

*British troops on the Burma border. (Reproduction by permission of the Imperial War Museum)*

*Mule convoys carrying supplies into Burma, 1945. (Reproduction by permission of the Imperial War Museum)*

*Indian troops in Burma, 1942. (Reproduction by permission of the Imperial War Museum)*

*A cluster of stupas in
an Inle village.*

*A crush of boats at
the floating market,
Ywama.*

written about the retreat and the long strenuous trek. Many will have read these and will know the agony, the trials and the wretchedness of it all. The world today being what it is, news reportage of wars on television has made us all only too well aware of what is to be a refugee fleeing for one's life.

The flight for these refugees was no different. The countless days of walking, shortages of food and water, plus malaria and dysentery, took their toll. Those who were weak and sick were unable to continue, many died by the roadside. People were fortunate if they arrived with a complete family or in comparative good health. In the end, for the many who succumbed, the dark dense jungles of the Hukawng valley became their graves.

While the terrible trek was going on, we in the Shan States were not spared. The rapid advance of the Japanese had disrupted all British plans. The disorganized Chinese forces of Chiang Kai-Shek, who were trying to hold the Burma Road, were also in retreat. They looted towns and villages and raped any woman they could find on their passage. Pretty soon, the invading Japanese forces arrived. They were everywhere and like driver ants made their way forward destroying any obstruction in their path.

Around March or April 1942 the first Japanese bombs fell on Heho, the airfield which lay twenty miles from us, then on Taunggyi. On that day, the family were all in Yawnghwe except for my father who was in Taunggyi. We stood in the garden watching the planes swoop down over Heho. Then we saw dark, black smoke wind up into the air in columns from the direction of the administrative capital. As it lay behind the hills we could not see the raging fires.

It was all very worrying, we were in tears, not daring to think the unthinkable, until my father returned late in the evening, safe but shattered. As soon as he came back, my father told us that his battalion was moving out and was retreating to India. Although asked to join them with the family, he had opted to stay behind. Having no more military responsibilities, but only those towards his family and his people, he decided that we should evacuate to one of the Inle villages that very night. A village nearest to the channel leading from Yawnghwe to the lake was chosen. It was also near Fort Stedman on the northwest shore, which gave us an option of going either by water or land to seek safety. Fort Stedman, you might remember, was where the British forces were stationed in 1886 when they had come to help the then Saopha of Yawnghwe.

The Japanese were advancing rapidly and Yawnghwe was considered no longer safe. Some people made for the nearest jungle and into the hills, while others made their way to the Inle villages. Those with foresight had left early, taking their belongings with them; others who had delayed found themselves fleeing for their lives, leaving all their possessions. Soon the town was empty but for the pye dogs.

After a few days my father took us to Ywama, one of the main villages in Inle, where we stayed for some weeks. Our next move was to an adjoining village called Thalay. I suspect my father did not want to be in one place for long, not knowing what the Japanese were intending. In both villages we stayed in the *salops* or rest houses in monastery compounds. Apart from our family, the group included our maids, bodyguards, cooks and serving boys with their own families, so we occupied three of four of these rest houses. It was in the long corrugated iron-roofed rest house, the largest, that our immediate family stayed. It had no rooms so the rich heavy, velvet embroidered curtains were used as partitions. We consisted of my father, my stepmother and her three children, Daw Daw, Daw Win and myself.

There were other people staying there too. Many of the refugees had come from as far away as Rangoon and Mandalay, but most were from Taunggyi, Kalaw and Yawnghwe. I suppose it was the great expanse of water, which gave us all a feeling of security. None of us dared to admit that it was quite possible for the Japanese to pursue us if they wished.

Sao U Hpa had taken precautions and had wisely instructed that boats were not to be left lying alongside the waterfront in Yawnghwe nor indeed were any to line the shores. In this way it was hoped that any Japanese attempt to pursue us might be hindered.

All the villages around were full of relatives and friends. Although we were all refugees, we seemed to have taken it as a holiday, and were in carnival mood. We had enough food and, for the moment, there were no shortages. The only worrying thing was not knowing how long we would have to stay in Inle.

We had no newspapers and our ancient wireless set which ran off a car battery had been left behind at the Haw. Our sole source of news was listening to rumours, of which there were many. The only way to keep sane was not to believe all we heard. Of course, some of the rumours did give us some idea of what was to be expected from the Japanese. Disquieting stories were that anyone who did not do what they were told by a Japanese was slapped across the face, or that one had to bow three times on meeting them. They liked being called *gyi gyi* master, meaning big, big master in Burmese. Soon no one was to worry about being

*Saohpa of Hsahtung in ceremonial dress escorting Japanese officers.*

slapped on the face – infinitely preferable to being arrested and tortured. Once that happened there was little hope for few came out alive from those torture chambers.

One of my father's younger brothers went back to Yawnghwe before us to deal with any urgent matters. He was also to assess the behaviour of the Japanese and see what they wanted from the Yawnghwe administration. In this manner, he was able to warn my father of the state of affairs.

Before long, the Commander-in-Chief in Taunggyi sent a message to my father saying he wished to see him. We were all frightened for him, and also for ourselves. We had known that one day he would have to go and meet the Japanese, but now that the time had come we were full of foreboding. One of the chief fears was that there would certainly be a big, black mark against him, for having been an officer in the British army. The other was that he had two sons in enemy territory. Finally, we could no longer put off the evil day, so we all returned to Yawnghwe after staying on the Lake for about three months.

A story my father loved telling was that when he arrived at the office of the Commander-in-Chief, he was puzzled to be greeted by an officer who had a familiar face. After his meeting with the Commander which turned out to be amicable, he was escorted back to our old, black Plymouth by the same officer. Showing great respect, he asked if my father recognised him. My father replied he could not, and that the officer in uniform had the advantage over him. Then the Japanese told him he was none other than Ai San, a 'Chinese' trader who had been living in Yawnghwe for some years and had a small noodle shop. Imagine my father's surprise.

It shows how efficiently the Japanese had organised themselves. Little did we imagine that the man who we thought was Chinese and who used to send us Peking duck at Chinese New Year, was in fact a Japanese abiding his time. He was rewarded by the Imperial Army for being a good and useful citizen, and was allowed to go back to Japan at his request.

By August 1942, the Japanese had control of Rangoon and the country. A Burma Executive Administration was set up to govern the country. A year later,

*Family with
Japanese officer,
Akira Yoshimura
c. 1944.*

my father and other Saohpas were called to Rangoon to meet the Japanese High
Command. Travelling during that period must have been hazardous, but the ruling
princes had little choice and could not disobey Japanese commands. They were
told that the Imperial Nipponese Government had decided to give the country
its independence. Dr Ba Maw, whom I have mentioned before, a leading politician and a Cambridge graduate, was to be the Head of State. He was to be called
Adipadi. Furthermore, the princes were told that the Japanese government was
incorporating the Shan States and Karenni State with Burma Proper, while Kengtung and Mongpan were to be given to Siam. They had also appointed Aung San
as the Minister of Defence.

There was no recourse as everything had been decided. It was certainly not a
happy situation for the Shan States, nor for other non-Burmans. In those days, the
Shan knew nothing of young U Aung San.

Whilst all these political developments were taking place in Rangoon, we
had news that at last the British were beginning to counter-attack. In early 1944,
Taunggyi, and Heho airfield were simultaneously bombed. At nights the sky was
ablaze with coloured flares which fell from the planes as they swooped down over
Heho airfield, bombing the Japanese army and their installations. As both places
were some miles away from us, we never had the slightest fear of standing outside
in the garden watching the red blaze which rose behind the western hills. Wickedly,
we whispered to each other how pleased we were to see the bombs falling on the
Japanese. When the noise of the planes receded, we came back into our house in
the glow of candle-lights and waited, listening for the next batch of planes.

## No news of my two brothers

We had had absolutely no news from my two brothers in England. We had heard
that Germany was victorious in Europe, and we feared for them. The Japanese,
however, had different ideas. They believed that both Sao Sai and Sai Hseng were
grown men and had been enlisted as pilots. They claimed that my brothers flew

reconnaissance planes over the Shan States, one in a plane with its fuselage painted red and the other painted blue.

My father denied all knowledge of this, but the Japanese believed that we were in touch. It was not very pleasant being confronted by the military police about my brothers every few days. In the end they became so suspicious that they had men who lived in to keep an eye on my father. We knew that my brothers were far too young to be in the Royal Air Force, so we had no worries of them being shot down or captured by the Japanese. What was a worry was not knowing where they were and what was happening. After the war we found out that the Japanese had mistaken one of my brothers for the Tawngpeng Saohpa's son, a fighter pilot, who unfortunately was killed in active service over Upper Burma.

During these years, there was a constant stream of Japanese officers who came to call on my father, and generally they had to be fed and entertained. They said they wanted to be our friends although their daily visits were obviously to check on my father and his administrative officers. At that time we had U Aung, a Burman, as our cook. He had a large paunch and was very jolly. Food was not only scare, it was also expensive, so when he had to feed more Japanese than he had cooked for, he would say "Add a little more water, they'll be none the wiser." Later on after the war, when he was feeding us and not the Japanese, we would have to remind him that the curry was not tasty as the sauce was too thin. Undoubtedly U Aung was hoping we had not noticed, but we knew he was up to his tricks again.

Sao U Hpa restricted my meetings with the Japanese to only a few officers. The few I met spoke English well as they had been educated in Germany or in America. Though they were proud of knowing English, they sometimes pretended they didn't and brought interpreters to translate. I expect until they knew us better, they were trying to catch us out. My father began to worry when they started bringing me presents – dark green seaweed sweets, bean curd cakes, fans and kimonos. It was curious how they delighted in telling us that the Japanese were better in all things. They often exaggerated, talking of large tomatoes which were the size of pomelos, a citrus fruit the size of a small football, and chrysanthemums the size of a dinner plate. Whatever grew in Japan was always bigger and better.

They were a friendly lot, but nevertheless one was always wary of them. We had heard grim and horrible stories of officers and soldiers alike raping and assaulting women, slapping and shooting down any fathers or husbands who went to their women's defence. We were fortunate that the Japanese administration behaved well towards us, and treated my father with respect.

Although the officers I met seemed harmless, my father decided that it was too risky having a young teenage daughter around. He decided I should return to Inle where I could learn to cook and sew, and train to be a perfect housewife.

## Sojourn in Inle

With my two aunts, we went to stay in Ywagyi, a village where my elder, paternal aunt lived with her husband, then the Myosa of Indein. We called them Sao Mye and Sao Paw meaning Princess Mother and Prince Father.

Ywagyi was built on a long spit of land on the western side of the lake, not very far from Thalay, the village we had fled to earlier. A river flowed down from the shore at Indein dividing Ywagyi from the acres and acres of paddy fields which lay in front. It gradually meandered down through forests of tall reeds making channels into the lake.

The river was fast flowing where it passed my aunt's house and though muddy was clean. This stretch of water became our private swimming pool. We didn't possess swimming costumes and anyway wearing one showing our legs would have been indecorous. Instead we swam with our *sin* knotted above the breasts. I loved jumping down from the little landing stage which filled the *sin* with air, before quickly tucking the bottom hem between my legs as it ballooned out. I could stay afloat as the current swept me a few feet until the balloon burst.

Daw Daw, Daw Win and myself were given a wing and we settled down to knitting and sewing. I was taught to cut and sew jackets on a treadle sewing machine and make Chinese buttons. These last needed neat and tidy stitches which I never managed to achieve. It soon became clear that there was a limit to making new clothes. Before long we were unravelling old jumpers and cardigans to knit new ones with different patterns. I learnt to knit socks, but never quite managed the heels. The days seemed to pass by without incident and a pleasant routine was established.

I can't understand why I did not make use of those days to read and write Shan, or try to improve my Burmese. It was forbidden to read or speak English by the Japanese, so we hadn't brought any books from my father's library, nor my school books. I yearned for the life at school and my friends. Although daily life was bearable, I felt our existence was becoming set in a pattern from which there was no escape. The British planes that came each night to make their raids seemed to be my only connection with the outside world. I was becoming lethargic and frustrated, and felt isolated. I was too lazy to read Burmese and I never once picked up the magazines such as *Myawadi* and other women's magazines which Daw Daw and Daw Win enjoyed reading. These were often worn and tattered as they had made the rounds of friends living near us.

Suddenly I became ill with a high fever. A friendly doctor whose sister was Daw Win's friend was at that time staying in Inpawkhone, a village about half-

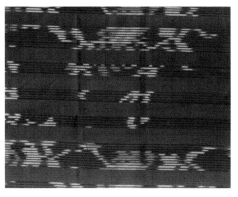

*Inle silk woven in the* zimme *pattern.*          *Inle silk woven in the* bankok *pattern.*

an-hour away in a sampan. He was sent for and first diagnosed malaria, before discovering later that it was typhoid. The doctor became worried, as it was difficult obtaining the necessary medicine to treat me. In the meantime, I had become quite deaf, with all the quinine I had taken previously. I was very ill and don't recall how many long days I lay on a lumpy mattress on the floor under the large mosquito net.

One day I heard hushed whispers, and recognised my father's voice. Perhaps that was the magical moment which pulled me round, knowing he had come all the way from Yawnghwe to see me. Anyway, some days later much to everyone's delight, I turned the corner, and began to show signs of improvement. Progress was slow. As I began feeling better, I also began to feel hungry. All through the days of my recovery I could think of nothing else but large platefuls of steaming rice, and delicious hot curries. Instead I was fed on rice gruel for a number of days. At last I was able to eat something solid. Though it was only a plateful of red, fragrant rice with a little salt to begin with, it tasted so good. Nothing else could have been more delicious. I had grown thin and weak, but my astonishing appetite soon put me back on my feet. I was once again my normal self – a plump, pimply teenager.

Before my illness, plans had been made for us to move to a village which was on the south-eastern side of the lake. Here an owner of some mechanical looms had kindly agreed to teach us his method of weaving. He dealt chiefly in cotton. The warp was imported, and the weft was spun cotton. We were to be taught to dye and spin the cotton, and learn to arrange the warp. It was a marvellous idea as it would give us practical knowledge and the ability to earn a living, if the war went on much longer. Although there were imported Japanese goods, the prices were too high for us to afford the clothes or the textiles.

After about a month or so we left Yawgyi and our swimming pool, much to my regret. The first thing when we got to the new village was to buy bundles of cotton which had already been cleaned and rolled, ready for spinning. I soon learnt to spin quite effectively and though I never got a very fine thread, I was able to weave with it. Spinning cotton was a tedious, but rather soothing job. My two aunts and I felt we were back at school. Each morning we would paddle from our small rented house to the factory. There were about ten or fifteen looms in the long bamboo shed which stood in the middle of the water. I do not know the name for these looms, but the metal reed was built into the slay or batten on which the shuttle ran from side to side. One had only to push the batten back, and the shuttle would fly across the warp. This made weaving faster and more efficient, as most looms used in the Inle were still hand looms.

We spent the day either dyeing or making up patterns. If the warp was on the loom, we wove lengths of plain and tartan-patterned material. To get the right size of square and rectangles on the material, one had either to count the rows of the weft as one wove, or judge it by eye. A new shuttle with a different coloured weft was put in to form the next square, then back to the former shuttle and so on. About half past three or four we returned to our house and spent the rest of the day spinning or sewing. We seemed to be learning well, but we had a long way to go to master the techniques of this kind of weaving.

The only other place where mechanical looms were used was in Inpawkhone, a larger village. Here the expert weavers wove lengths of *zimme* and *bankok* which were special patterned silk for *sins*. The terms *zimme* and *bankok* were imported from their namesakes Chiang Mai and Bangkok, by an enterprising merchant who liked the patterns which he had seen woven there.

The *zimme* patterns were brightly coloured in various designs such as flowers and geometric shapes. The soft silk was not printed but tied-dyed to make up the patterns. Since only three or four lengths of the *sin* were woven at one time, the patterns were unique for each length, which was about six or eight yards. As these weaving houses were not factories in the strict sense, there was no uniform method of using the different dyes and designs woven. Although they made beautiful *sins*, there was not a wide market for the silks.

It was slightly different with the *bankok* silk which was in two colours – white with green, blue or black. The pattern was of wriggling lines, and the combination of the two colours produced a softer shade of the green or blue, while the black and white produced a smart grey. These fabrics were usually exported to Mandalay for Burman men to wear on festive occasions. Women wore the *bankok* too, though they were somewhat stiff, making a swishing sound when one walked. How marvellous it would have been if there had someone like Jim Thompson, of Thai Silk fame, to rejuvenate the Inle silk industry.

The landlord of our house had extended his land, made up of floating islands of water hyacinths and weeds, so we had dry land to walk on around the house. One day while I was playing hop-scotch with our young maid, I cut the sole of my left foot on a piece of glass. It was a deep cut, and there was masses of blood. Both Daw Daw and Daw Win were very disturbed. They took this to be a bad omen and, as we had not heard from my father for some days, they feared the worse.

None of us could eat that night and there was a feeling of foreboding. Sure enough, about four o'clock in the early hours of the morning we were awakened by loud shouts. It was a message from my father saying that my third stepbrother had died of fever at only a few months old, and that we should pack up and come home. My stepmother was in a terrible state, and Daw Daw's calm presence was needed to run the affairs of the house and our family.

Feeling very sad, we came back to Yawnghwe. I have no recollection of the funeral nor of what happened immediately after. However, we had a welcome guest from Hsenwi. Evelyn, whom I had met earlier at Kingswood and who was Victoria's elder sister, had come to spend some time with us. They were both my stepmother's nieces.

By 1944, the British in India had managed to rebuild their forces, and nearly every night we had to run for cover into our trenches when the RAF launched bombing raids. This was no easy thing to do, for the trench was in the north garden and we slept in the south wing. When there was an alarm, we would put on whatever clothes we could lay our hands on, and barefooted we would race to my father's wing through the inner audience hall and down the stairs into the garden.

The L-shaped trench was a miserable affair five feet deep and some eight or ten feet long. A layer of wooden planks covered our heads, followed by sand, then mud, with sand bags on top. It was an odd mushroom-shaped object, and looking back now I wonder what made us have such faith in so flimsy and ineffectual a shelter. Every time there was an air raid I would fall into a fit of hysterical giggles.

When I was not giggling, I could never stop chattering about this or that – sheer fright, I suppose. My elders would be livid, because most were trying to say their prayers or tell their beads, and found that my nervous twittering disturbing.

On some nights, the sky used to be lit up with flares as bombs were dropped on the Heho airstrip, which had become a major Japanese communication centre. Inwardly I would rejoice, counting the flares of blue, yellow and red, I would pray hard that they went towards Taunggyi as well and hoped it would be bombed to bits as the Japanese had firmly entrenched themselves there.

## An earthquake

One night I was wakened by the monotonous drone of an aeroplane. I lay in bed trying to make up my mind whether to wake the others or to go back to sleep. Just then Daw Daw's voice cried out that we should go into the trench. My cousin and I leapt out of our beds and began running but before we had left our wing, the house began to sway and the floor moved under our feet. We suddenly realised it was an earthquake. We changed course, running instead through the back hall and down the steps. Once we reached ground level, we flung ourselves flat on our faces.

It was a moonlit night, and as we lay there we could see all the coconut palm trees lining the road swaying and the house creaking. One of our cars parked a little way down the drive was rolling gently first forwards, then backwards. Evelyn, who during all the air raids was never ruffled, held my hand tight as she trembled. It seemed an eternity lying there. Then it was over.

Upstairs once more we found that no one was hurt and all was well. Although a few minutes ago we were terrified of being squashed under the weight of our crumbling house, we felt quite relieved that it was only an earthquake and not a bomb.

Meanwhile, the Japanese insisted that we should all learn to write and read Japanese. Cousins and aunts, some of the State officials and I would sit in my father's office every evening learning everyday phrases and songs about the beautiful cherry blossoms. Our master, a small bespectacled Japanese, who looked exactly like a contemporary cartoon character, came from the Yawnghwe State School where he was teaching. I was not very interested; instead I wanted desperately to read and speak English, which I was rapidly beginning to forget.

I saw my father more often now and, although I began to know him better, I was perpetually afraid of him. He used to send for me from time to time, but when this happened my mind would start reeling, listing all the things I might have done wrong, or wondering whether I had said something to someone which might have displeased him. It was so easy to commit a solecism. Thank goodness, nine times out of ten, I was wrong and he had merely called me to help him add up columns of figures or to copy something he had written. My father had a serious countenence and, unless pleased with something, he hardly smiled. But when he was pleased his round face lit up with a big smile and he would give a grunt of approval. I began to feel more comfortable when meeting him and I started talking to him. Still, he was always a strict father who wanted his children to be obedient.

## Unwelcome attention

There were usually Japanese soldiers about in the town but they rarely wandered into our compound. One morning, however, one of the maids had gone to the back hall to fetch our breakfast of toast and coffee and without thinking had left the door connecting the south wing to the inner audience hall ajar. While she was away, we heard loud boot steps coming into the front room of our wing. Daw Daw, in whose room we were, remarked that it was odd for it didn't sound like my father's footsteps.

Fortunately for us, the main door which led to our rooms was locked, it had been re-bolted after the maid had gone out. In a moment, there was a loud banging on this door, followed by more hammerings and loud shouts in Japanese. We looked at each other, and realized there was not a moment to spare. We couldn't tell how long the door would hold out against the continual hammering. Once this door was down we would be lost, for the other two doors leading to Daw Daw's room and ours were not very strong. We dared not come out of my aunt's room into the corridor in case just at that very moment the big door might gave way.

Anyway we decided to take the risk and quickly ran out of the room and down the corridor into the back room through another door which we were able to secure. The maids had their room in this area and there were two bathrooms. We ran though to the second bathroom and down the flight of stairs that led into the back area of our large compound. These were the stairs the convicts used for carrying water up for washing and bathing, and the big, burly Indian sweeper who came to clear the commodes, for flush toilets had not been installed then.

Having reached the bottom, we decided not to go out into the open, in case there were more soldiers about. Luckily, the maid on hearing the banging had come back to take a look and, finding only two soldiers and not a score as she had thought, had run to the bodyguards for help. The bodyguards were in a state as they had no idea how the soldiers had got past them. The maid and two of the pages came down to tell us that something was being done.

The two or three bodyguards who had come to lead the soldiers away began by telling them there were no women in the rooms, as they had been shouting that they wanted women. This made one of them angry, as he said he had seen women, and knew they were hiding. It was all very tricky, and the situation only calmed down when an interpreter from the administrative office arrived and coaxed the soldiers to go with him into town, where he promised them more beautiful and younger girls. They at last agreed to go away.

The bodyguards on duty were given a good ticking off. I presume they were having their usual mid-morning nap and had therefore not seen or heard the two soldiers.

After this incident, my father decided that it was definitely too risky for us to go on staying in Yawnghwe. He, too, had on occasion been teased by some of the younger officers, who had called him 'father' and Sao U Hpa was not at all amused by this. I was only called to come down to help my father entertain guests when he was visited by some of the senior officers whom my father knew and liked. Sometimes, a perfect stranger would ask my father outright why he kept his daughter hidden. So, back to Inle Lake, my aunts and I went.

This time we went to Thalay where we rented a house, near to the same monastery we had stayed at during our first flight. The village was built partly on land and partly in the water. During the monsoon, the water rose some four or five feet reaching almost to the floors of the houses. When the water subsided we could walk from one house to the other over little bamboo bridges. The house in Thalay like any other in the village was built on stilts over floating islands and most of the villagers grew a variety of vegetables and ornamental plants with variegated leaves in a range of colours – mottled deep red leaves, round and long green leaves edged with white or yellow.

We built a room under the house to keep three looms. There was only one large bedroom and the front room served as the altar room, sitting and dining room, and a kitchen which had a large fireplace for cooking. When it was a chilly morning, we sat around a low round table, and had our breakfast (lunch) on the wide veranda in the sunshine.

Weaving and spinning were what we did during that period. Sometimes we would take a day off and row over to Ywagyi to see Sao Mye and have a wonderful swim in the swift river. Or go to Namhu to pay our respects to the Phaung Daw U Buddhas, rowing there in our sampans. We also made excursions to visit pagodas and monasteries: two outstanding ancient places with a multi-complex of *stupas* were at Indein and Kuk Ku, the former lying to the southeast corner of the Inle and the other to the northwest. Both have now become tourist attractions.

One day when we went to the Nampan market, I was able to pick up some coloured yarn with a woollen texture. It was an exciting discovery and I decided to weave into it some thick, white warp cotton I had spun. I was tired of making checks and squares and this piece came out well. It turned out to be a heavier material than we used for *sins*, and I thought it could be used for making jackets and coats for the chilly mornings. I was very pleased and decided to weave about twenty or thirty yards. Once the cloth came off the loom I was able to sell it for an enormous profit. Unfortunately soon after, the retreat of the Japanese began, and I found myself stuck with a suitcase full of useless Japanese notes. So much for my efforts at making money!

We stayed in Thalay for nearly a year, but it felt as if we were going to live there forever. It was a dismal thought. We were now at the end of 1944, and there were rumours that the British were at last on Burmese soil re-occupying the country. This piece of news cheered us up. At last, rumours were becoming fact. We heard that the Fourteenth Army in a fierce battle had almost wiped out the Japanese army which was trying to advance into India at Imphal. Then, that the Fourteenth Army was advancing into Burma and by March 1945, that they had re-taken Mandalay. Incredible as it seemed, the Japanese were now in retreat.

## The Japanese retreat

Not long after, my father and family came to join us at Thalay. The pressure of the British air attack was more seriously felt both at Heho and Taunggyi. They were bombed continuously, and no one felt safe. Yawnghwe town was practically empty and just the day before my father came to join us bombs fell around our house, but none directly on it. There were showers of shrapnel from the machine gun fire which made our roof look like a sieve. One bullet had actually gone right though my father's pillow, on the bed which he had vacated only a few minutes before to run down to the trench.

My father was extraordinarily lucky, and no one was hurt. This, of course, was put down to the Guardian *phii* of the Haw who had protected my father. The fact that bombs were dropped around our Haw and not on it, made everyone feel that the British did not really want to bomb Yawnghwe, but had done so to avoid any Japanese suspicions that we had connections with the British.

We felt we could breathe freely again with the Japanese in retreat and the British advancing. Some time later bombs fell on Inle, but only one exploded, so once again it was felt that the Guardian *phii* of Inle had protected us.

There were so many conflicting rumours about our friends and relations, and it was not easy sorting out the different stories. We had heard that the American 101 task force had contacted Sao Long Hpa, Saohpa of Hsenwi, and had offered their protection. Uncle Kyemmong with Ivan had gone to join them in the jungle. In the meantime, the Japanese had heard of their escape and in revenge had burnt down the entire town of Hsenwi and taken into custody some of his family. In fact, most of the family managed to escape in the end.

The Laikha, Lawksawk and Mong Pawn families were forced to escape from the retreating Japanese. We learnt later that they all had to make long and dangerous treks up north to eventual safety with British and American forces. The Saohpa of Mong Kung had been taken prisoner we were told. He was less fortunate, and had been made to ride bare-back along with the fleeing troops for a good hundred miles. So the news was not all good.

In this respect, Sao U Hpa was fortunate. Whilst he was still in Yawnghwe, a Japanese Colonel, whom he had got to know quite well, had kindly come from Taunggyi to tell him that it was time my father and his family found a safer place, for the Japanese army were now in retreat and the British were advancing very rapidly.

Our family was also lucky that we had the Inle to flee to, whereas the other princes who lived scattered across the Shan plateau in their states had to bear the brunt of the Japanese occupation and their retreat. There were a number of Japanese officers who, having observed how the many Saohpa families were suffering, were kind and sympathetic. They often gave advice and helped when these ruling families were in difficulty. Like the Japanese colonel who was kind to us, others turned a blind eye when the time came for families to escape from the withdrawing Imperial army. It was largely due to the warnings given by these few, who knew what devastation a retreating force could create, that made it possible for most of the Saohpa families to stay alive. To many of them we are grateful.

As soon as evacuation plans were ready, my father made it clear to the Japanese authorities that he had no intention of going anywhere but Inle. He did not want them to come looking for us and, finding the palace empty, assume that my father had gone off for protection to British forces in the vicinity. This step he took of making his whereabouts known, proved to be invaluable, as the Japanese had little excuse for saying that they did not know where he was, or that they were unable to find him, when they wanted to reach him.

*A leg rower. (Donnison Collection)*

Thus when a certain amount of rice was demanded for the troops, my father was able to arrange this, requesting that their soldiers go in an orderly manner and not to create havoc as they went. Each village on their route, he said, would be instructed to meet Japanese demands. Whether the Japanese listened to my father's request, or whether it was due to their complete weariness and low morale, we have no way of knowing, but they did not burn the villages as they retreated, which was what they were wont to do.

It was Sao U Hpa's fervent wish to ensure that his family and the people of his state escaped the horrors and destruction of the retreating forces. Happily, he was able to achieve this by being in constant touch with the Japanese authorities until the last moment of their departure from Taunggyi and Yawnghwe state.

## Another move

The house at Thalay was fine for a week or so, but we were all pretty cramped. My stepmother was pregnant with her fifth child who was due any day. So we moved out of Thalay, leaving Daw Win and her children Hayma and Papu there. Our next home was to be at a village called Min Chaung, close to the western shore. We made our move during the night because it was safer. Also, it meant we avoided being seen by British planes that now ruled the skies.

*Covered boat, with three rowers. (Donnison Collection)*

We started off in several boatloads. My father, stepmother, Ying, the fourth child and daughter, the midwife and myself, I seem to remember, were in the first boat. Daw Daw followed with the two younger brothers and, perhaps, the doctor. Maids, cook and servants with the luggage came in other boats. The vessels glided across the smooth surface of the water, with four leg-rowers manning each boat. It was about a two hour trip. My stepmother seemed quite well when we began for she had joined in making arrangements for the trip, and we were not unduly worried. But when we were about half way, she began having her labour pains. We immediately made room in the boat so that she could lie flat under the awning, while we sat outside under the twinkling stars.

My stepmother's moans became louder and louder. We thought she would give birth in the boat and became panicky. Fortunately, the baby waited until we arrived at the village and the mother had been carried into the house onto a make-shift bed. While my father held his wife's hand, the midwife began instructing us to boil water and to bring towels.

I was standing awkwardly in the doorway uncertain as to what I was expected to do next, when there was a very loud scream and the dark head of the baby appeared. I was rooted to the spot with fright. I suppose any other person would have rushed forward to help the midwife or done something useful. After another terrific groan the whole baby appeared. I turned around and dashed into the other room nearly knocking the doctor down. I was surprised to have seen the birth, but I was not certain whether I felt wonder or fright?

My behaviour most probably seems surprising, as it is generally believed that Eastern children became mature at an early age. This was said to be due mainly to the fact that the family, sometimes with an extended family, lived closely together in one or two rooms. Thus children living in villages soon learnt about sex as they often lived in communal rooms, and also observed the animals which they had to tend. That theory though did not apply to me. Although I was about fifteen or so at that time, no one had ever said anything about sex. I had firmly been told that I must under no circumstances allow any boy or man to touch me. Being a boarder at a co-educational school, it was not easy to carry out the instructions given to me by the family. We girls giggled and joked with the boys, and had infatuations, but none of us became seriously involved. So we never learnt very much from each other about falling in love, kissing or having sex.

The constant reminder from family elders was that one should never dishonour or disgrace the family. This actually meant that one could not fall in love with anyone one wished. I was warned that for social reasons of race, religion and position, it would not be a good idea to fall in love with someone whom I could never marry. When the time came for marriage, it would be to a person chosen by the family, not to someone I had chosen myself. Despite the lectures on matrimonial matters being dinned into my head, no one had prepared me for witnessing the birth of my brother.

When I went to see my stepmother and the baby the next morning, they were under a heavy mosquito net. The baby was swathed from top to toe, with only his little face showing. My stepmother was breast feeding him, and kept mopping her brow every other second. It was very hot and humid in the room. To keep the room at that temperature a large blazing fire was kept burning under an earthen ware pot, full of boiling water letting off a constant jet of steam.

The baby was called Myee Myee, meaning bear, and he became his father's favourite. I suppose since he was in attendance to see his son come into the world, he had a special attachment to him. When he became a teenager, Myee Myee was one of the most popular boys at his school and no one had a bad word to say against him. He had an open disposition and was always laughing and happy.

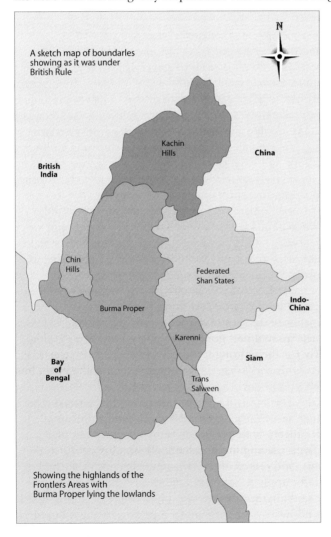

A sketch map of boundarles showing as it was under British Rule

Kachin Hills

China

British India

Chin Hills

Federated Shan States

Indo-China

Burma Proper

Karenni

Siam

Bay of Bengal

Trans Salween

Showing the highlands of the Frontlers Areas with Burma Proper lying the lowlands

*Sketch map of Burma under British Rule.*

Tragically, when the 1962 military coup took place, Myee Myee was to become a casualty of the whole horrendous affair.

## *Inle – British Contact*

While we were in this village, contact was made by the advancing British. They offered my father protection and asked him to join the guerrilla forces in the western hills, but my father refused. He saw no point in leaving his family, nor did he see any danger. He felt so long as he was staying in Inle, everybody – the British, the Japanese and the people of his state knew where he was. Since he was in one place, he could easily be contacted if they needed him.

The house where we were staying was a long, low-lying bamboo house. On one side it was on stilts above the water, and we all slept there. The other part was on land, and it was used as a kitchen and sitting room. The planes used to fly low over us on a raid, and we would then rush out of the kitchen along the bunds which divided the paddy fields and into the betel leaf plantations for cover. The emerald, green betel leaves climbed up bamboo stakes, like hops, and when they were several feet high entwined themselves together along the horizontal staves. So with the thick canopy over us, we could be certain that we would not be seen. But, as usual, we soon grew tired of running out for shelter, and just stayed indoors, praying we would be spared.

Unlike the previous evacuation, there was a definite shortage of food. White polished rice could not be bought, so we had to buy rice in their husks. Taking it in turns with the maids, I remember helping to pound the rice each day in a wooden mortar with a heavy pestle. When all the husks had come off the rice, it was put into a plaited bamboo tray. To winnow the rice, it was thrown into the air several times until all the husks were blown away. It was this coarse, red rice with a sprinkling of salt and sesamum oil which made many of our meals. But on some days we just had rice gruel and a pinch of salt. Since there were a number of us, it was not possible to eat rice and curry often. Fish, which was our only treat, had become more and more difficult to buy. No one dared to fish during the day for with so many planes overhead, they were frightened to be seen. At night, too, the fishermen were afraid their flickering oil lamps might attract the attention of passing planes.

The festive spirit with which we had first gone to Ywama three years ago had gone, and we waited anxiously for the fighting to be over. In the meantime, the British continued their contact with my father. They sent messages rolled up in a cheroot, or tucked inside the brim of a hat. All exchanges had to be made in a clandestine manner, since the Japanese had not retreated completely from our State. It was only when the Japanese eventually trailed across the border into Samka State, that two British officers came to see my father. It was a moment we thought we would never live to see. Quite unashamedly we all wept for joy. I could hardly believe it was true as I looked at the two white men, sun-tanned and bearded. At last the British had come back and we knew that war would soon be over. What euphoria!

We wanted to express our gratitude for their coming to see us to assure us that all would be well, but the only thing with which we could show our appreciation was a bunch of bananas. The officers had kindly brought us cigarettes and some ration packs. Sao U Hpa, who was the only smoker in the family was overjoyed, and the children could not have been happier as we munched the hard dry, bitter chocolate. We must have looked a pathetic group. I was sorry I never met either of them again, as it would have given me so much pleasure to find out what their impressions were of us, and to hear how they felt on being greeted with such a frenzied show of happiness. They also brought news of my brothers in England. We were overjoyed to know that they were both well and safe.

The prestige of the British rose again for they were beating the Japanese back. Other incidents also helped to make people feel more confident of the British, such as the following story. Until the war no one in our part of the country had ever seen a plane close up – when we saw them they were flying high and dropping bombs upon us. There were those, however, who were more fortunate. It appears that lorry drivers travelling along the stretch of flat road from Yawnghwe to Shwenyaung, laden with basketfuls of goods, on occasion used to see small planes swooping down and flying so low that the pilots were easily visible. At first the drivers were frightened, but they soon got used to the planes. Often the pilots used to wave to them and this filled the drivers with great pride. What an experience for them to see these "machines that flew in the air, which one could almost touch if standing on the roof of the lorry", they related to their friends.

Soon after the meeting with the British officers, Sao U Hpa decided it would be safe enough for us to return to Yawnghwe. The Inle, to our gratitude, had once again given us shelter and protection from the horrors of war and the retreating Japanese.

Now almost sixty years later, I dread to think what the Inle will be like in the future without the regular dredging of the silt from the numerous rivers flowing in and the clearing of water weeds and hyacinth from the choked channels. Over the years there naturally has been an increase in population, with more villages growing around the periphery of the lake. It seems by using the endless supply of floating islands, composed of rotted hyacinth, silt and other vegetation of the lake, to construct their homes, they have unwittingly encroached upon the waters of Inle.

A recent map of the Inle shows that the expanse of the waters is already smaller than it used to be fifty years ago. Therefore, there may be a real possibility of the lake disappearing within the next few decades. It would be sad to think of Inle no longer being the shimmering lake we used to know. There is also the danger of it ceasing to be a tourist attraction and a place of refuge in time of need.

Once we got back home we went from room to room, and wing to wing trying to find out how the retreating Japanese soldiers had treated the Haw. We were fortunate – it seemed that nothing was stolen or vandalised and the only damage was from the splinters of the earlier bomb which fell before the family fled to the lake. It appeared that senior Japanese officers out of respect for my father had managed to maintain control over their soldiers.

After all the excitement was over I rushed up to my room and my secret world. There below was Yawnghwe. It was a view I loved and nothing seemed to have changed. The glittering pagoda was still standing, the coconut palms waved in the breeze, and the houses still stood in their neat little squares. People walked in and out of their houses or were strolling on the roads talking and laughing. I could even make out the *dhobi* at work, washing clothes in the stream beside the city gate. Everything seemed to be back to normal. At last the war was over and we were all alive. Our hearts could once more be light and carefree.

In truth, the end of the war, had I realised it then, was also the end of my childhood. Gone forever were those simple days of innocence and enchantment.

## Back to school

After long ten years, in 1946 my eldest brother Sao Sai came back from England. From King's School, Canterbury, he had gone on to read engineering at St John's College in Cambridge. I hadn't seen him for so long and we had both grown up. There was little I remembered of him as a young boy. He was rather like my father somewhat reserved at first. Later I found him soft-spoken and gentle. Partly covering his mouth, he would often giggle to himself when something pleased him. He introduced me to classical music which I had never heard before. His favourite was Mozart's Eine Kleine Nachtmusik,  a 75 record played on the gramophone using wooden needles. I was fascinated by it all and soon found myself in charge of sharpening these needles on an emery board when they became blunt.

Then Sai Hseng, my other brother, came back for the long vacation. He was reading agriculture at Pembroke College in Cambridge. I was very envious of them, especially when they told us about England. I felt that being a girl, I would never be sent abroad. But my feelings proved to be wrong.

It must have been that year, just before Sao Sai's return, when the convents reopened. Since most of the nuns were Italians, they had remained in Kalaw and Taunggyi during the Japanese occupation. Soon I was sent off to St Agnes' Convent in Kalaw with my stepmother's nieces, Patricia and Nancy. Many of the girls were about sixteen or seventeen; suddenly throwing us into a convent after three years of independence and idleness was a little hard-hearted I thought.

The nuns made certain concessions such as letting us wear the dresses or *sins* we wanted instead of the drab blue pinafores, but one thing they were adamant about was religion. They insisted that, though we were not Catholics, we had to take part in all the prayers and church going. So we had to make our rounds each evening with 'Hail Mary' and go to church every day. Perhaps for the Sisters of St Agnes this one discipline gave them authority over us. We were no longer little girls but teenagers, and they were responsible for us in the absence of our parents.

Kalaw at that time was full of troops, and many of the day-scholars would tell us of the fun they had at dances and parties. We listened with dreamy eyes and envied them their jolly times. Ball-room dancing became a craze and older girls taught us the quick step and the waltz. My cousins and I would not have been allowed to go dancing, even if the nuns had given permission. Our parents had strong views on morality and boyfriends were forbidden, let alone being held in their arms. In fact, I never danced until I came to England, although I did go to one party. In those days a tradition had developed for the young daughters of Saohpas to 'come out' when they reached the age of a debutante. At such coming out parties the girls were introduced into the British official circle after careful selection and certain formalities. Apparently my turn had come, but there were various questions – was I a legitimate daughter, since no one in the Commissioner's office knew I existed and was I the daughter of the present Mahadevi?

My father, as can be imagined, was incensed, "How dare they question us in this manner?", he demanded. For the first time in my life I had been made aware that being my father's daughter was not enough, but I had also to be a Mahadevi's daughter if I wanted to get anywhere in British raj society. I suppose it was not so easy for the British authorities to work out "who was who" in our complicated polygamous society. They only knew that the current Mahadevi was my stepmother, Sao Hearn Hkam. Although they knew she had children, in 1947 only ten years after her marriage, she could hardly have had a daughter in her teens old enough to be presented. So, naturally, they were curious. If I had had my way, I would not have gone. But apparently it was only a hiccup and nothing serious, so on my father's insistence I went with him to my first British party. What an ordeal! I was tongue-tied and the English I had re-learnt at St Agnes went out of the window. It was an experience I never wanted to repeat.

I think it was at this party that I first met the two sisters of the young Kengtung Saohpa – Sao Noot, known at school as Marlene, and Sao Noom, Vera. They were relaxed and seemed to know everyone. Of course, the Kengtung family was a decade ahead of us in many spheres. They had close family ties with the aristocracy of Siam and Laos and, together with the Hsipaw and Tawngpeng families, many of the young had been educated at convents, private schools and had gone abroad. Also, the Saohpas themselves had travelled widely and had a more educated outlook on world affairs.

Kengtung's geographical position was always of great importance to the British since the annexation of Upper Burma. At the beginning there were uncertainties as to what the Siamese and the French intended to do on the borders, later it became a place from which political events could be monitored in war and peace. Therefore, Kengtung became better known to British administrators than the other Shan states that did not hold such a strategic position. It also meant the Commissioner gave it more attention by stationing a few officials there instead of only one.

The larger and economically viable states, with forests, mines and minerals were those which benefited more than the poorer states that were in the hinterland. These latter states had little to offer – no mines of gold or silver, no precious gems of rubies and sapphires, no teak forests – agriculture was their sole livelihood. Much of the cultivation was generally on small holdings and their produce were, therefore, of little commercial value.

On the whole it was the British government who held the rights to these natural resources and arranged with commercial firms to exploit them. Consequently, the larger states attracted investment and money. This in turn meant that any finance for future development went first to the larger states, thereby creating varying gaps in education and standard of living among the different states.

Although, each state received a percentage of the revenue gained from exploiting these natural resources, the princes wanted the opportunity of mining the minerals themselves. Unfortunately, the authorities felt that the small local companies set up by the princes were not sufficiently qualified to run such enterprises and their employees were ill-trained. Such an outlook was not appreciated and one can see the many complicated problems which must have arisen for the British administration in solving these disputes amicably.

Soon there was good news for me, Kingswood school was to be re-opened. My cousins and I immediately asked to be allowed to move from the convent. We had had enough of the nuns' discipline. Miss Reid, the new principal of Kingswood was glad to have us and I was especially happy to be back with teachers I had known. An earnest, young American, Dale Flinders was our only male teacher, so, as can be imagined, he had a number of fans.

Fifty years later, he was to turn up to meet us on the Isle of Dogs in London. It was marvellous to see him and his wife, and to find him still as keen on photography as he had been in Kalaw. Peter was glad to meet at last the legendary figure I had so often told him about. Dale had been back to Kalaw and had met many of his old students. There was much he had to tell us. It seemed that the time of our youth were certainly the best years for Kingswood and for Kalaw.

PANGLONG CONFERENCE. S.C.O.U.H.P.

Back Row L. to R.:  Thakin Wa Tin.  Duwa Shawng Gyung.  U Thang Lian.  U Sein.  Saohpalong of Baw.  Saohpalong of Loilong.
Saohpalong of Pangtara.  Saohpalong of Samka.  U Taikwel.
Front Row  "  Mr. Labang Grong.  U Tin Aye.  Duwa Dingra Tan.  Sama Duwa Sinwa Nawng.  Saohpalong of Pwela.  Saohpalong of Laihka.
Saohpalong of Yawnghwe.  Saohpalong of Tawngpeng.  Saohpalong of North Hsenwi.  Saohpalong of Hsamonghkam.
U Tun Myint.  Duwa Zau Lawn.
Sitting  "  U Po Han.  Capt. Mang Tung Nung.  U Thein Maung.  Sanda Thaike.  Mrs. Duwa Zau Lawn.  Mahadevi of Yawnhwe.
Sir. Maung Gyee.  Lady Maung Gyee.  Mrs. Shan Lone.  U Aung Zan Wai.  Major Shan Lone.

*Members of SCOUHP reunited, 1958.*

# VII
## *Crucial Years*

### *About Turn*

1946 and 1947 were two momentous years for the Shans, the other ethnic nationalities and the Burmans. The important events explained in this chapter will, I hope, give clarity to the complicated situation which existed then, as it does today. They were crucial years which shaped events that were to follow, leading up to the military takeover of the country in 1962.

We have first to look back to the time before the Japanese war, a period of contentment and relative prosperity for most people. However, the intense nationalism shown by radical university students and Burman politicians was a factor the colonial administration could no longer ignore. Japan was also aware of these sentiments and, long before the war, was already laying the ground for a greater Empire, introducing agents into Rangoon and elsewhere. Their assignments were to gather information and to recruit young students. Naturally, the young discontented fell into their arms and many were offered a chance to go to Japan for further studies. The Japanese also cleverly targeted the Thakins, the main nationalist and anti-British party formed in the early 1930s and composed of young impressionable politicians, whose lives were governed by politics.

As the call for independence gathered strength, some leading politicians made visits to neighbouring countries such as India and China. From India, they hoped to receive guidance from leading politicians there in their struggle against colonialism in Burma. British socialists, too, lent a hand with their support for the emerging politicians.

During 1939 and 1940, numerous strikes, political rallies and general agitation against the British colonial administration took place. The pressure exerted on the administration was such, that it felt it had to arrest many prominent members of these political groups. Aung San, already a leading member of the Thakin movement, managed to evade arrest and made his way on a ship to China. Japanese intelligence found him whilst he was in Amoy, and took him on to Japan with his companion.

A year later in 1941, when the British forces were beginning their long retreat, Aung San returned from Japan. He clandestinely recruited volunteers, chiefly from the Thakin party and shipped them out to Japan in great secrecy for military training. The group, including Aung San and Ne Win, came to be known as the Thirty Comrades. They were to become renowned as great heroes amongst their young Burman followers. According to plans which were made with the Japanese in Tokyo, a private army called the Burma Independence Army (BIA) was formed with the Thirty Comrades at its core.

From Japan, the BIA moved to Siam where their numbers expanded rapidly – by the end of the year over 3,000 men had joined the BIA. When the BIA entered Burma it was naturally on the side of the Japanese as they had pledged their allegiance to the Imperial Army's Supreme Command. It was, therefore, inevitable that as its soldiers marched towards Rangoon, they fought the British troops, who were moving northward. Regrettably, most of the soldiers were ill-disciplined. They fought pitched battles against any resistance they encountered, which included the Karens under British control. Horrific and inexcusable massacres took place in Karen areas as the BIA marched onward to the capital and these senseless acts perpetrated by the BIA have not been forgotten by the Karens.

With the Imperial Nipponese Government now in control, things began to gradually settle down. Although Aung San was the Minister of Defence, the Japanese deemed it prudent to disband the BIA. A little later, however, a new army was formed called the Burma National Army (BNA) under Major-General Aung San.

The years of Japanese occupation had not gone well in Burma. Despite ostensibly gaining independence under the Japanese administration, Burman political leaders were not pleased with the outcome. The young enthusiastic politicians had welcomed and helped the Japanese troops to fight the British in the belief that they were getting rid of colonialism, but somehow their aspirations had not been met. When Japan was seen to be losing the war, it seemed there was much re-thinking and new decisions to be made.

Aung San, always an able and resourceful politician, decided to turn to the British to seek assistance and to offer help in defeating the Japanese. The offer was accepted by the military who were eager to win back Burma from the Japanese. The senior British officers had no time to scrutinize the political situation in the country minutely.

To show that there was a change of heart, and a sincere desire to help, Major-General Aung San ingeniously managed to organize a secret revolt against the Japanese. One of the major ploys was carried out by the Burma National Army (BNA). The troops were ordered to march out of Rangoon to fight the enemy (the British) but then turned around and attacked the retreating Japanese army. The Nipponese troops were caught completely by surprise, and could do little in retaliation.

Due to this clever move, the BNA had the advantage over the withdrawing Japanese troops. In some places, it was able to lead the advancing British troops through Japanese lines, inflicting major damage on the enemy. Such military manoeuvres won over the British military and Aung San was to find in Lord Mountbatten, the Supreme Commander for Southeast Asia, his benefactor.

There were naturally rumbles from the older Burma civil service officials, who were with the Governor of Burma in the Indian hill station of Simla. These cautious senior civil servants were far-sighted and experienced men. Sceptical and unconvinced that Aung San was sincere, or trustworthy, they were somewhat shocked that they had not been consulted before Lord Mountbatten had made his hasty decision and given his blessing. To them, Aung San was a young upstart. Little did they realize that he was a man who would go a long way.

As soon as some form of British administration had returned to Rangoon, to begin the difficult task of re-establishing themselves, there were instructions from the Burma government in India to dissolve Aung San's Anti-Fascist Organization and the BNA. These orders had come too soon. There was still fighting against the retreating Japanese, while British forces on the ground were not sufficient to take over completely. As a result, these instructions were not carried out and the Anti-Fascist Organization and its army were left in situ.

One can sympathise with the feelings of the older colonial officials who, under extreme conditions, had to evacuate to India. Some of the officers must have been incensed at the way their troops had been brutally chased out of the country by the advancing Japanese with the help of the BIA. Now, the very man and the very organization who had supported the enemy, was making an about turn and offering its services to the British administration. These ICS officers must have asked themselves, how could he, Aung San, be trusted and relied upon.

When the British Military Administration ended in October 1945, the Governor, Sir Dorman-Smith, returned to Burma after three and a half years away in India. He announced that there would be little change in its administration and that the 1935 Constitution would be maintained as before the war. Burma Proper would keep its own administration, while full self-government within the Commonwealth was promised in three years time.

The administration of the Shan States and the Frontier Areas, meanwhile, would continue under a special regime controlled by the Governor. This meant that the Shan States, the Chin, Kachin and Karens would no longer be under the Burmans as the Japanese had decreed, when it gave Burma independence during its occupation. We were to be administered separately until we, the Frontier peoples, had found a suitable means of amalgamating with Burma Proper. The two Shan sub-states given to Siam by the Japanese were to be returned, so there were no foreseeable problems.

There were to be some changes, however, for the Saohpas. The powers of the ruling princes were to be further curtailed. It was unexpected, but it did not upset them too much, since they were glad that there were no longer Burmans lording it over them, as had been the case under the Japanese.

In Burma Proper, nationalism had greatly increased and the Act did not satisfy the political ambitions of those who espoused it. The Nationalists no longer wanted to be a British colony. With great impatience, they demanded immediate and complete independence. As Shelby Tucker has commented, "No one foresaw the power of Aung San's closed shop to alter the pace and the course of events."[19]

Unfortunately, Sir Dorman-Smith fell ill and, being unable to carry out his duties, left Burma. He had only been back as Governor for less than a year.

By now, Admiral Mountbatten had completely accepted Major-General Aung San, and had earlier warned of court-martial for any British military officer, who might have opposed the resistance groups, meaning the BNA and its affiliates. He also gave recognition to the Anti-Fascist Organization, which was later renamed Anti-Fascist People's Freedom League (AFPFL). The League, now firmly established, became the main organization through which all negotiations for the independence of the country were made with the British Government. Thus began the ingenious moves of a man who was to take on the British government alone, and to get his own way.

Although a few thousand of the Burma National Army had been integrated with the British troops, there was still a large number of armed young men roaming about the countryside. Before long, they were formed into the People's Volunteer Organization (PVO) said to be comprised of old wartime comrades. It eventually became apparent as these units spread throught the country, that they were under the central control of General Aung San and the Anti-Fascist People's Freedom League.

The war in Europe had ended and the Japanese war was now over for us. General elections in England had put the Labour Party in power. In its policy statement to Parliament in May 1945, the Secretary of State for Burma declared that: "The administration of the scheduled Areas, that is the Shan States and the tribal areas in the mountainous fringes of the country inhabited by peoples differing in language, social customs and degree of political development from the Burmans inhabiting the central areas, would for the time being be subject to a special regime under the Governor until such time as their inhabitants signify their desire for some suitable form of amalgamation of their territories with Burma proper."[20]

The British had thought that when they returned, the administration could go on as before with their plans for the country to be eventually granted self-rule. They were probably surprised to find that the 1935 administration Act was no longer acceptable to the leading Burmans. The idea of Dominion Status had ceased to be an option.

Shan Saohpas and ethnic leaders alike took the policy as declared to mean that the British administration was still conscious of their desire to preserve their own identities. They hoped that the British would continue to acknowledge their expectations which had been expressed in the past and which remained unchanged for the future. Unexpectedly, this policy never had a chance of being implemented.

For us in the Shan States, the Japanese occupation had left many states devastated and in urgent need of reconstruction. Time was needed to find the best ways and means of achieving progress for the people. Regrettably, groups of young people, incited by political propaganda from the plains, were impatient with the Saohpas and their administration. Little credit was accorded to them for bringing them through the harsh times of the Japanese occupation. Things were bad but it could have been worse.

The boundaries drawn between the Shan States and Burma Proper, which had kept the two races apart, and the earlier British ban on Burman political agitators from entering the Shan States no longer held. Young Shans who were willing to listen became easy prey. Agitators were quick to point out that "we were all brothers" and that any existing animosity between the Burman and the Shan was due primarily to the British. This was, of course, untrue. Hostility existed because it was the Burman who always wanted to have the upper hand in affairs concerning the Shan and other ethnic groups.

In respect of these developments, there arose the realisation that the Shans and other nationalities should come together to discuss their future. They wished to avoid what they had experienced during the years of Japanese rule, when the word equality had meant so little to the Burmans. Equality was what the ethnic peoples wanted.

Consequently, my father, together with Saohpas and other Shan leaders, held a conference at Panglong, in March 1946, to discuss the future. Chin, Kachin and Karen representatives were invited to attend. It was the first time that the different nationalities had come together in a way which was beneficial to them all. Although not much was achieved on that occasion in this village which lay in the middle of the Shan plateau, a precedent had been established. The different groups could now talk to each other and discuss their common problems. They realised that they had to stand together, as unity was the only way of gaining a better chance of dealing with the Burman politicians. The Supreme Council of United Hills Peoples, (SCOUHP), was formed, with my father as its president.

At that time, none of the Shan nor the ethnic leaders had any idea of the long-term plan the British Government had envisaged for a self-governing Burma with all its peoples united. The Frontier Areas Administration (FAA), created by the British when they were in Simla, realized that a great deal of diplomacy and tact would be needed if the British were to succeed in implementing such a plan. It would be essential for all the different peoples living in the country, including the Burmans, to join in to make a successful union.

Major General Hubert Rance arrived in the middle of 1946 as the new Governor. He was to be greeted with a strike first by the police, then by other government workers. There was much political upheaval and unrest for the next several months. At the end of these disturbances, Aung San accepted the numerous concessions the British made concerning the 1935 Act, including the formation of a new Executive Council which he was to head. Following these moves, the Governor handed over to the AFPFL the government of the country. General Aung San was now virtually Prime Minister.

Despite the conciliatory moves by the British administration, there was still a great deal of discontent in Burma. Meanwhile, General Aung San had gone to London for discussions with the new Labour government. Clement Attlee's ideas on the British Empire, as might be expected, differed hugely from those of the Winston Churchill and the Conservatives. Thus in January 1947, the signing of the Attlee-Aung San Agreement took place, and Aung San returned to Burma, flushed with success. Though no exact date had been given for the granting of independence, it was generally agreed that the British Government would recognize Aung San and his ministers as an interim government, and a Constituent Assembly would be established through elections. Full independence was to be granted within one year.

In spite of a telegram sent by my father and other Saohpas to the British Government that Aung San did not represent the majority of the peoples of the country, no notice was taken of this objection. This action by the Saohpas, of course, infuriated the AFPFL politicians who felt they were overstepping their mark.

The Shan and other non-Burmans suspected there had been hidden dealings between the British and the Burmans, which would not be made public. They felt aggrieved that they would never know what actually had been negotiated in the Attlee-Aung San Agreement.

There was also a fear that things were moving too fast, and that the ethnic nationalities were neither being consulted nor given a chance to put forward their views. The Japanese occupation had left a deep psychological scar on the different peoples, and, physically, the Shan States and Frontier Areas which had been the battle grounds between the Allies and the Japanese, had been left devastated. There were a great many problems, and most ethnic leaders realized that nothing could be solved in a hurry.

Like my father, many leaders were convinced that the country was not yet ready for independence. Everyone could see that the country was still in ruins having just come out of the Japanese war and its occupation. The Karens, who formed a large portion of the British fighting force in Burma had given their complete loyalty and were seeking recognition. Though many British officers who served alongside them realized their worth, little attention was paid at the higher levels. No one in the British administration wanted to acknowledge that the country was now in a worse disarray: economically, politically and militarily.

It is only after these many years that I have been able to understand what went on behind the scenes in Whitehall. Vernon Donnison clearly explained the situation: "In January 1947 when the British government conceded the principle of full Independence, they stipulated that inclusion of the minorities within independent Burma, which was an integral part of the demands presented by the Burmese must depend on the 'free consent' of those affected. Joint efforts were to be made by British and Burmese to obtain this consent. The Burmese demands were backed by an implicit threat of rebellion, of attacks upon Europeans, and of destruction of the government, if negotiations in London were to break down. The only thing that separated the parties was the question of the minority areas. Failure to gain the 'free consent' of the minorities was unthinkable for this could only result in the rejection of the offer by the AFPFL. In this case insurrection and chaos would result. In the circumstances both British and Burmese were deeply committed to obtaining that free consent. Indeed it is pretty clear that the British government was not prepared to take no for an answer from the frontier areas."[21]

Maung Maung in his book also confirms the fear the Burmans had, that if the Shan and the Frontiers Areas had refused to become part of Burma, the country could easily have become divided. "Independence without the frontier areas would be meaningless; a partition of Burma".[22] This was apparently, what neither the British nor the Burmans wanted.

## The Panglong Agreement

It is little wonder then that with such thoughts in mind the British administration was in a quandary. How could it satisfy the Burmans without hurting the Shan and other ethnic nationalities? Did it feel the time was ripe to grant independence? If so, it was a huge undertaking and a gamble. It had to ensure that Burma became independent with the whole country intact and all its ethnic groups in agreement. It would not be easy, but they had not reckoned on General Aung San being the answer.

There undoubtedly are several theories as to the importance of the Panglong Agreement and how the Union of Burma came about. Some believed it was the Shan, Kachin and Chin who pleaded to join Burma Proper. Others, that since the British already had a policy for the unification of all the peoples of the country, this was bulldozed through.[23] Still others believe, that Aung San, impatient to have independence from the British, had already prepared his ground. He is quoted as saying in an address to Shan students "that the Shan States being landlocked it would have no option but to conform, if lines of communication such as railway and telegraph were removed."[24] So he, at least knew how he could cajole the Shan, the Kachin and the Chin into joining with Burma Proper.

Whatever the truth is, it has become apparent that the British certainly were keen to see things pushed through, and, although the ethnic nationalities would have preferred to have stayed within the Commonwealth, as explained earlier, it appeared that the die was cast.

The director of the FAA at that time, Mr H. N. C. Stevenson was very knowledgeable about the people he had been dealing with over the years. He had seen a number of problems concerning the amalgamation of Ministerial Burma and the Frontier Areas, but as usual no one had the time nor the inclination to listen. "From the safe distance of London, government officials completely underestimated the depth of feeling amongst the minorities. 'Abysmally ignorant,'"[25] was Stevenson's view of his Burma Office colleagues.

When General Aung San came to the Shan States, he persuaded the Shans to ask for independence, and my father quoted him as saying: "When Independence was gained, it would be seen to, that the Shan States did not suffer and that it would have complete freedom. The Shan States were now backward, but with Independence it would be seen, that she was on equal footing with Burma, and as brothers would work together." My father added that "In most friendly and cordial manner he gave his promise."[26]

From these remarks, it can be seen that my father had no further doubts about Aung San's sincerity and joined with Burma Proper in demands for Independence. The conference was a turning point for the Shans, Kachins and Chins. From being highly suspicious of the Burmans, General Aung San managed to convince them that there would be no discrimination. Also, they had been persuaded that it was the best way out if they wanted to be free of colonial masters. Although the ethnic peoples did not feel they had been badly treated by the British, the pros and cons of colonialism was something they had been persuaded to think about.

I was there at Panglong, and seeing all these top leaders I was agog. I had come back to Yawnghwe straight from Inle, and had no idea of what was going on. I was a total ignoramus as far as politics was concerned, but I was very glad to be able to talk to the young Kachin and Chin leaders whom I was meeting for the first time.

In the past, I had never been allowed to talk to any man, so being able to carry on a sensible conversation with these young men was quite an experience. There

*Signing the Panglong Agreement, 12 February 1947.*
*Left: The Saohpa of Yawnghwe. Right: General Aung San.*
*(Courtesy of the Oriental and India Office Collection,*
*The British Library, London)*

was much to learn from them, and, in retrospect, I feel really disappointed that I was so green and lacked any political sense. Most of what I remember about the event was that there was a festive feeling and I had to serve hundreds of cups of tea, as I was put on the Messing Committee with my stepmother, the Mahadevi, and other wives of the other national leaders.

The conference was not serious discussions all day long, for there were exhibitions of cottage industries and people met informally to discuss agriculture or common problems they all faced in the villages. All in all there was a carnival atmosphere. Apparently, many of the Burmans were surprised that the Shans were not so backward and were amazed there was a working local press.

At the conclusion of the conference, the different nationalities had been won over and agreed to give Aung San and his interim government full co-operation. In return, an undertaking was given by Aung San that the Kachins would have a State, the Chins, material and social benefits, and the Shans their financial autonomy and the right of self-government. Thus in principle, the Union of Burma was established.

The Panglong Agreement was duly signed on 12 February 1947, by the representatives of the Shan, Kachin and Chin with General Aung San representing his AFPFL government. During the three-day conference, leaders such as Sima Duwa Sinwa Nawng and Zaw Lon of the Kachins, Vum Ko Hau of the Chins and the Shans were led to believe by the Burman general that he had their welfare at heart, since he gave assurances that there was to be no discrimination. He had emphasized that "If Burma receives one *kyat*, you will also get one *kyat*", a saying well remembered by many.

After the Panglong Conference, the general came to Yawnghwe to discuss the Agreement further with my father and some other Saohpas. This was to allay any

1947 PANGLONG CONFERENCE
MESSING COMMITTEE.

Sitting L. to R:   Sanda Thaike.   Mrs. Duwa Zau Lawn.   Mahadevi (Yawnghwe).   Lady Maung Gyee.   Mrs. Shan Lone.
Standing "          Duwa Dingra Tan.   U Tun Myint.   Mr. Lahung Grong.   U Po Han.   U Tin Aye.

*Panglong Conference
Messing Committee
reunited in 1958.*

*General Aung San (centre) at Yawnghwe Haw, after the Panglong*
*Conference. Saohpas in the front row from left to right are*
*Hsamongkham, Mong Pawn, Yawnghwe (in dark suit) and Pangmi.*

fears that the Shan and others might still have had regarding their status within
the Union of Burma. I recall the event, held in the visitor's apartment under my
father's wing, very well. I was kept busy bringing in cups of tea and cold drinks,
while the talks went on, but I do not remember being allowed to listen in.

Sadly, the key players in the great event of the Panglong Conference and the
later meetings at Yawnghwe Haw, are now long gone, and there is no way of
checking the finer points, of how or what they felt about these historic moments.
Those early months of 1947, sixty years ago, are more important than we may
think. For there is no denying that without the Panglong Conference and the
meeting of the different leaders, there would not have been a consensus for Independence from the British. Thus, it must be remembered that it was the Panglong
Agreement which made the Union of Burma possible.

The ethnic nationalities knew implicitly that without their co-operation, there
would have been neither Independence nor the Union of Burma. I fear though that
most disgruntled Burma politicians have refused to see its importance.

One wonders what might have happened had the Shan and Frontier peoples
taken a firmer stand. I suppose they had little choice. It was no small feat for
Burma to have gained Independence within a year and a half of its coming out
from the wreckage of the Japanese war. But at what cost?

Immediately following the Panglong Agreement, in order to have a clear
conscience, the British government sent D. R. Rees-Williams M. P. to the country.
He led the Frontier Areas Committee, which came to find out what the different
nationalities really wanted. During the various meetings, the committee interviewed
representatives from all groups.

The following is an interview Rees-Williams had with my father:[27]

Chairman: *Would you let us know the views of SCOUHP, as to the future as-*
*sociation of the Frontier Areas with Ministerial Burma?*

Sawbwa of Yawnghwe: *We want to associate with Burma on the condition that full autonomy is guaranteed in our internal administration.*

After questions on common grounds with Burma, my father was asked:

Chairman: *What form of Government do you suggest to deal with them?*

Sawbwa of Yawnghwe: *A Federal Government.*

Chairman: *What is the Federal Government to consist of?*

Sawbwa of Yawnghwe: *It will consist of representatives of Burmese, Shans, Kachins, Chins and Karens.*

Chairman: *Should it be a form similar to the United States of America system or will it be in a simpler form of Government?*

Sawbwa of Yawnghwe: *It is possible that it may be similar to the United States System.*

My father was not a politician, neither were the other leaders. They did not have clever words to persuade the Committee. Presumably, lacking oratorial skills, they had difficulty in arguing their case for equality within the Union. The princes, in every way loyal to the British, had been persuaded to join a union in which they were to be given equal opportunities – how could they refuse?

The Committee dutifully listened and went away feeling that at least it had made an effort to understand the situation. No one, though, seriously considered the ethnic problem, nor how it should be dealt with. In view of the fact that all discussions were speedily concluded, decisions were finalized before people could even stop and think. One can even question whether the Parliamentary Inquiry was merely a confidence trick to ally the fears of the ethnic groups. No further attention was given to these matters, although in reality close consideration was very much needed.

Hugh Tinker says of the conclusions made that: "The Committee has often been criticized for the cavalier way in which it appeared to dispose of the future of the hill peoples, but in reality the whole issue had been prejudged under the Attlee-Aung San Agreement."[28] This shows that my father was certainly right to have had misgivings about the Attlee-Aung San Agreement.

However, the Panglong Agreement, the creation of the Union of Burma and clause 201 in the Constitution for secession, appeared to satisfy the Shan politicians, though many Saohpas and ethnic leader remained doubtful.

Then in July, General Aung San, the Premier, was assassinated with his newly-appointed Cabinet. It was a great loss, leaving a huge gap in the politics and government of the country. With his tragic death, many felt their dreams and aspirations for the future of their independent country were completed shattered.

Splits had already appeared among the politicians and their different parties. Now Aung San's untimely death produced serious struggles. Trouble was probably foreseen by aficionados of the political scene, but no way was found to curtail these disasters which arose spontaneously.

U Nu, who was already President of the Constituent Assembly, succeeded as leader of the Anti-Fascist Freedom League and was immediately asked to replace General Aung San as Prime Minister, although he had been earmarked to become President. At this point, my father became the President of the Constituent Assembly. Later, the Assembly appointed him to the Presidency of the newly independent Union of Burma. According to Vernon Donnison, in the agreement reached with General Aung San, the non-Burmans were apparently promised that the first

President of independent Burma, would be a Shan. This then was how my father came to be chosen.[29]

As a Shan ruler who had endeavoured to make Yawnghwe a better place for his people, and had the well-being of the Shan States at heart, it could not have been an easy decision for my father to accept this exalted position. Perhaps he genuinely felt that his acceptance would help keep the Union together. He may have also felt that amongst his colleagues, both Burman and non-Burman, there were enough like-minded men to make the Union a success.

With hindsight, I wonder what options he had? Was he beguiled into taking the prestigious appointment by the promise of the ten year right of secession clause for the Shan and the Karenni states in the Constitution becoming a reality? Even if he had realized that being isolated in a non-political role meant he could at no time stand up for the Shans, he may have felt it was already an impossible situation and as President, there may still have been an opportunity to help. My father was an advocate of federalism and with the creation of the Union of Burma, he had perhaps been persuaded to believe it was a hopeful sign.

I wonder how much time he had to consult his brother Saohpas or the non-Burman leaders when he was chosen? Surely, the Shans should have foreseen the problems that lay ahead, for without unity and someone strong enough to speak for them, theirs was a lost cause. Here perhaps lay the crux of the matter. It would appear that the thinking by the Burman politicians was that once my father was removed from the politically active Shan scene, it would become easier for them to control and to manipulate the Shan.

Indeed, there were also those Shans, who may have favoured my father's absence, as it would give them an opportunity to show that they were capable of dealing with problems themselves. Whatever these men may have planned, they had not realized how powerful their opponents were. There never was a chance for the Shans nor the non-Burmans after independence was granted to achieve equal status with the Burman in their newly formed Union of Burma.

The years after independence were not ones of peace or prosperity. In fact, there were a number of armed insurrections and communist uprisings. Nearly every section of the community had something to grouse about. In the Shan States, there were the Kachin, Karen and the Pa-O who were in revolt. Unfortunately, the Union government did not question why the country was in such turmoil and did not try to work out solutions. Instead, the Burma army was sent in to contain the rebellions.

Unfortunately, due to the unrest, the might of the army began to grow. Starting as early as the 1950s, the Shan States came under military administration. The Saohpas and the leading Shans, who had supported first General Aung San and later U Nu's AFPFL government, were helpless and could only watch as the army began a campaign to stamp out the rebels, using brutal means to do so.

Due to the presence of KMT refugee forces from China, mentioned before, encamped along the Mekong river on the Shan State side, the military justified its administration within the Shan States. However, although most of the KMT were within the Kengtung area, it did not come under military administration. Instead the military centred itself around Taunggyi and other interior states. The KMT had indeed become a force to be reckoned with, since Taiwan, with the help of the United States, were reinforcing them against Communist China during that period.

As far as the family was concerned, soon after the Panglong conference, there were new arrangements. As my father became more and more absorbed with his new work and politics, he and my stepmother left Yawnghwe for Rangoon. It was there that everything was happening. My two younger brothers, Hso and Tzang, were sent off to a school in Hsenwi and it was decided that I should stay behind at Kingswood to continue with my education. The remaining younger members of the family were to join the parents later.

Then, before long I had to go back to Yawnghwe and under the watchful eye of Daw Daw at the Haw, I was given special tuition in Burmese. The intention was that I should attend Rangoon University once I had passed my matriculation. I began to study seriously for these examinations, but found the subject more difficult than expected and I wondered if I might ever make the grade. Perhaps Burmese would be my downfall.

As it happened, I need not have been worried so much, as certain events were to take place in the near future to whisk me away from Yawnghwe and Rangoon University.

*Sao Mye with children in formal dress at President's House. In front: Harn, Leun and Hayma. Standing behind: Ying, Hso, Tzang and Myee.*

*The ex-Governor Sir Hubert Rance during the handover ceremony Sao Shwe Thaike, the President of the Union of Burma, 1948.*

*Governor Sir Hubert Rance with General Aung San and other Burmese dignitaries 1945.*
*(Reproduction by permission of the Imperial War Museum)*

# VIIII

## *A New Life*

### *To England*

By the middle of 1947, my father had been elected President of the Union of Burma. As head of state of independent Burma, he was invited to attend the royal wedding of the then Princess Elizabeth to Prince Philip in November of that year. The invitation had been extended to include a companion for my stepmother, and two Secretaries for my father. So it was decided I should go along as the companion. I was excited, but not overly so since I had no idea what was expected of me. It was rather a gentle, cautious excitement, a wait and see attitude. I was curious though, to know what I might find in England.

Anyway, the day arrived and we left Rangoon in a Sunderland Flying boat, a seaplane which took a few days to fly us from Rangoon to Poole in southern England. Our flying boat was named 'Hunter' and was commanded by Captain George Stead, a New Zealander, who for his services in the Royal Air Force during World War II had been awarded the Distinguished Flying Cross (DFC) and the 1939/1945 Star. We were honoured to have him as our pilot. He was a friendly, pleasant person who soon put his passengers at ease for the long flight.

Our route took us to Calcutta, Karachi, Bahrain, Cairo, Augusta and Marseilles. The night at the Shepherd's hotel in Cairo, the visit to the Pyramids and the museum made a great impression upon me. I was overwhelmed by everything I experienced, even though now with the passing years I have forgotten much of the detail. One thing I remember was the camel ride, which most tourists have to endure. The bright neon lights were exciting and thrilled me, but I imagined that as England was a bigger nation, everything there would be bigger and better, that the neon lights would be brighter. At the beginning, London did not outshine Cairo's neon lights, but later I was not disappointed, when the effects of the Second World War had worn off, and London was once more a bright and sparkling city.

Although it was the first time I was to fly, I felt no fear. However, I was prone to motion sickness, so spent much of the flying time during the day lying in a bunk on the upper deck, while others were enjoying the wonderful food and wine, and the comfort of the plane. Looking back I think I was in shock, as I only remember snatches of the whole flight and the nights we spent at the splendid hotels. There are, however, vivid scenes I recall of our arrival at Poole. I was groggy and green in the face as I unsteadily alighted from the plane. I was put under the care of Mrs George Stead, the Captain's wife, and she made me feel a little better. I felt I just wanted to sink to the ground and even the joy of seeing Sai Hseng with a beaming smile on his handsome face, couldn't revive me.

*Sanda, at graduation 1953.*

*With Captain George Stead who flew us from*
*Rangoon to Poole, and wife, Marjorie.*

*Mr and Mrs Frank Neal,*
*my guardians.*

The fact that I had missed a first glance of England through the window of the plane because I was feeling so ill, made me feel miserable. It was hardly the right way to arrive in a country one had been anxious to see, a place one had thought and puzzled about. Yet, here I was thoroughly sick, tired and confused. I had no time to reflect that the moment I boarded the plane in Rangoon was to be the end of my carefree days of childhood and youth. It was also a whole way of life which had been left behind. Neither did it occur to me then that it would be the last time that I was ever to live in the Haw at Yawnghwe. Without realizing it, the moment I stepped onto English soil was the beginning of a new life for me in an unfamiliar and uncertain world.

It was a grey, shadowy November day, the first of many I was to experience. After a short rest, we left Poole by train for London. When we came to our first stop, I was completely taken aback to see white men, who were railway workers, carrying picks and shovels, with dirty smutty faces. I could not help exclaiming that I thought there would be other people, either Indian or Chinese, like we had in Rangoon who were menial workers. My father laughed at my astonishment. He told me not to be silly, as after all it was their country, so naturally there were labourers who were white and English. I was so used to seeing the English as *pukka sahibs* and *memsabs* that I had never imagined they could be anything else.

My father and stepmother went to Westminster Abbey for the magnificent regal wedding. They wore Shan ceremonial dress, resplendent in their silks to suit the occasion. My father wore the *sa-lwe*, one of his pieces of regalia worn on special official occasions. It was a sash made of chains of gold. Four large decorated medallions held the strands in place, the whole worn over the left shoulder like an Officer's sash. Later I was taken to St James' Palace to see the gorgeous wedding presents. Both my stepmother and I dressed in the long ceremonial *longyi* adapted from the Mandalay Court for the various occasions, with jewels and trailing flowers in our chignons. Then a day or so later to commemorate the royal wedding, we had our portraits taken at the studio in Swan & Edgar, which then occupied the corner between Piccadilly and Regent Street. Although Swan & Edgar no longer exists the photographs do.

Mr and Mrs Frank Neal, guardians to my two brothers, were invited to London to meet Sao U Hpa. They were a typical Yorkshire couple who had had no previous contact with Asia and had only become guardian to my brothers, as their Housemaster at King's School in Canterbury, Mr Ronald Groves, lived in Bradford. He was a friend of the Neals and knowing they had no children, proposed them as guardians for my brothers.

*London 1947, The Mahadevi of Yawnghwe attending the wedding of Princess Elizabeth.*

Frank Neal, was a trim middle-aged man, who worked at the City Hall in Bradford. His wife, Annie, was a handsome, large woman of jolly nature, who taught Arts and Crafts at night school. Although I remember very little about the meeting, I think it was slightly embarrassing with no one quite knowing how to keep the conversation going. One thing I do remember is that Mrs Neal wore a pretty pink hat and a fur stole. However, at the end of the visit, it was arranged for me to become their ward and to go to Bradford to attend the Bradford Girls' Grammar School.

Amongst a host of official activities organised for us was a drive to Sheen near Richmond to see Colonel and Mrs Jimmy Green so we could renew our friendship. It was a wonderful reunion, especially as we had not expected to see them again after Jimmy's retirement and their return to England. They, too, promised to look after me. It must have been a great relief for my father to know that I now had two English families who were there to keep an eye on me.

Like my father who was greatly impressed by his first visit to London in 1930 and 1931, so was I. It was fascinating and I was dazzled for I had never seen such grand buildings. As for the traffic, the buses, trams and all manner of motor cars took me by surprise. I was disappointed though that, on our trips out into the countryside during those few days, I never saw thatched cottages with hollyhocks growing in their gardens, nor snow on the ground and robins with red breasts hopping around, as I used to see on Christmas cards. Had I known then about the

*With Auntie Annie in Bradford.*

seasons, I might have understood why there were no hollyhocks growing in winter! Though there was no snow to welcome us, there certainly was snow awaiting me in the north of England, and a great deal of it too.

When my parents had left, Sai Hseng took me to Bradford to start a new stage of my life. What could have been an ordeal for me in adjusting to the western way of life was made easier by his being there. In addition, the Neals were a warm, kind-hearted couple who treated me as one of their family. Auntie Annie was a marvellous cook and her Yorkshire puddings for Sunday lunches were not to be missed. I can still hear her persuasive voice urging me to eat up, "Come on love, you're a growing girl you'd better finish it up". Since I liked her food and probably never refused a second or third helping, I found myself soon weighing nine stone. Though we were still on rations, our Sunday table for high tea was always laden with platefuls of delicious home-made buns and cakes.

Auntie Annie had a large family. All the aunts and uncles took me into their circle and soon I was quite at home. I warmed to their way of speech ending every sentence with 'love'. Most weekends were spent with Vera, a niece, who could not have been a better friend and whom I have rediscovered after all these years. I was also introduced to fish and chips, a favourite dish of Yorkshire, which used to be sold wrapped in newspaper in those days. On evenings when Aunty Annie had a class, Uncle Frank and I would walk up the steep hill from the house to meet her at the bus stop which was next to the fish and chip shop. It was a treat to eat the steaming, hot food out of the newspaper packet on those cold and windy nights.

I had absolutely no idea what to expect when I was thrown into a class of young girls. But thanks to the Headmistress of the Bradford Girls' Grammar School, Miss Hooke, and the teachers, with their patience and encouragement, I managed to adapt effortlessly to the school. Although I was the oldest pupil and a foreigner, the pupils were well-mannered enough to take me in their stride, although what they really thought of me I shall never know. Later, learning that I was a princess, some were disappointed that I didn't wear silks, satins and a tiara. I am sure I was pretty much a curiosity, as in those days there were hardly any Orientals around. Nor were there Indian or Chinese restaurants and takeaways, as English palates were not yet accustomed to spicy curries and soya sauce.

Once in a while, to help relieve my homesickness, I was allowed to cook rice, and something to accompany it. There was a great deal of trial and error as I had never cooked on a gas stove before, since at home there was only a wood fire. Auntie Annie would complain at times of the smell of the rice cooking and the garlic I used. I don't think the Neals had ever tasted garlic, though onions were used for the stews. The only form of cooked rice they had ever eaten was the rice pudding so beloved by the British. At school we were served great dollops of this lumpy stodge which I suppose kept me going until teatime.

During my first years in England, Sir Maung Gyi was still Burmese Ambassador, and he and his family were kind enough to look after me during the school holidays when I used to stay with them in London. Once, when Independence Day celebrations were held at the Embassy, Dora Than E, whom I had met earlier with my parents, was there. She was a svelte and attractive person, who was the belle of Rangoon University before the Japanese war. Her melodious voice made her a popular figure within Rangoon society. In London, she was a friendly and helpful person within the community. Everyone called her Ma Ma Gyi, meaning elder sister in Burmese. That evening she was surrounded by a happy group, one of them being Kitty Ba Than, later to become one of General Ne Win's wives. Also on this occasion I met the four beautiful daughters of Prince Svasti of Thailand, when the princesses performed a Thai dance.

*Independence Day 1948, Dora Than E (centre) and Kitty Ba Than, (extreme left) who became General Ne Win's wife.*

*Sir Stafford Cripps at Independence Day 1948, London.*

*Independence Day 1948, the four Svasti Princesses, London.*

*The approach to Girton College. (By courtesy of Girton College, Cambridge)*

*Opposite: The Emily Davies Court. The room to the left of the clock was my room for the first year. (By courtesy of Girton College, Cambridge)*

## Cambridge

Two years at Bradford and some months of private tuition in London prepared me for my university entrance exam for Cambridge. How elated I was when I heard I had been accepted by Girton. How delighted Miss Hooke and the teachers at school must have been to know that their efforts had not been in vain. I was to read Geography and, as I loved topography, it appeared all was set.

There were only two women's residential colleges when I went up; Girton was founded in 1869 and Newham a few years later. Girton is situated up-hill about two and a half miles from the centre of Cambridge. A large red brick building, it stands in beautiful grounds of gardens and orchards. Then it was entirely a female establishment and male undergraduates were only admitted in 1979.

I was fortunate to have a room in Emily Davies Court near the large clock for the first year, looking out onto the grounds. A great campaigner for the emancipation of women, Emily Davies founded Girton which started as a women's college in Hitchen. Our rooms facing the Court were reached through a long corridor. The gyp rooms and the bathrooms were on the other side. I lived in for the whole three years moving rooms each year to different parts of the college. In this way I became acquainted with new neighbours yearly.

There weren't many rules and regulations. We could pretty much do what we liked during the day, but had to be in to dine in Hall wearing our flowing black gowns. When going out in the evenings gowns were obligatory, so that the Proctors could distinguish us from the townspeople. By ten o'clock we had to be in before the porters closed the gates and special permission was needed from our tutors to stay out late. Similar rules applied to men's colleges, but some undergraduates liked to boast of climbing in after the ban.

Once settled into college, I even went to two or three of our Geography tutor, Mrs Andersen's famous tea parties. So it came as a shock when I was told I had to change to Economics for the First Tripos. This was a parental wish, or should I say a command? Both my father and stepmother thought I should read either Economics or Law, since most young Asians who came to England read these subject, which they had been told were prestigious. If I read Economics, I would be properly trained for getting a job when I returned home.

Indeed, many Asian undergraduates I met did read these two preferred subjects and not a few of them became successful businessmen and lawyers back in their countries. What my parents, unfortunately, did not realize was that one had to have an understanding of economics and a flair for business to be successful in the world of commerce. Alas, I possessed neither of those qualities.

I was disappointed. Economics was definitely not my scene and changing suddenly to read the subject meant I had to start from scratch – preparing for tutorials, lectures and trying to catch up with my reading. I found that year a difficult time. I can remember Mrs Holland, my supervisor, trying to make me understand the principles of economics. She was always immaculately dressed and used to smoke with a long cigarette holder. She could not have been more patient or kinder to me. After my first year reading Economics which I did not enjoy, I was allowed to change to Anthropology, a two year Tripos. Although I knew nothing about the subject and realised it would be hard going, I felt it was preferable to continuing with Economics, a subject in which I had no interest.

My brother, Sai Hseng, had already left for Trinidad and I no longer had his company to cheer me up when I was feeling unhappy. In looks, even to this day, he is a younger version of my father, dark brown eyes with a broad forehead. Though serious at times, we laughed a lot as we do now. Before he left, feeling responsible for me, he took me for a long walk and attempted to explain to me about the facts of life. My poor brother, what an undertaking for him! Although I was in my late teens, the protective life I had led at home made me vulnerable and he had every reason to fear for me. After all, I was a Saturday born. But he need not have worried. There were certainly many attractive and charming men around, but I did not fall under their spell, nor did I fall in love until some time later.

Despite the hard work I had to put in, I decided to let two friends of my brothers from Burma, Reggie Mya Maung and Richard Sein Min, introduce me to their friends and help me integrate into college life. I was taken out on the river Cam and taught to punt. I never quite mastered the art of punting but relied on others to take me up the river to Grantchester where we would have afternoon tea at the Orchard, a place made famous by Rupert Brooke's poem, *The Old Vicarage, Grantchester*.

When they went down and back to Burma, I met a number of other Burman undergraduates, too many to recall. Kathleen Ba Han who read Medicine was with me at Girton. She was Dr Ba Maw's niece. Her cousin, Zali Maw was the son of Dr Ba Maw who read Law. Two others were Richard and Albert Ba U, sons of Dr Ba U, who became President after my father in 1952.

Our large group of friends of all nationalities spanned the colleges and faculties. In between and after lectures we crowded into the Copper Kettle on King's Parade for coffee. In the afternoon if there were no tutorials, we went to tea-dances at the Dorothy's, now Marks and Spencers or tea in the men's colleges and ate sticky Fitzbillies buns. Sometimes we would have picnics in the grounds of Girton or tea parties in our rooms. I remember also lazily walking along the Backs in early Spring admiring the daffodils and crocus growing in colourful patches.

Heffers in Petty Cury, was one of my favourite bookshops where I spent hours browsing. When we felt rich a group of us would go to the small Chinese restaurant here and to an Indian place in All Saints Passage. Often the male undergraduates paid for us – although emancipated we let them be chivalrous. I found the May Balls exciting and delightful, and went to a number of them. I loved dancing all night and ending up with breakfast at Grantchester after being punted there.

*With Chit Wha and other friends, before a May Ball,
Cambridge 1950.*

Our group enjoyed each other's company, usually doing things together. Sometimes when we paired off to have tea or coffee, we behaved with formality and modesty, making them pleasant, friendly occasions. I thoroughly enjoyed the many social activities offered and I loved doing every thing short of beagling (I felt sorry for the poor hares), or joining a political party.

I cannot recall how many times I must have cycled up and down from Girton in a day for lectures, tutorials, meetings and parties. It was a long cycle ride into town so one could easily have clocked up seven or eight miles daily. Neither the winds blowing across the Fens nor the cold, affected me and, happily, the exercise seemed to keep me fit.

During my first year at Girton, it was Chit Wha Gunn, now Datin Chit Wha Lau, who made sure that I enjoyed college life. We became firm friends and have kept in touch. A great traveller, Chit Wha took Julia Hua, also in her first year, and I during our Christmas vacation to Cannes la Bocca. It was my first visit to France and our holiday left me with a desire to return one day to absorb its romance and beauty. While my husband, Peter and I were living in Mandelieu, Chit Wha and Julia came to see us and we were able to celebrate the 50 years' anniversary of our Cannes la Bocca holiday. Alas, much had changed on the Cote d'Azur, and we could no longer find the part of the town in which we had stayed and had enjoyed such a memorable time.

Later, game for more adventure, during one of our short vacations, Julia and I decided to go fruit-picking at Wisbech north of Cambridge in the flat Fenlands. We thought we could munch on the strawberries as we picked them and have some wonderful fresh air. Little did we realise what back-breaking work it was. Instead of strawberries, we found ourselves picking gooseberries which were really sour if one tried to eat one. Bitter winds blew across the Fens making us, with our inadequate clothing, cold and miserable. The bunks were hard to sleep on and it was not the holiday we had thought we would enjoy. Although we were engaged for a fortnight we managed to escape after one week. The only good thing was earning our first wages of five pounds. I framed my crisp white fiver-pound note for a while, but must have spent it as I never set eyes on it again after the holidays.

*Sanda, Julia and Chit Wha in France.*

*Cambridge friends: Ted Williams, Princess Dina Abdel Hamid, Richard Sein Min, Chit Wha Gunn and Reggie Mya Maung.*

Not many friends who came up to Cambridge to see Kathleen and myself liked coming to Girton, considering it too far away. Instead, I would spend time with them going round some of the colleges along the River Cam, starting with St John's, Trinity and King's, or sometimes as far as Queen's. After numerous photographs had been taken of the splendid buildings and courtyards, gardens and people punting on the river, there would be complaints of tired feet so we never got further. Everyone was taken to see King's College Chapel and no matter how many times I visited, I always found something new to look at and absorb.

In 1952, my father was asked to continue serving the Union of Burma for another few years as Speaker of the House of Nationalities. Many leaders of the ethnic groups were representatives in the House of Nationalities, each working with the other in an effort to keep the Union intact. It would seem he was doing what he could, but he must have known in his heart of hearts, that politically it was not a happy situation. There were many political upheavals too in the Shan States, and he must have been quite upset about the state of affairs all over the country. He may have thought when his Speaker's term came to an end, and he no longer held such a high and responsible post, he could once again make his Shan voice heard.

I had already been in England for over five years when, grudgingly after a great deal of discussion within the family, a decision was made for me to go home for the long vacation.

When my father left the President's House, the family moved into Golden Valley, a pleasant residential area. It was here that I had come for my holidays. I was not at ease, and it was not a carefree time. My father was not best pleased with me as gossip mongers had been at work, and he had heard that I was not studying as hard as I should. My decision to give up Economics and to read Anthropology instead, made him even more cross. Perhaps he was right to be angry with me in this instance, but as Economics did not appeal to me, I did not think it wrong to read what I wanted and to enjoy myself at Cambridge.

Added to this situation I had another problem. In London at one of the Burmese Embassy parties I had met a young, engaging Burman. I was infatuated with him, despite the fact that I also liked another English undergraduate whom I had seen off and on. John read Anthropology and played the piano beautifully. Now, since I was in Rangoon, Eddie asked to see me. My father was infuriated, but nevertheless gave permission for a visit. When I met him again, although it didn't feel quite right I meekly agreed to a secret engagement. I was perhaps not really taking it seriously and unconsciously thought it would not work, since he was in Burma and I was going back to England. Anyway, after the visit, there was an icy atmosphere in the house – no one said a word but I knew there was definite disapproval.

My stay in Rangoon continued and I was kindly invited to various diplomatic parties. I had the distinct feeling that I was being sized up as to whether I fitted into the social scene. Perhaps it was because I wasn't encouraged to go out to these parties or because I didn't enjoy them, that I recall so little about them. One thing I do remember though was going to the Rangoon Races at the Tuft Club. It was the first time I had ever been to a race meeting and I was caught up in the excitement of the crowd. A Burmese friend of the family, Mrs. Shane, acting as chaperone, took me there. We didn't place any bets, but just sat enjoying talking to her many friends. The atmosphere was pleasantly relaxed and it was a very different side of society I was seeing. It was here that I caught my first glimpse of General Ne Win. One can imagine everyone's surprise when the military took over, that horse racing, one of the General's favourite sports, was banned for ever.

On this short visit, I do not remember seeing my eldest brother, Sao Sai, who was up in the Shan States. Due to the sudden rush of events in late 1947, Sao Sai had to stay on instead of going back to Cambridge. With my father away in Rangoon, as heir apparent, the Kyemmong, he had to stand in for his father. He was now in charge of the administration of Yawnghwe and became acting Saohpa.

It was not the easiest of times as he had not only to learn the ropes of the administration, but was also faced with insurgencies within the state. Taunggyi[30] was overrun for a while. It certainly threw him in at the deep-end of the complex political situation existing at that time. Soon after independence, different groups of insurgents had begun to gather strength, spreading in various directions. In the Shan States, Kachin mutineers were joined by Karen and Pa-O groups and occupied Taunggyi. By the end of 1949, the administrative centre was retaken by the army, supported by loyal Saohpas who felt such behaviour against an elected government was wrong. These sentiments were readily accepted by the Burmans then, but in 1961-1962, though these sentiments of loyalty to the Union remained unchanged, they were branded as traitors and made scapegoats.

Sao Sai had married Sao Shwe Ohn, my stepmother's niece, and daughter of the heir apparent of Hsenwi. We generally called her Pat, which was her school name. She was a school friend of mine, petite and vivacious, whom I've mentioned before. I wasn't surprised that Sao Sai had fallen for her. They lived most of the time in Taunggyi and Yawnghwe with their two young daughters.

My elder brother, Sai Hseng had been with the Shan State Government in their Agricultural Department. Like his brother, during the uprisings he found it difficult to carry out his work, especially as he needed to travel from one agricultural station to the next. He was married to the second daughter of the Saohpa of Lawksawk. She was slim and attractive, and was often the belle of the party. Her school name was Audrey, though her Shan name was Sao Hom Noan.

*Sao Sai and his wife Sao Shwe Ohn, or Pat.*

*Sai Hseng and his wife Sao Hom Noan, or Audrey.*

I remember meeting Audrey in Lawksawk at the funeral of her grandfather, the old Saohpa, during the war. It was in 1943, so I must have been about fourteen or fifteen, and remember that Audrey had taken a group of us to the orange groves where we sat and ate quantities of sweet, succulent oranges which were like tangerines. There was a large gathering of all the Saohpa families who had travelled from afar, so I presume that during the first year of Japanese occupation it was a fairly peaceful time.

By 1952, the family had grown to ten, and I remember the fun I had with my younger brothers, Tzang, Myee Myee and Pyee and sisters, Ying, Hayma and Leun. The older children were at the Rangoon Methodist School, which was a sister school to Kingswood in Kalaw. The two youngest Pyee and Leun were still very young. Hso was on a mountain climbing expedition with his Dera Doon school in northern India, so I did not see him. I was glad to catch up with Sai Hseng and his family, as he had just come from the Shan States to Rangoon to work for ICI and was living at our family house in Kokine Road.

My holidays soon came to an end and it was good to get back to my studies and Girton, though the hard work ahead worried me. It was a frustrating time as I had to catch up on my reading for the term. Switching from one subject to another had its complications. First it was Geography, next Economics and then Anthropology, no wonder I was often in a daze. Professor Fortes gave lectures on the Ashanti and other African societies, while Dr Fortune taught us about the Trobiand islanders and other Pacific islanders.

One of the many books Dr Fortune recommended was *Coming of Age in Samoa*[31], which was a study Margaret Mead, the famous American anthropologist had made of the islanders and their social habits. In many ways, this helped me to appreciate the new subject I had to choose. I began to see how the kinship organizations and social structure of Samoa could be related to our own. This then set me off in preparing kinship charts for our family and other princes.

I found anthropology fascinating, but it was also very confusing for me. The teaching staff were understanding and considerate in helping me to grasp the subject. Similarly friendly undergraduates were always willing to explain certain points I did not understand or pick up in the lectures. Amongst them were two I would like to mention: Venetia Brewis, also at Girton, and Anthony Forge, who already knew Peter, my future husband. Venetia Pollock, as she was later known, became an editor with Secker and Warburg and later Penguin, and we met whenever I returned from our foreign travels. She was always full of ideas and I would come away planning my next project. Anthony went on to teach anthropology at one of the universities in Australia. So we never caught up with him in later years. Sadly they have both passed away which was a great loss to us.

*Hso (at the back third from right) and other Doon School students on their Banderpunch Expedition.*

Sometimes I wished I had been given a choice of reading History or Modern Languages. The latter would have suited me well since later we lived both in France and in Spain where I needed to know the languages. Nevertheless, though reading Anthropology was a *force majeure*, I have no regrets. Perhaps at that time I did not enjoy having the subject pushed on to me, but in the end I learnt a great deal.

Only when I had left the university did I begin to acknowledge that in many ways it didn't matter what subject one read – it was the whole experience of being at Cambridge that was important. Many of us take the privilege of being at university for granted. It was only when I ceased to be an undergraduate at Girton that I began to realize what an outstanding experience it had been. There was no one pressuring me or telling me what to do, I had been left to myself and the decisions I made were my own. Certainly, it was very special being at Girton College. As the years have sped by, I have begun to appreciate more and more the knowledge and the wider outlook on life I gained by being there.

I know that without the sympathetic understanding of my tutor, Miss Rosemary Murray, it would have been a pretty daunting life for me. Both she and the Mistress, were well aware of the difficulties faced by those of us who had come from different backgrounds and from homes thousands of miles away. There was a great deal of adjustment to be made both in education and in culture. With remarkable ease she gave us confidence and made us feel able to face any challenge. Her skill in dealing with us 'lost' undergraduates was recognized when she went on to become Mistress of New Hall, the third women's college in Cambridge founded in 1954. Later in 1975 she become vice-Chancellor of Cambridge University, the first woman ever to hold such a high post in its 766 years' history.

Ever since I can remember, my father used to say to me that although other Saohpas gave their daughters gold and jewellery, he would not give these to me. Instead, he would give me something more precious and lasting, something which would make me independent and give me a living throughout my life. Education, he said, was this gift. When I was younger I couldn't quite understand what he meant – after all I was a vain young girl and would much rather have had those blue, blue sapphires and dazzling rubies. I envied the other princesses who used to show off their jewellery.

Then in 1953, when I received my degree, my father's dream that I should have an education and become independent came true. The three years at Cambridge went by in a flash. I am amazed now to think how I fitted so many things into those few years. Many undergraduates I met and got to know well went on to join their governments becoming ministers, prominent citizens and successful entrepreneurs. I kept in contact with a number of them for a while but gradually have lost touch. On the other hand, from time to time someone turns up to renew a friendship from those distant years.

## *Peter*

I met Peter Simms for the first time in late 1951 at a Buddhist Society meeting I had been persuaded to attend by my friend Anthony. When he told me about Peter I thought he must be a crank, since I had not had the chance to meet any truly serious western Buddhists. Nevertheless, Anthony was determined that I should meet his friend who was running the Cambridge Buddhist Society with the blessing of Christmas Humphreys, an authority on Buddhism and President of the British Buddhist Society. Althought not particularly interested, I went along.

Imagine my surprise to see that our speaker was a tall, blonde and handsome man. On being introduced I saw how blue his eyes were, that he was polite and asked us to take our seats. "Gosh, how handsome he is", I thought to myself. At the end of the talk I realized that my preconceived ideas about Peter was wrong and that he knew more about Buddhism than I did. Indeed, what I know about Buddhism today is what Peter taught me over the years. Until then, my knowledge of Buddhism was confined to the active side, which consisted of merit making ceremonies and rituals. Being young and steeped in tradition, I never once questioned these rites nor did I think there were other ways of practising Buddhism. Now I was to learn that there are many schools and aspects of Buddhism, and saw how Peter, through his reading and meetings with eminent Buddhists, was able to take the intellectual approach. Apart from Christmas Humphreys, there was also Dr Edward Conze, scholar and lecturer who had written and translated Buddhist literature, and Daisetz Teitaro Suzuki who introduced Zen Buddhism to the West. Both were his mentors. In addition, Peter had read Sanskrit for a year, so he was able to explain much of the Buddhist terminology of which I had very little knowledge.

At our first encounter I also met a Burmese friend of Peter's, Dr Hla Pe who was then compiling an English-Burmese dictionary at the School of Oriental and African Studies, University of London. He was on hand to give advice on Buddhism. At that time his friends thought Dr Hla Pe was a confirmed bachelor. He was, however, later to marry an heiress from Moulmein. When I eventually met her, she turned out to be one of Daw Win's best friends when they were together at Rangoon University, before the Japanese war. After living in England for several decades, Dr Hla Pe returned to Burma and took up residence in Moulmein, the home of his wife. I am told that the locals find him quite anglicised and he is called the 'Englishman' by them.

As we were leaving Peter asked us to tea the following week. Anthony said he was busy so I agreed to go alone. I was quite excited at the prospect of seeing Peter again. When I went to tea, I learnt he was teaching English to foreign students and was sharing a house with two young attractive Scandinavian students. Perhaps I thought the arrangement slightly unusual and not proper from my restricted point of view. He asked to see me again, but I said I was going away and we left it at that. Although I was attracted to Peter, I did not think of him that much – there was John in Cambridge and Eddie who came up to see me from London.

When I returned from Rangoon after the long vacation the following year, my feelings for Eddie became uncertain. I knew I had to make up my mind soon if I was to concentrate on my studies. After a few weeks I broke off the engagement,

*Sanda with Peter and two of his students in*
*Cambridge.*

and I felt easier. With piles of books on my desk I began to study earnestly, but when I could began seeing John again. Then Peter turned up one day with a bunch of red roses. I was embarrassed but also delighted. In this way began our fifty-year relationship. I found out that he was a parson's son, his father had died but his mother was still alive. After some months, I was to meet this gentle, kindly person. Sadly, she died a few years later.

Peter had had one year at Jesus College reading Mechanical Sciences before he joined the army and was commissioned in the Royal Engineers in 1943. He was seconded to the Royal Bombay Sapper and Miners at Poona as a Lieutenant. It was then that he became interested in Hinduism. Just twenty-two when he was demobbed in 1947, he came back to Cambridge and read English for the next two years, then Sanskrit for a year. Engrossed in reading about Buddhism, he decided to become a Buddhist. Although we didn't talk much about it, I can imagine the heated conversations between father and son, his father was a strict Church of England priest, when Peter decided to change his faith.

We became great friends. Peter had warmth and understanding, he was polite, kind-hearted, and cheerful. He had a great enthusiasm for everything and we had fun doing things together. Peter was quite frank and told me that he was separated from his wife. They had married soon after his return from India, but the marriage had not worked out. They had a son and he was in the process of getting divorced. I wondered if it mattered that he was a married man? I knew in my hearts of hearts it didn't make the slightest difference but my conscience debated whether it was ethically right to carry on.

By this time Peter had moved into a barn which was behind a pub and above a stables on Trumpington Street, diagonally opposite Fitzwilliam Museum. Today modern flats stand in its place and it is difficult to imagine that there was once an old wooden barn here. It was a spacious studio with books lining the whole of

*John Blofeld with his family. He became a great friend to us in Bangkok.*

one wall, and wooden stairs leading up to it. Probably it was where the stable boy lived in former days.

Peter was still teaching English to foreign students and I was studying hard, but I found myself spending more and more time with him. We were now hopelessly in love with each other but knew once exams were over and term ended, decisions would have to be made. The eternal question was : what should we do?

During 1953, Peter was offered a teaching post in Bangkok at the Prasarnmitr College and, deciding to take it, left in September. After graduation, I, on the other hand, went on to London to the School of Oriental and African Studies to study Thai with the expectation that I would be joining Peter, but when? Our separation was made more difficult, as I had little idea of what I felt was the right thing to do. Was it my duty to go back to Rangoon and teach Anthropology or perhaps become a diplomat? Would that make Sao U Hpa happy? I knew that he was not pleased with me as I had not expressed my wish to go back to Rangoon as soon as I had graduated. Worse still, if he knew I was in love with an Englishman, a foreigner, he would certainly be furious. I was torn between not wanting to be disloyal to my family, and at the same time wanting only to be with the man I loved.

I suppose my father had taken a great risk in deciding that I should have an English education and a Cambridge degree. As a Shan girl of eighteen, I was already of marriageable age. Although he did not wish it, surely he must have imagined that by my spending some six years alone away from home, it was quite possible that I might meet someone and end up marrying him. Therefore, why should he object? It didn't make sense. Having obtained my degree, as he wanted me to do, he could hardly grouse about that. Still there were nagging doubts that left me undecided.

My indecision made me extremely unhappy and I stopped writing to Peter. After two or three weeks Dr Hla Pe telephoned me saying he wanted to see me urgently. I went to see him and he said that Peter had sent a telegram saying he was very worried as I had not replied to his letters. Peter wanted me to join him in Bangkok. Peter's telegram woke me up and I realized that I really wanted to be with him. His following letters suggested I should go to him as soon as I could and bear the brunt of my father's anger.

*Peter at the World Fellowship of Buddhists Conference, Rangoon 1954.*

It was a testing time for me, but once I had made up my mind to be with Peter, I left when term ended. We had a Buddhist ceremony and received a blessing from one of the monks John Blofeld knew when I arrived. Since the divorce hadn't come through we didn't have the official Consular wedding until a year later. We stayed with John for a while until we found a house on the river.

Soon after my arrival, we took one of the coastal vessels down to Songkhla. It was a pleasant uneventful sail south, but on our return we called at several ports to load big jars of *nam-pla*, fish sauce, and at others dried fish and *kapi*, fermented fish paste. We were overwhelmed by the strong smell of the cargo and despite moving around the ship we could not avoid the pong. It slightly marred our sail back. One evening when we were sitting down to have a drink of Mekong, the Captain offered us some bats' blood and crispy fried bats. I was too squeamish to have any but Peter gave the Captain great pleasure in joining him. Many glasses of Mekong were drank that evening to wash it all down. It was a wonderful introduction to Thailand for me, seeing the coastal towns and enjoying the occasional swim on one of the beaches. I can hardly believe that it was fifty-three years ago that we made our trip.

When we talked about the potential rift with my father and family, Peter was philosophical, saying he was sure things would work out and we would find a way to appease Sao U Hpa. Fortunately, this opportunity came, when Christmas Humphreys asked Peter to attend the Conference of the World Fellowship of Buddhists as a delegate for the Society. The Conference was being held in Rangoon and since we were living in Bangkok it was easier for us to make the short flight, than someone coming all the way from London.

I was not at all happy, but Peter said we had better get it over with, and accept Mr Humphreys' proposal to go to Rangoon. Peter felt that it was time he met my father and what better opportunity than now? So it was decided. It was only a two hour flight from Bangkok and soon we were in Burma.

In a dilapidated jeep we went straight from Mingaladon Airport to the house at 74 Kokine Road. When people were told of our arrival, my aunt Daw Daw came rushing out to meet us, with tears streaming down her cheeks. My stepmother who was only a few steps behind smiled at us, but said nothing. My brothers and sister dashed out to see if we were real. Someone said "He's very angry with you." It was a tense moment. Then one of the children ran and hugged me.

On asking where my father was they said he was in the front room working at his desk. With little smiles of encouragement, we were told to go through to where he sat at his desk bent over some papers he was working on.

Peter and I made the customary *wai*, and touched the floor three times with our foreheads. My father looked up and seemed to show a slight acknowledgement of our presence but went on writing. Peter and I sat some distance from his desk where a few arm chairs stood in a half circle.

The time seemed interminable. Sao U Hpa continued with his work and did not look up again from his papers. The minutes ticked by. I was getting more nervous and becoming restless. Every time I made a move to get up or open my mouth to say something, Peter would signal me to be quiet. We must have sat in this way very silently, for well over an hour.

Then very slowly Sao U Hpa put his pen down and looked up, as if noticing us for the first time. We began answering the formal questions he put to us. Where were we staying and how long were we going to be in Rangoon? We told him about the Buddhist Conference at Kaba Aye and that Peter had come as the United Kingdom delegate. He seemed pleased with the news, but did not say anything except to nod approval.

Then he told us that the family had just moved into Kokine Road, and the place was still under repairs. He said we couldn't stay with him and the family this time, but asked my stepmother, who had by then come to join us, to get us accommodation at the Strand Hotel. It was a relief for all the family to see that Sao U Hpa was not in a rage. Everyone had been fearful of what he might have said or done to me in his anger. Though I was also relieved, my emotions were still pent up within me and I couldn't speak a word without my voice trembling. As for Peter, I think he knew it was going to be all right.

My father had met his match. He realized that Peter respected him but that at the same time he was prepared to stand up to him if he was in the right.

During that visit, we called at the house a number of times. At the Conference, my father and Peter sat opposite each other. Peter sat with the then British Ambassador, Sir Paul Gore-Booth and his wife on the British side. So for the duration of the meeting, we saw my father every day. Sometimes we exchanged a few words, at other times it was a nod and a smile. I began to feel a bit more confident and was hopeful for our future relationship.

Our stay in Rangoon gave us an opportunity to renew our acquaintance with a colourful Burman, Bo Setkya, whom we had met recently in Bangkok. Bo Setkya was one of the Thirty Comrades of the Thakin party during the early 1940s. I had met him previously in London, when he was involved in the filming of *The Purple Plain* with Gregory Peck and Win Min Than who was playing the female lead. He told me he had known my father since 1930, as they had both attended the Round Table Conference. He wanted to help in smoothing things over between my father and ourselves and he invited us to come and spend one of our holidays with him in Rangoon. By that time, Jimmy, as his friends called him, had married the lovely Win Min Than.

*View from the house of boats on*
*Chao Phraya river.*

## Bangkok in the 1950s

In Bangkok, Peter continued teaching at the Prasarnmitr College for Teachers. I found a job at Trium Udom School for Girls. To help the students speak English, Peter started an English Club which met fortnightly. We organized tea parties and invited English friends from the British Embassy and business circles, so the students would have the opportunity of speaking the language. As well, we decided to run a magazine called *Thought and Word* to encourage the students further.

Soon, Peter began writing a weekly article for the English edition of *Siam Rath* newspaper. Mom Rajawongse Kukrit Pramoj, the Editor approved of *Thought and Word* and said he would like to contribute to it. We were delighted. Peter had a keen interest in Siamese culture and art, so he wrote a series of articles on Siamese royal titles and other Thai subjects. Kukrit was a kindly man and not only took an interest in our project, but also offered us his friendship. In the 1970s he was to become Thailand's Prime Minister during a difficult period for the country.

When Peter first arrived in Bangkok, he had been taken under the wing of Prince Svasti and his family, whose four attractive daughters we had met in London. They introduced him to Thai life and culture. There was Prince Prem too, who was fond of amateur dramatics and used to ask young diplomats from the British Embassy and Peter to participate in his plays.

Little did I realize when talking to Thai friends in London what Bangkok would be like. I was thrilled to find so many things that were common to our Shan way of life. The many temples overwhelmed me and being in a society where I was able to speak a mixture of Shan and Thai, and to be understood was wonderful. I felt as if I was back in the Shan States

I don't suppose anyone could have adequately described to me, what I might find in the Bangkok of the 1950s. It was a charming and romantic city with its splendid Buddhist temples, fine palaces, museums and extensive parks. Boats on the many *klongs*, the waterways, and the *sam loh*, the three-wheel pedicab, whose

*Our Bangkok house
on the Menam Chao
Phraya, 1954.*

drivers used the jingling bells of their bicycles for a horn, were the main means of transport. There were far less motor cars then and despite the numerous motorised *sam-loh*, known as put-puts because of the noise they made, there was little pollution and hardly any traffic jams.

Whilst living there, we frequently went to the Sunday morning market at Sanam Luang, the large open ground near Wat Phra Kaeo and the National Museum. In those days everyone took their time to walk around gently without being pushed. People seemed happy and one was greeted with smiles everywhere. It was an amazing market full of merchandise of every kind.

I always made a point of buying a bird or two that were kept captive, wanting to give it its freedom. Also I felt I would gain some merit by doing so. I was to learn later that these little birds were quite tame and after they had been freed, they would fly around and then come back to the vendor. The only person who was gaining anything was the vendor.

Then there was the floating market on the Chao Phraya which nostalgically took me back to Yawnghwe and the Inle Lake.

We used also to go off for weekends to the closer seaside resorts of Pattaya and Bang Saen. In those days, there few crowds and we used to have most of the beach to ourselves. Hua Hin was also a favourite place of ours. The sandy beach stretched for miles. Once we were there during full moon, and saw an enormously pale, golden moon rising from the sea. It was an astonishing sight.

In Bangkok, we had rented a delightful house on the Chao Phraya river in one of the smaller palace complexes. It was a wooden house on piles with large French doors through which the river breezes blew in cooling the rooms. We never needed air-conditioning or fans. The only problem was it was said to be haunted.

I don't think Peter believed in spirits but it left him unsure. Not long after we had moved in, Peter found that whenever he worked late writing an article or correcting student papers, he would suddenly feel someone standing behind him. On turning round he found nobody, which disturbed him. Leaving the work unfinished he would come to bed saying he couldn't continue. It was quite scary.

The study was next to our bedroom and had a safe. On some nights when we were trying to sleep, we would hear the combination to the safe whizzing around, and the door of the safe would open and slam shut again. Occasionally the keys of the typewriter hitting paper with the carriage return would be heard. After checking the first few times we gave up since there was no one there and we suspected a ghost.

Then one evening when our maid went upstairs where there was a large room with a balcony, she had a fright. She came running down saying that a prince was standing on the balcony looking at the sunset dressed in full uniform. We ran up the stairs hoping to catch sight of him but he had disappeared by the time we got there. Things were getting serious and we realised that whether we believed in spirits or not, one was certainly active in our house.

We told John Blofeld about the incidents since he was knowledgeable about such things. He recommended that the house be exorcised. This we did as soon as we could. After the Buddhist monk had made his incantations, he said he believed the late prince's possessions were still stored in the cupboards under the eves and this was the reason why his spirit was unable to leave. Following his advice, the belongings were duly removed and, we never again had sleepless nights.

Every so often groups of families who lived in boats would come and anchor under the house. Their arrival meant that for the next few days we would be pervaded by whiffs of smoke and cooking smells seeping up from below. They were a friendly group so we never minded their being there.

One of the unpleasant things one had to put up with living on the river, was when a dead animal floated down. We would race to close all the doors and windows as soon as we got a whiff in an attempt to keep out the stench until it had gone past our house. Fortunately it didn't happen all that often.

When we lived in Bangkok, the river was still used intensively to ply goods to and from the inland towns. The major *klongs*, were originally dug in the reign of Rama I to facilitate shipping from the sea up to Ayutthaya. Later, *klongs* were dug in Bangkok as short cuts between one point of the river to the other as it meandered around. Now, of course, many of the *klongs* have been filled in.

From time to time, we would hire an outboard motor to take us down river to the Oriental Hotel, which was one of the larger hotels in Bangkok. Here we met friends at the Bamboo Bar which was air-conditioned – a luxury in those days. When Daw Daw came to visit us we also took her on the boat to the Oriental. She loved these trips as it reminded her of Inle. We had some happy times at the Bamboo Bar which will always be remembered.

Our stay in Bangkok was made all the more enjoyable by the friendship extended to us by various other members of the Royal Family such as Prince Dhani, who also contributed to *Thought and Word*. He used to hold literary lunches every Saturday which we attended. The Thai dishes served were taken from old Thai recipes and were delicate in flavour. Another family, Prince Piya and Princess Vipawadi Rangsit could not have been more generous and gracious.

We were all relatively young in those days, and Bangkok was the right place for us at that time. It was a period when the number of foreigners was still small, mostly composed of English lecturers from Chulalongkorn University, diplomats from various Embassies, and young businessmen. The families readily accepted us into their fold, and gave us the opportunity to learn about Thai culture. It made us feel that Bangkok was a special city, with little hassle and a slow tempo of life, quite unlike the bustling metropolis of today.

Then, we were able to spend time together and to form lasting friendships. Even after our respective departures from Bangkok, we often managed to keep in touch and to meet many of these friends again in different parts of the world.

Among these friends were two young diplomats, Robert Swann and Christopher Curwen, who both spoke Thai and were easily integrated into Thai society. When Robert left Bangkok, we lost touch. However, several years after, we found him living not too far from us in the south of France, and were able to resume our friendship. Chris had been with us in Cambridge and we were delighted when he arrived in Bangkok. From time to time we used to go together to the seaside, and I remember one occasion clearly when we were trying to find a place for lunch. Driving along the coast road, we came upon a lonely shop house on the beach. Here we were served tiny Thai oysters cooked in an omelette and were overjoyed to find some half-bottles of Guinness sitting on a dusty shelf coated with cobwebs, looking very neglected. It made little difference to the Guinness though, and we had a splendid lunch.

The English lecturers in those days were wonderfully attuned to the Thai way of life. One who befriended us was John Blofeld. Peter had heard of him even before he reached Bangkok. On one of his train trips from London to Cambridge, he had met one of John's fellow Embassy friends from Peking, who recommended him to Peter. John was well versed in Mahayana Buddhism and wrote a number of books and became well known. He was as tall as Peter, but broader and was forthright in his views. He was well-liked by his pupils at Chula and many a time we sat listening to John as he expounded on Buddhism.

Many years later when we came back to live in Bangkok, John, having retired from the university, was working in the Economic Commission for Asia and the Far East (ECAFE). I was fortunate enough to work also in this United Nations organization in the Information Department. Some years later it changed its name to Economic and Social Commission for Asia (ESCAP), and is still based in Bangkok. John was a great gourmet and an authority on Chinese food and I think it was every other Friday, when a group of colleagues used to go with him for the most delicious lunches. We must have had a meal at all the best Chinese restaurants existing in town at that time, including sumptuous dinners to which Peter and I were invited when Peter was in town.

John also took a kindly interest in the Shan States and my family, and travelled two or three times to Yawnghwe and Taunggyi to see them. Whenever a brother or sister visited Bangkok, they always made it a point of going to see him. He was always helpful and gave sound advice when there was a problem.

## Silver cup – Jim Thompson

After Taunggyi was bombed and the Japanese were getting nearer, we had had to leave Yawnghwe in a hurry, leaving a great many things behind. I am not sure what was done about the royal regalia, but a quantity of silverware was buried in the gardens. When we returned from the lake and dug up our treasures, we found some of them were missing and no one knew who had taken them. The family decided not to worry too much – after all we were safe from harm and back home.

Then, on one of the times when Peter and I visited Bangkok while we were living in Rangoon, Jim Thompson invited us to dinner. He had some antiques he had bought in Rangoon and wanted us to have a look at them to see if we could tell him of their provenance. In looking through the various objects and silver ware, he picked up one particular bowl and turning it over said, "There is writing on the base. Can you read it?" Imagine my surprise when I read my stepmother's name, Sao Hearn Hkam, written in Shan on the bottom of the bowl. Jim, too, was astonished.

At once he said, "It belongs to your family and you must take it back to her." He was very insistent and we could not refuse. We found out that indeed it was one of the silver pieces that had been stolen during the war. My stepmother was very pleased to get her silver bowl back, as it had been a wedding present. What a coincidence! Jim was considered a hard-headed businessman and his generosity towards us was thought by some of his friends to have been very unusual.

At the end of the Second World War, Jim Thompson, an American working in the OSS, had found himself in Thailand. Growing fond of the country and its people, he decided to stay on. He began taking an interest in the ailing Thai silk industry, and rejuvenated it by creating designs with an incredible colour scheme, which immediately became popular. Thai silk, all of a sudden, became an international success.

Jim also became well known for his superb Thai house, one of the first of its kind to be constructed in Bangkok. Six old, Thai style, teak houses were put together to form one magnificent house. The doors were beautifully carved, while the house was decorated with Thai furniture and his own Thai silk furnishings,

*Jim Thompson in his shop in Bangkok.*

which gave the house a luxurious and sumptuous atmosphere. If he wasn't entertaining friends, tourist were welcome to look around. Later, it became one of Bangkok's major tourist attractions and a museum.

Many years later in 1972 while we were living in Singapore, Jim, who was visiting some friends in the Highlands of Malaysia, disappeared under mysterious circumstances. It made world headlines, and there were a number of theories about his disappearance. For a while, there were sightings of him and it was reported he was variously in different countries. The story then died out, and it seems that no one has ever been able to fathom out what had really happened to him.

## Travels in Laos

When Peter and I finished our teaching contracts at our respective colleges in Bangkok, we decided it would be interesting to visit neighbouring Laos, another Tai country, which we did not know. We felt that we needed about six months if Peter was to collect data and to write something about Buddhism in Laos.

In 1954 after the fall of the Dien Bien Phu garrison and the retreat of the French army, a Conference concerning Indochina was held in Geneva. From being a country nobody knew, Laos suddenly came into the international spotlight which gave the great powers an excuse for intervening. The Geneva Convention established the International Control Commission (ICC), composed of Indian, Canadian and Polish delegations, who were to supervise the withdrawal of Viet Minh troops in the north of Laos and to maintain peace within the country. A charming

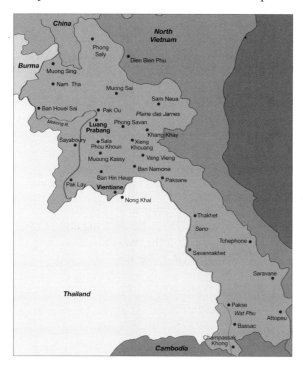

*A sketch map of the Kingdom of Laos.*

*Peter, 1955 near Nam Tha.*

*Sanda with porters near Nam Tha, 1955.*

man, Samar Sen, was the first Indian Chairman. The French were gradually forced to leave their protectorate, and the United States began to cast a greater influence on Laos and Indochina as a whole. With the French out of the way, the Americans took on military sponsorship and full economic aid for the Laotian economy.

In the same year, the South-East Asia Treaty Organization (SEATO) was founded to protect the Southeast Asia region against the encroachment of Communism. The offices were in Bangkok and the signatories included the US, UK, France, Australia, New Zealand, Pakistan, Thailand and the Philippines. It was the time of the domino theory, wherein if one Southeast Asian country fell to Communism, it was thought the rest would follow. SEATO being based in Bangkok was highly worried and extended its protection to the three Indochinese countries.

It was in 1955, a year later, when the political situation seemed a little more stable, that we decided to go to Laos. Arriving in Vientiane I liked the atmosphere and the look of the place and immediately adopted it as my second home. With little transport and few viable roads, many having been destroyed during the Japanese war, it appeared we would have to travel the best way we could – walking, on horse back and in army vehicles. So we walked and rode over northern Laos and travelled with the help of the military in the south. It was so like the Shan States and I felt really at home. Speaking in Shan and Thai, as explained earlier, I was able to get us around in the villages without having to learn Lao, while Peter spoke French with Laotian officials. In those days, very few people spoke English so we had quite a struggle at times trying to make ourselves understood completely.

One day in a village close to Vang Vieng, we went to a monastery and two young novices came to greet us. I asked for the abbot in my best Tai mixture of languages, but after five minutes one of the novices returned with a big chopper for chopping wood. I realize that I had put the stress on the word for monk in the wrong place. Though our languages are closely related it was not easy finding the correct pronunciation for a word with several tones and meanings.

For our first week in Vientiane we were allowed to stay at the Setha Palace, often called the Bungalow. Permission was given only after a long plea with the ICC, who had commandeered all the rooms. Fortunately, one of the rooms belonging to a Canadian Officer was free as he was away, so we were able to spend the few days looking around Vientiane and preparing ourselves for our long trek to Luang Prabang without worrying about accommodation.

*Mong Kassy, with the French engineers, who rescued us.*

After being in Vientiane for a week or two, the military told us an army convoy that took supplies north to the outposts was leaving for Vang Vieng and we could travel with them. Here we met a party of American Aid people who were planning to drive all the way to Luang Prabang. We were happy to meet them and thought perhaps we could join their party, which would be splendid as then we won't have to walk all the way.

The route to the royal capital was still being prepared by the French engineers and much of the road had yet to be finished. The recent heavy rains had created gigantic and numerous potholes which made it impassable for the jeeps. While the American party turned back to Vientiane, we went up to the French genie camp at Mong Kassy where they looked after us for two or three days. We walked on from there to Luang Prabang, spending many nights in villages inhabited by the Meo, now referred to as the Hmong and the Kha, or Lao Theung.

From Luang Prabang we flew up to Nam Tha on one of the small planes carrying families back to the provincial town. The plane was filled with baskets of chickens, bags of rice and mothers with babies on their backs, and two or three soldiers with their guns. We left for our next destination, after a few days in Nam Tha enjoying the hospitality of the Chao Khoueng, the governor, which included visiting Tai Dam villages where we danced to the beat of a drum, the rhythm sounding a bit like a samba.

When we were in Mong Sing, Laos celebrated its entry into the United Nations and there was a great amount of *mao-tai*, a home brew, vodka-like rice spirit, which Peter had to drink as the Chao Mong had asked him to be co-host. It was 'bottoms up' for every guest he welcomed, so one can imagine what his head felt like the next day.

Mong Sing, the north-westernmost point of Laos, borders on Kengtung. Here we met two or three men from there, one of whom had married into the former Mong Sing Chaofa's family, and had become a respected, senior member of the town. When the time came for us to depart, he provided horses and porters for us to go back to Nam Tha. It was a hard day's ride climbing almost 3,000 feet and riding along narrow ledges with a sheer drop on one side. Having made one ridge we had to climb down to the valley only to ascend another. The porters enjoyed taking us up one hillside and down the other. They would shout gleefully "Tang

*The Mekong at Houie Sai.*

luk, tang luk," when we came to what they called 'short-cuts'. At times, Peter would have to dismount and help to push the horse up the hill, as he was too tall for the small horses to carry him up the inclines. With each crest, the landscape changed from thick tropical jungle to semi-tropical deciduous tress and pampas grass which swayed with the slightest breeze stretching for several miles.

By sundown we reached the broad plain of Nam Tha and the dust road which led into the town. There we found a number of members of parliament campaigning for the election, and Tiao Somsanith took us under his wing and helped to arrange the next stage of our trip. Despite his kind help, we could find no horses, so we had to walk all the way to Houie Sai.

We met a host of Kwii, Akha, Kwen, Yao and other peoples during our trek who couldn't believe their eyes when they saw us – one tall *farang* and one small Asian trudging along side by side, mile after mile. To them a white man was usually a missionary or a doctor, so sometimes when we stopped at a village Peter would be asked for medicine. Fortunately, we had been given some aspirins and anti-septic ointment by the American Aid group, so we were able to dispense these. It made us realize what these out-lying villagers lacked and we could see that even in peaceful times, life was difficult for them. I wonder what is happening now in these uncertain times? Governments and armies come and go, but in these villages there is little change – a situation probably not dissimilar to in our Shan villages.

Our companions were all in family groups with little toddlers, their different costumes distinguishing them from each other. They kept pace with their parents until they were really tired, then they were carried piggy-back. When we got to Houie Sai, we were quite sorry to part with them. Many were going further north or crossing the Mekong to Thailand to see their families. No doubt had we been able to converse with them properly, we might have found out that some of them were going as far as the Shan hills.

*Luang Prabang,
the Royal Palace.*

*Wat Visoun.*

*Wat Xiengthong,
Luang Prabang.*

*Champasak family, Chao Siromé and three Princesses.*

From Houie Sai, with the help of the Chao Khouang, the governor of the province, we booked passages on a boat sailing down to Luang Prabang. It took three or more days to prepare the boat. Even then it took several hours on the day of departure for the engineer to decide it was fit to sail. I am glad that in 1995 UNESCO declared the royal capital, Luang Prabang, a World Heritage Site. It was then a city far removed from the hustle and bustle of busy Vientiane. Sedate and calm it gave the impression of a Laos of many centuries ago. We stayed there long enough to climb up the Phou Si hill and to go up river to Pak Ou, the holy caves full of thousands of Buddha images of all sizes. We also went to see the famous Blind Bonze, who stated that Peter would return to Laos a number of times, a prediction which proved to be correct.

Vientiane, the administrative and commercial city was completely different. What was special about Vientiane was the delicately balanced mix of French and Lao cultures, which produced the sophisticated life style of its inhabitants. In those days, there were still a fair number of French families living in the city, including the military which contributed to a feeling of being in a small French town some-where in the Midi. The avenues were tree lined and behind the trees were colonial style houses, and in town there were French bars and restaurants. There was an atmosphere of *joie de vivre*. Only the highly decorated *wats*, standing in their neat squares on most roads which ran through the town, were a reminder that we were indeed in Laos. There was a certain charm – people didn't stand on ceremony and there was none of the stiffness of the British. Everyone was relaxed, – I found the Lao speaking and behaving like the French, effervescent and informal, and it made us feel that we were amongst friends.

Our travel through the villages of the north opened our eyes to so many cultur-al, educational and political problems. No amount of reading about the situation in Laos would have helped us to understand its complexities. The south seemed a different country. We no longer walked but went in army trucks when they were available. We had a *laissez passer* organised for us by Colonel Phoumi Nosavan. This permitted us to travel anywhere with the military convoys. Later, Colonel Phoumi, as General, was destined to become Laos' strongman and leading mem-ber of the right-wing government supported by America.

*Wat Phu,*
*a general view of ruins.*

Travelling in army convoys was not always comfortable nor did they go at sensible times. But we travelled with them nevertheless, as they took us to the places we wanted to visit. I was usually given a seat by the driver and sometimes Peter came in the front as well. But most of the time, he had to ride in the back with the soldiers. The roads were bumpy and uneven, and we were covered with dust when we arrived at our destination. It was wonderful when the camp was near a stream or river, as we could have a proper wash and get rid of the heavy dust.

When we went to Champasak we stayed with Chao Siromé and members of the Royal House of Champasak. Chao Siromé's elder brother was Prince Boun Oum, who was head of the family. In the 1960s, he was one of the Three Princes who were trying to bring a stable government to Laos – Prince Souvanna Phouma, the Neutralist; Prince Boun Oum, leader of the Right-wing faction and Prince Souphanouvong, Left-wing and leader of the Pathet Lao. Despite earlier hopeful signs nothing came out of these meeting and talks as the divisions were too deep.

I had arrived at Bassac in a pair of trousers and not looking as respectfully dressed as I should have been. The three princesses, and sisters of Chao Siromé took one look at me and politely said I should change. They led me to their room upstairs and put me into a Laotian *sarong/phasin* with its beautiful colourful border. Giving me a look of approval, the elder sister said "You are now our sister."

We spent some days with them and were taken to see Wat Phu, a sanctuary of great importance for Champasak. The *wat* is built some way from the Mekong river on a hill. It was believed to have once been an ancient capital of Chenla but little of it remains. Some stone figures and steles had been found earlier on the plain we walked across, though we only saw a few.

Wat Phu had a magical and unknown quality as we gently walked up the steep steps to the top. Over the whole side of the mountain, the trees and jungle creepers had pushed their way through the stairs and the retaining walls of the terraces.

*Wat Phu, a Khmer-style lintel carved with the
Churning of the Ocean of Milk.*

Some attempt at restoration had been made in order to preserve and uncover what
lay beneath the mounds of greenery. Everywhere we walked there protruded an
arm of a statue, heads or feet from the ground, disclosing a wealth of archaeological treasures. No doubt, today with the boom of tourism, some of what has been
excavated will have gone to fill the shelves of antique shops.

The temple itself lies on a large terrace half-way up the hill. Rising behind it
was the grey-black wall of the mountain leaving only enough space for a small
path that zig-zagged up towards some holy place further up. It had become a Buddhist *wat* with serene Buddha images sitting on the altar filled with flowers. The
scent of the frangipani was very strong. Like Luang Prabang, UNESCO has now
given World Heritage status to the temple and its surroundings.

We spent a wonderfully relaxed day wandering around and saw the Buddha's
Footprint and the Divine Spring, amongst other sights. When 5.30 came, the truck
which was to have picked us up, did not appear. Flashes of lightning and thunder
brought on a sudden storm soaking us completely. Eventually when sunlight had
faded into dusk, Chao Siromé led us back towards town. It was a good thirteen
mile walk in the dark, with only the light from a million stars to guide us. We
trudged along the dust road stumbling now and then on stones, or walking into
potholes and, since we were wearing only flip flops our feet were getting sore.
When we saw some lights ahead, we all cheered thinking we were quite close, and
since the straps were rubbing we decided to walk barefoot. But that was not the
best idea, as there was still some kilometres to go. Although we soaked our feet
and massaged them, we suffered from very sore feet for the next few days.

A day or two later, we continued our travels and went to the Khong Falls,
further south. They are called in Lao Si Phan Don meaning the Four Thousand
Islands. These falls stretch over 14,000 yards or nearly 8 km and are the widest in
the world. Six large islands and innumerable small ones lie across the actual falls,

*A sacrifice in a southern
Laotian village.*

dividing the river into a number of rapids, with only two places where a single fall stretches for a thousand yards or half a kilometre wide. Water tumbling down here was an impressive sight.

In the past, the French had invested large amounts of money marking out the channels in an attempt to make the Mekong navigable. They eventually came to the conclusion that it was not feasible while the river was still untamed, since at times its waters can rise twenty or thirty feet with alarming suddenness. During the years before the Japanese war, barges from Saigon and Phnom Penh filled with goods came to the southern tip of Done Khone where the French had built gantries and quays. Across the island they constructed a small gauge railway leading to the northern end, from where the goods were reloaded on to barges and carried up to Vientiane, Luang Prabang and in the wet season, north or Houei Sai.

Nowadays, the Chinese and Vietnamese traders have found it cheaper to carry goods overland from Thailand to Laos. Unfortunately, the little railway at Khone which had been the only one in Laos was no longer used and had become derelict and left to rust.

Near the town of Saravane, we witnessed an annual sacrifice of some ten or more buffaloes in one of the Kha villages. Sacrificial posts had been erected in the middle of the village where the animals were tied. The buffaloes stood solid and impassive as if accepting their fate, while a single cow kept bellowing. Some ten or fifteen warriors carrying long swords in one hand and round wooden shields in the other, danced around the circle of posts to the beat of some gongs and a drum. A glass of *shaum*, a rice liquor, was knocked back whenever the circle had been completed, then they continued their ceremonial dance again. The drinking presumably was to give them courage for what followed – hacking, slashing and plunging of swords into the animals as they sank onto the ground, rolling over and dying. It was a horrifying and upsetting experience.

I hadn't expected such a performance and, unable to continue watching any longer, retired to the other side of the village for the rest of the ceremony. For days after I used to still hear the low call of the tied-up animals, waiting their turn to be slaughtered. We were told that it was an annual ritual demanded of this tribe to ensure that the spirits favoured them for the year with a good harvest. It was also to keep them free from illness and natural disasters. Of course, it also gave the villagers a supply of meat for the whole year.

When our six months in Laos came to an end we were overwhelmed by the kindness and help that so many people had given to us, the number of places we had managed to see, the events we had participated in and the experiences we had gained. It was extraordinary. We had walked, ridden on horses, travelled in pirogues, river boats, small Cessna planes and Air America planes which took us rice dropping. There had also been an assortment of army vehicles and commercial trucks and buses, which took us around the south. Only too well do I remember one bus trip when it had broken down, leaving us sitting in the heat of the day. Peter had no hat on and suffered sun stroke, which put him in bed for some days. We had seen almost all of Laos except for the two provinces of Phong Saly and Samneua, which were under the sole power of the Communist Pathet Lao.

We had made many Laotian friends, as well as friends in the International Control Commission and the diplomatic services. We were sad to say good-bye to all of them, but we knew that we would be returning to Laos, for the Blind Bonze had so predicted. Indeed, we went back to live in Laos twice and Peter spent most of the early 1970s there, covering the war in Cambodia, Laos and Vietnam.

While Peter and I were in Thailand and in Laos, in Burma there had been more political activity and the different splits in the AFPFL were getting worse. A general election had been held and the AFPFL was re-elected. My stepmother who had become increasingly interested in politics and Shan affairs stood for Parliament and was elected as a member of Parliament for Hsenwi, her home state. She had the backing of my father and her brother the Saohpa. At last, she was in her element – an ambition had been fulfilled. It was an opportunity she had been waiting for to make a stand for the Shan people. She was outspoken, and not many politicians accepted her taunting frankness. A somewhat jokey relationship with the Burman politicians was to develop, and I wonder how seriously they took her speeches.

Much later, I was to discover that her sometimes contemptuous manner did not please the Burmans. They may have smiled and laughed with her, but underneath lay a veneer of distrust. Politicians were always watching her, as were the military, waiting for her to make a wrong move. Therefore, in many ways, it was a very good thing she was in England when the coup of 1962 took place. For without a doubt, she would not have been spared and would have had to bear the indignity of being imprisoned.

*Peter and Sanda, a picture taken for a* Sunday
Pictorial *article about their travels in Laos.*

# IX

# *Overland to Rangoon*

## *The Adventure begins*

After we left Laos we first went back to England, with the intention of then returning to Burma, as my father had said he was quite content for us to come back there to live and work. We were pleased and began discussing various ways of getting there.

During our short holiday, the *Sunday Pictorial* having heard we had been to Laos, as yet undiscovered by tourists, decided to do a story on us. They thought its readers would find our trekking through the little-known country hazardous and exciting. When my father saw the series, he told Daw Daw happily, "They had quite an adventure, didn't they?" So I learnt with joy that at last Sao U Hpa had accepted Peter and our marriage.

As luck would have it, while still trying to make up our minds on dates and different airlines, we were told that there was to be a conference of the World Fellowship of Buddhists at Kathmandu in Nepal towards the end of 1956. Christmas Humphreys, who was attending the conference, invited Peter to join the British Buddhist Society delegation. It was such a splendid idea and a good opportunity for us to visit Nepal, so the invitation was accepted happily.

Peter, who was always adventurous and loved travelling, wondered if we might think of driving overland as flying to Kathmandu was somewhat boring and by driving, we could visit several countries which we wouldn't otherwise see. If we started sometime in September, we could spend two month travelling and taking in the beauty and history of each country. Peter's additional argument for making such a trip was that once we had attended the conference, we could see Nepal at our leisure. Then driving on to Burma, we would see the tea plantations in Assam, the Stilwell Road, the Kachin hills and the northern Shan States. What's more after that long trip, we would have a Land Rover to use in Rangoon while living there. Peter was persuasive and it sounded like a good idea. Nevertheless, I accepted the plan with some apprehension.

Having made the decision, we went to Solihull and bought a long wheel-base Land Rover for the journey. Since it was our first Land Rover, the company took a paternal interest, with technicians at Solihull offering to give Peter some tips, while I was given a few lessons on how to use the gears properly and handle the car in four-wheel drive. They were kind enough also to give us the necessary tools we might need on the marathon trip.

Peter had always talked about Land Rovers, saying they had the best engines, and once he had owned one, he invariably insisted on buying a Land Rover each time we needed a new car. I suppose Hong Kong was the only place in our years in Southeast Asia, where we didn't drive around in a Land Rover. Even when we

*At Land Rover's in Solihull,
with instructor.*

*Filling up our jerry cans.*

*Jimmy and Dorothy
Green, centre, at the
farewell party.*

lived in England, and later in Spain and France, the Land Rover was always our car. Peter had no difficulty with its size. It fitted him beautifully. As for me, I loved driving a Land Rover, because I felt very safe and it was great when smaller cars gave way to me.

Peter was in his element preparing for the trip. We spent long hours at Embassies getting our visas, followed by jabs for yellow fever and the rest. We laid out maps and began planning out our route. Mobilgas and Metal Box decided to sponsor us, the former giving us petrol, the later a carton or two of tinned soup. The tins were very convenient as when the wick in the middle of the can was lit, it warmed up the soup. Though perfectly safe, I wondered if an odd tin might blow up, but luckily it never happened.

The Oxford and Cambridge-Far Eastern Expedition had gone a year or so before, paving the way not only for us, but for numerous others who were keen to make the overland journey. Many Australians and New Zealanders went as far as India, then shipped themselves home through Singapore.

The next person to follow the Oxford and Cambridge expedition to Singapore, was Group Captain Peter Townsend, who was some weeks ahead of us. Unlike the Far Eastern Expedition, we did not have to make elaborate plans as by then many of the routes were open. Also the countries we had feared might be strict or difficult about visas and permits, were not. The customs and police at the frontiers also seemed to have become used to seeing enthusiasts such as us wanting to drive for hundreds of miles. They probably thought that we were all quite mad, wanting to make these uncomfortable journeys.

Before setting off we had a small leaving party attended by some twenty of our friends, including Jimmy and Dorothy Green, who had been friends to my family in the Shan States. We took about ten days or so to drive across Europe. We stayed a few days in Paris, then drove on to Munich where we stayed for four or five days. It was my first visit to Germany and I was impressed by the little hotel which was spotlessly clean. We visited the mediaeval castle which Peter described as being an old building "heavily romantic and full of strength, massive and huge, with an ability to defend itself against all comers". It was indeed imposing. We went to a Hofbrauhaus too, having heard so much about them, and found the place filled with jolly, friendly people.

Then on to Stuttgart and to Graz. Once we crossed the frontier into Yugoslavia, we began to feel uncomfortable and drove on to Zagreb and Belgrade. During our first day, we had parked our car near the museum, but when we returned we found one of our windows broken. Before we could have it mended, another window was broken during the night. It was a nuisance. The Land Rover agent kept the car for a few days, since he had to order new glass panes to have them fixed. In the meantime, the Tourist agency put us into the care of a young student, who was eager to learn English. He had been instructed to show us around the city. I suppose he was in fact our minder. We tried to make the most of the sightseeing, but we didn't feel in the mood nor very cheerful. It was a relief when the windows were replaced, and a greater joy when we got our passports back from the hotel. We were at last able to leave Belgrade.

Although we were still in Yugoslavia, we felt free being able to continue on our journey, but our joy was short lived. On our drive down to Skopje, we realized there was a black saloon car behind us, which did not overtake though there were a number of opportunities to do so. Were we being followed, we wondered feeling somewhat annoyed. When we stopped to have a picnic lunch by the roadside, we were glad to see the car drive past. Then when we continued, we found them parked a few kilometres ahead. It was becoming unnerving, but we decided not to worry and carried on driving. There was not much traffic that day but towards dusk as we were nearing Skopje, we found groups of families trudging along the road. Most of the women wore long black skirts and shawls over their heads. They looked drab and solemn, making us feel sorry for their gloom and the sombre atmosphere created. They were quite unlike a crowd one would have seen in Asia when everyone talks all at the same time. Even on sad occasions, there were generally cheerful faces and excited chatter.

The black saloon was again parked on the side of the road, and, passing by, we saw them start following us again. When we got to the suburbs of the city, the black limousine drove past. The two men waved at us as the car disappeared into the distance. Who were they? Anyway, whoever they were, they must have found it dull following us, as we hadn't stopped to talk to anyone or even to take photographs of the lovely scenery. Maybe we were in a sensitive area we had not been told about.

In Skopje, we came across eight Australians who were in a large van making the same overland drive as ourselves. They were a pleasant group. There was also a New Zealand couple, a brother and a sister, who turned up in a Land Rover. They were monarchists, and didn't like rude remarks being made about royalty. Anyway, since we kept to our own schedules, driving along at our own speed and time, we didn't meet them again until Kerman where they were buying a carpet.

We were certainly glad to cross into Greece where we found the customs officials in good humour and very helpful. What a contrast to the Yugoslav officials who looked glum and despondent. It was late afternoon when we reached Salonika. The sparkling sea looked so inviting that we jumped in and had a quick swim. We didn't find the water all that warm though. The Mobilgas representative who had come to meet us had also brought a photographer along. After a few poses, and a discussion on where we might spend the night, the men went off. So, we were very surprised the next morning to see ourselves in the newspapers.

We drove along the picturesque coast admiring the dazzling Aegean Sea as we crossed into Turkey. The view of Istanbul was breathtaking. We managed to get ourselves to the Park Hotel after several wrong turnings. The hotel received us in a grand manner, as if it was a daily occurrence for them to welcome two apparently dirty, dusty looking people in an equally dusty Land Rover. It was a luxury and we felt we deserved it after spending nights in the car on route. Our stay was so enjoyable, that we decided we would sleep in the Land Rover for a few nights as we travelled, but when we came to a city we would splash out and treat ourselves to a good hotel. As it turned out, these were the only times when we could get a decent night's sleep, and get ourselves and our clothes washed.

For our stay of three or four days in Istanbul we became tourists going to the museums and visiting both Saint Sophia, the magnificent domed structure and the Blue Mosque, with its spectacular minarets. We only managed to see the outside of the Topkapi Palace as the place was closed to visitors that day. It was such a shame as I was looking forward to seeing the famous gems. Galata market was enormous – so full of glitter and thousands of tempting things, it was bewildering to walk through.

*Mapping our route with the Mobilgas representative, Salonika.*

Apart from Land Rover agents, Peter had arranged with the Automobile Association and Mobilgas in London, that we could contact their representatives whenever we reached one of the major cities. We had also asked if the British Consul could keep our mail for us. It was reassuring for us to have someone we could turn to if and when we needed help. The assistance these people gave us was invaluable, as we made our way across the different countries of the Middle East.

Peter recorded how after leaving Istanbul and crossing the Bosphorus, we lost our way several times, wasting precious time, before we reached the main road to the capital, Ankara. It was a good road and we pushed on as rapidly as possible as there were probably as many as 300 miles to go. "The country was rolling, it being plateau land and the driving was easy, we did not eat again, but kept on until we were pretty certain that the lights of Ankara were ahead of us and going by the map, stopped at a Mobilgas station on the left of the aerodrome. As soon as it was light, Sanda was awake and we drove on over the hill top until we could find a quieter place to have breakfast ..." Presumably it was a long hard drive, with Peter at the wheel all through the night, while he kindly let me sleep.

From Ankara, we began our drive towards Adana in the south, on the Mediterranean coast. Though the road was over hilly terrain, it had a good surface and Peter drove at full speed for we seemed to be the only ones on the road. Ankara had been somewhat depressing, with all the restrictions and permits we had to acquire to drive through the military zones. So we felt free and happy to be on our way again in the brilliant sun.

By the time we reached the Cilician gorge it was evening. We had still a long way to go so we drove on though the narrow and very twisty gorge, its mighty cliffs towering above us. It was a precipitous road and we went on and on, finding nowhere to park as we continued climbing. Then suddenly in front of us was a bus full of people, stranded, having run out of petrol. It was fortunate that we carried extra petrol so we were able to give them a full jerry can.

We drove on in search of a place to stop for the night and eventually found a small hotel standing on the edge of a precipice. It seemed a scary place to live, deep in the middle of the mountains. The proprietor came out and invited us in, but we declined. He, however, was a kindly man and brought us coffee to keep us warm.

Next day we continued through the gorge, gradually descending to the plateau. At Adana, we crossed the stone bridge which spanned the Seyhan river, and joined groups of men down below who were washing their horses in the river. We decided to wash the Land Rover too and spent a leisurely hour paddling around.

As we drove on, we were tempted to stop at one or two castles which we could see perched on top of the hills. We attempted to reach one but saw that the hill was going to be too steep to drive down. Also a river lay at the bottom whose banks sloped down at right angles. We realized that if we were really keen to see it, we would have to walk up, so regrettably gave up that idea. This medieval Crusader castle seemed as impregnable as it must have been in the olden days.

## On guard

At the Turkish border we had no trouble, but there was a small incident on the other side, which put us on our guard. While Peter was inside the Syrian Sûreté building, I sat waiting in our fully loaded car looking at a map of the area, when a guard walked over and asked to see the map too. For a moment he seemed to be pondering something, then suddenly taking out a pen he began scratching out Israel, shouting "no! no! no!". He would probably have destroyed the map, had Peter not come back to the car at that moment. Peter saw that we were in one of those tricky situations where tact was needed. He surmised that the best solution was to say nothing and to act as if nothing had happened. With a friendly gesture he offered him a cigarette. Taking it, the soldier walked off quite content, waving to us as we drove away. It made us realize the extent of hatred and tension which existed, and how even though not provoked, anger can easily spring up. Since we had several more days driving through the Middle East, we decided to try and be extra careful not to say anything that might upset anyone.

Eventually we got to Damascus at about midnight. The next morning Peter went out to buy *The Times*, but he was to be disappointed. After finding the Street called Straight, we decided to leave Damascus. As it was a Friday and a holiday, there was little we could do. We drove on to Jordan where we spent a night or two in the capital, Amman, and went on to the Dead Sea. Here, we went for a swim and found ourselves floating with no effort, which was a strange sensation.

We drove further south to Al-Aqaba as we wanted to see Petra. We were not to be disappointed. "The rose-red city, half as old as time" as Petra is popularly called, was an amazing place. Approaching it from the east riding through a narrow, darkened gorge or *siq*, it was magnificent to see facing us a stunning building of changing colours. First it looked rose, then it became red with a tinge of yellow and streaks of purple in the sandstone rocks from which it was built. Behind it, and around, were other buildings of varying sizes, some temples others tombs, all in the same hue glistening in the bright sunshine. It was a superb day of exploration.

Back in Amman we spent another day or two, then crossed over to Iraq. From Baghdad we went straight on to Kirkuk, where we were to spend a few days with the oil companies. We learnt a great deal about the oil industry as we were taken around the oil fields and oil wells. The towering structures were indeed remarkable. We were very well cared for and had a few days of luxury in this remote region of north-eastern Iraq. Much of the area is considered Kurdish territory and today Kirkuk is claimed by the Kurds. We also went to see the "ever-lasting fires" which supposedly had been burning since time immemorial. In fact, there wasn't much to see except for two flames which spouted about six inches high from the ground within an enclosure.

In 1956 it was still possible to drive through these countries fairly safely, and we made our way through the Middle East without much fear. Although we had to keep going to arrive in Kathmandu in time for the conference, we did not hurry unduly. Most of the roads in Iran were good and we went around visiting the various historical sites. Persepolis was one place we wanted to see in particular. It lay just over 30 miles northeast of Shiraz, in south-western Iran.

In those days, before the restoration that was carried out later, it was an incredible sight. The tall columns gave a feeling of majesty, the wide terrace held proud sculptures and carvings which had been wrecked. Huge marble-like rocks that had once formed parts of buildings, lay around in ruins. We wandered through the remains trying to recapture their ancient splendour. It was Darius the Great (r. 522-486 BC), who built this magnificent place and Alexander the Great, who destroyed it.

We went on to Kerman, the city best known for Persian carpets. We spent a day or two watching carpets being woven and found the rocks along the river side covered by all sizes of carpets which had been washed and left to dry in the sun. It was a colourful picture. We couldn't afford to buy a carpet, but the New Zealand couple we had met earlier, found one to take home. "Seventy-five pounds!", we exclaimed, saying we thought the price quite exorbitant. Today's price undoubtedly would be much more.

When we left Kerman, on a mad impulse, we decided it would be quicker to drive straight across the desert rather than the over 330 miles to get to Zahedan. Many had done that drive following other people's tire marks, and we were told there were oases on the way where villagers were helpful. We were, therefore, confidant we could do the same. The trouble was that after some hours, we were lost. We cursed our stupidity, but there was little we could do but press on. Luckily, Peter had brought a compass, so at least we could head east towards Zahedan.

Suddenly we saw clouds of dust coming from different directions, and when two cars came into view, we thought we were in luck. Now we could ask for directions. But they didn't look at all friendly. Before we knew it, they had got out of their cars, and pointing guns at us, signalled for us to step down from the Land Rover.

One of them shouted something which we didn't understand. Then Peter shouted back saying, "We are English".

"You Israelis? Where you come from? You got guns?"

"No!" we both shouted back.

They seemed to relax then and one of them came over to us. It must have been the English speaker. He wanted to search our car, so we said go ahead. But instead, he went back to his group and they had a conference. The guns were no longer pointed at us but they wanted more questions answered. We told the young man we had driven from England and had just come from Kerman. We had lost our way and we wanted to go to Zahedan. He called back to his friends and they laughed. In reality, we must have looked a harmless pair – Peter in his

*Persepolis, the great arches.*

shorts and bare feet, while I must have looked very small and frightened. What an unusual couple they must have thought. Then the English speaker with a grand gesture said that one of the cars would take us to the road which led to Zahedan. What a relief!

We thanked them and once in the car, Peter said what a good thing it was that we had decided not to carry any weapons. How right he was. It was quite a few hours before we got to the main road and we were grateful to have been brought all the way. With a wave from the men, their car drove off in a different direction. We couldn't work out who they were, but were grateful to be back on a road, thanks to them, with the knowledge that we were going in the right direction.

There is an extraordinary feeling of exhilaration driving through deserts – the endless expanse of land that stretches towards the horizon as it meets the deep blue of the sky. Unbelievably, we felt free and as if we were floating on air. There was hardly any traffic and we could drive at any speed we wanted. With the windows wide open, a warm, soft breeze blew across our faces, sweeping back our hair as we drove. It was a joy. Sometimes we slowed down, when a shimmering on the road surface looked as if something might be approaching, but after the car had gone some distance, we would find that it was only a mirage. Sometimes whiffs of cloud arose which then evaporated into thin air.

It is an experience one does not easily forget, and we were lucky enough to drive through the Middle East three times – first in 1956, then in 1959, when we took the Land Rover back to London, and the last long drive when we left Oman for London, about 1987.

On the last occasion, once we had left Abu Dhabi, we soon found ourselves driving along mile after mile of excellent road with the pipeline on one side, and vast stretches of desert on the other. Along some stretches of the country, there were endless fields of green, watered by giant water sprays which stretched to lengths of twenty metres or more. Imagine fields of corn in the middle of the desert. It was incredible. At other times when we stopped for a break, we would see a mass of tiny flowers covering patches of the desert. Here the mirages appeared as sheets of glass suspended in mid-air. We felt we were drifting above the vast sea of sand.


## The Suez Crisis

We arrived at Zahedan, on the Iran-Pakistan border about dusk. As we drove through the small town, people stopped and looked at us. We slowed down, hoping to ask someone where we could find a hotel. But just then we came across a group of young boys who began throwing stones at us. We wondered why they were behaving in this manner and drove off quickly. It seemed very strange, since it was the first time we had ever been greeted in this way. We felt the urgency of seeking out either the Pakistani or Indian Consulates, to find out why they were so unfriendly here.

It wasn't long before we found the Indian Embassy. The Consul told us that the crisis over Suez had created a lot of anti-British feeling, and he wasn't surprised we had had trouble. Not having read a newspaper for some time, the Suez affair was unwelcome news to us. We were relieved, however, that we were no longer driving across the Middle East.

He explained that seeing a strange vehicle, an English Land Rover at that, the frustrated boys probably felt they had the right to take it out on us. Not looking forward to having more trouble, we asked " If that is the case, will you please let us park in your compound for the night?" He got into a panic, shaking his head from side to side in an agitated manner and said, "No, the best possible place, you know, I think, is in the school compound. It is not far from here, only a little way from the town".

Neither Peter nor I liked the idea, but there was nothing else we could do. We thought perhaps it would be safe, since it was on the outskirts of the town. We also understood his feelings – if anything were to happen to us, he would prefer it to happen elsewhere, rather than inside his compound. Anyway, he probably didn't want his Consulate to be wrecked by irresponsible youths.

Gone were our dreams of having a comfortable night on a bed and a hot meal of rice and mutton curry. Instead we had a tin of spam, our last tin as it turned out, and some *nan* we had bought in Kerman. We couldn't even console ourselves with a glass of wine, as we carried neither beer or wine since we were travelling through Muslim countries.

The next morning when we called on the Consul, he seemed pleased to see that we were still alive and well. Without hesitation, he helped us with formalities and various passes we needed to carry on with our journey. It was a long drive through desolate terrain with both rocky and sandy stretches, though the road itself was fairly good.

The one-time British fort of the North West Frontier, Quetta, is situated some 5,500 ft above sea level and retains much of its military atmosphere. In earlier times, the Baluchi were nomads but nowadays they have settled with a province of their own, and Quetta is a divisional and district headquarters of Baluchistan. Most of the men are tough looking with thick black beards, their rifles slung across their shoulders. Watching the television news or documentaries on Afghanistan these days, I would find it difficult to distinguish them from the Baluchis.

Since we were in this region of the great Indus civilization, we felt we should go to Harappa, which was further along our route to Lahore. Peter had been keen to see Mohenjo-daro, a similar archaeological site which was better known and larger on the Indus River. However, as it was some 400 miles to the southeast, we knew we didn't have enough time. Harappa was excavated by the archaeologist Sir John Marshall in the early 1920s. His findings revealed that Indian prehistory dated back to about 3,500 BC, further than previously thought.

There are other remains of the Indus Valley culture to be found around the valley itself and in the Punjab. It was thought that these mainly agricultural people at the height of their civilization had links with ancient Mesopotamia. Their trade was carried out by sea and overland through present Baluchistan. No one is quite certain why this civilization mysteriously disappeared. Two theories have been put forward – the destructive flooding of the Indus could have been one cause, the other that a considerable influx of Aryans, the Indo-Europeans, centuries ago, could have swamped these peoples of whom little is known.

The remains of the ruins were not as exciting as expected. What we saw was a citadel surrounded by mud-brick constructions forming low walls and ramparts. Some uniform and rectangular remains were said to be workers' quarters, while other larger complexes were thought to be public buildings. Some of the limestone sculptures, along with seals, had been removed to a museum in Delhi, so it was not surprising that we did not find a great deal to see at Harappa. However, there was still some excavation work being done at that time, so presumably they may now have found some other sculptures, structures and artefacts.

We spent a few days in Lahore and continued the over 300 mile drive to Delhi. We had planned to stop there for a day or two, before driving up to Kathmandu. Peter, however, began feeling unwell with no idea of what was causing it. So we thought the best thing to do was to fly, instead of making the strenuous drive up the mountains, for Kathmandu is situated some 7,000 ft above sea level. We left the Land Rover behind in Delhi to pick up when the conference was over.

## Kathmandu

On the first day of the Conference, while Peter was taping one of the speeches, he suddenly said, "I don't think I can go on making the recording, I really feel worse than I did in Delhi." When I looked at him, his face was quite yellow.

We didn't try to guess what it could be, but left everything and immediately went in search of a doctor. We found Dr Price, an American doctor, who took one gasp and sent Peter straight to bed saying it was a bad attack of hepatitis, and that he must stay horizontal for at least the next six weeks. What a blessing to find an efficient and capable doctor. Peter was relieved to know what he was suffering from, but unhappy that he had to give up his work at the conference.

Although the conquest of Mount Everest by Sir Edmund Hilary and Tenzing Norgay in 1956 had popularised Nepal, the hordes of tourists and 'flower children' had not yet arrived. So the only large hotel then was the Royal Hotel.

*Christmas Humphreys, seated centre and other delegates to the World Fellowship of Buddhists Conference, Kathmandu.*

*Chinese premier Chou En-lai visiting*
*Kathmandu while we were there.*

A former royal palace of the Rana Family, it was run by Boris, a White Russian. Boris was somewhat stout and heavy by the time we met him, but he had once danced in Diaghilev's ballet troupe, the Ballet Russe. The hotel was large and richly decorated with spacious rooms and marble baths in the bathrooms. As it was winter, and there was no heating in the bathroom, I found that there was always a problem having a long, hot bath in the marble tub, as the marble soon cooled down the bath water, and left me freezing.

The Yak and Yeti bar was a great meeting place for residents and travellers alike, where everyone relaxed and listened to Boris, as he entertained us with his delightful reminiscences of his earlier days as a ballet dancer, his hunts with the Princes or his encounters with his first American tourists. The last often refused to eat any local food, but Boris' mouth-watering dish of wild boar soon won them over. We used to sit around a big, cheerful fire which was kept burning all day.

The Yak and Yeti was well-known throughout India and the rest of Asia, becoming synonymous with its owner. He was a great character and extremely kind. When Peter took ill, Boris told us we could stay for as long as it took him to get well. During the three months that we were there he took personal care of Peter, making sure that Dr Price's suggested diet was strictly followed. He called on Peter nearly very day and they became great friends. When we eventually left, Boris let us pay only a minimum for our stay, saying that when we had made our fortune, we could repay him everything we owed. In 1976, he visited us in Singapore and we had a marvellous reunion. It was the last time that we ever saw him.

*Kathmandu, prayer wheels.*

*Kathmandu, Kali figure.*

*Kathmandu, Peter with Boris, the white Russian Manager of the Royal Hotel.*

*Kathmandu, Bodhnath temple with streamers and the all-seeing eyes of the Buddha.*

Some weeks later, Peter began feeling better so he sent me down to Delhi to to collect our mail and attend to any administrative chores which we had left undone, thinking we'd be back in a week or so. It was fortunate, too, that Group Captain Peter Townsend happened to be in town. When I went to see him he was very helpful, giving me the addresses of people I should contact in Delhi for the next stage of our journey to Burma. As he was coming up to Kathmandu, it was arranged that we should meet again, since he wanted to talk to Peter as well. Peter Townsend was charming and courteous, and gave us much encouragement. He left about six weeks before us so we never caught up with him to thank him for his kindness. However, twenty years later the two Peters met in the air, when they were both flying to Singapore. Since we were living in Singapore then, we were able to invite him home to repay him for his kindness and help.

As soon as Peter was allowed to be up and about, we took walks around Kathmandu to see the many temples that were scattered in and around the capital. Worshippers came from all over Nepal, India and Tibet to these Buddhist and Hindu temples which were regarded as very sacred. The temple at Bodhnath, with its enormous painted eyes on all four sides of the base of the spire, looked out protectively over the valleys and the mountains. It was said to represent the "all seeing eyes of the Buddha". We went several times as well to the Pashupati temple on the Baghmati River, which was built like a pagoda, though it was a Hindu temple.

There was also much to see in the Hanuman Dhoka, where the old palaces of the Nepalese kings stood. There were temples with differing architecture, and a tall column which supported a bronze kneeling image of the eighteenth century ruler, King Bhupatindra. By the temples, there were usually a number of Tibetan monks in their dark brown-purplish robes, walking round and round with their prayer wheels. There were also other Tibetans who had come to sell their wares of herbs and semi-precious stones, such as turquoise.

Walking through the older parts of the city was always enjoyable as we watched the young men in their Nepali caps, dressed similarly in tight, white trousers, long flowing shirts and dark waist-coats as they strolled down the streets. An occasional person supported a *kukris*, the lethal curved, Nepali knife, which the Gurkha troops used against their enemies. In the older streets of Kathmandu anyone walking through the narrow lanes could see into the first floor through the highly decorated windows, as the houses were built low. Elsewhere around town and in the market, the brightly dressed women chatted happily. Gurkha men and women, their heavy loads on their backs, were also a familiar sight.

A week or so before we left, there was a scare. It was rumoured that a Yeti, an abominable snowman, had come down from the Himalayas for villagers had seen his footprints. Of course with a story like that, journalists flew in to authenticate the tale. All-night excursions were made by some, but no one found the Yeti and the story died out as quickly as it had sprung up. One of the journalists, Desmond Doig, from the *New Statesman* of India stayed behind. He was a walking encyclopaedia of Nepal and its neighbouring kingdoms of Sikkim and Bhutan. Whenever a question was asked about these countries, Desmond always had the answer.

We had had a marvellous time in Kathmandu, but by mid-February it was time to continue our journey. We decided to divert from our planned route and to go to Darjeeling, one of India's famous hill stations. An introduction to a Mrs

Morgan, a long-time resident of Darjeeling was given to us by Desmond. It was quite a climb, but, once there, the view was spectacular with massive mountain ranges on one side and the sheer drop on the other to the valley of the great Rangit River. Darjeeling sits on a long, narrow ridge on the side of the Sikkim Himalayas rising to well over 2,500 metres. Rhododendron and magnolias grew in abundance and the air was fresh and clean.

We had not known that Mrs Morgan was a women who still thought and lived in the old style of the British Raj. Now she was confronted by a couple, an Englishman and an Asian woman, who were actually married. To be fair to her, she accepted us with good grace and sat us down to tea in a beautifully laid-out garden. She told the butler to bring our suitcases in and to lay out our evening clothes. Normally, we would have been shattered. But fortunately Peter was pre-pared with his black tie and jacket, as we had hoped to see Queen Dina of Jordan in Amman when we passed through. Dina had been two years ahead of me at Girton, and, when she heard we were going to make the overland trip, she invited us to call on her when we reached Amman. Regrettably, we arrived too late, for she had just left the capital when we got to Jordan. When we went to the palace to make an appointment, we were told that she had gone away, and it was not known when she would return. Of course, she never did return.

Mrs Morgan gave us two very enjoyable days. Peter charmed her completely, and we must have gone up in her estimation when she saw that Peter travelled with his dinner jacket and black tie. It certainly put him in her good books. When we left, she gave us a letter of introduction to one of her tea-planter friends in Shil-long. Driving through the tea plantations of Assam was tremendously restful as we looked out onto a never-ending expanse of green.

## The Hukawng Valley

After a couple of days we started on our drive down the Ledo or Stilwell road. Ledo was its original name but during the war it was renamed after General Stil-well, an American general working with the Chinese troops of Chiang Kai-Shek, who were rebuilding this section of the 478 mile stretch which went through Myitkyina and on to Lashio in Hsenwi State. From Lashio, the 717 mile road linked with the Burma Road which led up to Kunming in China.

Having obtained our exit passes from the North East Frontier Agency, we drove to the Pang Sau Pass which was about 56 miles from Digboi, the Indian out-post. Once inside the Burma border, we began our drive through no man's land.

The roads we had travelled on up to now, had still been roads, whatever their condition. We had driven along good asphalt and gravel roads, and some distances along dust roads – the road we were now facing wasn't really a road at all. It seemed that since the Japanese war, no Rangoon government had thought of its upkeep. However, it was again thanks to the Far Eastern Expedition and to Group Captain Townsend who had driven over these parts only three months earlier, that Peter and I were able to pick our way through the undergrowth, despite it being difficult to see where the jungle ended and the road began.

Some bridges were passable while others had deteriorated. We took it in turns to check if we could drive across a bridge or not, but most of the time we used to drive down to the river bed then through the river, which sometimes was a gently-flowing stream, but at others a rushing torrent. With no way of knowing how deep the water was, one of us always wadded across. On these occasions, it was Peter who did the driving since we didn't want to get stuck in the middle of a river.

Earlier on, when we had to drive downstream across some rice fields to find a suitable spot to cross, I had stranded the Land Rover on a bund. Beautifully balanced right in the middle, it was not my moment of glory. "Now you've done it. Why weren't you looking where you were going?" Peter shouted, when he had got out of the car and saw our predicament. We had a winch, but we had to find a suitable tree. Peter having served in the army as a Bombay Sapper and Miner, soon worked out what we could do. We had fortunately been given two *kukris* by Nepalese friends, so we were able first to cut branches, then pile them up on either side of the bund, in order to ease the wheels over the edge. I am not sure how long we spent working on this, but once when Peter looked up he saw a Naga observing him from a distance.

"Don't look now, but I think we have company. Don't show any fear.", Peter muttered, adding as an afterthought to reassure me: "We are nearly finished."

Of course, in the days before the war, the Nagas were known to be headhunters. For the first time since driving along this forsaken road, I did begin to feel a little frightened. I began to wonder if he was alone, or if there were also others watching us. Then I reminded myself, that they must also have watched Peter Townsend struggling along by himself; if he had got through, we must be all right. It probably took another ten minutes or so, which seemed much longer, before Peter could drive the car off the bund and winch it across the wet field. We took no risks after that, often using the winch whenever we felt it was necessary.

We were to learn later that Fred Warner, at that time the First Secretary at the British Embassy in Rangoon, had gone up to escort Peter Townsend over the rough jungle road and eastwards through the Shan States to Kengtung. They spent several days repairing various bridges here and there, and making stretches of road passable as they drove through the dense jungle. On New Year's Eve 1956-1957, they found themselves in a bamboo hut with three Chinese muleteers and five Nagas, which was hardly where either of these two elegant gentlemen would have wished to be on such a night.

Fred was full of energy and fun and we became firm friends. We were to meet him again at his other postings after he had left Rangoon. At one, he gave us a never-to-be-forgotten seafood lunch in Piraeus when we called on him in Athens on our second overland trip with Martin Morland. When we went back to Laos later in 1966, he was then the British Ambassador. There he became not only our friend, but also that of my family.

When we came to the Burma border, the troops stationed there were surprised and soon surrounded us. They couldn't believe we had driven from India, let alone from England. Here was a six-foot plus Englishman and a not quite five-foot Shan woman, saying they had driven for miles and wanted to go to Rangoon. They took our passports and, looking through mine slowly, one of the officers asked, "So you are the daughter of our President?"

"Yes, he is now the Speaker of the House of Nationalities", I replied.

They decided to ring through to their HQ to check. Then after another telephone call, we were told it was all right for us to continue.

In the meantime, one or two of the younger officers told us that they hadn't been paid for months, "*Amah gyi*, (big sister in Burmese), will you please tell our commander in Mandalay, to send us our pay?" they pleaded. I am afraid we never did manage to pass on the message to their superiors.

We followed the road to Myitkyina, remembering the terrible trek thousands had made fleeing from the advancing Japanese. Many had hopes and dreams for the future as they tried to escape from what they imagined they might face if they stayed behind. Little did they know that it was not only disease and hunger, but the environment itself, with its unfriendly climatic conditions and its teeming insects, which were the killers. In places, it was sinister and uncanny,  as if the ghosts of the thousands who had died in this valley were still wandering around.

In November 2005, the Oxford and Cambridge team came together to celebrate the 50th anniversary of their overland journey. The six enterprising undergraduates, five from Cambridge and one from Oxford, certainly inspired many of us to follow suit. In his book *First Overland*[32] published in 1957, Tim Slessor recounts their exciting journey and the division of labour and responsibilities shared amongst the six of them. The book was reprinted to commemorate the occasion and they were pleased to sell a large number of copies on that night. It was marvellous listening to their accounts and seeing the photographs and film taken of the expedition by Antony Barrington Brown. Many of the brilliant shots so reminded me of our own journey – the river crossings, the unmade roads, the shared memories of no man's land and the Burma Road. Alas for me, there were no such souvenirs as the few pictures Peter took were lost when we posted them to England by sea mail.

Once we had crossed the border, our minds were set on reaching Rangoon as soon as possible. It felt unreal that we had driven all those miles and were at last in Burma. We kept saying to each other, another few days and we should be there. I am not too sure, but I don't think we even contemplated sightseeing in Mandalay or driving to Maymyo. It was March, and it was very, very hot, even for Peter, who lapped up the heat. We thought that we could come to these places another time – as we all know too well that 'sometime' rarely ever happens.

It was a wonderful journey to have made. The overland trip was not only an adventure but it had taught us a great deal, giving us a wider perspective on the countries we passed though and their peoples. How fortunate we were, for, although we were to drive back overland two years later, there is little doubt that today such journeys are not easy to make, until sensitive political issues are settled in the Middle East.

In some ways, I think that, unconsciously, we had wanted to prove to my father that we were prepared for any challenges we might have to face. Although he had accepted our marriage and was content to have us come to Burma to live, we felt we had to be worthy of his acceptance.

Many of our conversations during the journey were of the people we had met, of those who had shown us much kindness and were to become friends. Through-out our six months, we had not met any of our friends, so imagine our great surprise when filling up our Land Rover at the petrol pump in Lashio, that the other person doing the same thing was Oz Robinson, a Cambridge friend we had not seen since coming down. He was now in the Foreign Office and had been posted to Rangoon. He told us that the Consulate in Maymyo was closed for the time being, and any consular matters were conducted from Rangoon. For this reason he was travelling in the area, and it was our good luck to have met him. It was wonderful to know that Oz was stationed in Rangoon. How fortunate to have met him, as it made our task of finding directions for the route to Rangoon so much easier. Armed with his instructions, we proceeded happily on our way.

When we arrived in Rangoon our speedometer showed 14,522 miles. We had left London on 9th September, 1956, and had arrived on 11th March, 1957. What a journey! What an experience!

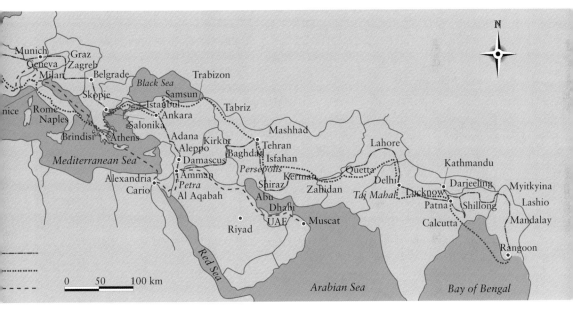

*A sketch map showing our three overland journeys: 1956, 1959 and 1987.*

*The Shwe Dagon Pagoda,*
*Rangoon.*

# X

# *Return to Burma*

## *Living in Rangoon*

We reached Rangoon in less than a month after leaving Kathmandu. It was a marvellous homecoming, as even Sao U Hpa came out to meet us as we drove in to the compound. He was happy we had made the overland journey safely and proudly took us to a flat he was giving us, behind the big house above the garages. Peter and I were overjoyed by this gesture of generosity.

We had arrived and so began our life in Rangoon where we thought we would be living for the rest of our lives. In fact, we only had four years, but they were four years of happiness in which I re-discovered my family. Peter too found himself enveloped by the family and to me, Sao U Hpa was no longer just a father in name only or a father I feared. True, behind those gold-rimmed spectacles, he wore a stern impassive face and was reserved, but behind the mask he never missed a good joke and enjoyed a laugh.

*Family in Rangoon, including
Peter and myself, 1960.*

I found him more relaxed and more lenient. I assumed it was because he had for the last ten years been living with a younger family. When the family came to live in Rangoon, Myee Myee, the third son, was about three years old and the younger two were born while he was President. They had moved into the present house on Kokine Road in 1953. It was a large house, with a history of Jewish and Indian riches, and possibly evil spirits lurking from the time when it was a Kempeitai headquarters during the Japanese occupation.

The house, however, was certainly much, much smaller than the Haw, where there were many more rooms and halls. In my childhood, I had been relegated to the women's quarters or to the halls if I wanted to run around. Later, going to boarding school, I naturally saw my father infrequently. But now the younger children had the advantage of being around him daily, which led to their having an informal and normal family life. Much of the "dos and don'ts" had been relaxed, and there was less rigidity in the upbringing of these siblings.

Leun, my youngest sister once said to me, "Pyi Sanda, elder sister, I believe when you were children, Sao U Hpa used to be very strict with you and all the other older brothers and sisters. Is that true? He was more lenient with us, the younger ones."

My reply was, "Yes, it certainly was very different." But then there was a good twenty year's gap between Leun and myself. Also by then, Sao U Hpa had adapted to living in a smaller house and had learnt how to cope with a young family.

Being back in Burma also gave me an opportunity to take Peter to visit Yawnghwe and Taunggyi. We stayed with my elder brother who was living in the Haw as acting Saohpa and Daw Daw was also living there at that time. Peter was thrilled to see where I had grown up and loved walking in the grounds and gardens. As far as I was concerned, nothing had changed except that we now had electricity. Little did I know that this was the last time I was to see my beloved home.

*Peter and I visit family in Yawnghwe 1958.*

*Daw Daw with my young brother Papu, in Taunggyi.*

*Sao U Hpa's visit to Moscow.*

My father was always a devout Buddhist, but now he had taken up meditation seriously. He used to take his young sons, and sometimes Peter, to meditate together. One of his major aims was to get the *Tripitaka* translated into Shan and published. As his official duties became lighter, he was able to oversee this work being done in a Buddhist Centre in Panglong. His enthusiasm for this venture led young Sangha and students alike to make further attempts at reviving Shan language and literature.

Soon to be free from his state duties as the Speaker of the House of Nationalities, Sao U Hpa was able to take a deeper look around him and to access conditions within the Shan States and his own state of Yawnghwe. Since the formation of the Union, there had been a growing number of problems and disputes, one of them being discrepancies in the allotment of revenue, for the different components of the Union. It was clear that the Shan States was not being given enough, since the amount per head for every man in each state, for defence, education, medical services and public health, was hardly sufficient for the upkeep of these services, let alone achieving any progress.

As a result of the lack of funds, the situation in the Shan States was no better even though they were now independent. The reasons were simple – the Japanese war had devastated much of the states, then after 1948 there were uprisings and, finally the heavy-handed treatment of the villagers by the army, had been disheartening and distressing to the Shans. It was only natural that people should have aspirations and a desire for prosperity after becoming independent.

How these goals were to be achieved was a worry, not only for my father, but for the other princes as well. Many of them came to see him to discuss these matters and to seek his advice. I am sure he was glad that at last he was once again able to concentrate on Shan problems. As an elder, he was naturally pushed to the fore, but he would have preferred to stay in the background, leaving much of the running to the younger Saohpas and politicians. My stepmother as an MP, became more and more politically and actively involved in Shan affairs.

My father was courted by both the Chinese and the Russians and was invited to visit the two countries. Meanwhile, family members were invited to go and swim in the Embassy pools whenever they wanted. The children were happy to have a large pool to swim in, and went often to the Chinese Embassy. Later, on the one or two occasions we accompanied the children the Chinese officials did not know quite what to do with the *gwelio* who had arrived with the children. However, when they were told that Peter was the son-in-law of the Speaker, there were smiles all around.

About April and May of 1957, my father was invited to visit China. It was a private visit made with his family. With all eight younger children, their ages varying from about twenty to five years, their nannies and the secretaries, it probably made a good plane load. They were first flown to Kunming to see the Dai or Tai peoples, the other branch of our Tai family. They met Chairman Mao, Chou En Lai, who had instigated the invitation, and other notable Communist leaders. The children came back ecstatic with red scarves around their necks and very impressed by Mao Tse Tung's China. It was a successful trip for the family.

Since I am writing about fifty years ago, I have kept the old Chinese spellings for those personalities mentioned.

On their return from China, Tzang, my stepmother's second son, became interested in politics and the Shan issues his mother was involved in as a member of Parliament for Hsenwi. Having joined Rangoon University, he acquired a wider view of politics. There were Burman, Shan and other ethnic students he met who had varying ideas on communism, socialism and nationalism. Many of them were understandably anti-government, since politicians were not at that time governing the country, but quibbling amongst themselves. Best of all, for both Tzang and his sister, Ying, they were able to meet and talk with other Shan students, who appeared to hold the same views on matters concerning the welfare of Mong Tai as a whole. Being young and optimistic, they were full of ideals.

Peter and I found that Rangoon in the late 1950s was still an harmonious mixture of East and West. The golden-spired temples and monasteries, the wide roads lined with flowering tropical trees, the monumental Edwardian brick government buildings, the wood and plaster shop-houses and the private residences in their large gardens, were all a living memory of the colonial civilisation of this great mercantile city. It had not been overtaken by the modern world. Bicycles and trishaws dominated the streets, their silent process broken only by the raucous horns of the brightly coloured, but very ramshackle, buses. Life moved at a gentle pace.

Rangoon was considered the metropolis with all its foreign inhabitants, whilst Mandalay was the cultural centre. Towns like Maymyo and Kalaw were the hill stations, where weary officials and families

*The President's House, as it was in 1950s, Rangoon.*

*The famous Strand
Hotel in the 1950s.*

retired to recoup
from the heat of the
plains in the summer.
The country as a
whole was perhaps a
little too sedate, but
Thailand was within
easy reach for excite-
ment and the latest
attractions. Bangkok
offered a range of hotels and nightclubs with beguiling neon lights, while Pattaya's
beautiful, palm-lined beaches, were empty and stunningly beautiful. Later, it was
to become famous as an R&R centre for American soldiers during the Vietnam
war. Still Rangoon, the stately aunt, was the place that most people preferred for
living and working.

Its one luxurious hotel, at least by pre-war standards, was the Strand. Faced
with stone, it was in those days an imposing three-storey building overlooking
Rangoon river. It knew nothing of tourists, as only a few travellers dropped by
each year, and most of its clients were on business. At that time much of the
country's trade depended on the large foreign companies, such as Bombay
Burmah, Steele Brothers, Burmah Oil Company, and the multitude of Indian and
Chinese business houses who traded in rice, teak and other hard woods, silk,
rubies and jade and a vast range of agricultural products.

After World War II, business found itself restricted by the government of this
newly-independent Burma, but while frustration was ever present, the business
world remained a gentlemanly occupation where, at least for those at the top,
their lifetime's work would leave them riches to enjoy in their old age. If, in the
immediate post-war years the returns were meagre, the natural wealth of the country appeared to leave no doubt that the rewards of the future would be as great, or
even greater, than when the country was governed by the British.

In pre-war days, Burma was known as the rice bowl of the world and, even
after the war, neither poverty nor starvation was known. Economists forecast that
by the mid-1950s Burma would be the richest of the Southeast Asian nations.
These forecasts regrettably were proved to be wrong, as no one could have predicted what would happen politically over the next few years.

Although Rangoon was small, compared to western capitals, it had a rich
social life. One of the social centres, as mentioned before, was the racecourse,
known as the Rangoon Turf Club. I never managed to get back there during
our stay in Rangoon as neither Peter nor I found the sport exciting. Against that
was the Pegu Club, the home of the white Burra Sahib. A single-storey, wooden
building, its long verandas provided cool and silent shade, while its polished teak
bars never ran out of ice cold beer, Singapore slings, pink gins or whisky. In the

shadows were the Boys, still Boys even if they were 50 or 60 years old, who stood quietly in the background, always ready to anticipate a need and to refill an empty glass. There was also the Sailing Club which, although I did not know then, was a prestigious club to join. It was quite exclusive and on the whole non-whites were not allowed to join it. Though with the political transition, things changed.

After the war, the Pegu Club, with great reluctance, began to open its membership to allow a few Burmese and other non-westerners to join. One can understand though, why in the early days, the Burra Sahibs wanted their clubs to be exclusive, as it was the only place where they could let their hair down. They could grumble about their jobs, the unbearable heat, the non-whites they had to work with, calling them by any derogatory names they wanted, and they did not have to stand on their dignity. They could get drunk and behave badly, since it was generally accepted behaviour. But this attitude was already becoming an anachronism.

The social life of Rangoon began largely to revolve around the embassies and new business enterprises. While the Burra Sahibs of Bombay Burmah and Steele Brothers might still have had great commercial leverage, in cocktail parties and dinners they were gradually taking second place to the elite politicians, the Shan and other national leaders, and senior civil servants who were Burmans and Anglo-Burmans.

Things were changing in this post-independence period and they were changing fast. But not it seemed at Rangoon's only large department store, Rowe and Company. I loved going to Rowe's. Here one was still served by Britishers behind the counters, and Rowe's proud boast was that there was nothing in the world that could not be bought from them. If they did not have it, Rowe's would obtain it wherever it came from. A veritable Harrods's of the East.

There were also two excellent bookshops, Smart & Mookerdum and the Peoples' Bookshop. The latter was run by a communist, who appeared to sell his extreme left-wing material more out of duty than desire, and showed a real flair in his selection of academic and literary books. They were our weekly haunts.

Burma Cold Stores provided European provisions mostly in tins. The butter was semi-melted and prone to go rancid unless it was put on ice immediately. Some of the goods such as tinned ham were pretty pricey. There was no problem as far as whisky and beer were concerned, but wine was still expensive and we hardly drank it except at diplomatic parties. Of course, the embassies had their own commissariats, so the Russians were never short of caviar nor the French, their Champagne.

It was always fun to go to the Scott Market, also known as Bokyoke market where under one roof there were stalls selling gold and silverware, jewellery of rubies and sapphires straight from the Mogok mines, silks and clothing at one end and food at the other. There was the prevailing smell of *nga-pi*, same as the *ka-pi* of Thailand and the *ngoc-nam* of Vietnam, the rotten fish paste and fish sauce. Like these the durian was an acquired taste. During its season the whole place would stink of ripe cheese. Unappetising as the durian smelt, its flesh, with the texture of a soft, French cheese, just melted in the mouth. For many people of Southeast Asia it is a prized fruit. Today when durian is in season it can now be

*A group of pagodas on the platform
of Shwe Dagon Pagoda, Rangoon.*

found in London, in most Filipino and Thai supermarkets. Many Europeans have
also acquired a taste for this delicious fruit. Some prefer the durian preserve sold
in long cylindrical tubes wrapped in plastic, as there is hardly any smell to them.

On a Sunday, or when we had visitors, we went to the Shwe Dagon Pagoda.
This ancient pagoda is said to have been built over seven strands of hair from
Gautama Buddha and is one of the most sacred shrines in Asia. Legend has it that
when a casket with the strands of hair was presented to King Okkalapa, it burst
open and the strands of hair grew to a great height at the same time emitting a
dazzling light. All at once the dumb began to speak, the deaf to hear and the lame
could walk again. Then a shower of gems fell knee deep. The king built a golden
pagoda and up to the 14th century little is known of its history. Then, but successive Burman and Mon kings over the last five centuries built it up to its present
magnificent size. The little town of Okkala also grew through the ages to become
Rangoon as we know it today.

A large platform forms the basis of the *chedi*. There are four covered stairways
leading up from the north, south, east and west giving protection from the heat of
the sun. It is a steep climb and as we mounted step by step in bare feet, we stopped
now and again to select flowers, candles and joss-sticks from the shops lining the
stairway, and also to get our breath back. Once at the top of the vast platform
we made our way to the main shrine to pray, walking past several smaller shrines
built around it. The marble floors we sat on soon cooled us down. Listening to the
prayer bells tinkling in the breeze and enveloped in the fragrance of the frangipani
and jasmine flowers, one felt at peace.

When the first *Golden Guide to South & East Asia* was published by the *Far
Eastern Economic Review* in 1961, Peter and I contributed an article on Burma.
Looking at it again, I was interested to find these statistics: the base of the pagoda
has a circumference of 1,420 ft and the stupa rises 320 ft above the platform. The
*stupa* is covered with gold leaf up to the Plantain Bud which is about two thirds

up. From there onwards, there are 8,688 gold plates, measuring a foot each, that sheathe the Plantain Bud. The *htee* or the umbrella right up at the top is decorated with 5,448 diamonds and 2,000 precious and semi-precious stones.

Little wonder that under the blazing sun, the shimmering gold and gems of the spire of the Shwe Dagon serve as a landmark and a beacon for fishermen and ships at sea. It is also the first glimmering sight one sees from the air, either when flying over Rangoon, or coming down to land at Mingaladon.

Life in Rangoon went gently on and, at first, the slow recovery of the economy could be blamed on the disruption caused by the Japanese invasion. But as the years went by, it became apparent that Burma, the so-called rice bowl of Asia, could no longer maintain that status. The production of rice remained still barely sufficient for the country's own needs, and the export of teak and other agricultural products failed to come anywhere near pre-war levels. It became clear that the failure had to be placed at the door of the government, where widespread corruption, inefficiency and incompetence were turning Burma into one of the poorest nations in Asia.

Numerous reasons can perhaps be given for this state of affairs, but in reviewing these years, maybe one could say that it was the virtual collapse of the structure of government which brought about these calamities. Once the country gained Independence, it was to become somewhat difficult for the civil servants, who were chiefly British, Anglo-Indians and Anglo-Burmans, to continue working at their posts. The newly independence Burma was impatiently anxious to establish itself and to follow though its main aim – to Burmanize. Altogether, it is difficult to visualize the short-sightedness of these nationalistic policies.

Despite the economic disasters towards the end of the 1950s, a new programme of construction had begun. Soon there was the Inya Hotel, built beside the Royal Lake in a joint venture with the Russians. A new air-conditioned cinema called The President had also sprung up and we all flocked there. Rowe & Co, together with the Burma Cold Store, continued to meet our demands, though there were also other smaller shops and stores which were coming up. Later, a major competitor was a supermarket, established by the military and the first of its kind in Rangoon.


## Teaching and Broadcasting

We each found work we were interested in. Peter began writing articles for an English language newspaper in Rangoon. Later, he joined the English Department at Rangoon University, where he met men such as Dr Hla Myint, Dr Tha Hla and Dr Nyi Nyi, to name but a few, who were dedicated educationists. There was also a notable Englishman, Gordon Luce, who was both a Burmese and Chinese scholar. Over the years through his studies, he contributed a great deal to academic research at Rangoon University. He was married to a Burmese and had lived in Rangoon for a long time. He was much respected for his scholarly work and many regarded him as their *Sayagyi*, great teacher.

Unfortunately, when the military coup took place in 1962, an unbelievable and unforgivable thing happened. Gordon was to find himself an exile. It appeared the

**SHAN LITERARY SOCIETY, UNIVERSITY OF RANGOON.**
EXECUTIVE COMMITTEE MEMBERS (1960-61.)

*1st Row: (L to R)—* Sao Mya Kyi. Sao Mon Hsar. Sao Lao Leing. Sai Kyaw, *(President)* Sai Yawt Ngurn, *(Secretary)* Nang Dong, *(Treasurer)* Nang Nu Nu Myint. Nang Khin May Win.
*2nd Row: (L to R)—* Sai Mg Nyunt. Nang Marie. Nang Yawt Seng Lao. Sao Ying Sita. Nang Kitty Hkam. Nang Nwe Ni. Sai Hsam.
*3rd Row: (L to R)—* Sai Moong Tip. Sai Hfun. Sai Hsam Hlat. Sai Aye. Sao Kan Kywe. Sai Sengs Boac Bong. Sai Hkun Ohn Tai. Sao Tzang.
*4th Row: (L to R)—* Sai Tong. Sai Kyaw Zan. Sai Seng Lwe. Sai Sang Yee. Sai Sai Sinn. Sai Noom Som Muong. Sai Win Tin.
*Absentees:* — Sai Nyo Myint. Sai San Lun Mg. Sai Win Aung. Oscar Hkun Ohn. Nang Hsai Sinn.

*Committee of the Shan Literary Society, Rangoon University with Tzang and Ying amongst the young students. Ying middle second row. Tzang right in 3rd row.*

regime did not want him in the country. He had never dreamt that one day he would be forced to leave his adopted country which he loved and had done so much for.

Amongst Peter's many pupils then were my brother Tzang, and Ying, my sister. Tzang and Ying belonged to a young group of Shans who had great ambitions for the Shan people and Mong Tai. The Shan Literary Society at Rangoon University, of which they were members, was enthusiastic about the Shan language and writings. After the coup it became impossible for such activities to continue.

About once a month, we would have a party at our house for the Shan students and they used to bring their friends who were an ethnically mixed group. With each conscious of their heritage, they found common ground to discuss their own plans and ideals for the future. I suppose these young students, had they been given the chance, once they had graduated and taken on responsible jobs, might have been able to contribute a great deal to the country. As future leaders they might have been able

*With members of the Burmese Section of the BBS 1959; left to right, U Tin Maung, Mr H Horsley and U San Win.*

*With our BBS English Section guru Percy Hla Bu and his wife, Olive.*

to sustain the Union and followed in their elders' footsteps. This, alas was not to be.

My choice was not to teach again but to do something different, so I joined the Burma Broadcasting Service (BBS) and read the news in English. It was a wonderful experience. At that time, English news was broadcast only three times a day and the English language programmes were limited to a few hours.

Writing about it now, I may give the impression that there was nothing to reading the news, but I remember my very first news broadcast. Peter had gone with me to the BBS to lend moral support but found himself having to read the news instead, as I had stage fright and lost my voice. Once I had made a few broadcasts, I was less nervous and it all became easier. Thank goodness, we didn't have television then, as I didn't have to worry how to look or act in front of the cameras.

Percy Hla Bu was the main linguist of our small unit. He was a Karen, who with a young group of students had been sent to Japan during the occupation. Later, when the country became independent, he was sent by the Burma Broadcasting Service to the BBC in London to be trained. With his BBC experience, he was our guru telling us how to pronounce the difficult names of the various international leaders or answering questions on classical music and composers, which we broadcast each day.

From time to time, I tried to arrange short features and plays for broadcasting and a number of friends helped in lending their voices. Of course, this meant that we had to steal time from the music programmes, which didn't always please the presenters. It was great fun though working at the BBS.

The new Broadcasting House was still being built then, and though we were somewhat cramped in Windermere Road, we were a harmonious unit full of laughter and fun. I left before the new station was opened and by then the English programmes unit had been enlarged. Despite the uncertainties of life, Percy and his family stayed on in Burma but he sadly died in the late 1990s. As for my other colleagues I have lost contact with them and have no idea where they might be.

My work kept me busy at odd hours since our English broadcasts were early in the mornings, the afternoons and evenings. There were three of us who took it in turns to read the news. Sometimes our driver was occupied and I had to drive to work. As I am a small person and I was driving a Land Rover, it used to surprise oncoming drivers to see just a head over the steering wheel. Later, driving in France with a Land Rover which was a left-hand drive, with our boxer dog Bertie sitting on my right, people would look twice to make sure that it was not Bertie who was the driver.

Once again, with Peter's love for writing and publishing we decided to start a magazine called *New Burma Weekly*. We had a number of academics and other young professionals who joined us and contributed articles each week. It became well-known for its collection of seriously thought-out articles and our readership increased. Every fortnight or so, a group of us would go off and have dinner after our editorial meetings at the Szechuan restaurant, the Nam Sin, just on the outskirts of Rangoon on the way to Mingaladon airport. Here the food was superb. One of the dishes it was well known for which we never failed to order was the eel with garlic and chillies. We were able to taste the dish again many years later at the Pine and Bamboo, in Happy Valley in Hong Kong.

We never had a routine at weekends but when we had no visitors, Sunday became a day devoted to photography and music. Early in the morning before the sun had got too hot, Peter and I would drive around trying to find the right angle to take a stunning photograph of the Shwe Dagon pagoda. We weren't professional photographers, but it became a challenge trying to get a really good picture of the pagoda. In this way our interest grew in photography, and, due to the high expense involved in having films developed, we began developing them ourselves.

Naturally, we wanted the pictures in colour, but we had to use black and white instead as we found Kodachrome transparencies extremely expensive in those days. However, Ektachrome came to our rescue. Developing these transparencies was not too difficult to manage and though we didn't have a dark room or air conditioning in our flat, we went ahead. It was difficult, of course, working with the chemicals as they had to be at the right temperature. We used to stand the bottles of developing mixture in a basin filled with broken ice, which had been bought in a large block. By keeping a close eye on the thermometer floating in the water and adding a piece of ice whenever necessary, we were able to keep the temperature steady.

Peter became quite an expert working with Ektachrome films, while I enjoyed cutting up the strips and putting the negatives into their paper frames. It was always exciting when the time came for viewing our handiwork. I don't think any of our friends were ever subjected to these viewings, and it was only the children, my brothers and sisters, our loyal spectators, who used to crowd around the projector, taking turns in working it.

I don't remember grumbling too much about the heat. Most of the time Peter, who was usually dressed in a white shirt and white trousers with a tie to go to the university, looked cool and relaxed. As I wore a short-sleeved *ingyi* or blouse of thin lawn or cotton and a *longyi* of a light material, the heat never bothered me. At work there were large overhead fans to keep us cool, but since they regularly swept our papers off the tables, they were off most of the time. In later years, as one became accustomed to air conditioning, I wondered how we could have ever lived without it, and why we hadn't found both Bangkok and Rangoon unbearably hot in the earlier days?

It was always exciting when we had visitors from elsewhere, as apart from taking them around Rangoon sightseeing, we would also hold parties in honour of their visits. These parties were invariably made up of diplomats, university friends and journalists so there was any amount of serious talk, as well as gossip. The evenings were much enjoyed and as each group departed, Peter would, without fail, see them all down our long flight of stairs to their cars. I think that was why he kept slim in those days.

A number of foreign correspondents came when U Nu gave his great political rallies and several of them used to call on us. One was Dennis Bloodworth, the highly regarded foreign correspondent for the London *Observer*, who covered all of Asia. Throughout our years in Southeast Asia, we met up with Dennis whenever there was a major breaking story. When we went to live in Singapore he couldn't have been more helpful in getting us settled in. We could not have had better friends. Dennis continued living in Singapore and was the author of many books, including those he wrote with his Chinese wife, Liang Ching Ping, whom we always called Judy.

As we were living in my father's compound, the police who had a guard house at the gate used to stop and check visitors. I have a feeling one or two of them rather objected to being stopped and used to have the guards running after them. But any feeling of annoyance dissipated, when they reached the top of our stairs and found a large glass of cold Mandalay beer or an ice-cool gin and lime awaiting them. Also the calm and cool atmosphere of our flat, created mainly by the plants on the veranda shielding the brightness of the sun, made them soon relax.

Our flat above the garages proved to be pleasantly cool. There were two verandas, one at the front and the other at the back, that ran its entire length. The large doors into the rooms were kept open so there was always a breeze. Like my stepmother, I had become an orchid enthusiast. The whole front veranda was full of beautiful sprays of the golden, white and purple hanging orchids, which had been collected from the hills between Shwenyaung and Taunggyi, and had been given to us by relatives. Then there were ground orchids, which we used to bring back whenever we went to Bangkok, which grew in pots along the side of the veranda. What with the green of the ferns, rubber plants and palms, it was a lovely miniature garden.

We found the four years we lived in Rangoon thoroughly enjoyable, as we moved around from one social circle to another. It was an in-between period. Although British colonial rule had ended in 1948, there were still certain vestiges of those times, which were gradually giving way to a liberated Burmese society. The up and coming young men and women, children of the former Indian Civil Service, (ICS) and the Burma Civil Service, were beginning to find their niche in society.

Rangoon society then was not large, so one got to know the personalities in both the university and government circles, the socialites of Rangoon and those from the diplomat corps. Everyone mixed freely and there were endless cocktail and dinners parties, not forgetting, of course, the many National Day celebrations. Some of the parties had mad themes, and I recall a Pyjama party we were invited to at one of the British Embassy houses.

One year, organizers of a charity ball asked if we could help by producing an item for the floor show. After some thought, Peter and I decided that the fast jumps and swishing of Shan swords might make an exciting spectacle, since normally one could only see such performances in a Shan village. Luckily there was a Shan village just a few miles out of Rangoon, so we went there to ask the village elder's help in finding someone.

In ancient days swords were used for defence and figured prominently in battles. With no more wars to fight, the movements which were made in this kind of combat became an exhibition piece. A single performer will use two of the long, thin swords to show his dexterity in the manoeuvres, but when two display their skills they generally perform a mock fight. The dance is performed to the beat of a collection of gongs and a long drum slung over the shoulders and played with both hands. The arousing music is loud and monotonous and becomes hypnotic after a time.

With sword in hand the men make a *wai* and begin the performance. Crouching down their feet slightly apart, each man takes a calculated jump as their swords clash mid-air. Next they take a step towards each other, then with a jump pass back to back. A thrust is seldom made, but each man tries to dislodge the sword of his opponent from his grasp as the movements become faster and faster. As the swords cut through the air with swift strokes, the gongs beat faster. The men's baggy Shan trousers are rolled up to the groin exposing their legs and their torsos of blue and red tattoos. These usually represent magical spells of strength and power while figures of tigers and *nagas* symbolise fierceness and might.

The steps of the sword dance and the movement of the swords though seemingly easy need special training. The training is taken seriously as an unqualified person could easily cause an accident. Even then it is usual for each man before such a performance to make obeisance to the *phii* concerned, asking for protection. It is sad to think that as older generations pass away, knowledge of these skills will gradually disappear with them.

You can imagine what a din the gongs and the drums made in an enclosed space, as usually such displays take place in the open, in a village square. There was great excitement when one of the swords slipped and fell in front of the Yugoslav Ambassador's wife. There was a tense moment, but luckily it did not create a diplomatic incident.

A few years back, Peter and I were invited to a Buddhist New Year, *Pii Mai*, celebration in London by Laotian friends. There was the long drum, especially long with a deep boom which was accompanied by several gongs varying in size.

*British Ambassador Sir Richard Allen and Embassy staff with President Dr Ba U, 1956. Included in the group are Fred Warner, Peter Murray, Elizabeth Barraclough and back row far left is Oz Robinson.*

As they played, it brought back all those memories of happier times with family and friends so many years ago. This feeling of nostalgia took me back to my childhood and also to our days in Laos. I realized that it did not matter whether we were Laotian or Shan, for the music being played was a reminder that we were of the same culture and origin, and had a common Tai heritage

One of the highlights of the year was the New Year's Eve party at Jimmy Bo Setkya's. Nearly all of Rangoon society attended and he entertained us lavishly, with the band playing until dawn. They were wonderful, unforgettable parties. His tall and willowy Anglo-Burman wife, of course, was the main attraction. Perhaps, that was the only time when men, both young and old, ever had the chance of admiring her and dancing with her, the beautiful lead actress of *The Purple Plain*.

We had many Burman friends who were well-educated, sensible people. In those days we all seemed to accept who or what we were, each respecting the other. Peter and I felt that many of these Burmans were good friends with whom we could talk to freely. Several were people I had met in London and Cambridge, who had come back to serve in the Foreign Office and other government departments. In the Planning and Statistics Department were such bright and enthusiastic men as Tony Thet Tun and Richard Win Pe, to name only two. However, I never met again those young officers from the armed forces whom I had known earlier and who had had such high hopes for their country.

Peter and I were very much wrapped up in our own work and we did not follow too closely or really take in the explosive political conditions around us. I had been away for ten years and living abroad I had not kept abreast of what was happening in the Shan States nor did I realize the depth of hostility between the Burman political elite and the ethnic nationalities. In fact, I was quite off-hand and cavalier about the whole political scene.

Then when Peter became stringer for the *Far Eastern Economic Review* and *Time Magazine* our interests in politics deepened. Although I was working in the BBS, the English newscasts were chiefly concerned with foreign news. The little news we had on Burma dealt generally with the comings and goings of the Prime Minister or the General, or the visits of foreign dignitaries.

I learnt more about what was happening politically, when I began to stand in for Peter. When he had a lecture, I stood in for him by attending press conferences and briefings given by the Information Ministry and various Embassies. With so much happening around us and newspapers full of politics, it was difficult not to begin thinking about the situation within the country. I did not, however, make a serious study of these happenings, so at times I missed the nuances. Somehow I felt that problems which existed between the Burmans and the Shans were not insurmountable and that with some give and take, things would be solved. How naive I was! How little did I know of the darker side of human nature.

It began to look as if Peter and I had come to live in Burma at a time when the country, though it had the appearance of stability and a flourishing economy, was in fact in a state of economic and political flux. There were many plans and much talk, but little happened. Although politically the country was in turmoil, the lid was still on. A sense of breakdown was emerging, but much remained hidden. Not being personally involved, we watched the political scene from the sidelines.

*Peter and Jimmy
Bo Setkya.*

Most people in Burma are superstitious though they may deny it. There are always signs and omens for different incidents, and I well remember one of these. One evening in early 1961, when we were at a cocktail party, streaks of lighting flashed across the sky. I recall us all sitting on the balcony of a diplomat's house watching this fantastic phenomenon. It was dusk, and the sky was tinged with orange and silver. This ever-changing spectacle, which went on for a long while, was something we had never seen before. Some older people told us later that it was an inauspicious omen and there would be great upheaval. I wonder if anyone else remembers that evening and if one should have been superstitious enough to read the signs.

Perhaps in that period most of us thought the Union would work out some-how. We felt that despite the political rows and the fighting that was going on against the Communists, and the Karens fighting for their rights, that an under-standing could be reached and we could all go on with our day-to-day lives.

Clearly, we misjudged the tensions that lay behind the smiling, sometimes benign faces of the various politicians and military men. We were to find that unlike its Thai neighbour where political disputes and coup d'état were dealt with in an Asian way, it was to be different in Burma. Over the years, too many under-currents of distrust, inequality and hatred had been built up, and confrontation became inevitable. No one though suspected the way it would happen.

*Acting as commentator for Independence*
*Day Parade, Rangoon.*

# XI

# *Politics*

## *The right of secession*

1958 was the year in which the right of secession of the Shans from the Union of Burma could take place. After ten years of a 'united' government, people began to feel that it was not working out. It was, therefore, understandable that many Shans, be they Saohpas, parliamentarians or ordinary people, felt they should speak out expressing their disappointment. There were a few, more hot-headed than others, who spoke strongly of disillusionment and aired their views on secession at meetings and rallies in the different states. The demands for Shan autonomy became louder, but much of it was hot air. Nevertheless, a great deal of the distrust and anger people felt arose from the way in which the army was conducting itself in villages.

Since the early 1950s the Shan States had come under military administration, and villagers suffered rape, torture and general bad behaviour from officers and soldiers alike. Neither the Saohpas nor the Shan government could help alleviate the misery of their people. Since their loyalty lay with the Union government, they were in no position to act unilaterally against the might of the military. Although the AFPFL recognised the situation, it did not want to take responsibility for curbing the Tamadaw (the military).

In September 1958, U Nu, the then Prime Minister, began to realize that his laissez-faire policies were being blamed for an increasingly serious economic situation. Politically, some members of his party wished to see him forced out of active politics, making him answerable for the current state of affairs. As a result he began to acknowledge that despite the legality of the clause in the 1947 Constitution, there was no way in which the Burman politicians nor the military, would now agree to secession.

*Premier U Nu, with visiting Chou En-lai, Rangoon.*

When the granting of Independence was discussed, the British had only made a half-hearted attempt to accommodate the demands of the ethnic nationalities within the future framework of the Union of Burma, with no safeguards provided. It soon became apparent that they had failed, since the British administration though conscious of disparities, did not look too deeply into the real divisions existing between the Burman and the non-Burmans.

The British had only administered Burma as a whole country for some sixty years when the Japanese invasion ended colonial rule. They had provided education for the rich lowland towns, but in the hills, advanced education was only available for the families of the Shan rulers and, to a lesser extent, to leaders of other ethnic groups. This educational inequality undoubtedly was to become one of the major problems facing Shans and those from other ethnic groups.

The British administration in those days before Burma's separation from British India, naturally used the Indian Civil Service (ICS) to govern the country. It was mainly composed of British, Indian and Anglo-Indian officers. There were only a few Burmans amongst the ICS then, a fact that was to cause growing discontent. Later, as Burmans became better educated, its Civil Service came into its own as the favoured elite of the administration and professional classes.

Over the years, many educated Burmans began to develop a degree of political acumen, taking their cue from Indian politicians and other Europeans who were interested in Burmese affairs. It was this group of Burmans who naturally formed the political parties and shouted the loudest. When Independence came, the Burmans quickly demonstrated that they considered themselves the 'big brothers' who had to lead the way, claiming that the ethnic nationalities were uneducated and backward. In many ways, of course, this was true. But these discrepancies did not mean the uneducated were in any way inferior nor that they should be considered as second-class citizens.

*General and Mrs Ne Win at*
*the Independence Parade, Rangoon.*

The myth that Burma has always been a country populated by one race or ethnic group, the Burmans, is quite untrue. Other ethnic nationalities make up some forty per cent of the population. The term Burmese, is an accepted generic name, meaning those who live within the country. It does not, however, mean that because I, a Shan, am said to be Burmese, my mother tongue is the same nor that I have the same traditions as a Burman. Since we are close neighbours and being Buddhists, we have naturally maintained a certain common form of culture assimilated from either side over the centuries, but we definitely are two peoples of distinct origins.

Another disagreement concerned the economy – basically who owned what? In the colonial period, before the Japanese war, British enterprises had made enormous profits from the natural resources of the country. Burma Proper, as mentioned before, lies in the lowlands along the banks of the great Irrawaddy River whose tributaries flow into the Bay of Bengal. Here were immensely rich, fertile rice lands, oil fields, minerals and teak forests, where most Burmans lived. Surrounding this area on three sides are the highlands and plateau land, where the ethnic nationalities live. These regions also hold invaluable resources – minerals such as silver and tin, ruby and jade, vast teak forests of economic importance, not forgetting the mighty Salween River with its potential to generate electricity.

When Independence was considered, it became obvious that the Burman political elite wanted to claim these resources as their own, to make similar fortunes as the British. In U Pe Khin's book, the foreword by U Tun E, a Shan AFPFL politician, acknowledged that the natural wealth of the Frontier Areas was of great importance to an independent Burma, "The geo-political significance is easily appreciated. The economy of Burma Proper without the forest and mineral resources of the States would not be very significant".[33]

Once independent, all such natural resources became the property of the Union and whichever government was in power then benefited from these riches.

In the late 1950s, the many problems facing the incumbent government became extremely serious, especially with the approach of a general election. A complex group of conflicts had dragged on for ten years, while communists and other extremists had gone underground to express their dissatisfaction with the AFPFL government through armed struggle.

Then unexpectedly, due to unreconcilable issues, the AFPFL split – U Nu and his followers called themselves the 'Clean AFPFL' and the opposition, the 'Stable AFPFL'. The split marked the beginning of Burma's present situation. In September 1958, parliament was dissolved. U Nu, perhaps feeling that as a civilian he could not solve the problems himself, asked General Ne Win, the head of the Army, for help in organising free and fair political elections for April 1959.

One wonders though, whether U Nu realized that by asking the military to step in, he was opening Pandora's box to military rule. But what he presumably thought then, was that with the military in charge, all political unrest and revolts would be brought under control, after which he could easily step back into power. He reckoned that by making such a move, it would save both his political power and his position. But he also knew the army was breathing down his neck, itching to control the disarray within the country. U Nu, therefore, had little choice but to give way to Ne Win.

By October 1958, General Ne Win agreed to take on the task and became Prime Minister. It was the first military coup d'état to take place in the country. Unlike its Thai neighbour where army coups were habitual, the Burmese army had in former days kept its distance from the politicians. Now, the army in power called their new government, the 'Caretaker Government'.

Modern writers commenting upon those days have been quick to observe that the Caretaker Government laid the foundations for the major military coup of 1962. Of course, they are correct. But at the time many did not see it that way. It was felt that they were implementing what the politicians were unable to achieve, thus the public were grateful to the military. Although there may have been initial fears, most people put their minds at rest finding little to complain about.

During its tenure, the Caretaker Government achieved a number of things. Importantly, it restored law and order and ruthlessly quelled rebellions. Moving more soldiers into the Shan States and Frontier Areas, the army began establishing themselves permanently in these areas.

In the economic sphere, young motivated colonels led by officers such as Maung Maung and Aung Gyi were able to make the country's economy viable again, both in agriculture and industry. Within this short period, internal and external trade once again began to thrive.

The army regime was able to show off its efficiency and capability as the months went by and people were impressed. They were noticeably beginning to win hearts and minds. That was why, at that time, no one really thought that there would be another coup after the army had handed back power to U Nu. In addition, because the Caretaker government had been benign, when they did come back in 1962, few expected the army to behave in a cruel and exacting manner. When April 1959 arrived, General Ne Win found it was too soon to return power to the politicians, and no one objected.

One of General Ne Win's *bête noires* was the Saohpas. He had always had a great loathing for the princes. I am not sure why he disliked them so much, especially as he had been to stay at our palace in Yawnghwe when he and Kitty had first married. He wasn't the only one to harbour such feelings. Burma had become independent, but the long-standing hatred towards the Shan and the Saohpas was still instilled in the minds of many a Burman.

The future for the Shan people did not look good, and disturbances going on in other parts of the country were soon to effect us. For centuries people who lived in the Shan States had only known the feudal system. Villagers were dependent on the ruling prince as the only person they could look to for help. In times of trouble, he was there to give them his protection and to them it mattered little whether the Saohpa was a good or bad ruler, they relied on him.

However, as young Shans became educated and came into contact with the world outside of their states, they began to see things differently. Naturally none of their major towns had the facilities nor the grandeur of Rangoon or Mandalay or even lesser towns. There was no comparison. They blamed their comparatively low standard of living on the feudal system and the oppression of the princes who in their view only cared for themselves.

Their political awakening easily gave Burman politicians an opportunity to guide them since they were anti-Saohpa and anti-feudal. Soon, rightly or wrongly, the young began making demands for the abolition of the feudal system, their favourite slogan being "Down with the Saohpas". They were obviously not aware that the paternal system could work well, and that there was a special relationship between the ordinary people of the states and their ruling princes, each with a responsibility towards the other. It was interesting to find Hugh Tinker describing this rapport as "a paternal, benevolent-despot relationship".[34]

In some ways, one could say that the Saohpa acted as a bulwark for his people. Once he was gone, there was no longer anyone to represent them, or to stand between them and an aggressor. Apart from that, any new form of government taking over from the "traditional, hereditary system of authority"[35] had to be carefully thought out. It should not be a question of throwing out the old feudal practices for new ones whatever the cost. During that period there were few educated and qualified Shan officials, but in time the transition from feudal to Shan government control could have been carried out without bringing in outside administrators who regrettably were young Burmans. Some were sympathetic and fitted in well, but others had little empathy for the Shan.

Many Shan politicians were influenced and highly dependent on their fellow Burman AFPFL members, who were wont to blame the Saohpas for every wrong. Subsequently Shan politicians began to believe that their hereditary princes were useless and were to be despised. It was a sad state of affairs.

My father had had the foresight to recognise that feudal rule was becoming out-dated – an easy target for politicians and army alike. In 1952, he initiated and prepared the princes for the transfer of their feudal powers to the Shan State Government of the day. Yet, he has been accused of being one of the Saohpas who did not want to give up his powers. Such unjust criticism of an enlightened man is unfounded.

It can be proved that some fifteen years earlier he had already renounced his Saohpaship. During the Japanese occupation when the country had been given Independence in September 1943, Dr Ba Maw, the Adipadi made a speech at a banquet in Rangoon. He cited unified Germany and Japan, and called upon the Saohpas to follow their lead.

He said "Shan Sawbwas should make a note of this example and be prepared to sacrifice for the good of one's country and one's people."

Naturally, it was an oblique warning to the Shan princes of what was to happen in the near future. A month later, my father submitted a letter to the 'Nipponese' Governor when he visited the Shan States (the Japanese liked to refer to themselves as the Nipponese at that time). In it he made clear that he was quite willing to give up his powers, writing: "That for the honour of proving that I have no self interest whatever and that I am prepared to willingly sacrifice for the cause of the Greater East Asiatic Co-prosperity, to kindly accept my renunciation of the Saohpaship of Yawnghwe State."[36]

Surely these words prove that my father had decided as far back as 1943 to renounce his powers. Since that was his decision then, why should it have been any different in 1959? He had no cause nor the desire to hang on to the feudal powers of the Saohpas, for he was aware that time had come for everyone to join the twentieth century.

The on-going negotiations concerning the surrender of heriditary rule by the Saohpas came to an end. In April 1959, General Ne Win, as the Prime Minister of the Caretaker Government triumphantly went up to Taunggyi to accept the surrender of these powers. The signing of the Renunciation Treaty was overseen by the then Head of Shan State, Sao Hom Hpa, the Hsenwi Saohpa. The princes were offered compensation, said to be amounts large enough for the maintenance of their states and their families. Lamentably, these sums were not massive and were considerably less than those received by Indian princes, who had also to renounce their powers. In fact, there was a great discrepancy in what was actually received by the Saohpas, and what the general public believed they had been awarded. Nevertheless, the anti-feudal group were satisfied to be rid of the Saohpas.

It became clear that General Ne Win could hardly wait to go further, for as soon as the ceremony was over, demands were immediately made to persuade the new Shan State government to surrender altogether the legal right of secession from the Union. Most Shans began to ask whether the 1947 Constitution was still valid?

## Respite from politics

The Caretaker government was now in control of the country and it seemed there would be a peaceful period. So about the same time in the summer of 1959, we decided to drive our long-wheelbase Land Rover back to London. It was the long vacation for Peter, and I took time off from the BBS. The Burma-India border had been closed since we had made our 1957 overland journey, so we had to ship the car to Calcutta. Martin Morland, who was then a Third Secretary at the British Embassy joined us and we flew to Calcutta. The Indian Customs took several days to clear the Land Rover. Each day, there was always seem to be one small matter which had to be resolved. We finally left with a sheaf of papers, to show to any official who might have been interested enough to look at them as we drove across the country.

We made a quick trip to Kathmandu, to recapture the charm of the place. Then back to India and onward along the Trunk road. We took it in turns to drive, and there was generally a lot of cursing, when one had to suddenly slow down to avoid hitting the holy cows that stood along the verge or the middle of the road. Before we made our stop at dusk, we would drive through a haze of smoke which came from cow dung being burnt by villagers. We managed to stay at dak-bungalows along the way and had comfortable nights.

Martin has reminded me that even as early as crossing India, we used to get tetchy with each other. It was after just such a long drive, that we suddenly came upon the Taj Mahal by moonlight. He remembers "all our fatigue and irritation falling away in an instant at the sheer magic of the sight". People who had visited this incredible place had told us, "You must see the Taj Mahal by moonlight to catch its enchantment". They had not exaggerated. The air was heavy with perfume from the burning incense, and my imagination transported me centuries back, as I thought of the great love of the Mogul prince, who had dedicated this most beautiful monument to his beloved wife.

*Martin at a soiree, Rangoon.*

*Martin, Peter and I with an unknown person on our overland trip.*

We had applied to travel through Afghanistan, but Peter and I were not given visas as our passports showed we were journalists. However, our drive through Baluchistan was of breathtaking beauty with deep gorges and sheer mountains rising above. Often on mountain tops we could clearly see tribesmen with guns slung across their shoulders keeping watch. I felt it was probably a bit like going through Red Indian territory as one used to see in films.

Later, as we travelled through the deserts, Martin often slept on the roof of the car and was occasionally nibbled by a camel, but he didn't grumble much.

We had crossed Turkey two years previously travelling along the southern routes, so we decided to take a northern route this time to Ankara and Istanbul. We drove though mountainous terrain making our way across to the Black Sea. It was early Spring and in places there was snow. It was exciting to see snow for the first time in many years, but our excitement was greater still, when near Erzerum we found mountainsides covered with crocuses, forming patches of colour, as they peeped out in their thousands from their glistening white covering.

Another adventure Martin remembers was when the Land Rover slid into a ditch without any warning as we drove along the coast road in the dark. We seemed to be stranded in the middle of nowhere with no passing traffic on the deserted road. Suddenly a car full of young Turks appeared. They kindly pulled us out and led us into Samsun which was some twenty miles away. I recall their asking us all sorts of questions and graciously giving us dinner. We were total strangers, yet they were friendly and made us feel at home.

There was still exchange control in those days, and we were usually short of cash when we left the sterling area. Martin was our treasurer, and there was often a tiff as to whether we should spend our last piece of money on buying food, or *The Times*, which Peter demanded. When I pleaded with Martin in Isfahan market, he relented, and allowed me to buy a lovely, slightly worn carpet for all of ten pounds. I don't remember whether we had to deny ourselves other luxuries – a delicious meal in a village or a good hotel bed – for the rest of the journey because of my rash purchase.

When we arrived at Ankara we were in luck. As Martin was going up the British Embassy steps he bumped into an old school and Foreign Office friend, who helped us out of our difficulties.

Our drive though Europe was done in easy stages, calling in to see friends at Athens, Rome and Florence. When we got to France we decided to go to St Paul de Vence, to see another old friend. Peter had taken me to see Joan Smith before in 1953 and now four years later, we felt it was time to visit her again. She was an outstandingly brave woman, for during the war she had helped a Jewish friend by hiding him in her loft. She was a young English artist, when she first came to this spectacular place in the 1930s.

St Paul de Vence was a delightful enclave of artists and writers in those days with little commercialisation. Joan's tiny house stood on a corner near the neat little square by the village fountain. Since there were three of us, she offered us a few days rest at her cottage, which was outside the village in the pine woods. It was peaceful there, and the air was fresh and soothing for us weary travellers. Sadly enough, the St Paul de Vence we knew then no longer exists. Having such excellent views, as it sits perched on the ridge, the rich and the famous have gradually moved into this mountain village and its surroundings, developing it out of all proportion. The quiet, narrow streets are filled with art galleries, tourist shops and cafes, changing its unassuming character completely.

We had a good journey back to London and we seem to have made it in very good time. Then as we were dropping Martin off at his parents' flat in Buckingham Palace Road, we saw the Grenadier Guard of Honour for the visit of President General De Gaulle pass by. There at the head was Dominic Morland, who waved his sword at his brother Martin in a "quite unmilitary way". What a coincidence, as if we planned our arrival for that moment.

Despite the uncomfortable times on the roof and some petty squabbles, Martin has remained a firm friend. He was later to become Ambassador in Rangoon during the rise of Aung San Suu Kyi, and the start of the democracy movement. She became a popular figure with her outspoken speeches against the regime which led to her house arrest. In the 1990 elections the National League for Democracy (NLD) won the majority of the seats but the army refused to honour the results. Later in 1991, with the Nobel Peace Prize awarded to her, she became world renowned for her stance on democracy. Despite hopes for her release in 2007, she still remains in military custody.

Aung San Suu Kyi, as one might have guessed, is the daughter of General Aung San who initiated Independence for Burma and was one of the signatories of the Panglong Agreement, bringing about the creation of the Union of Burma. There is little doubt that General Aung San, as the founding father of the present day Burma army, the Tamadaw, would be appalled by its behaviour nor could he have foreseen his country's present predicament, least of all, the manner in which his daughter is being treated by the military regime.

Suu Kyi continues as an icon for democracy both inside and outside the country, and has given hope for the future to the people of Burma. The eleven years of incarceration have not dampened her spirits though they have been difficult and trying times personally for her and her party. It has been equally hard for the peoples of the country, be they of any ethnic group, including the Burmans themselves. The military have absolute power to change the unhappy situation,

*Aung San Suu Kyi beside a photograph of her father, General Aung San.*

but they are at this moment unwilling to respond to any sensible suggestions put forward to ease the hardship and suffering of the people.

I suspect the army regime finds itself in an embarrassing situation in trying to resolve the present political stalemate, since on the one hand there is the national hero, General Aung San, it respects and worships, and on the other, the daughter it despises and considers its enemy for her defiant stance. The military regime I believe will not take any action, until some face-saving solution is found to get them out of this impasse.

To return to 1959, after spending the last weeks of our vacation in London, Peter and I flew back to Rangoon to continue with our respective work. Six months after our return we received a letter from an Officer in the Gurkhas to say that he had driven our Land Rover back overland to Kathmandu where he was then stationed. It was a lovely surprise and it was wonderful to know that our beloved Land Rover was still in good condition and in safe hands.

## The General Elections

Once more in Rangoon and after three months away we found the politicians still bickering among themselves. Somehow life went on without too much disruption. People reluctantly accepted the falling standard of living and enjoyed such peace as there was.

In the early months of 1960, General Ne Win had a busy schedule. A long drawn out border dispute with Communist China was at last settled. The General flew off to Peking on 1st February to meet Premier Chou En-lai. While there, he signed the Treaty of Friendship and Mutual non-Aggression and at the same time the Sino-Burma Boundary Agreement was published.

A fortnight later, Prime Minister, Nikita Khrushchev came on an official visit. His main objective was to inspect two of the several projects that the Soviet Union had given to Burma. They were the Technological Institute for some one thousand students, and the over 200-room Inya Lake Hotel, which was to include twenty-five luxury suites. Then, at the beginning of March, the military regime hosted a goodwill and friendship visit by their Majesties, the King and Queen of Thailand.

All visible cracks in the political world of the country appeared to have been cemented over, and the future the Union of Burma was looking rosy and bright. We joined others at these social events and toasted the future. By April and eighteen months since he had taken power, General Ne Win was able to show that the country was in good running order. The Caretaker Government lived up to its promise, and the General gallantly handed back the country to U Nu and his politicians.

Most people were impressed, and praised the military highly for keeping its word and bringing peace and prosperity back to the strife-torn country. These achievements undoubtedly gave General Ne Win grand ideas and the impetus to prepare a hidden agenda which became apparent in 1962.

The *Far Eastern Economic Review* of March 1960 in a special Supplement entitled 'Burma Today, 1948-1960', commented that "Burma stands to emerge as one of the healthiest economies of South East Asia if sound and able administrators are encouraged ..." it then hoped that in the future "political battles (would be) fought out across the floor of the House rather than in armed warfare". Unfortunately, neither of these observations were ever to happen.

The general elections were held and U Nu was swept back to power and was once again Prime Minister. His party, now renamed Pyidaungsu or Union Party won a vast majority. He had based his platform on what he expected to be popular measures: Buddhism as the State Religion, and statehood for the various minority groups who were being administered directly under the central government. The Stable AFPFL, the opposition, had firmly decided to ally themselves with the Army. Its aim was to continue the economic rejuvenation of the country, begun by the military government during its eighteen-month rule.

However, after the general elections, it did not take long before the politicians were fighting amongst themselves again. Whilst all this political turmoil was going on, we carried on with our daily life and work, and continued publishing the *New Burma Weekly*.

In August, the German government offered Peter a trip with other journalists to Germany. It was university term time, so Peter could not go but suggested I went in his stead, as a representative of the broadcasting service. This I did, and it was a wonderful jaunt for me, going to the different cities including a visit to East Germany. It was a strange, uncomfortable feeling going from West Berlin with is prosperity to the drab and ruined side of East Berlin.

While I was away, Peter suddenly fell ill but swore everyone to secrecy, so it would not spoil my trip – as always the thoughtful Peter. Had I been told, I would certainly have returned immediately. It was during this time lying in bed, that he began reading Marcel Proust's *À la Recherche du Temps Perdu*. He read much of it in French before going on to C.K. Scott Moncrieff's English translation *Remembrance of Things Past*, reading all twelve volumes. On my return, I was encouraged to read Proust as well. Although it took me longer than Peter to read the twelve volumes, I began to appreciate why Peter found Proust a sheer delight. Eventually, we were to work together on a book on Proust, a kind of handbook "to enable the reader to make his way through these first difficult pages, by providing a key for those who have found it was too full of obstacles to be enjoyable". We spent three years, which were to be Peter's last, working on the book deriving great pleasure in reading out our favourite passages. But this is going ahead, for there is still much to tell about the happenings of those years back in the early 1960s.

## *Politics Again*

Squabbles between the politicians, regardless of which party they belonged to, continued and the newspapers were full of their in-fighting. It was a relief when the university term ended and schools broke up for the holidays. Yawnghwe was the family's destination, but we decided to take a cruise to Singapore and Hong Kong for the vacation.

Before Sao U Hpa departed, he showed us a letter he had written to U Nu. It set out the discouraging economic and social conditions in the Shan States with no improvement over the past several years, and how help was needed urgently to alleviate them. The letter ends by reminding the Prime Minister that:

"If we look back into the history of Burma, we see that we are of different cultures and races, but our religion is the same, and in the past they have helped each other without delay, when they were needed. At the present moment, it is even more important to help one another, therefore, if one of them is backward and in difficulties, the other would not be satisfied to look on and be contentious. As in the instance of a household and family, if one of them should be in need, it is the responsibility of the others to look after him. Likewise, it is believed, that within the Union, if the Shan States is not up to the standard required, it is therefore the responsibility of Burma and the other states of the Union to help. Thus, as brothers, if one prospers, the others too should prosper with help given to them, and so achieve their goal. Believing in this, it is hoped, that the Honourable Prime Minister will be able to consider the problem, and suggest ways and means by which the Shan people will be able to attain progress and prosperity".[37]

The letter showed that matters were getting serious in the Shan States, and the relationship between the Shan and the Burmans were not going smoothly. Naturally there was much concern among the princes, as the elite politicians were creating divisions between the Saohpas and the young Shan politicians. There was no sharing of views nor attempts to understand each other. The gap which already existed was getting ever wider. The Shan States Peoples Freedom Party, took its orders directly from the AFPFL in Rangoon, as did the Shan States Youth League, formed in 1942 under the Japanese, with an office in Yawnghwe.

The political situation was all very disturbing. Peter and I wondered how we could help and resolved to ponder the issue during our cruise. On our way back to Rangoon, we diverted for a visit to Bangkok for a few days. Whilst we were there, we were told by some friends that the U Nu government did not want us back in Burma. No reason was given and we were very puzzled. Peter had to get back to prepare his lectures for the new term, and I, to my work at the BBS. We couldn't understand who had circulated this news, nor what was happening in Burma.

We went to check at the Burmese Embassy and were told to wait for a few days while they found out if what we had heard was true. Day after day we had no news. Then, after we had been in Bangkok for about ten days, Peter's re-entry visa to Burma expired and the Burmese Embassy refused to renew it. Never told the official reason for the refusal, we were now stranded in Bangkok. We felt dejected and couldn't understand why this was happening. We wondered whether we should have returned regardless of the warning, since Peter's re-entry visa was still valid then? Yet, had we done so, there was no telling what might have happened.

The Burmese Ambassador, though he knew us, was no help at all. I was later to find out that he had no love for Saohpas, and least of all for my father. He had been one of the chief political instigators, who had come to Taunggyi at the time of the Panglong Conference to cause a rift between the young Shan politicians and their rulers.

No further clarification of why we were not allowed to return was given. I remember, one of the senior Embassy official, the Consul, saying on one of our many visits, "You know Sanda, there is nothing to stop you from going back to Rangoon, as you don't need a re-entry visa, you know". We gathered that what he really meant was that I was still a Burmese citizen even though I didn't carry a Burmese passport but a British one. We ignored his remark.

## Back to Laos

As a result, we were left in Bangkok with no job and with everything we possessed in Rangoon. Stan Karnow, who was *Time* Bureau Chief in Hong Kong, was visiting Bangkok at that time. By good chance we met him at a cocktail party, and he asked Peter whether he would be willing to go to Laos as the *Time Magazine* stringer. Since Peter was already their stringer in Rangoon, we immediately accepted. No strangers to Laos, we were delighted to be going back there.

Laos had become centre stage once more. Little had been achieved politically for peace since our last visit in 1959. When we arrived we found that Vientiane had become a relatively busy city, with a spate of construction going on, including one or two new hotels. The streets were congested and many of the cars causing traffic jams were Mercedes and army jeeps.

We noticed that compared to 1955 and 1959, there were more Americans to be seen. Their presence was felt in various administrative departments and in the army. Apart from the diplomats, there were attachés and advisors from the American Aid programmes, and a number of Air America personnel. Though the French were still around, they were less visible. Politically, the atmosphere was full of intrigue and manoeuvring, with each faction – the Neutralists, the Right-wing Royalist Faction and the Left-wing Faction – trying to dominate the other.

To understand something of the Laotian situation, one must look back to the intervening years from 1955 to 1962. During this period, a great deal had happened to change Laos, most notably the events which occurred during 1959 and 1962.

At the beginning of 1959, the National Assembly gave the Royal Laotian Government of Phoui Sananikone special powers for one year to rectify problems which had arisen with the North Vietnamese along its borders. Since there was supposed to be a coalition government, during the early part of that year an ultimatum was given to the two Pathet Lao battalions under Prince Souphanouvong, often called the 'Red Prince', to integrate with the Royal Lao Army. One battalion did join, but the other battalion escaped making its way towards the North Vietnamese frontier. Prince Souphanouvong and other Pathet Lao leaders, considered to be Communists, were in Vientiane at that time and so were arrested. They were released, but in July were re-arrested, creating more bad blood.

Although the North Vietnamese, accused of supporting the Pathet Lao, denied having troops within Laos, there were frequent skirmishes between the Royal Lao army and North Vietnamese troops stationed within Laos. Due to this situation, in August a state of emergency was proclaimed in the northern provinces. The Royal Lao Government then requested help from the United Nations, and Dag Hammarskjold, the UN Secretary General visited Laos in November. A month later, the reigning monarch, King Sisavang Vong passed away, and was succeeded by his son, King Savang Vattana.

Though new elections were scheduled to be held in November, the Prime Minister decided against it and instead formed a new government. However, there was opposition to extending the present mandate of the National Assembly, and he resigned on 30 December. On the following day, New Year's Eve, senior generals of the Royal Army carried out a coup, saying they were safeguarding the unity of the country; at the same time, the National Assembly was dissolved.

Behind the scenes diplomacy produced some semblance of peace once more, and a civilian government was brought into power in January, 1960.

In the meantime, Prince Souvanna Phouma resigned his Embassy in Paris to stand for the up-coming elections, which took place in April, when he won the seat for Luang Prabang and a month later, was elected President of the National Assembly. In May, his half brother, Prince Souphanouvong, managed to escape and marched back north to his Pathet Lao stronghold.

A new Prime Minister was elected in June, but his government only lasted for three months, as on the night of August 9, Captain Kong Lae, head of the elite Second Paratroops Battalion of the Royal Army, staged a coup. His stated justification was objection to the "politics of an allegedly corrupt government".[38] Other reasons were that the soldiers under his command were extremely disgruntled due to exhaustion and exasperation at continual operations against the Pathet Lao forces.

He also advocated neutralism and requested that Prince Souvanna Phouma become Prime Minister. The Neutralist leader, a much respected and able politician, formed his seventh government incorporating two right-wing figures, Prince Boun Oum and General Phoumi Nosavan, though the two never took up their posts.

Instead, General Phoumi Nosavan, the right-wing general, flew south to Savannakhet, and with Prince Boun Oum, formed a Revolutionary Committee, to combat the insubordinate, Captain Kong Lae. The general also refused to recognize Souvanna's government, although it was approved by the National Assembly.

During the last months of 1960, there was little to stabilize the country as fighting commenced between the Royal Lao army and troops loyal to Kong Lae. An attempt by one of the generals was made to unseat the young captain and to seize control of Vientiane. At this point, Prince Souvanna Phouma, losing patience with all the wrangling between the different political factions and the army, departed for Cambodia. From there, he embarked on a world tour trying to gain support for his government of neutrality. Meanwhile, the King declared that Prince Souvanna Phouma's government was no longer legal.

In January 1961, the National Assembly met and gave its support to Prince Boun Oum. No longer able to hold out in Vientiane, Kong Lae departed northward with his troops, giving little thought to a reconciliation with the right-wing.

*Laotian Royal Family c. 1958-1959*
*Sitting centre: King Sisavang Vong and*
*Queen.*
*Standing: Crown Prince Savang Vattana*
*and Consort, with Princess Savivan,*
*their eldest daughter.*
*Furthest right is Prince Souvanna*
*Phouma.*

*Three Princes meeting at Ban Hin Heup,*
*Prince Souvanna Phouma with right-wing*
*strongman General Phoumi Nosavan.*

*General Kong Lae, Commander-in-*
*Chief of Neutralist Forces, Khang*
*Khay, in foreground.*

*Peter with Prince Boun Oum na*
*Champasak on the Plaine des Jarres.*

There were calls for the return of the International Control Commission, (ICC) which had 'adjourned *sin die*', two years before. Eventually in May it returned. A de facto cease fire was declared and the proposed resumption of inspections along the north-eastern borders began.

By May, representatives of the three factions began a series of meetings, primarily to declare a full ceasefire. By October, there had been some progress and the Three Princes met at Ban Hin Heup, to hold discussions on how best to achieve a peace settlement for the country.

In the midst of these happenings, we were able to find a house by the Mekong, which we promptly rented. The spacious two-storey wooden house once painted a pale lime green had faded with only a glimmer of the original colour showing. It had a wide veranda on one side on the first floor which became our dining and living area during the day.

In the large upstairs sitting room Peter and I sat facing each other and we could be seen pounding out our stories furiously on our typewriters after a press conference, in an effort to get to the PTT, the telegraphic office, first, before our competitors could file their stories. Since the PTT closed its door firmly between noon and three in the afternoon there was always an urgency to get there on time to meet European and American deadlines

We felt happy to be back in Laos and as soon as we were settled in, we went to the Ministry of Information to register ourselves. Peter for *Time Magazine*, the *New York Times* and *The Observer*, and I, for Reuters and *The Daily Mail*.

Stringing for Reuters meant I had to file every day whether there was a story or not, and when a story broke, it had to be filed immediately. So I was kept very much on my toes trying to beat the other agencies.

By now, the Neutralist faction, with its leader Prince Souvanna Phouma, was based in Khang Khay, in the middle of Laos on the plateau known as the Plaine des Jarres. This was where Kong Lae, now a General, and his army were also. Members of the left-wing Pathet Lao headed by Prince Souphanouvong were there as well. The Royal Lao Government with its leader, Prince Boun Oum of Champasak, remained in the capital, Vientiane.

Britain, France, the United States and Russia, vigorously manoeuvred behind the scenes to try and make peace between the three Princes. The objective was to produce a stable government for the country. Their task was not an easy one. All these political goings on naturally gave us a great deal to write about. As the political situation became more tense, Vientiane filled up with other journalists and foreign correspondents.

Reporting on these complicated machinations was not always easy and many of us were in and out of the American and British Embassies, seeking clarification on certain points. Press briefings, held almost daily by either embassy, helped us to understand the position of the Three Princes and the views of these four Western powers. Trevor Wilson from the British Information was always willing to help, as was Colin McColl, who took us under his wing to explain the intricacy of the changing political scene. Norris Smith from the American Embassy had a busy time too, looking after a large number of American newsmen who had descended en masse upon Vientiane.

As well, we had language difficulties. There were few Laotian officials who spoke English, since Laotian and French were the two languages mainly used for all administrative purposes. Peter, who spoke fluent French often found himself interpreting for a speaker at many of the press conferences given by Laotian officials.

There was a feeling of camaraderie amongst us newspeople, and once we had filed our stories for the day, many would congregate at the Constellation Hotel buying drinks for each other. At other times, we used to have a houseful of journalists who drifted in to have a post mortem after a particularly long speech given by one of the princes. There were so many nuances that none of us wanted to get it wrong.

Many of us made monthly helicopter flights over Pathet Lao territory either to attend the Three Princes' Meetings, as they became known, or to the headquarters of the Neutralists at Khang Khay for Prince Souvanna Phouma's press conferences.

Additional interviews were also accorded to Peter and I, whenever Prince Souvanna Phouma had something to say, or when there was a political rally of the Neutralists. In this manner, we became acquainted with the Neutralists, politicians and military personalities alike.

Once when we were invited to a special military parade held by General Kong Lae at Phongsavan, there were no rooms left at the small Chinese hotel run by a fat Madame where we usually stayed. Kong Lae, beaming happily said he had arranged for us to stay with the family of a French restaurateur. Little did we know when we arrived that we would be sharing an eight-foot wide bed with a family of six. "What we have to do to get a story!", I complained to Peter, who grinned mischievously and taking the outside edge of the bed, replied "Worth it, for a scoop! Come, lie close to me, and don't fret", as we clambered under the tent like mosquito net and the giant quilt. Anyway, I suppose it was preferable to sharing either a room or a bed with Kong Lae's bawdy young officers who frequented Madame's establishment.

Prince Souvanna Phouma from time to time used to warn us, "I hope you understand, I will not be able to save you, should the plane in which you are travelling crash, and you should fall into Pathet Lao hands".

*View of the large, heavy jars spread over the plateau of Plaine des Jarres.*

*Three Princes Meeting, Plaine des Jarres.*
*L to R: Prince Boun Oum na Champasak, former Right-wing Premier,*
*(with hat), Prince Souvanna Phouma, Neutralist Prime Minister of*
*Laos, (centre) and Prince Souphannouvong, Leader of the left-wing*
*Pathet Lao Party.*

In those times, there were no clear demarcation as to which of the factions controlled which area. One never knew what might happen, and the prince's warning was apt. Though we did know there were risks making those dangerous trips, we felt that the ideas and thoughts Prince Souvanna Phouma and his Neutralists wanted to convey to the world, were worth reporting. Then, of course, there was Prince Souphanouvong, the half-brother and leader of the Pathet Lao, who would sometimes add a comment or two.

Laotians both in Vientiane and in Phongsavan, used to say to Peter, "Thank goodness you are here. At least, you understand our problems, and maybe people will listen to sense." Our many visits to Laos somehow had given them confidence in Peter, and we shared with them their ups and downs. Peter also won the trust of some of the diplomatic corps for his accurate and measured reporting on the prevailing situation.

The Laotians, regardless of whichever faction they belonged to were always kind and hospitable. It was like being back amongst one's family and friends in the Shan States. We made a large number of friends, too many to name, who treated us as one of their family. Our friendships have continued from our first visit in 1955 to the present, as many of them have come to live in Europe in exile.

By December, the Three Princes had met variously in Zurich, on the Plaine des Jarres and in Vientiane, but nothing concrete had come out of these meetings.

In January, 1962, the Co-chairmen of the 1954 Geneva Conference, invited the Three Princes to Geneva to find out more about their disagreements. But it was yet another failure. This time, objections were raised from the right-wing group.

Over the next months, it became clear that each faction was now holding firm to its position, determined not to give in. During this period, both Ambassador Averell Harriman, sent by President Kennedy, and Malcolm Macdonald, the British co-chairman of the Geneva Conference came to Vientiane, to help ease tensions and to try to solve some continuing problems.

*Dinner at Lang Xang, Vientiane with Tony
Beamish of the BBC and other journalists.*

Going ahead with what happened later, June saw the resumption of negotiations between the Three Princes on the Plaine des Jarres. At last, we thought, there was hope for peace, which had eluded Laos for so long.

Then in July, 1962 in Geneva, an Agreement was finally signed. The Agreement, said Hugh Toye "was comprehensive, embodying a formal statement of intent by Laos herself and solemn undertaking to respect the neutrality of the country by all the nations represented." He was to add that by the end of the year "the hope that the Laotian dilemma was indeed solved began to fade."[39]

We had all worked together with the hope of finding a solution for lasting peace and a stable government for Laos, and people had pinned their hopes on the Three Princes. No one wanted to consider neutrality for Laos in the 1960s as the United States was in fear of a neutral government turning Communist. For that period, the right-wing and the military triumphed. By the 1970s, Laos was to be swept into the orbit of the Vietnam war. Nothing could stop this fall. Events moved too fast and people were helpless.

This whole period in Southeast Asia was a very interesting one and, looking back to the early 1960s, one finds that each country had its own political troubles. Peter and I were lucky to have been in Laos to see the initial stages of political change. In addition, what had happened and was happening in Laos was useful to compare with the situation which was developing in Burma at that time.

Today the country is no longer the Royal Kingdom of Laos, but the Republic of Democratic Laos. It is ruled by a regime with Communist beliefs. Though the regime in Burma is not Communist, there is no longer a freely-elected government, but an army regime which is in power.

During 1961-1962 in Laos, whatever little news we received about Burma from time to time was never good. Reports were that Burman politicians and newspapers were trying to undermine the prestige of the Saohpas, accusing them of being disloyal citizens. They were said to have been plotting against the U Nu government and had been called traitors. No one was spared, even Sao Hkun Hkio, the Saohpa of Mong Mit and one time Foreign Minister of the Union of Burma Government, was criticised. Like my father, he was a loyal citizen.

This was hard to take, since it was an unfair one-sided campaign, and it made me extremely unhappy. It must have been very trying for Sao U Hpa, since you could not have found a more law-abiding person than he, nor one who could ever be disloyal. Coming from an old princely family and having been in the army and trained by the British, he certainly knew the meaning of honour, duty and loyalty.

Despite the furore against the Saohpas from the Burmans, U Nu and his wife continued being friendly with the family, as did General Aung San's wife. In addition, my stepmother continued her acquaintance with Kitty, General Ne Win's wife. So it must have been a time of uneasiness for these relationships.

Many years later, in trying to work out why Peter and I were not allowed to return to our jobs in Rangoon, one of our many conclusions was that it may have been because U Nu's government did not like the economic articles Peter had previously been writing for the local *Guardian* newspaper. In some of the articles he had pointed out the mistakes that had been made and the problems which existed within the fragile economy. Also he had been writing for the *Far Eastern Economic Review* and *Time Magazine*, and it was quite possible that they did not approve of some of those articles either.

We also recalled the number of times, we used to be asked quite casually, "Have you been to Thailand or Laos recently?" by some friendly political figures we knew. Did these people think that our visits to Bangkok and Vientiane were not merely holidays but that we were involved in some political manoeuvres? Perhaps by refusing to give Peter a re-entry visa, the Burmese government was hoping that we would leave Asia and go back to Europe. Did whatever suspicions they had of us deepen because we did not return to Europe, but stayed on in Laos? We will perhaps never know.

In February 1962, while there was a flurry of negotiations and meetings between the Three Princes, out of the blue after almost a year, we were told Peter had been given a visa by the U Nu government. It was for one month only, in order that we could clear up our affairs in Rangoon. This was a blow to us, because it meant that Peter would not be allowed to return to his post at the university, and, obviously, I would no longer be working with the Burma Broadcasting Service. There was no question of an extension to the one month stay. Despite this disappointment, we were glad to learn that both the British Embassy, and the Rangoon University had kindly continued pressing for Peter's return. Now our return to which we had so looked forward was only to be for a disappointingly short time.

I could feel that there was some political motive in all this. Certainly, it was a loss of face for my father not to be able to bring his daughter and son-in-law back into the country. We learnt later that there was much political activity going on in the Shan States, as finally the Shan and other ethnic nationalities were beginning to think for themselves. They were putting forward ideas and trying to work together towards unity. A sharp eye and a close watch was kept on them as these moves were seen by Burman politicians, newspapers and the army as treacherous and dangerous.

Though we had not made up our minds when to return to Burma, we felt this might be the time to do so. There were no concrete conclusions from the princely meetings at the present, and since we had only a month's stay in Rangoon, it seemed probable that we would be back before the next session of important meetings.

*Sao Shwe Thaike,*
*formal portrait.*

# XII

## *Problems ahead*

### *Undercurrents*

We did not fully realize that the year we were away, 1961-62, had been one of continuous political and economic upheaval for the country. Although U Nu was back in power, he was not really in control. It appeared that things were beginning to disintegrate again.

Unlike his predecessor, General Aung San, who knew what he wanted and how to obtain it, U Nu had wide-ranging ideals which perhaps were not always easy to implement. He was also a man who tried to please everybody. Nor like his successor, General Ne Win, was he tough and ruthless. Somehow, U Nu seemed to have neither the temperament, nor the understanding, to continue the army's policies, and he soon found himself facing one crisis after another. His election promises had been broad and appealed to so many different communities, that when he tried to implement them, he created even greater divisions.

In one of the editorials of a national English-language newspaper of that period on 28 June 1960, it said that there was a growing doubt about U Nu's ability to govern the country, commenting "U Nu is running true to form of injecting misplaced sentiment and religion into the day to day administration of the country … and perhaps unwittingly making a mess of things."

One can sympathise with the difficulties that U Nu had to face. Most of the politicians were men with whom he had grown up and there was a bond of camaraderie; together they had gone through the heady days of anti-colonialism, the Japanese occupation, the liberation and independence. On the other hand, since a latent rivalry existed between them, none could be considered a real friend he could rely on. Each had their own agenda, with differing ideas for their country and there was a proliferation of political parties.

His own party, the Union Party, was itself in turmoil, the members quarrelling amongst themselves for positions in the government. As things stood, many felt they were not benefiting, and were even in danger of losing their privileged positions. As Prime Minister, U Nu's position was hardly an enviable one.

The promise of Buddhism as the State religion, naturally did not go down well with those of other religious denominations, such as the Christians, Hindus, Moslems, and Animists. So even this issue created concern and distress.

As far as the possibility of statehood for Arakan and the Mon were concerned, talks were already going ahead and smoothly. The amnesty being offered to many rebel groups, including the Communists, was slowly taking effect.

Though the army was only observing from the sidelines they became increasingly infuriated with U Nu and the politicians. They were extremely proud of their achievements. The expectant brigadiers and colonels watched aghast, as seemingly their brilliant economic and social accomplishments carried out with military precision over the last eighteen months, were being dismantled. It was not certain why at this stage, the quarrelling politicians were not more conscious of the havoc they were creating, especially with the army looking on. The military had given U Nu and the politicians a second chance by handing back power. But the latter were unaware that they had to prove themselves capable of running the country. What U Nu failed to notice, was that the army's patience was wearing thin. Soon it would not matter which direction he took, for the military were already preparing to overthrow him.

Around that time, one of the top army colonels is quoted as saying to the foreign press that despite twelve years of independence the politicians had contributed nothing, "At this rate our country will go to the dogs sooner or later". Unfortunately, these pronouncements were to come true. Neither the civilian government nor the military could prevent the future disarray of the country.

One must not forget the ferocity and the manner in which the Tamadaw had dealt with the Communist insurgents (CPU) and the Karens (KNU) earlier. Such draconian methods became practiced tactics used later, when fighting against the real or imagined rebels often known as the 'multi-coloured rebel groups'. Many of the techniques were incorporated from military procedures used in various different friendly countries, including Israel.

For the last almost 50 years, the army has fought running battles with the Karen in the south, and with the Shan, the Kachin and the Chin in the north. Any ceasefires have been ineffectual and the fighting goes on. Initially, it had been chiefly due to harsh and cruel treatment by the Tamadaw, that the nationalist groups took up arms and went underground.

Over the years these groups have been termed 'rebels' and 'terrorists', but they are in fact nationalists, fighting against repression. It naturally suits the military regime to categorize them as the former, since the mention of terrorism was more likely to gain them international support and munitions.

The aims of these nationalist groups have been to win equal status and responsibilities within the government of the country. It was a goal that men of my father's generation tried to achieve in vain.

The unrestrained animosity mainly in the army towards other ethnic nationalities has gradually become so intense that it has spilled out into blatant savagery. The Tamadaw has no respect for those who are not Burmans. Their attitude towards minorities is expressed by one army officer, who was quoted as saying that the only thing he knew about minorities was "how to kill them".[40] With such attitudes prevelant among the majority of the military, how can the Shan and other ethnic groups ever trust and live peacefully together again with the Burmans?

The years of the AFPFL government had not been a successful time for our ethnic nationalities. Year after year, the deviations from the principles upon which the Panglong Agreement had been drawn up with General Aung San became ever more blatant. In 1961, therefore, the Shan, together with other nationalities, began seeking reforms to the 1947 Constitution which they felt had been drawn up too hastily and was now in need of amendments.

My eldest brother, Sao Sai, who had been in the Shan States at the time of these first discussions in early 1961, told me that the talks had been initiated by my father to discuss the demarcation of the frontier with China, since the land involved concerned Chin, Kachin and Shan State areas. A request was then made to U Nu seeking alteration to some sections of the Constitution regarding the border. The Chief Justice of the country saw nothing wrong in asking for these changes and gave his consent to go ahead. At this point, other states such as Kayah, Mon and Arakan also decided to join in, since they too had points to make and it seemed an opportune moment.

The proposed changes were sensibly and lawfully presented under the aegis of the legally-constituted Shan Government, an action that was taken only after seeking advice from leading judicial and legal members of the profession, who were mainly Burmans.

As was to be expected, these proposals to amend the Constitution quite naturally led to discussions on common problems and unanimous agreement for federation. Whatever may have been believed by the Burman politicians, newspapers and foreign embassies, I understand no serious reference was ever made by the Shan then on the question of secession. The requests for constitutional changes were in fact, recommendations for strengthening the Union, to give ethnic nationalities unity and an equal voice within the country's parliament.

Although alarm bells rang for the military when they observed these political activities, there need not have been any fear. What was being put forward for consideration was to reinstate in part agreements, reached earlier, for a loose form of federation as General Aung San had envisaged. It was also thought that through reform, widespread discontent could be stemmed, thus averting further uprisings.

The ethnic nationalities firmly believed there was discrimination against them with many long-standing problems. Over the years, whenever discussions on development projects for the country were held, they invariably focussed on improvements for cities and larger towns which were naturally situated in Burma Proper. Since these places were largely populated by Burmans, with a smattering of Anglo-Burmans, Indians and Chinese, they were the ones who benefited most.

Perhaps it was not intentional, but once the projects had been put in motion they were not enlarged to include outlying regions such as the Shan States and the Frontier Areas. No doubt there were similar projects for these areas but it took longer for them to be implemented. The bureaucratic outlook from central government was generally that there was no urgency to carry out these projects, which meant that little happened. There was more talk than action.

Many foreign experts in the field of education and the economy often tended to talk in overall terms of assisting the people of the country, when they were really talking about the Burmans. No one seems to have insisted that these projects, whatever they might be, should include help for other ethnic nationalities.

Ever since Independence, the ethnic nationalities had found that the central administration was not sympathetic to their problems but only wanted to gain control over them. They became sceptical and suspicious of any moves made by the Union government and, consequently, the return to a federal government as envisaged earlier became more and more attractive.

General Aung San's memorable promise – "If Burma receives one *kyat*, you will also get one *kyat*" – became a motto for the different nationalities. At the Panglong Agreement, General Aung San was the sole signatory for the Burmese

Government, but after he was assassinated, did the AFPFL take this to mean that they no longer needed to honour the letter of the agreement? Although not stated publicly, there might have been a secret understanding to forget Aung San's pledge. Could this be the reason then, as now, that the ruling powers continue to disregard the Panglong Agreement?

When the first Constitutional Amendment Meetings were taking place in December 1960, my father handed a letter to the then Minister of Justice, expressing his personal view of why he felt such amendments were of paramount importance. He wrote "of the practice of racism", which I have termed Burmanization; of the Shan States and others being under the "subordination of Burma proper"; and of the inadequate finances given to the States for development, since purse strings were controlled by the central government. He reiterated, in reference to federalism, that "No one in the States has the intention of destroying the Union". and concluded:"If Burma proper becomes a Constituent State of the Union, on equal footing with other States, the dissatisfaction will gradually disappear."[41]

On the Burman side there appeared to be a stone wall – no politician or military man took my father's statement into consideration, despite the fact, that many non-Burmans also held the same sentiments.

Unlike the military, U Nu did not think that having a federation would have broken up the Union, since he had been given assurances by Shan and other ethnic leaders that that was not their intention. Nor did he believe the damaging rumours being circulated about the Saohpas and Shan leaders, since they had always backed him and were loyal to the Union. He knew my father's position on federalism, and I am sure, they must have discussed this subject in private a number of times.

Although U Nu might have been listening to the ideas on federalism, he was fully aware that there would be strong opposition from his own party and people, had he ever thought of granting any form of federation or equal status to non-Burmans. He knew that it was not what the Burman political elite nor the military wanted, and was soon to learn the military's strategy.

The propaganda of the day was that the military had to take over in 1962, because of the 'federal movement'. The truth of the matter was that the ethnic proposal for a Federated State of equal partners, composed of "Burma Proper and the Frontier Areas", was what the military did not like. It did not want to consider any kind of constitutional reform, since to General Ne Win these proposals were unconstitutional. Thus the army proclaimed that the federal movement was a dissident organization out to break up the Union of Burma.

They were quick to condemn such proposals, saying to foreign correspondents that, "Federation is impossible, it will destroy the Union" and that "Burma cannot afford such a luxury as federalism." [42] The idea of federation was totally abhorrent since they did not want to share power, believing then, as now, that other people living in Burma were underdogs, and only the Tamadaw had the right to rule the country.

Contrary to what the army claimed, any sensible person could have seen that there would not have been any advantage in seeking to dismantle the Union. It was, after all, the much revered Panglong Agreement of February 1947, which had brought about the formation of the Union of Burma. The Shan, Kachins, and Chin leaders had then given their trust and loyalty to the Union, as had General Aung

San himself, who had made pledges and signed this important Agreement, for the country's independence and its creation.

Nevertheless, during 1961 and the beginning of 1962, there were cryptic and vicious remarks in the newspapers, seemingly questioning my father's position, with veiled accusations insinuating that he had been in touch with SEATO and the KMT, seeking their help to dismantle the Union. It appeared that some of these newsmen were passing judgement and indulging in naive speculations, without trying or even wanting to understand my father's viewpoint.

It would be an ill-informed military, indeed, if it were to continue to insist that the real reason for throwing out U Nu's government was solely because of the Federal Movement. At that moment there were a multitude of alarming internal problems. There was rising insurgency throughout the country, with political and social unrest spreading in cities; there was the problem of the KMT, whom the army had yet to evict; externally there was an aggressive Communist China on Burma's borders despite the treaties of goodwill and friendship signed between the two countries.

Rumours of discussions among Union Party leaders of wanting to curb the excesses of the military and of a possible reduction in their numbers also did not go down well with army officers. Whether these latter stories were true or false, such proposals would not have been entertained by the military.

General Ne Win, who was no fool, most certainly was also influenced by outside events. Looking back on 1961 and 1962, it wasn't only in the Union that there was trouble. Neighbouring Laos, as mentioned earlier, was in the middle of political chaos and there had been a coup d'état which eventually divided the country into three factions. Thailand also was politically unstable. Such a climate undoubtedly made the army nervous.

SEATO was also becoming concerned about the political situation in South-east Asia. In those days, the domino theory of Communism was much in vogue. One must not forget that since the Second World War, America has always had a powerful influence on the military of these Southeast Asian countries, and the Tamadaw, in those days, was no exception.

Once the General had made up his mind to act, he obviously did not need any reason for his actions. However, seeking a scapegoat, he decided to blame the Saohpas, the Federal Movement. The people of the country were made to believe this lie.

The constitutional seminar held in March 1962 with U Nu's blessing had been approved the previous year after he had been swept back to power. Despite his uncertainty on the reactions from his party and the military, perhaps he believed then that he was strong enough to fight the opposition. Fatefully, his calculations proved wrong. Leaders and representatives of all nationalities had travelled to Rangoon from their respective States to attend the convention. It was a godsend for the army to have everyone they wanted in the capital at the same time, making it simpler for Ne Win to overthrow U Nu's government. The coup was suddenly and brilliantly executed. The prime minister, including his cabinet and all parliamentarians, were swiftly detained. Although there may have been rumours of an army takeover, I have a feeling that people were not unduly concerned at that moment and were taken by surprise.

## *Coup d'état*

The coup d'état of 1962 was completely different from that of 1958. The Caretaker Government had been a benign, efficient military government. The general public had been greatly impressed by its earlier achievements. To many, its 1958 shining reputation could never be tarnished and the public regarded it as a saviour. Thus when the 1962 coup came, many thought that military rule might not be so bad. People had had enough of politicians who never kept their word, and they wanted change.

Never did the unsuspecting public imagine that the military regime they thought might deliver them from political bedlam had come in a different guise. Before long people were to find out that it was not the same benign authority which ruled previously and was nothing like the highly praised Caretaker Government. Although they did not know it, the military regime had come to stay.

On the fateful day of 2nd March, we were still in Laos and had just finished breakfast, when I turned on the radio to listen to the short wave broadcast from Burma, as I generally did every morning. I could not believe the news I heard – a coup d'état had taken place in Rangoon, and the army under General Ne Win had taken control. The news also said that my father had been taken into detention. The only casualty of the coup was one of my younger brothers, Myee Myee. He had been shot by the soldiers who had come to arrest my father. I was devastated to hear the appalling news.

When the news of the coup in Burma broke, some of the foreign correspondents who were with us in Vientiane, naturally headed immediately for Rangoon. We arranged to follow them as soon as we had picked up Peter's visa at the Burmese Embassy in Bangkok. But when we arrived in Bangkok, some of our friends who had already got to Rangoon warned us that our presence might not be welcomed by the military and advised us to think again about going on to Rangoon.

Peter and I decided that whatever awaited us, we had to go back to Rangoon. We wanted desperately to see my father and to find out how he was fairing. We also wanted to be at Myee Myee's funeral but were not able to start out for Rangoon until a day later. I really felt desperate not being there.

A two hour flight from Bangkok turned out to be a nightmare. Every time we were about to depart, they reported something wrong with the aeroplane. We had been trying to leave since 2 o'clock in the afternoon, but we did not take off until well past midnight. We finally landed, but with all the formalities on the plane, did not arrive at the airport building until after 3.00 am in the morning. It was clear that a state of high security existed, and it looked as if we would not be cleared for another hour or two. It was also obvious we wouldn't get home until about 5.00 am, and we felt the noise of our arrival might terrify the family. Peter, therefore, asked to be allowed to telephone the Strand Hotel to book a room. An American diplomat and his very pregnant wife were on the plane with us and it was their first visit to Rangoon. They were stranded as there was no one to meet them, so we gave them the number of the Strand Hotel to make their reservation.

Our arrival, as can be expected, caused considerable interest. There was much too-ing and fro-ing as the security officials checked Peter's visa. They were making doubly sure that he really had permission to return.

By the time we were allowed to leave, the other passengers who had been cleared were sitting in the bus waiting for us. Everyone looked exhausted, but the young American wife was almost in tears. We asked her why, and she said that we had taken the last room at the Strand, and they didn't know what they could do. She seemed even more pregnant than before, so Peter and I decided that the only decent thing was to offer them our room and have the airline bus drop us off at our house, which fortunately lay on the route into town. Little did we know the problems we were laying up for ourselves.

There were guards all around the compound, and they reluctantly let us in. Daw Daw and the children heard the noise of the vehicle at the gate and came out of the house to find out what was happening. As may be imagined, our meeting was one of great joy, mixed with sorrow over Sao U Hpa's arrest and the death of Myee Myee.

Hugging me Daw Daw wept, asking over and over again, "What is happening?", "What is going to happen to all of us?" We huddled together spending a long time, talking, sobbing and worrying about Sao U Hpa. The children looked forlorn, the whole experience of the shooting and seeing their father being taken away so unceremoniously, was traumatic. It all seemed senseless, with no reasons to be found.

Peter and I had had no idea that my stepmother was not in Rangoon and that she had gone to London for health reasons. It seemed a terrible time for my father not to have her there in the house with his children. I was sick at heart wondering how Sao U Hpa might be feeling, and whether he was right in sending his wife away when he needed her most. Perhaps restless behaviour by the military had given some clues as to its intentions, and my father had been thinking ahead. As it happened it was a wise move, and very fortunate, that Sao Mye was not in Rangoon.

I don't remember how closely we kept in touch with my stepmother at that difficult time – we had no reliable international telephonic service and telegrams were the fastest form of communication. It was worrying for both the children and their mother being so far apart.

We woke Gopal, our Indian house boy, and went up to our flat above the garages. One would have thought that we had never been away. Everything was spotless and every book and picture were exactly where we had left them nearly a year ago.

The first thing next morning, I telephoned Colonel Lwin, head of Burma's Military Intelligence Service (MIS), to ask his permission to see my father. Known to most people as 'the moustachio', he was considered tough and was feared. As in the past he had been cordial to us and at times even friendly, he seemed the best person to contact. As soon as he came to the phone, he began by asking where we were staying. When I told him we were at home, he wouldn't believe me. He kept saying, "So you are not at the Strand Hotel then?".

It became clear that Peter's telephone conversation with the hotel had been intercepted, and he couldn't understand why we weren't there. In their search for us, the poor guests at the hotel had been turned out of their rooms, while they made certain we weren't hiding in one of the rooms.

When I asked if I might be given permission to see my father, he did not give a direct no, but said the request would be considered. I am afraid for the four whole weeks that we had permission to stay, my frequent requests to see my father were turned down. It was very upsetting and I couldn't believe that the authorities could be so heartless.

I have no idea what they suspected us of, but Peter and I were under surveillance all the time. One day, the MIS man assigned to us came to ask if Peter had been out the day before, when my aunt, the children and I went to the monastery. We had gone in two cars, but Peter had decided not to go with us. When we told the agent that Peter stayed behind, he kept insisting that there were two cars, so he must have been in one of them. It took sometime to convince him that Peter had indeed been at home all morning.

After that incident, Peter asked the agent to come and have breakfast with us each morning to compare notes. We felt that his reports to the MIS would be more accurate, if we filled in the gaps for him. There were very few nights during our stay, when we could have a good night's sleep. Three or four times a night there was always a car or a jeep, that would come to the corner where our house was, screech to a stop then turn around and revving its engine speed off. Sometimes, what seemed like truckloads of soldiers would come belting down the road, tooting their horn if they wished. It was nerve wracking not knowing what they were up to.

Since we were back only to stay in Rangoon temporarily, Sai Hseng decided to take the two youngest children, Harn and Leun, to be with him and his family. Daw Daw stayed on in the family house while we were there with Tzang and Ying. No real plans could be made for the children, especially with their mother being away. I remember the long conversations we used to have with Tzang and Ying, as we walked around the compound. We could not work out why the coup had taken place nor why the army had acted so forcefully. The questions were always why, why, why?

Soon, the army were to give their answer – one which seemed utterly incredible. I could hardly believe that they pointed their finger at federalism and to those connected with it. The Saohpas and the ethnic leaders were blamed once more.

When our month was up, we left, having booked ourselves on a Polish cargo boat to Singapore. Just as we were about to board, a voice called out "Mr. Simms, Mr. Simms". Peter gave me a glance as if to say, "This is what we have been expecting," and my heart sank. A man came running out with a piece of paper, which turned out to be a receipt that we had not picked up. What a relief. All our fears which had been bottled up inside and never discussed during the month, seemed to go the moment the anchor was hoisted. It was only when we sailed away and had arrived in Singapore that we felt really safe.

Of course it was distressing, packing up to leave our home, but I seriously thought we would be back before too long – how wrong I was.

After a brief stay in Singapore, we returned to Vientiane in time for the visits of the two dignitaries, Averell Harriman and Malcolm Macdonald, mentioned before. After the June meeting of the Three Princes on the Plaine des Jarres, the venue was shifted to Geneva in July. To have the satisfaction of seeing the completion of these meetings we had followed for so long, we decided it would be good to attend the Geneva Conference for the signing of the important Agreement.

With some sadness, we began making preparations and packing our belongings in the lovely riverside house. It stood looking out on the gently flowing Mekong,

*Siblings perched on a rock in
Kunming, 1957.*

*Myee Myee, a casualty
of 1962 coup.*

*With my siblings:
from left to right: Myee, Htila, Sanda,
Harn, Leun and Hso.*

where we had had a busy, but happy stay in Vientiane. Within a short space of time so much had changed in our lives. We were leaving the many friends we had made and a country I had adopted as my own.

Would we ever return to the Laos we had got to know and love? We did in 1966, but much happened in the intervening years.

## *Reflections*

Thinking back ever the past years a great many questions come to mind. What would Burma have been like if General Aung San had not been assassinated? Would he have kept his promise of all partners being equal? Was the secession clause merely a ploy to make us join so he could achieve his own demands for Independence from the British? Did he feel that once the Shan and the Frontier peoples were part of the Union, it would be easier to deal with them?

How much should we have trusted him? One wonders, too, if he would have had control over the military, or, would he being a Burman, have sided with them? With so much power, would he have become corrupt like so many others?

Other questions concern the role of my father. If he had not become President would the Shans have been in a better position? If Sao Sam Htun had lived, and had not been assassinated together with General Aung San, would the Shan State with his advice and guidance progressed along the lines that had been envisaged? Such troubling questions can never be answered.

I know that my father was always conscious that the Saohpas and eminent Shan leaders had to stand together if they wanted to achieve progress for their people. He realized, too, that the Japanese war and its aftermath, and subsequent independence for Burma, had brought the outside world into our own in a rush. He knew that whilst he was the President, and later the Speaker of the House of Nationalities, he could do little as his hands were tied . He had to wait until he had finished his duties for the Union. Perhaps he hoped that once free of state duties, he could work again for the Shan cause wholeheartedly, albeit treading carefully.

There is no doubt that as Saohpalong of Yawnghwe he was already a powerful figure, without becoming President of the Union of Burma. As one of the elder statesmen and a much respected ruler within the Shan States, he could have helped in forging stronger ties amongst the Shan and other ethnic nationalities enabling them to speak with confidence and with one voice.

I suspect that by the time he was able to take up Shan affairs again, it was already too late. After fifteen years of Independence the Union was in a state of flux. My father reappearing on the scene to fight for the cause of the Shan in union with other ethnic nationalities, began to appear to the elite Burman politicians as a force to be reckoned with. Although it was a legitimate force, they wanted to be-lieve my father was in the wrong for speaking out for the Shan. Ultimately, what they probably did not wish to see was a united front of ethnic peoples.

I have never understood why the Burman politicians have since 1931, and probably even earlier, been so against the Saohpas, the feudal system and feder-alism? What was it that made the elite Burman politicians, the intellectuals, the newspapers and the army so opposed to these concepts?

Although there may be various reasons for such antagonism, some of the following factors may have contributed. Most Burmans generally believed that during the reign of the Burman kings, the same frontiers existed as in the present day and therefore the Shan States were always within its domain. In reality, continual wars between ancient neighbours created shifting alliances with no fixed borders. When one was strong others accepted suzerainty, when others became strong, one became weak and had to let go. King Thibaw's kingdom was at its ebb when the British annexed Upper Burma and the Shan Sates in 1886.

Having made peace with China, Laos and Siam, the demarcation of frontiers became necessary for the inclusion of Burma within the British Empire. Once this was accomplished and the country was under control, the British unceremoniously exiled reigning King Thibaw and his Queen to India leaving a vacuum without a replacement. The Burmans were appalled and angered by the action, even though no suitable leading prince or important minister was found to take over the throne, since they had already been exterminated by the royal couple. Consequently the country became a colony, ruled jointly with India, hurting the pride of the Burmans who always considered themselves conquerors and not the vanquished.

Next, the British decided to rule Ministerial Burma separately leaving the Saohpas to their own devices but answerable directly to the Governor. For the Burmans this added insult to injury and they called this policy a diarchy or a government of divide and rule. The anti-British feeling grew gradually to become intense nationalism.

For the Burmans, it was galling to see Shan princes holding power, respected and looked up to by their subjects. The Shans had always been considered 'barbarians' yet now the princes could continue to lead their own lives in their States having little to do with the plains people. When they met in Rangoon, Burman politicians would address the ruling princes as 'Sawbwagyi', *gyi* meaning great in Burmese. While flattering them on the surface, deep down they felt resentment, which grew over time until the Saohpas became an anathema to the Burman. Understandably there was much rejoicing in 1959 when the Saohpas relinquished their powers, but another hurdle arose when the Shan State government began cooperating with the princes. This coming together to speak with one voice, was viewed with great suspicions.

The British were blamed for the earlier separation, the argument being that the Shan States would have been less primitive and better assimilated had the Burmans been allowed to travel freely within the Shan States. Is this really true? Or were they set on Burmanization even then?

In 1947, the Panglong Agreement had created the Union of Burma formed by a federation of states. Without such a form of government, I doubt the Shans and other ethnic nationalities would have joined the Union. The Burmans, however, objected to the union of different states, saying it had colonial undertones of the divide and rule policy. In fact, the main Burman hostility to such a system was having to share power with a concomitant decrease in their own supremacy.

During the period of the Caretaker government, in 1959, Josef Silverstein[43] wrote, "Officially the government supported the constitution and its objectives; unofficially it sponsored and advocated policies which ran counter to the formal pronouncements and sought to create unity through the Burmanization of the people." He rightly concludes that, "Only by ending the policy of forced Burmanization and by encouraging the gradual growth of a Burmese culture which recognizes its rich and diverse sources can people be drawn together in a viable national unity."

The days and months that followed the military's seizure of power in 1962 were obviously full of anxiety and uncertainty for the population as a whole. Buddhism had guided our lives and destinies, taught us to have reverence for the Buddha, the Dhamma and the Sangha. People throughout the centuries had accepted its teachings of humility, tolerance, civility and politeness. It was a way of life. The coming of the military, however, was a major transformation for the different societies within the country.

The Tamadaw was at last showing its true colours. People suddenly found themselves unexpectedly under the harsh edicts of a new alien order. It was hard to accept that those now giving the orders were not arrogant foreigners, but had once been 'uncles' and 'brothers'. Gone, it appeared, were the days when one could come and go as one liked, say what one wanted, or laugh and joke. The freedom that had once existed was gone.

Right up to the coup, the British, the Anglo-Burmans and Anglo-Indians in Rangoon provided most of the civil servants and professionals who maintained the infrastructure of government and society, while big British companies, together with Indian and Chinese traders, mainly ran the economy. The latter wealthy businesses had established themselves soon after colonialism was imposed and had gradually expanded to become monopolies. As a result of their riches and power Indian money-lenders and Chinese rice traders were generally detested.

General Ne Win held similar views to the general population but in addition he became paranoid. Adopting an extreme dislike for all non-Burmans, he expelled them regardless of who they were. Perhaps things could still have been different for the country if he had not taken such drastic measures. Subsequently, his policy developed into rejecting anyone he did not like – be they experienced men or women, Burman, or non Burman, or even some in the military. He preferred to have only those he trusted, however inexperienced they might be, to run the country. Accordingly, the organization of government became a fiasco and the existing administrative structure was destroyed. Instead military men were installed to govern the country, though they had no administrative knowledge or background. In this manner, they extended their coercive influence throughout the country. Having established a firm grip, they were in no hurry to relinquish their power.

General Ne Win, the instigator of the terrible coup d'état, has now departed this world with little pomp and ceremony. Tragically, his heritage of mayhem and unhappiness continues. Few mourned his passing, including the army, even though it was because of him that the Tamadaw came into power.

Today apparently, much to the pride of the Burman, it is the Burmese themselves who are in control of the economy. Civilian entrepreneurs operate only with the blessing of the military regime, who form the elite in today's Burmese society living reasonably well and in comfort. Though some realize that there are a host of others who are less fortunate than themselves, they feel powerless to help. Most have chosen the easy way out of turning a blind eye to the plight of others, since to survive under the present regime, they must pretend not to see, nor to hear nor speak of the terrible state of affairs that exists within the country.

*The family house at 74 Kokine Road, Rangoon.*

*An elaborate pandol,*
*awaits Sao U Hpa's body.*

# XIII
## *End of an Era*

### *Aftermath of the coup*

About four months after the coup we were back in London hoping that the night-mare would soon be over. Since my stepmother was in England and living with us, we felt there was still hope and that perhaps when my father was released, he would come over to be with us.

Dorin Court, a large house with gardens bordering Richmond Park, had been divided into four. We bought the tower part of the house, which had been converted to have two bedrooms one on top of the other, plus one other bedroom and a lovely lounge looking out onto the garden. It stood near Robin Hood Gate at the bottom of Richmond Hill. A high wall separated us from Richmond Park and we could hear, from time to time, a deer bark as we sat in the garden.

Despite our beautiful living accomodation, we were not a happy household during that period, so to cheer me up, Peter decided to give me our first Boxer dog on my birthday, having spent several hours at the pet shop in Harrods, finding a little brindled pedigree. Marcus was adorable, and while he was still very young Peter used to carry him under his overcoat when we walked down the hill to the pub near Robin Hood Gate. He grew into a large muscular dog, and with his black face gave the impression of being really fierce. But he was gentle and loving. The only thing he hated was cats. It was the same with the three Boxers that followed, Diggy, Bouncie and Bertie. So four Boxers spanned our married life.

Our month in Rangoon had been extremely unpleasant. Everyone was afraid and we hardly saw any of our friends, as nobody knew whether we were to be considered friend or foe. Many years later, some of our Burman friends were surprised to learn that the army had attacked my father's house on false information, and had shot my brother, mistaking him for a rebel. These friends had been told by the authorities that our house was being guarded by a rebel force and was full of men and ammunition. When we told them that what they had been told was a total fabrication, they were taken aback. The military had done their work well in convincing our friends that my father was a rebel.

What actually happened was that when the soldiers went to arrest my father, they surrounded the house and began to open fire. The shooting went on for a long time. My young brother Harn, who was only fourteen then, remembers the ferocity with which the firing continued. The soldiers were crying out at the same time saying "Shan ma, (Shan woman), come out!, Come out! Open up or we will shoot with cannons!" Incidentally, *Shan ma* in Burmese is a derogatory term for Shan women. It is indeed incredible that, if they thought there were only Shan women in the house, they went on shooting, or even began shooting in the first instance.

Of course, when the soldiers entered the house, they were to find only one man – Sao U Hpa, alone with a group of women and children. Instead of guns, they found pile upon pile of the *Tripitaka* books, the Buddhist scriptures, which my father had had translated into Shan from the Pali. These books were what saved him from being shot, as the thick volumes took the impact of the bullets. Myee Myee, his favourite son, was not so lucky. He was shot down when he opened the front door hoping to go for help. Our Burman friends could hardly believe that Myee Myee's death was in vain and that my father was not leading a rebellion. Of course, no apology was ever given for coming and shooting up the house.

My father, other Saohpas, Shan and other Members of Parliament and Burmese political leaders of U Nu's government were taken into detention and kept in Mingaladon. Later, they were transferred to the terrible Insein jail. But U Nu and some other senior members of the government were only under house arrest. Why was my father, who had once held the highest position in the land and was much respected, subjected to senseless ignominy? Undoubtedly, there was some racial discrimination. Mercifully, he did not last out the detention. The other detainees who survived were released only after six and seven years, many in ill health.

Throughout the months of waiting, we had had no news of Sao U Hpa from the family in Burma, which was very worrying. Sai Hseng told me years later, that he was allowed to see Sao U Hpa only once during those months. It was a brief visit in which he had expressed concern for the welfare of his wife and young children. It was a nightmare occasion, and Sao U Hpa could not comprehend what had happened. My brother was heart broken to see his father in such a state of bewilderment.

I often wonder what my father's thoughts could have been apart from worries about his immediate family? Did he feel let down? Did he question his former trust and loyalty to the Union? He had given so many years to the state but what was there to show for it? What had he and the others done that they were all in this predicament? Where was the democracy they had believed in?

Surely there was no law against requesting an amendment to the 1947 Constitution? Nor one against discussing the formation of a federal state? Yet the army claimed that these talks were against the law and as the disintegration of the Union was being planned, such a movement had to be crushed. Its claim, as mentioned before, was ridiculous. But Ne Win had his way and silenced all voices.

One can only assume that what the army did not like was the coming together of the different ethnic nationalities speaking with one voice in their demand for a Union with equal rights.

On November 21st, we heard that my father had passed away. We stood by the telephone numb with shock and despair. He had died in detention in the notorious Insein jail. We could not understand how or why Sao U Hpa had died. So many terrible thoughts crossed our minds. It was agonising to be thousands of miles away in London, and completely helpless unable to do anything.

Apparently, two of my brothers, Sai Hseng and Tzang, were summoned by the military and told of my father's death. But each was told separately and at different times. I fail to understand what the point was. What did they hope to glean from two shattered people, who had just been told that their beloved father had died? Did they think they might learn something different from each of my brothers, by using such a tactic? One will never know.

The Revolutionary Council asked my stepmother to return to Burma for the funeral. She went alone leaving Hso, her eldest son, to stay behind with us. It seemed better that way, as it was term time and he was due to go to Keele University. The military allowed the family to take Sao U Hpa's body back to Yawnghwe. Permission was granted to give him the traditional state funeral with the honour and respect that was befitting a Saohpa, the Lord of the Sky. Though we were all grateful to the authorities for this gesture, we felt it had only been granted because my father was no longer alive. Sao U Hpa in life as in death was loved and respected by his people, and many thousands of his subjects came to attend the funeral. It did not matter if he was not considered a Saohpa any longer, having given up his rights to the bureaucratic government. To his people he was still their Saohpalong, the Great Lord of the Sky. It was he who had cared for them and had given them his protection during all the harsh times, including those of the Japanese occupation.

Many years later, I was asked whether I knew that my father may have been murdered. But how? I had actually tried not to think of his death in that way.

*Sao U Hpa's funeral: a sole black umbrella amongst the white signifies the sad occasion.*

*The cortege with the family walking behind.*

*Sao U Hpa on his final journey, mourners pulling the chariot.*

*Below: Family tombs.*

Perhaps there was some truth in what I was told. I do not know. It opened up many avenues of thought. But who could tell us the circumstances of his death? Since he was kept in isolation, the real nature of my father's death may never be known. Officially, he was said to have died of heart failure whilst he was in meditation. If this were the truth, one can only believe that, for one who was a devout Buddhist, my father could not have met his death in a better way. Maybe it is better not to speculate and just believe that that was the way it had happened.

Most coup d'états, wherever they take place, affect people similarly. The opposition are generally tortured, imprisoned or shot. Those who are able flee from their homes trying to find refuge within their own countries, while others flee to safer foreign countries. Families are torn apart no one knowing for how long. Some lose all they have in the world, some suffer more, others less. Undoubtedly, it is the same feeling of despair and sadness for all of us. When these monumental devastations occur, there is little one can do except survive and tell the tale.

I cannot help feeling sad that what happened to my father and family, also occurred in Laos, affecting our good friends. Most of the royal family including the then ruling King and Queen perished at the re-education camps. The king had been a benign ruler and Laos was a happy country. Neither my father nor the Shan Saohpas were despots or rebels, all they wanted were equal rights, peace and freedom, and to be left alone. What a distressing state of affairs when politics and ideology take over our lives.

During the years that Peter and I lived and worked in Rangoon, Sao U Hpa's large family of seven sons and five daughters was pretty scattered. We saw my eldest brother, Sao Sai and his family, only rarely since he resided in Taunggyi and Yawnghwe. When Sai Hseng joined Imperial Chemical Industries (ICI), he and his family moved down to Rangoon, so we were fortunate to see more of them.

Of the younger brothers and sisters, Hso, ten years younger than me, was being educated first in India, then in England. Tzang, the fourth son, and Ying, the second daughter, were at Rangoon University and doing very well in their studies. Tzang won a gold medal for being the best student at the university and had started teaching there. The three younger ones, two sons and a daughter, Myee Myee, Harn and Leun were at the Methodist school. Then the other two, Hayma and Papu, were with their mother, Daw Win, in Taunggyi, though Hayma did go to the Methodist school with the others in Rangoon. As well, we had an additional sister, Htila, who had been adopted.

Since most of the time we were involved with our own lives, it was always a wonderful occasion when this large family managed to meet. The weekends were the time when Peter and I went shopping with my brothers and sisters, or when they came over to our house to listen to music or to join in a party. They were happy times. The coup, however, was to split our family asunder.

Tzang found it difficult to continue teaching at the Rangoon university under the constrains of the military regime. A few months after the coup he decided to go underground and join the Shan Resistance.

*Tzang, seated left in dark
shirt, in the jungle.*

Back in London, Peter and I decided that it was too early for us to return to Southeast Asia. The loss of Sao U Hpa had been a heavy blow, and our feelings were in a turmoil over the family not knowing what was happening to them and where they might consider going. Peter and I had also been deeply hurt by the way U Nu's government had treated us, leaving us without a home and without a live-lihood. So we decided that it might be a good idea to look westwards and to go somewhere we did not know, which was far away. Some time later, an opportu-nity came when Peter was offered a lecturing post at the newly-created University of Guyana, in Georgetown. It was then known as British Guiana (B. G.), as it was still a colony. Thus began another adventure in our lives.

Later talking to Sai Hseng, I was to discover that he had already visited B. G. before us, when he went to Trinidad for his practical year from Cambridge. He went with the university football team and found the Guyanese a happy and hospitable people. It was then about 1950, before the real political troubles began.

## *Lastly*

The consequences of these last four decades or more have not been kind to the Shan nor to the other ethnic nationalities. It has also been a trial for the Burmans themselves.

After General Ne Win and the military took power in Burma, the country was ruled through the Revolutionary Council, under the name of the Burma Socialist Programme Party. The military claimed that through their policy of the Burmese Way to Socialism, Burma would be at peace once more and would prosper.

Dr Htin Aung[44] comments in his *A History of Burma*, that General Ne Win when he came to power "had looked to the Burmese past to create the Burmese future" and his aim was "to follow the 'Burmese way' in all aspects of life". Did he then set a trend for others to follow? Is this the reason why the present regime nostalgically longs to return to the epoch of monarchy?

For although we are in the 21st century, we might as well still be in the dark ages. When dialogue appears to be the only sane solution, the Tamadaw continues to show its military might by oppressing people, heedless of their sufferings. It persistently refuses to consider proposals put forward by other political parties, ethnic nationalities and regional bodies. The military regime may have its own agenda for a free and peaceful country pursuing the 'Burmese way'. However, the manner in which it conducts itself is hardly conducive to winning hearts and minds. There is little show of goodwill nor signs of a move towards democracy.

From the very beginning the Burmese army's aim has been pointedly to subdue non-Burmans. It claims that its persistent rallying cry of "One blood, one voice, one command", is a call for unity within a one nation state. To the army, Myan-mar as the country is now called, is to be peopled only by the Burmans. To this end the soldiers make sure that wherever they are, villagers recognize this slogan and comply. One risks one's life to say one is anything other than a Burman.

However, in the civilian world a less obvious way is being used to intimidate the Shans. Nowadays Shans are usually taunted with "Why are you wearing those baggy trousers?" when they are dressed in their native clothes. I suppose Shan men are expected to wear sarongs as the Burmans do, although they consider a sarong feminine attire. Yet to keep a low profile and to stay out of trouble, many have had to adopt the Burmese sarong. Shans have also learnt not to speak their own language in public so as not to draw attention to themselves. In villages, teaching of the Shan language is forbidden, even in the *phong gyi gaungs*, Buddhist monasteries. Clearly this is a less than subtle form of Burmanization.

Dr Robert Taylor in a paper presented in 2002 and published in 2005,[45] was to confirm that "The central policy tenets of the Revolutionary Council government and its constitutional successor were socialism, equality and neutrality", but their "efforts at equality was to disband any ethnic basis upon which political rights were granted. The ethnically designated separate administrative units, created under the 1948 constitution, were maintained but their administrations increasingly came under the control of central, often army and ex-army, personnel ... Similarly, in an effort to create national unity out of the plethora of languages, cultures and religions that exist in Myanmar's multi-ethnic society, the government halted the teaching of languages other than Bamar (Myanmar)".

Naturally as a Shan, I feel strongly about the way in which the military regime has imposed its will on the ethnic peoples.

I find it remarkable that even intelligent and educated Burmans fail to understand that each of us who are born a Shan, a Karen, a Kachin, or any other ethnic nationality are proud of our heritage and wish to retain our own identities. Just as a Burman is proud of his birthright and would not like to change, so it is with us. We wish to remain Shan as our forefathers have done for centuries.

Burma in 2007, is a very different country, even compared to ten or twenty years ago. It was hard-going then under Ne Win's repressive rule, but is no better today. Burma is becoming more isolated as its successive ruling generals reshape its destiny. Cities and towns, roads and streets are renamed making places unrecognisable, and even the centuries-old capital has been abandoned. Similarly, all non-Burmans have had to change their names to be officially acknowledged, whether they be Anglo-Burman, Shan, or any other nationality.

People who read about the country or visit it may not know that it has not always been ruled by a military regime nor that its people have been as poor or as isolated as they are today. Tourists who spend fleeting holidays in Vietnam, Cambodia and Laos, have little knowledge of their recent past, of their wars and suffering. So it is with those who visit Burma, where they see only what the authorities want them to see with few or no military in sight. Thus, many go away with little idea of what lies behind the façade of tourism.

Regarding the debate as to whether one should visit Burma, my feeling is that it is undoubtedly better for tourists to go and to have seen something of the country and its peoples, rather than not to have been there at all. Contact with the people, be they porters, waiters, or taxi drivers, though only brief encounters, may give them some happiness, something to think about, some respite from the restricted world in which they are forced to live. Also small amounts of money given by tourists will be of help for their families.

The side not seen is how people have to live daily in a world where they have to watch each word and step they take in order to remain within the limits prescribed by the military. Though people still smile and pretend their lives are normal, they are becoming more and more oppressed and poorer than ever before. If everything is as fine as is claimed, why are people not able to travel freely nor have freedom of speech and action as before?

When the British arrived over a century ago, they found people still in a 'primitive' state with little knowledge of the outside world. As a colony, people began to learn the ways of the west and soon found themselves in a cosmopolitan world. Of course, colonialism was a mixture of good and bad but the British in their time brought peace, and the country was able to prosper on various levels and in different directions. Even after the country had become independent, there was still a veneer of prosperity.

After the Japanese war my father knew that there was no turning back and the Saohpas had to move with the times. The princes were very concerned and looked to the British for guidance. The British, however, had a long-term plan for the amalgamation of the Shan States and the Frontier Areas, with Burma Proper. Although the British government was conscious that the ethnic nationalities were content to remain within the Dominion, it felt it had to convince them that joining with Burma Proper was in their best interest when independence came. Ultimately, when the time came, any idea of a smooth transition was wrecked by the speed with which events towards Independence began to move.

Time was of the essence and everything was too rushed. Maybe in the Shan States, with less tension and pressure on the princes and the Shan State government, things could have worked out. In today's world, it can be seen that where there have been wars, civil or otherwise, miracles do not happen. It generally takes decades for things to evolve and no devastated or underdeveloped country has ever been able to rehabilitate itself or achieve its goal of self-rule or Independence within a matter of one or two years.

U Maung Maung has written in his book[46] that the Burma Independence Bill passed in Parliament, "would be the first of its kind and probably also the last, for an ex-colony to decide to leave the Empire explicitly, and on the part of the British to grant such a wish without a struggle involving military intervention."

The Labour Government at that time considered Burma as one of its difficult colonies and was not willing to spend time trying to sort out the complex problems. That may perhaps explain why Independence was gained in so short a time. I remember many old British Burma hands saying that "Burma had been given a raw deal". But had it? Then again, Aung San and the politicians were jubilant to achieve Independence within such a short time.

With Independence, everyone looked to the future with high hopes for peace, progress and prosperity. But transition came too rapidly for adjustment. Young Shans were at first content while they were in full-time education, but soon became impatient for reform and progress. After a decade with nothing much to show in the way of development, the Saohpas were blamed for not doing more for their people even though their hands were tied.

During these years there was little peace and the expected prosperity evaded the villagers. The only modern equipment they were ever to know, and to become familiar with, were the tools of warfare. The Burman army came and went, as did the Shan nationalists, both armed to the teeth. The fighting showed the villagers how potent these arms were as they became pawns in other peoples' battles.

My younger brother, Tzang,[47] who witnessed all the rape and brutality, displacement and death, became sick of the carnage. He wrote twenty years ago, in 1987, that, "The time has come for Burma's leaders, both in Rangoon and jungle headquarters to re-think seriously and practically their ambitions, and prejudices. For much too long, the people of the Union of Burma have been entrapped in a politics of violence. All efforts must be undertaken to break the vicious cycle which has made the Burman (or Burmese), Shan, Mon, Karen, Karenni, Kachin, Chin and Arakanese, pitiable victims of war and violence."

It seems that everything Sao U Hpa and his generation strived to achieve has been in vain. The older generation of those times, many of them honourable men who gave their trust and loyalty to their country, have left this world.

Some ten years ago, Martin Smith[48] recorded in detail the many problems existing between the military, the Burmans and the non-Burmans in his book *Burma: Insurgency and the Politics of Ethnicity*. He commented that, "One day the idealism and rhetoric on all sides must marry with the harsh social realities, and then it will be recognized that no side has a monopoly on righteousness or political values.

"Thus, while the future is increasingly in the new generation's hands, it is also vital to reflect on the lessons of the past."

What then of the second and third generation exiles, be they Shan or others, whose parents gave up everything to start new lives abroad, giving them education and a decent standard of living, expecting that one day their children would return to help reconstruct their homeland. On the premise that there are those willing to make sacrifices and return, will they not find it difficult living in a country where their daily lives are filled with uncertainty and apprehension – a country whose leaders who are totally out of step with the outside world? Many may, of course, never return despite their birthright and prefer to live in exile.

What too of the children of the military personnel? What do they, the generations who have grown up since 1962, think when they travel and see other Asian countries? Do they travel with blinkers on? Don't they want their own country to progress? Are they not willing to do something about the present circumstances?

Nothing has improved over these forty or more years. At each conference when so-called negotiations have taken place between the present regime and the ethnic nationalities, their requests have always been the same – for the reinstatement of the Union of Burma within which a federal system based on equality, self-determination and democracy is contained. The military government simply rejects such demands out of hand.

Compared with the cruel environment of today, and looking back at my childhood days in Mong Tai and in Yawnghwe, it seems like Arcadia. Things happened at leisure without rush and hurry. People lived by modest means, leading simple lives. There was all the time in the world. They were slow and gentle days.

As a child, the Court of Yawnghwe was the only world I knew. It was the centre of my universe. Our lives were filled with ceremonies and festivals, they were carefree times with smiles and laughter. All year round there was excitement and fun. It seemed that my days at home were never dull. I expect what really made my childhood an enchantment, was the number of people who were around me, warm-hearted and caring, giving me serenity and security.

A simple pleasure for me, was going to the five-day bazaar when I was home from boarding school. Armed with my pocket money of a few pence, I would wonder around with my cousins looking at different peoples from various out-lying villages, all in colourful costumes to rival the wares they sold. There were chillies and tomatoes piled up in heaps, their reds and greens vying with the yellow of the papayas and bunches of bananas. There were hundreds of things on display full of bright colours to attract a child. These were moments of happiness for me.

It was a time when we had as yet to learn of machines and the materialistic way of life. One cannot deny that new technology and modernity are a boon, but their coming has changed the whole pattern of life. It is no longer the protected, peaceful world in which I had been brought up as a child.

The Court of Yawnghwe as we knew it with its pageantry and ceremonies ceased to function with the outbreak of the Japanese war and its occupation. Afterwards, due to constant political pressures and work involving the Panglong conferences, life for Sao U Hpa never regained its gentle tempo. The years in Rangoon kept him away from his capital, and his eventual return was all too brief. There was much achieved during his life time of sixty-six years, though there were also many disappointments. When my father's life came to an end in 1962, it was to be the end of an era for Yawnghwe and the Shan States.

Although our Yawnghwe kingdom of over six hundred years may fade into the mists of time, we can still be proud of our heritage. Through the coming years, there will be changes, since all is impermanence. But for Yawnghwe and the Phaung Daw U festival and the other Buddhist festivals, so long as Buddhism prevails, they will endure, albeit under different conditions.

The Haw in its dignity will stand looking out on to the town of Yawnghwe, as it has done for the last century. One will no longer hear voices and laughter that filled the air, but as a monument, with a bit of luck it will survive.

The ambitious ideas my father had of founding a new capital up on the eastern mountains, free of swamps and mosquitoes, as Sai Hseng remembers, will remain unfulfilled. Certainly, the many expectations, hopes and dreams of Sao U Hpa will lie as secrets within the walls of the Haw. There, too, remaining hidden in every nook and corner of the rambling palace will be the many memories of our family, even when we have left this world.

This book is a homage to the two men who shaped my life. Firstly, to my father, who brought me into this world and gave me, what he termed the most priceless gem, my education. Secondly, to my husband Peter, with an enduring and everlasting gratitude for having been my mentor and sharing his life with me.

*The vacant thrones in the Royal Throne
Audience Hall.*

*A faraway view of the Haw
from the east.*

# *Epilogue*

Little has changed in Burma since the coming to power of the military regime over forty decades ago. Generals have come and gone, but it is the same set up that runs the country harshly. Internal and external attempts at persuading the incumbent government to be less draconian, to accept Aung San Su Kyi's position on democracy and the ethnic nationalities' request for fundamental equal rights, has so far fallen on deaf ears.

Life, however, has to continue and people make the most of what little they can muster, content to live day by day, and grateful to be alive. Others leave hoping to find better lives abroad, but in their hearts of hearts yearning to be back in familiar surroundings, amongst family and friends.

In my family, after the fiasco of 1962, my eldest brother, Sao Sai, decided to stay on in Burma with his family. Daw Daw and Daw Win and her children, Hayma and Papu also remained. Sai Hseng, my elder brother, and his family, no longer able to stand the pressures and prejudices came over to England in the late 1960s.

My stepmother and her three children after their escape from Burma in 1963, lived in Thailand until 1969 when they emigrated to Canada to join Hso in Toronto. Harn and Leun, still in their teens remained with their mother while Ying went off to New York to start a new life. Tzang, discouraged at seeing despair and carnage in the jungle, left the Shan State Army before emigrating to Canada with his family some years later.

Peter and I began a peripatetic life after we left British Guiana, spending most of our working years in Laos, Thailand, Singapore and Hong Kong with our last four years before retiring in the Sultanate of Oman.

Our two years in British Guiana, now known as Guyana, produced a book on the political situation there. Georgetown was an enchanting city with imposing wooden public buildings such as the cathedral and the city hall, and elegant houses. The latter were many-roomed mansions, usually painted white, standing proud in large green gardens. The population was made up of descendents of early African slaves followed, when slavery was abolished, by indentured labourers from India. There were also some Portuguese and Chinese. They had all been brought over to work in the bauxite mines and sugar cane plantations of the white capitalists.

Peter joined the English Department of the newly founded University of Guyana while I did some field work in the sugar plantations. Unfortunately, we were there at a politically charged time just before the country gained its Independence from the British. The two major ethnic groups, the African-Guyanese and the Indians, formed two distinct political parties violently opposed towards each other, leading the British Government to fear that the country might disintegrate. We found bombs going off from time to time, added to which there could be a sudden flaring of tempers that often led to disturbances, strikes and riots. When we were caught up in these commotions it was not always easy to extricate ourselves from the jeering and shouting crowds, police with truncheons and tear gas. Peter being white and tall stood out amongst the crowd making him an easy target. However, sometimes this had advantages as a policeman, mistaking him for a government official, would lead us to safety.

But between these violent outbursts, people in the capital went about their daily chores cheerfully. The civil servants such as policemen, postal workers and town clerks were usually African-Guyanese, while businessmen and shopkeepers were generally of Indian, Chinese and Portuguese extraction. Colourfully dressed African-Guyanese women would be seen in the markets selling their wares quite happily with everyone mixing in good humour, as if they were all the best of friends. It was an extraordinary state of affairs.

In 1966, Peter accepted a *Time Magazine* offer to go back to Laos and I became a stringer for the *Daily Mail*. Peter had to travel so we were put into the newly-built Lang Xang Hotel as a temporary measure, but we ended up staying there for the whole year. One dramatic event during our stay happened a day after a wonderful birthday party Peter gave for me in October. Amongst our guests had been one General Kouprasit Abhay, who escaped the bombs on his headquarters, as he was still in bed and was not sitting in his office as he should have been. The bombing was carried out by one of the top pilots of the Royal Laotian Air Force who had held a grudge. There were a few casualties but no fatalities. Everyone was shocked and scandalized by this appalling action. Eventually brought back to Vientiane he was given a heavy sentence, and later, died, although we were not told how.

It was fantastic to be back in Thailand in 1968, when once more we were to meet the gracious Rangsit family and through them Evelyn, the Earl of Cromer. Later, like us, Evelyn and his wife Plern moved to Singapore and Hong Kong, where we continued our friendship. At *Time*, Peter worked with David Greenway who went on to Hong Kong where we caught up with him and JB, his wife, a few years later.

In Bangkok, we had the most lovely one-storey wooden house designed by an Italian architect, with a *klong* running through the bottom of the garden in Sri Ayuttaya Road. Here we played exciting games of croquet, and when it became serious, an opponent's ball would suddenly find itself in the *klong*. Marcus, our Boxer, was happy to jump into the water to retrieve the balls and our cries of 'No! Marcus, no!' never deterred him from showering us as he shook off the *klong* water. I joined UNESCO in the Information Department and would ask John Blofeld, who was heading the Editorial Department, whenever we needed our articles perfected for English.

Then in 1970, *Time* decided to send Peter as Bureau Chief to Toronto. This proved to be not such a good move as by the end of the year non-Canadians were posted elsewhere. What did turn out well was being re-united with my family. Leaving Canada we went to live in our Spanish house in Javea. Peter wrote a thriller but it was turned down as literary agents said the plot was too close to a Fleming book. However, people make places, and the two years we spent there were truly delightful. We met up again with families we knew in Laos, Singapore and Hong Kong and became firm friends with others who had already retired in the congenial atmosphere of Costa de Blanca.

Casa St Ramon, a typical barn-like Spanish finca, which we shared with Jerry Schecter, a *Time* colleague, provided the most perfect place for parties with its long patio looking out over the vines, almond trees and the countryside beyond. Long walks amongst the pine woods or along the coast, picnics and lazy afternoons on half empty beaches were wonderful ways to spend our time. All too soon the pleasurable days came to an end and we were off again, this time to Singapore and Hong Kong.

Two years ago visiting Javea, with my brother Harn, I went in search of St Ramon and found it still standing, a lone farm house, surrounded by new 21st century bricks and mortar. It was a moment of mixed feelings, I didn't know whether to shout hurrah or to just sit down and cry. I was glad that Jerry who took over the house, had decided to keep it pretty much as it was when we had left in 1972. But for how long?

Once again with *Time*, Peter began travelling around Southeast Asia going wherever there was a story to be covered. I, on the other hand, joined Singapore University Press and found myself managing, editing and generally running the office. Charles Letts, an astute businessman, generous to a fault, came into our lives through friends from Bangkok. Sometime in 1974, after working in Cambodia and Vietnam, Peter came back for a few days. Evelyn and Plern, who had also moved there, invited us to join them on their boat and while going down the slipway Peter fell and broke his arm. As we waited for the doctor, Evelyn thought a good slug of cognac would do Peter some good. This apparently was the wrong thing to do as it delayed an immediate operation. The arm, which was badly broken, had to be in plaster for weeks, and Peter thought it best to leave *Time*.

David Cornwell, John le Carré, was looking for a researcher for his latest book, *The Honourable Schoolboy*, and once they had met Peter was given the job. This provided an opportunity for them to spend time together travelling. Peter was delighted to show David around the countries he knew so well and to introduce him to personalities of interest.

In 1975 we moved to Hong Kong as Peter had been offered a job with the Hong Kong Government. Then, not long after our arrival, I joined the Government Information Service, which meant that we both had pretty busy lives. That was why the best thing we did soon after we were in Hong Kong was to buy a small yacht which we sailed at weekends with our two Boxer dogs, Diggy and Bouncie. Sailing to nearby islands for a picnic and a swim liberated us from the noise and crush of people on Hong Kong island. Sometimes we spent a night on board anchored in a small cove off one of the many islands and watched the twinkling stars as we lay on deck. So long as we went sailing or out driving in the New Territories, life was bearable and I did not feel unduly claustrophobic. Our sailing companions, Bob Allen and Stephen Entwistle, who worked with Peter, were competent sailors and loved the rough seas. On cloudy, windy days I generally stayed home with the dogs much to their annoyance, while the three men went off into the wind with the sails taut and the boat at an angle, feeling exhilarated and free.

Hong Kong had its own hierarchy of government servants as did the business tycoons forming their own jet-sets. As we belonged to the Hong Kong Club, a bastion of Britishness, we, at times met civil servants of the top echelon, but never had the chance of entering the much talked about glittering society of the Chinese *hongs.* Most of the Hong Kong Chinese we knew were our colleagues at work, who were serious and thoughtful about Hong Kong's future and 1997.

After some six years in Hong Kong, we felt it was time to move and in looking around for jobs we found two posts with the Omani Government. I was overjoyed when the time came for us to leave Hong Kong and found life in Oman very different. The Omanis we worked with were kind and hospitable. Both men and women were open and relaxed, with no woman wearing a veil or burkha. However, the wives hardly came out to parties we had, and when invited back to their houses, I would eat with the men first, before being ushered into the backroom to join the women. Since it was mostly the men who spoke English, there was no common language, though with signs and an occasional word from the children who were learning English at school, I was able to communicate with them.

The joy of Oman was that it was not only desert but a land of contrasts with multi-coloured ranges of mountains, plateaux, soft green hills and valleys. The wadis, dry valley beds, with their rocky outcrops, home to flora and fauna, were our favourite spots for picnics on a Sunday. After some rainfall, we would come into a wadi and find it fragrant from the mass of pink and white oleander on the rocks and bulrushes flourishing in puddles left by the rain.

Oman is scattered with numerous ruins of forts and castles. Renovation work continues on these but most famous is the seventeenth century Jabrin Castle. This towering sandstone building standing in the middle of the desert, surrounded by a sea of green date palms, is an enthralling sight. One can still see the ancient ceiling of one of the principal halls which is exquisitely painted with flower patterns of red and ochre, curves and Arabic writings, while wooden windows and doors are delicately carved. Once restored to its former glory, Jabrin will certainly become one of the finest in the land.

We had been in Oman from 1982 to 1987 and it was time to retire. For the next fifteen years in France and England, we spent our time researching and writing books. La Petite Domergue on the Canal du Midi, a charming house between Castlenaudary and Toulouse was an ideal house for that purpose. Its grounds and garden gave us the inspiration we needed to write a brief history on the City of Carcassonne and a small book on the wines of the Corbières and Fitou.

One day in 1992, Harn telephoned Peter saying that he was in touch with someone said to be his son, who wanted to contact him. Subsequently, Christopher came to see us in France. For father and son it was an emotional reunion as it was forty years since they had last met. After so many years of separation, it was probably not easy coming to terms with the many unanswered questions between them. Nonetheless, neither of them showed any signs of anxiety or strain, and the week went off pleasantly. Christopher and I were surprised and please to find we shared the same birthday. Since Peter's death Christopher and I have kept in touch.

When our fourth Boxer, Bertie, died we decided to come back and live in London. From our flat on the Isle of Dogs we watched the Millennium Dome being built on the opposite bank of the Thames. Each day provided a new spectacle. There was a variety of traffic on the river and when we were not at our computers, we would sit to watch the different crafts plying the river. In 1998, our book, *The Kingdoms of Laos* was published, and we felt elated to have produced something worthwhile for our Laotian friends.

In spite of our travels we kept in touch with my family, many visiting us at La Petite Domergue and in London. The more motivated of the siblings have spent their years contributing their time and energy, according to their ideals and beliefs, working for the Shan cause and the right for equality and freedom for all. Over the last forty-five years members of the family have gradually declined. Both Daw Daw and Sao Mye, my stepmother, have passed away, including four brothers, Sao Sai, Tzang, Myee Myee and Papu. Now instead of twelve siblings, only seven of us remain – Sai Hseng, Hso, Ying, Harn, Hayma, Leun and myself – plus our adopt sister Htila.

Tiring of the grey skies and the cold, Peter wanted to return to sunshine and warmth. Although Peter was not in the best of health he enjoyed living on the Cotes d'Azur. They were three stimulating years as we progressed with the book on Marcel Proust. Little did we realize that the end would come so soon. It is now almost five years since Peter's departure.

I sit at my desk looking out onto the brilliant blue waters of the Solent, gathering together my thoughts as I write. Beyond, on the opposite shores lie Gosport and Portsmouth and the horizon is tinged with a warm glow of pink. It is a moment in the late afternoon and all is quiet. Neither the car ferry or the foot-passenger ferry can be seen plying past. But before long and before the sun sinks low in the sky, a lone yacht will sail by and traffic will resume including a cruise ship making its way from Southampton towards the Channel and the open sea.

As I watch, a thousand memories flash by of joy, of excitement, of sadness and sorrow – a past gone forever, but to remember and reflect upon, reminding me that all is transient.

## Recent happening in Burma
### Valiant efforts

On Tuesday 18th September 2007 several hundred Buddhist monks in Rangoon began peaceful marches which attracted a large number of civilians, culminating in as many as 100,000 protesters on the ninth day. In other cities, too, monks marched in support. On that same day, a crackdown came with shooting, arrests and death. A curfew was then imposed, clearing the streets. In the early hours of the next morning authorities raided monasteries, maltreated and arrested a large number of the Sangha, causing death in some instances. In order to prevent any fresh protests, riot police and heavily armed soldiers continued patrolling the streets of Rangoon for several days after. The brutal and outrageous behaviour of the military regime against peaceful demonstrators, was widely broadcast and reported throughout the world which brought the UN representative, Ibrahim Gambari to Burma for consultations with both Aung San Suu Kyi and General Than Shwe, the head of the junta, in early October.

It had all started in mid-August when a small group of political activists protested against a sudden price increase in fuel that concurrently led to a rise in the cost of living which the already destitute people could ill afford. The young demonstrators were beaten up and promptly arrested by the authorities. Buddhist monks from the Federation of All Burma Young Monks, unable to continue

watching such repression, began their marches in support of the protests believing they could help alleviate the suffering of the people.

The courage shown by these monks and what they have had to endure since, may, it is hoped, stir consciousness in bringing about serious political dialogue. Continued background manoeuvring by the UN might help. But much may ultimately depend on how much the generals value world opinion. In the meantime, reconciliation between the Sangha and the military may take some time, since merit-making alone cannot absolve the sins they have committed.

## Appendix I

### *Sao On's letter, 1886*

Quoting from Sao Saimong Mangrai's book
*The Shan States and the British Annexation*, page 114

His first letter to the British reached the Deputy Commissioner of Kyaukse by about the end of April. The letter itself bore no date but the Deputy Commissioner of Kyaukse reported to his superiors at Mandalay on May 3, 1886. It is reproduced in full below:

Sao Maung, formerly Sawbwa of Nyaung-ywe, brought up from Mandalay the Legya Queen and her son Kodawgyi, and began to issue orders and requisitions to all myosas, and Shwe Guns and Ngwe Guns, saying that he would fight the English and take Mandalay. Meanwhile he was attacked by forces from:

| | |
|---|---|
| Thaton | Nankok |
| Banyin | Hopon |
| Nawngmun | Ponmu and In |

He was wounded and had to flee to Kyauktat. While he was there these forces, having set Saw Chit Su up as Chief of Nyaung-ywe, again plotted against Saw Maung. I got to know this, and saved his life by taking him away to Hlaingdet district. The Ngwe Gun Min of In and other States mentioned above then invited the Legya Queen and her son Kodawgyi and again planned to fight the English and take Mandalay.

Meantime the Nyaung-ywe Sawbwa, Sao Maung, handed over Nyaung-ywe to me, bidding me take possession of it as best I could. Relying on your favour and by your goodwill I did so and I am now in possession of Nyaung-ywe and Inle Ywa (In). Various princes have tried to persuade me to join them, but I have declined and have obeyed no such summons, replying that we cannot fight the British. I now beg for a reply to say what you wish me to do, and so that the hereditary rights of the Chiefs may be upheld.

As for the present state of affairs in the Shan States, the Thibaw Chief has returned to Thibaw. The old Sawbwa of Mone has retaken his State, and with the old Myoza of Maingnaung, old Sawbwa of Yatsauk, old Myoza of Maingpyin, and the Limbin Prince has established himself in Mone. Thence he is sending letters to all Sawbwas and Myozas to say that he intends to conquer the English and take Mandalay and is demanding men and arms. He has demanded 100 muskets and Rs. 20,000 of Legya, to guard the Prince, as he says, the Sawbwa of Mone-Kyaingtaung has left his own territory and taken refuge in Legya, and Mone demands his extradition also. So the old Sawbwa of Yatsauk and the old Myoza of Maingpyin are not received back by their people. Maung Shwe Gan, the old Sawbwa of Maingnaung, has left his State and taken refuge in Kyethi Bansan, and he too is demanded.

The Chiefs of     Mone)
                 Maingriaung)
                 Maingseik)
                 Maingpun)     A
                 Maukme)
                 Yatsauk)
                 Maingpyin)

have made a firm resolve to oppress the rest of us, and seeing that we could not endure it,
                 Legya)
                 Yatsauk)
                 Maingkaing)     B
                 Kyethe)
                 Bansan and I )

consulted together and joined forces and are now attacking the former.

The Ywangan Myoza and the Bawzaing Ngwegunhrau are the only people who are on the side of the Myinzaing Prince. The supporters of the Legya Queen's son are dispersed and the Prince himself with the Yewun Sayadaw, has taken refuge and is living in Thamaing-gan.

Of the other States none dares to join in any other's plan. Each is severally keeping his own territory in order as well as he can.

Although there are many hereditary claimants to States, yet, unless the people consent and unless the hereditary Chiefs can agree with their neighbours, even they at the present time cannot keep their footing and hold possession of their States.

In consequence of the Mayangyaung pongyi's assembling of dacoits and raising disturbances in Toungoo, Shwegyin and Martaban districts, on one bad man's account the whole of the clergy, we hear, are in straits and are disturbed. The clergy in the Shan States are disturbed and alarmed in consequence.

How to come under the British flag and obtain British protection so that our hereditary claims may be respected? What policy we ought to adopt? Whether we ought to join the Chiefs of the 57 States of Siam and so obtain British protection? All these questions I have never faced before and cannot solve.

I look to no quarter for aid and protection but you, and I therefore beg for your instructions and guidance as to the course I am to adopt.

(Source: Burma Foreign Department Proceeding No. 1, May 1886)

## Appendix II

### From Sao Shwe Thaike, Saohpa of Yawnghwe State

Dated 23rd October 1943

1. By the virtues of hereditary rights I have been Sawbwa of Yawnghwe for the last sixteen years and it is now the seventeenth year of my Sawbwaship.

2. Having descended from the ruling family of Yawnghwe State and thereby having realised that the general welfare of the Yawnghwe State people rest in my hands, my sole aim and only main object has been not for my own self-interests but for the betterment of Yawnghwe State and the advancement of the Shan States as a whole.

3. With such intentions since 1936, I have organised a committee termed as the Peoples Council to act as an Advisory Board. This is the first of its kind in Yawnghwe and the Shan States introduced with a view to give the people a share in the State Government. It has been of no little help to me and at present it still exists.

4. For the uplift of religion and to defend the faith I have held annual examinations for the *Phongyis* for the last twelve years incessantly. This year under the kind auspices of their Excellencies, Major General Tanihuji Ngahide and Lieut. General Nishimura Takuma I was able to hold a general authorization of the *Vinnayas* for all the *Phongyis* residing in the Shan States, for which act of kindness all the *Phongyis*, and Buddhists are for ever indebted to their Excellencies and would also add a vote of hearty thanks to theirs.

5. During the time of the British Government with its strict economic and political control, I had been able only up to a certain extent in my efforts for the advancement of Yawnghwe State and also that of the Shan States. Now since the Nippon Government has successfully driven the English people back from the East Asiatic lands and proclaimed the Greater East Asiatic Co-prosperity I found that it only coincides with my desire for the betterment of the Yawnghwe State and the Shan States, but by far exceeds in greatness of heart and generosity for which I thank the Nippon Government very gladly and heartily.

6. The scheme of amalgamation of the Shan States to Burma for the unity and Co-prosperity of the Greater East Asia will be not only an asset towards the achievement of the high ideal but at the same time as it also will fulfil my own wishes for the prosperity of Yawnghwe and the Shan State – as the Shan States is an integral part of the Greater East Asia – I would again tender my thanks to the Nippon Government.

7. Having realised in good faith that as the political scheme arrived at at present will agree with my own wishes for the Yawnghwe and Shan States, I have been trying to think of the means and ways as to how I should give a substantial help, and thus the speech made by Dr. Ba Maw, the Adipadi of Burma on the night of the 29th, September 1943 at the Rangoon State House on the occasion of the State Banquet, was recalled to my mind.

The gist of his speech, I believe would be as follows:-

"The Shan Sawbwas should take an interest and study the history of the Unification of Japan and Germany. Formerly Japan was besetted into a number of States under different Feudal Lords and there was no unity whatsoever thus impeding co-prosperity. It is now just only a little over seventy years that Japan was brought under control as a unit by the then August Emperor. Similarly the unification of Germany was effected only in 1830. Since then both the countries have acted under one command in one effort with one voice, hence their greatness and achievements. The Shan Sawbwas should make a note of this example and be prepared to sacrifice for the good of one's country and one's people."

8. I quite appreciate and understand the value of the Adipadi's speech. Since I have been prepared to do any form of sacrifice, even my very life itself, for the good of my State and the Shan States; as well heretofore I am very glad that at present an opportunity has been offered in which I may prove myself; and that even on a far greater cause namely the Greater East Asiatic Co-prosperity.

9. For fear that the Shan Saohpas will only serve as an obstacle in the unity of Shan States and Burma; and as there exist the historical examples of the feudal lords in Japan and Germany who had to forsake their positions towards the unification of their respective countries; also to prove to the Nippon and Burma Governments that I have no self interests; and having explicit faith that my desire for the prosperity of Yawnghwe and the Shan States will finally be attained together with the prosperity of the Greater East Asia of which they are an integral part, I beg you to kindly concede to me the following:-

a.) That for the honour of proving that I have no self interest whatsoever and that I am prepared to willingly sacrifice for the cause of the Greater East Asiatic Co-prosperity, to kindly accept my renunciation of the Saohpaship of Yawnghwe State,

b.) That as is customary my family and self are entitled to State pensions or allowances but we would gladly return them to the Government to be used for the cause of the Greater East Asiatic Co-prosperity. Other State pensions and relative allowances may kindly be maintained, as usual.

c.) That after my renunciation. I may be allowed to  enjoy the protection given by both the Nippon and Burma Governments as an ordinary common person is entitled to.

d.) That after my renunciation as it would be very difficult for my family and self to earn a living either in the Shan States or Burma as a commoner through previous position and status and also as my hereditary right of respect from my people and those with whom I have had dealings heretofore would only serve to make things more awkward, I would like to leave the Shan States and Burma, but at present as there is no other suitable country to which I may turn to, I beg the Nippon Government and Burma Governments to kindly arrange with the Thai Government in order that I may be able to reside in Thailand with my family and also to kindly give me the protection as an ordinary commoner is entitled to in Thailand.

e.) That regardless of my position I have most willingly and gladly sacrificed myself for the of the Greater East Asiatic Co-prosperity by renouncing from the Saohpaship of the State, but this will not prevent me from bounden duty to serve the noble cause from wherever I may happen to be.

Furthermore I would beg that the Nippon Government will consider the facts enumerated above with sympathy and kindness and allow me to prove my lack of self interest by accepting the renunciation tendered and that the Burma Government also will approve and support me in the above mentioned concessions claimed for.

Saohpa of Yawnghwe State,
Yawnghwe

## Appendix III

### *The Panglong Agreement 1947*

Dated: Panglong, 12 February 1947

A Conference having been held at Panglong, attended by certain members of the Executive Council of the Governor of Burma, all Saohpa and representatives of the Shan State, the Kachin Hills, and the Chin Hills.

The members of the Conference, believing that freedom will be more speedily achieved by the Shans, the Kachins, and the Chins by their immediate co-operation with the Interim Burmese Government.

The members of the Conference have accordingly, and without dissidents, agreed as follows:

1. A representative of the Hill Peoples, selected by the Governor on the recommendation of representatives of the Supreme Council of the United Hill Peoples (SCOUHP), shall be appointed a Counsellor to the Governor to deal with the Frontier Areas.

2. The said Counsellor shall also be appointed a member of the Governor's Executive Council without portfolio, and the subject of Frontier Areas brought within the purview of the Executive Council by Constitutional Convention as in the case of Defence and External Affairs. The Counsellor for Frontier Areas shall be given executive authority by similar means.

3. The said Counsellor shall be assisted by two Deputy Counsellors representing races of which he is not member. While the two Deputy Counsellors should deal in the first instance with the affairs of their respective areas and the Counsellor with all the remaining parts of the Frontier Areas, they should on Constitutional Convention act on the principle of joint responsibility.

4. While the Counsellor, in this capacity as Member of the Executive Council, will be the only representative of the Frontier Areas on the Council, the Deputy Counsellors shall be entitled to attend the meetings of the Council when subjects pertaining to the Frontier Areas are discussed.

5. Though the Governor's Executive Council will be augmented as agreed above, it will not operate in respect of the Frontier Areas in any manner which would deprive any portion of these areas of the autonomy which it now enjoys in internal administration. Full autonomy in internal administration for the Frontier Areas is accepted in principle.

6. Though the question of demarcating and establishing a separate Kachin State within a Unified Burma is one which must be regulated for decision by the Constituent Assembly, it is agreed that such a State is desirable. As a first step towards this end, the Counsellors for Frontier Areas and the Deputy Counsellors shall be consulted in the administration of such areas in the Myitkyina and the Bhamo Districts as are Part II Scheduled Areas under the Government of Burma Act of 1935.

7. Citizens of the Frontier Areas shall enjoy rights and privileges which are regarded as fundamental in democratic countries.

8. The arrangements accepted in this Agreement are without prejudice to the financial autonomy now vested in the Federated Shan States.

9. The arrangement accepted in this Agreement are without prejudice to the financial assistance which the Kachin Hills and the Chin Hills are entitled to receive from the revenues of Burma, and the Executive Council will examine with the Frontier Areas Counsellor and Deputy Counsellors the feasibility of adopting for the Kachin Hills and the Chin Hills financial arrangements similar to those between Burma and the Federated Shan States.

*Shan Committee* {Signatories]
Khun Pan Sing, Tawngpeng Saohpa Long
Sao Shwe Thaike, Yawnghwe Saopha Long
Sao Hom Hpa, Hsenwi Saohpa Long
Sao Noom, Laikha Saohpa Long
Sao Sam Htun, Muang Pawn Saohpa Long
Sao Htun E, Hsa-Muang Kham Saohpa Long
Khun Pung, Representative of Panglawng Saohpa Long

*People's Representatives:*
U Tin E
U Htun Myint
U Kya Bu
Khun Saw
Khun Htee
Sao Yape Hpa

*Kachin Committee* [Signatories]
Sinwa Naw (Myitkyina)          Zau Rip (Myitkyina)
Dinra Tang (Myitkyina)         Zau La (Bhamo)
Zau Lawn (Bhamo)               Labang Grong (Bhamo)

*Chin Committee* [Signatories]
U Hlur Hmang (Falam)           U Thawng Za Khup (Tiddim)
U Kio Mang (Haka)

*Burmese Government* [Signatory]
Aung San

## Appendix IV

### Sao Shwe Thaike's letter, 1960

A letter presented to the Dr E Maung, the Minster for Justice at the opening of the Constitutional Amendment Committee, 22 December 1960, Rangoon, in which he sets out his personal views with regard to the amendment of the Constitution.
    In the letter, he stated:

> "During the practical application of the Constitution of the Union of Burma, for the past 13 years, it was found that the Constitution permitted the practice of racism it appeared that Burma proper had not become a constituent state of the Union, but had taken the place of the British in the administration of the Constituent States. It also appeared as if these States did not join together in a voluntary union but were brought into subordination of Burma proper. These Constituent States had to request Burma proper to provide for their needs. There is not a single right of self-determination given to the States by the Constitution and all administrative matters

have had to be undertaken in accordance with the wishes of the Union Government. As no financial powers were given to the States, nothing could be done for the development of the States; for example, as only *Kyats* 125 *lakhs* had been allotted as annual contribution to the Shan State, it appeared that the Shan State deserved only that amount, and no more. The Shan State had no voice in matters relating to the benefits accruing from the finances of the Union Government. All other States were also in the same position.

According to the principle of federation, Burma proper should be one of the Constituent States and enjoy only those rights which the other States enjoyed. But because, under the present Constitution, Burma proper exercised the power and rights of the Union Government, which are greater than those enjoyed by the States, the States are dissatisfied. No one in the States has the intention of destroying the Union. If Burma proper becomes a Constituent State of the Union, on an equal footing with other States, the dissatisfaction will gradually disappear. Therefore a true Federal Constitution should be drawn up in all sincerity"

## Appendix V

### *A Paper Submitted to the Prime Minister*
### by Sao Shwe Thaike

From 1922, the Shan States has been ruled and advised by the Federal Council. During the two years of 1930 and 1931, the Round Table Conference was held in London, in connection with the establishment of a government for Burma, and the question of Burma's separation from India. For the first meeting, the Sawbwa of Mong Mit, Sao Khin Maung, and the writer, the Sawbwa of Yawnghwe, Sao Shwe Thaike, were chosen as representatives for the Shan States and attended the Conference as Observers. On the second occasion, the Hsipaw Sawbwa, Sao Ohn Kya, and the writer, Sawbwa of Yawnghwe, Sao Shwe Thaike, were chosen by the Federal Council as delegates. The Sawbwa of North Hsenwi, Sao Hom Hpa, and the Kyemmong of Kengtung, Sao Kawng Tai, attended the Conference as Advisors. At the present time Mong Mit Sawbwa, Sao Khin Maung, the Hsipaw Sawbwa, Sao Ohn Kya, and the Kengtung Kyemmong (Sawbwa) Sao Kawng Tai, are no longer alive.

In 1935 according to a legislative act, India and Burma were separated, and the Shan States also had the opportunity of breaking away from India at the same time. India then transferred to them the revenues it obtained from them, the Central Revenues, and the powers of administration.

From that time until 1942, at the time of the second World War, when the Japanese occupied Burma, the Shan States administration never neglected its duty. After the separation from India, the Central Revenue was distributed according to the population to Burma and the Shan States. It had been said that it was possible for the Shan States to try to become a Dominion Status within the British Empire. So with this aim in view, the Shan Administration knowing that there was not enough teachers, doctors or nurses and there were difficulties set to work on education, health, public works, construction and giving these items priority. The Shan people are very devout Buddhists, and are contented people and because of this attitude, the country was unable to become as prosperous and progressive as it was hoped. Not only in the matter of health and medicine when they did not dare to go to hospitals for treatment, but even for their children to go to school, it needed coaxing, and frightening them, before the children were sent to school.

In 1938, at the time when the second World War was spreading, that only if the British had won the war, could keep its promises. Therefore money from the Shan States treasury were put into expenses incurred for military purposes: forming the Territorial Force 13 and Territorial Force 14 and the M.T. section (1-16). Many Shans however took part in the war, either as fighting soldiers or ordinary men. From 1939 until 1942 when the Japanese came, their duties were satisfactorily carried out. From 1942 to 1945, when the British came back, the Shans had in no way benefited from the Independence which the Japanese were supposed to have given, nor did they prosper in any direction, instead they suffered severely in the end.

When the English came back and saw the low conditions of living and the backwardness of the Shan States, the British Government then said that it would consider raising the Shan States to the level of Dominion Status, and would keep that promise. The war brought great difficulties and the disastrous results of the war, consequently brought the Shan people to feel that had they been independent they could have decided their own fate. It was at this time when General Aung San came to the Shan States, and persuaded the Shans, that Burma and the Shan States should ask for Independence. When Independence was gained, it would be seen to that the Shan States did not suffer and that it would have complete freedom.

The Shan States were now backward but with Independence it would be seen that she was on equal footing with Burma, and as brothers would work together. In most friendly and cordial manner he gave his promise. So in 1947, at the second Panglong Conference, the idea of ever achieving a Dominion Status within the British Empire was abandoned and together with Burma a treaty was signed to ask for Independence, which was duly granted in 1948.

Before Independence and when the Shan States was still under the yoke of imperialism, laws made by the Federal Council which were considered unfit for the Shan States could therefore be rejected, under the Power of Rejection. The six counsellors elected by the Federal Council had meetings with the Governor every six months, at which all existing problems were discussed, and apart from that, the Shan States being considered a Saluted State, the Sawbwas were able to see and consult with the Governor at any time. On foreign and International matters direct conferences with the Governor would be held. As far as problems on defence, forming of military units, and recruiting of soldiers were concerned there was a special representative within this organization.

After four years of Independence this was the situation that could be seen. In the 1952-1953 Budget in which the expenditure for the four main items being the police force education, medical services and public health were shown for the whole country, these are the figures which can be seen allotted to one man for the one year:-

|        | Burma | Shan | Kachin | Kayah |
|--------|-------|------|--------|-------|
| *Kyats* | 9.98  | 3.30 | 10.07  | 12.58 |

Out of all these, Shan States' figure is the least. Taking this as an example if this was the figure at which the expenditure allotment for one man in the Shan States was to continue, without doubt, the already low standards of living would get considerably lower. In fact the writer seeing this situation had commented on it. Now after nine years of Independence, the 1956-1957 Budget shows for one man his allotment for the four same items

|        | Burma | Shan | Kachin | Kayah |
|--------|-------|------|--------|-------|
| *Kyats* | 17.45 | 5.23 | 14.41  | 13.64 |

Again it can be seen that the allotment for that of the Shan States is much smaller than the other three. If this is the amount per head for every man in the Shan States, for his defence, education, medical services and public health, there is no way in which the Shan States can advance or progress in the next ten years, it will go from the yoke of colonialism to ..., thus from bad to worse. The writer felt that the only way for the Shan States and its people to be equal with other countries was to join Burma and to become Independent. The present situation however, is most disheartening. Thus like the writer, the Shan people feel the urge to be untied and to act as one body to achieve progress and prosperity. Because of this situation in the Shan States, it is only natural that the people should desire and plan for prosperity and well being. If the present conditions were not presented to our brother government and it were to be kept quiet, it may become the fault of the writer for not having put the matter before the public. That is why it is hoped that the Honourable Prime Minister will give this matter some consideration and to suggest the best method by which the present disheartening condition can be uplifted.

In calculating the whole central revenue, it has been found that the Shan States according to its population is entitled to 314,000 *kyats* for one year. Burma is supposed to have spent on the Shan States, 350,000 *kyats*, or even 360,000 *kyats*, but nothing can be seen of this great expenditure. Although it has been said that the amount of *kyats* 350,000 was spent on the Shan States, only *kyats* 125,000 was received, what happened to the remaining 225,000 has not been made known.

The profits of the rice trade to the amount of 200,000,000 *kyats* was not used for the progress of the nation. For the Shan States Budget to be on the same level with Burma respectively, it is necessary that the Shan States gets not less than 25,000,000 *kyats* a year. Although it is able to raise 10,000,000 *kyats* it is unable to raise the necessary 15,000,000 *kyats* by itself. It therefore, needs the help of Burma annually, if it is to attain its goal for progress and prosperity. It in however, a great and heavy responsibility.

If we look back into the history of Burma, we see that we are of different cultures and races, but our religion is the same, and in the past they have helped each other without delay when they were needed. At the present moment, it is even more important to help one another, therefore if one of them is backward and in difficulties, the other would not be satisfied to look on and be contentious. As in the instance of a household and family, if one of them should be in need, it is the responsibility of the others to look after him. Likewise, it is believed, that within the Union, if the Shan States is not up to the standard required, it is therefore the responsibility of Burma and the other states of the Union to help. Thus, as brothers, if one prospers, the others too should prosper with help given to them, and so achieve their goal. Believing in this, it is hoped that the Honourable Prime Minister will be able to consider the problem and suggest ways and means by which the Shan people will be able to attain progress and prosperity.

(Sao Shwe Thaike, c. 1961)

## Group of Saohpas

Some of the Saohpas remembered. The informal groups were taken early 1947 before the Mong Pawn Saohpa was assassinated in July.

1. *Yawnghwe*; 2. *Loilong*; 3. *Mong Yai*; 4. *Pwela*; 5. *Kengtung*;
6. *Tawngpeng*; 7. *Hsahtung*; 8. *Monghsu*; 9. *Hsipaw*; 10. *Mongnai*;
11. *Hsenwi*; 12. *Pantara*; and four unidentified.

1. *Mong Pawn*; 2. *Samka*; 3. *Hsamongkham*; 4. *Kesi-Mansam*; 5. *Hopong*;
6. *Laikha*; 7. *Pangmi*; and three unidentified.

# Appendix VI

## *List of Shan Saohpas*

Saohpas through Sao U Hpa's reign from 1927 to 1959,
the year in which all ruling princes had to abdicate.

| STATES | 1927-1945 | 1946-1959 |
|---|---|---|
| 1. Baw | Sao Hkam Sein | Sao Hkun Aung |
| 2. Hopong | Sao Hkun Law | Sao Hkun O, Kyemmong |
| 3. Hsahtung | Sao Hkun Kyi | Sao Aung Myint |
| 4. Hsamongkham | Sao Hkun Po | Sao Htun Aye |
| 5. Hsenwi | Sao Hom Hpa | Sao Hom Hpa |
| 6. Hsipaw | Sao Ohn Kya | Sao Kya Saing |
| 7. Kengtung | Sao Kawng Tai | Sao Sai Long |
| 8. Kesi-Mansam | Hkam Lu | Sao Shwe Hmon |
| 9. Kokang | Yang Win Pyin | Yang Chi Sein |
| 10. Kyong | U Po Tin | Sao Hkun San |
| 11. Laikha | Hkun Lai | Sao Noom |
| 12. Lawksawk | Sao Hkun Suk | Sao Hkun Hsa |
| 13. Loilong, Pinlong | Hkun Hkam Chok | Sao Moe Kyaw. |
| 14. Mawkmai | Hkun Hkawng | Sao Htun Hpu, Kyemmong |
| 15. Monghsu | Hkun Htun | Sao Hman Hpa |
| 16. Mongkung | Sao Noom | Sao Kyi |
| 17. Monglon, Monglin | Sao Khanam | Sao Hman Lek |
| 18. Mong Mit | Sao Khin Maung | Sao Hkun Hkio |
| 19. Mongnai | Sao Kyaw Ho | |
| 20. Mongnawn | Sao Hkun Sa | Sao Ohn Maung |
| 21. Mongpai | Sao Pin Nya | |
| 22. Mongpan | Sao Hkun Ong | Sao Shwe Kyi |
| 23. Mong Pawn | Sao Hsam Htun | Sao Hso Hom |
| 24. Mong Yai | Sao Naw Mong | |
| 25. Namkhok-Nawngmawn | | Sao Thaung Shwe, Kyemmong |
| 26. Pangmi | Sao Hkun Min | Sao Hkun U |
| 27. Pangtara | Hkun San Nyo | Sao Win Kyi |
| 28. Pwela | Sao San Mya | Sao Htun Sein |
| 29. Sakoi | Sao Sein Bwint | Sao Hkun Nyunt |
| 30. Samka | Sao Hkun Kyi | Sao Hkun Kyi |
| 31. Tawngpeng | Sao Hkun Pan Sein | Sao Hkun Pan Sein |
| 32. Wanyin | Sao Hkun Yo | Sao Sein Nyunt |
| 33. Yawnghwe | Sao Shwe Thaike | Sao Shwe Thaike |
| 34. Ywangan | Sao Hla Paw | Sao Hkun Yi |

## END NOTES

*Chapter I – From Early Times*

1. Yawnghwe, Chao Tzang, The Shan of Burma, ISEAS, Singapore, 1987.
2. The Shan States, including the Karenni, in the 1890's covered 59,363 sq. miles, while England and Wales today have an area of 57,832 sq. miles.
3. Crosthwaite, Sir Charles, *The Pacification of Burma*, Frank Cass, London 1912, p. 134.
4. Wyatt, David K., *Thailand*, Yale University Press, New Haven, 1984.
5. Marshall, Andrew, *The Trouser People*, Penguin, London 2004, p. 146
6. Maung Maung, U, *Burmese Nationalist Movements 1940-1948*, Kiscadale Publications. 1989, p. 283
7. To the east the borders stretched to the Nampawn river and Mong Nai; to the west from Paunglong river, Hlaingdet and Yamethin; to the south from Mong Pai to Toungoo; and to the north, up to Myitnge river, at Namtu, Hsipaw and Mong Mit. Both Yamethin and Toungoo are well known towns on the main Rangoon to Mandalay railway line.
8. Yawnghwe, Chao Tzang, *The Shan of Burma*, ISEAS, Singapore, 1987, p. 75.
9. Mangrai, Sao Saimong, *The Shan States and the British Annexation*, Connell University, NY, 1965.
See Appendices: Appendix I
10. Scott, J. George, *Scott of the Shan Hills*, ed. Mitton, G. E., John Murray, London, 1936 p. 80.

*Chapter II – 1896-1930's*

11. Donnison, David, *Last of the Guardians*, Superscript, Newtown 2005.
12. Burma Round Table Conference, Proceedings, Govt. Printing and Stationery, Burma, 1932, p. 3.
13. Scott, J. George, *Scott of the Shan Hills*, ed. Mitton, GE, John Murray, London, 1936, p. 294.

*Chapter III – Growing up*

14. Sargent, Inge, *Twilight over Burma: My Life as a Shan Princess*, University of Hawaii Press, 1994.
15. The Green Centre for Non-Western Art, Brighton, *Burma, Frontier Photographs 1918-1935*, Merrell, London, 2000.

*Chapter V – Duties of a Saohpa*

16. Memorandum of the Federated Shan States, London, December, 1930.
17. Memorandum of the Federated Shan States, London, December, 1930.
18. Seagrave, Gordon S., *The Life of a Burma Surgeon*, Ballantine Books, New York, 1960.

*Chapter VII – Crucial Years*

19. Tucker, Selby, *Burma, The Curse of Independence*, Pluto Press, London, 2001, p. 89.
20. Burma, Statement of Policy of His Majesty's Government, May 1945, HMSO.
21. Donnison, F. S.V., *Burma*, Ernest Benn, London, 1970, p. 135.

22. Maung Maung, U, *Burmese Nationalist Movements 1940-1948*, Kiscadale, 1989.
23. Glass, Leslie, *The Changing of Kings*, Peter Owen, London, 1985, p. 205.
24. Pe Kin, *Pinlon, An Inside Story*, ed. By Guardian Press, Rangoon. Feb. 1994, p. 28.
25. Smith, Martin, *Burma*, Zed Books, London, 1999, p. 75.
26. See Appendices: Appendix V.
27. Frontier Areas Committee of Enquiry, 1947, Rangoon, Govt. Printing and Stationery, Burma, 1947.
28. Tinker, Hugh, *The Union of Burma*, OUP London, 1957.
29. Donnison, Vernon, *Burma*, Ernest Ben, London p. 136.

*Chapter VIII – A New Life*

30. Tinker, Hugh, *The Union of Burma*, Oxford University Press, Oxford, 1957, p. 47, p. 49.
31. Mead, Margaret, *Coming of Age in Samoa*, Penguin, London 1943.

*Chapter IX – Overland to Rangoon*

32. Slessor, Tim, *First Overland*, George G. Harrap & Co., London 1957.

*Chapter XI – Politics*

33. Pe Kin, *Pinlon, An Inside Story,* ed. By Guardian Press, Rangoon. Feb. 1994, p. 28.
34. Tinker, Hugh, *The Union of Burma*, Oxford University Press, London 1957, p. 161.
35. ibid p. 163.
36. See Appendices: Appendix II.
37. See Appendices: Appendix V.
38. Dommen, Arthur J., *Conflict in Laos*, Pall Mall Press, London 1964, p. 275.
39. Toye, Hugh, *Laos, Buffer State or Battleground*, OUP, London, 1968, p. 187.

*Chapter XII – Problems ahead*

40. Marshall, Andrew, *The Trouser People*, Penguin, London, 2002, p. 152.
41. See Appendices: Appendix IV.
42. Smith, Martin, *Burma*, Zed Books, London, 1999, p. 196.
43. Silverstein, Josef, *The Federal Dilemma in Burma*, Far Eastern Survey, American Institute of Pacific Relations, New York, 1959.

*Chapter XIII – End of an Era*

44. Htin Aung, Dr. *A History of Burma*, Columbia University Press, New York, 1967.
45. Taylor, Robert, *Myanmar, Beyond Politics to Societal Imperatives*, ISEAS, Singapore 2005.
46. Maung Maung, U, *Burmese Nationalist Movements 1940-1948*, Kiscadale.
47. Yawnghwe, Chao Tzang, *The Shan of Burma*, Institute of Southeast Asian Studies, Singapore 1987.
48. Smith, Martin, *Burma, Insurgency and The Politics of Ethnicity,* Zed Books, London, 1991, p. 452-3.

# GLOSSARY

All are Shan words where indicated otherwise, except for those pointed out as being in other languages.

*daw* (Burmese) – aunt or equivalent of Mrs
*gweilo* (Chinese) – foreigner
*farang* (Thai) – foreigner
*haw* – palace
*hsala* – medicine man, astrologer
*hto nau* – fermented black beans
*ingyi* (Burmese) – jacket, blouse
*inle* (Burmese) – lake small
*Intha* (Burmese) – lake dweller
*kham* – gold or golden
*kham san* – ordination ceremony
*khao lam* – glutinous rice stick
*khao neo* – glutinous rice, sticky rice
*kyat* – Burmese currency
*kyemmong* – heir apparent
*Mahadevi* (Sanskrit) – Great Goddess, senior Consort of a *Saohpa*
*mintha* (Burmese) – male dancer
*minthami* (Burmese) – female dancer
*mong* – kingdom, country, principality or state
*nang* – female, of nobility
*neua yong* – dried beef or buffalo meat
*phaso* (Burmese) – sarong for ment
*Phaung Daw U* (Bumese) – front of royal barge
*phii* – a spirit, *nat* (Burmese)
*phongyi kaung* (Burmese) – Buddhist monastery
*poy* – festival, *pwe* (Burmese)
*sai* – male
*sala* – rest house, *zayat* (Burmese)
*sanad* – a grant awarded by the British
*Sangha* (Pali) – the community of Buddhist monks
*Sao* – prince or princess
*Saohpa* – Lord of the Sky, Prince, Ruler, *Sawbwa* (Burmese)
*Saohpa Long* – Great Lord of the Sky, Great Prince
*Sao Mye Mong* – Princess Mother of the Kingdom
*Sao U Hpa* – Lord Father of the Sky
*sin* – sarong, *longyi* (Burmese)
*tang luk* – short cut
*tawmaw* – pavilion
*thakin* (Burmese) – master
*thakin-ma* (Burmese) – mistress
*thanakha* (Burmese) – bark from the tree known as *Limonia acidissima*
*U* (Burmese) – Mister, Mr
*zat* (Burmese) – theatrical performance
*zayat* (Burmese) – rest house

## SELECT BIBLIOGRAPHY

Ba Maw, *Breakthrough in Burma,* Yale University Press, New Haven & London 1968.
Bayly, Christopher & Harper, Tim, *Forgotten Armies,* Allen Lane, London, 2004.
Callahan, Mary P, *Making Enemies, War and State Building in Burma,* Cornell University Press, Ithaca, 2003.
Cochrane, Wilbur W., *The Shans,* Government Publication, Rangoon, 1910.
Collis, Maurice, *Lords of the Sunset,* Faber & Faber, London, 1938.
Collis, Maurice, *Trials in Burma,* Faber & Faber, London.
Collis, Maurice, *The Journey Outward,* Faber & Faber, London, MCMLII.
Conway, Susan, *The Shan: Culture, Art and Crafts,* River Books, Bangkok, 2006.
Crosthwaite, Charles, *The Pacification of Burma,* Frank Cass, London, 1968.
Diran, Richard K., *The Vanishing Tribes of Burma,* Weidenfeld & Nicolson, London, 1997.
Dommen, Arthur, *Conflict in Laos,* Pall Mall Press, London, 1964.
Donnison, David. *Last of the Guardians,* Superscript, Newtown, 2005.
Donnison, F. S.V., *Burma,* Ernest Benn, London, 1970.
Enriquez, C. M., *A Burmese Arcady,* Selley, London 1923.
Furnivall, J. S., *The Governance of Modern Burma,* Institute of Pacific Relations, 1960.
Glass, Leslie, *The Changing of Kings,* Peter Owen Publishers, 1985.
Hall, D. G. E., *A History of South-East Asia,* Macmillian, 1994.
Hall, H. Fielding, *The Soul of a People,* Macmillan, London, 1920.
Harvey, G. E., *Outline of Burmese History,* Orient Longmans, 1954.
Htin Aung, Maung, *A History of Burma,* Columbia University Press, New York 1967.
Leach, E. R, *Political Systems of Highland Burma,* The Athlone Press, London 1964.
Mangrai, Sao Saimong, *The Paungtaw-U Festival,* The Siam Society, Bangkok, 1980.
Mangrai, Sao Saimong, *The Shan States and the British Annexation,* Connell University, NY, 1965.
Marshall, Andrew, *The Trouser People,* Penguin, London, 2002.
Maung Maung, U, *Burmese Nationalist Movement 1940-1948,* Kiscadale Publications, 1989.
Mead, Margaret, *Coming of Age in Samoa,* Penguin, London 1943.
Milne, Leslie and Cochrane, Wilbur W., *Shans at Home,* John Murray, London, 1910.
Mitton, G. E., *Scott of the Shan Hills,* John Murray, London, 1936.
Orwell, George, *Burmese Days,* Penguin, 1944.
Sargent, Inge, *Twilight over Burma: My Life as a Shan Princess,* Univeristy of Hawaii Press, 1994.
Scott, J. George, *Scott of the Shan Hills,* ed. Mitton, G. E., John Murray, London, 1936.
Scott, J. George, *Gazetteer of Upper Burma and the Shan States.*
Scott, J. George, *Burma: A Handbook of Practical Information,* The de la More Press, London, 1921.
Scott, J. George, *British Burma Gazetteer,* Government Publication, Rangoon, 1889.
Scott O'Connor, V. C., *The Silken East,* Hutchinson, London, 1904.
Seagrave, Gordon S., *The Life of a Burma Surgeon,* Ballantine Books, New York, 1960.
Seidenfaden, Major Erik, *The Thai Peoples,* Book 1 The Siam Society, Bangkok, 1958.
Shway Yoe, *The Burman: His Life and Notions,* London, 1937.
Silverstein, Josef, *The Federal Dilemma in Burma,* Far Eastern Survey, American Institute.
    of Pacific Relations, New York, 1959.
Slessor, Tim, *First Overland,* Harrap, London, 1957.
Smith, Martin, *Burma: Insurgency and The Politics of Ethnicity,* Zed Books, London, 1999.
Steinburg, David, *Burma: The state of Myanmar,* Georgetown University, Washington DC.
Stevenson, H. N. C., *The Hill Peoples of Burma,* Longmans, 1944.
Tinker, Hugh, *The Union of Burma,* Oxford University Press, London 1957.
Townsend, Peter, *Time and Chance, An Autobiography,* Collins, London 1978.
Toye, Hugh, *Laos: Buffer State or Battleground,* Oxford University Press, London, 1968.
Tucker, Selby, *Burma: The Curse of Independence,* Pluto Press, London, 2001.
Warren, William, *Jim Thompson: The Legendary American of Thailand,* Asia Books Co. Bangkok, 1976.

Wyatt, David K., *Thailand*, Yale University Press, New Haven, 1984.
Yawnghwe, Chao Tzang, *The Shan of Burma*, ISEAS, Singapore, 1987.
Yawnghwe, Chao Tzang, *Ne Win's Tamadaw Dictatorship*, University of British Columbia, 1990.
Young, Gordon, *The Hill Tribes of Northern Thailand*, The Siam Society, Bangkok, 1974.


## OFFICIAL & OTHER PUBLICATIONS

*Burma Handbook*, Government of India Press, Simla, 1944.
*Burma Round Table Conference*, Proceedings, Govt. Printing and Stationery, Burma, 1932.
*Frontier Affairs Administration*, Stevenson, H. N. C.
*Frontier Areas Committee of Enquiry*, 1947, Rangoon, Govt. Printing and Stationery, Burma, 1947.
*Government of Burma, His Excellency The Governor's Speech at Panglong*, on 26th March 1946,
    Govt. Printing and Stationery, Burma, 1946.
*Shan States and Karenni, List of Chiefs and Leading Families*, Government of India Press, Simla, 1943.
*The Constitution of the Union of Burma*, Rangoon 1947 Govt. Printing and Stationery, Burma, 1947.
*Vietnam, Laos, Cambodia: Chronology of Events 1945-68*, BIS, Central Office of Information,
    London, 1968.
*The Burma Year-Book & Directory, 1957-58*, Student Press, Rangoon.
*Chronology of the Great War*, Greenhill Books, 1988.
*Golden Guide*, Far Eastern Economic Review, Hong Kong 1961.
The Green Centre for Non-Western Art, Brighton, *Burma: Frontier Photographs 1918-1935*,
    Merrell, London, 2000.
Institute of Southeast Asia, *Myanmar: Beyond Politics to Societal Imperatives*, ISEAS, Singapore.
*Siam Society Journal*, Relationship with Burma, Part l & Part ll, The Siam Society, Bangkok, 1959, 2 vols.

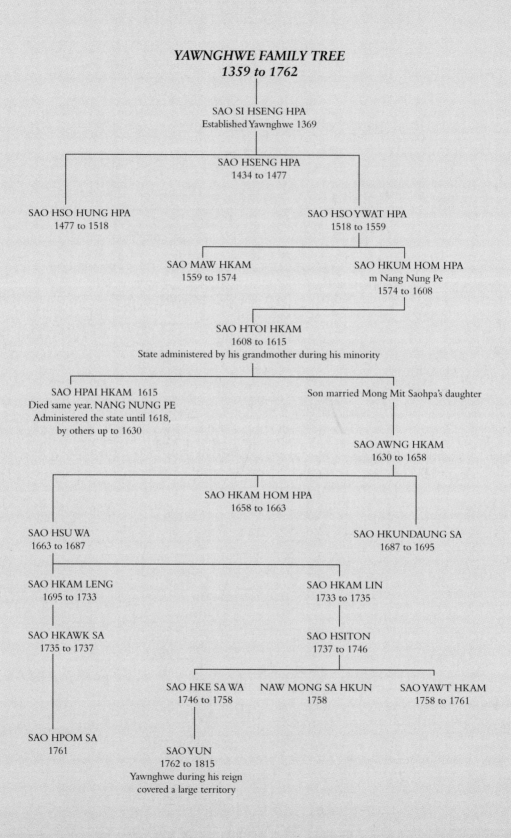

**YAWNGHWE FAMILY TREE**
*1359 to 1762*

SAO SI HSENG HPA
Established Yawnghwe 1369

SAO HSENG HPA
1434 to 1477

SAO HSO HUNG HPA
1477 to 1518

SAO HSO YWAT HPA
1518 to 1559

SAO MAW HKAM
1559 to 1574

SAO HKUM HOM HPA
m Nang Nung Pe
1574 to 1608

SAO HTOI HKAM
1608 to 1615
State administered by his grandmother during his minority

SAO HPAI HKAM  1615
Died same year. NANG NUNG PE
Administered the state until 1618,
by others up to 1630

Son married Mong Mit Saohpa's daughter

SAO AWNG HKAM
1630 to 1658

SAO HKAM HOM HPA
1658 to 1663

SAO HSU WA
1663 to 1687

SAO HKUNDAUNG SA
1687 to 1695

SAO HKAM LENG
1695 to 1733

SAO HKAM LIN
1733 to 1735

SAO HKAWK SA
1735 to 1737

SAO HSITON
1737 to 1746

SAO HKE SA WA
1746 to 1758

NAW MONG SA HKUN
1758

SAO YAWT HKAM
1758 to 1761

SAO HPOM SA
1761

SAO YUN
1762 to 1815
Yawnghwe during his reign
covered a large territory

## YAWNGHWE FAMILIY TREE
### 1762 to 1927

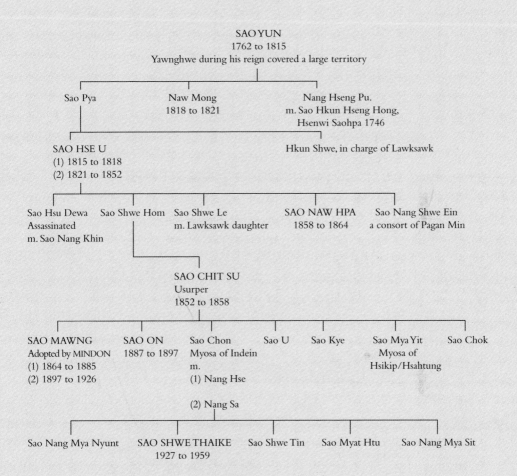

SAO YUN
1762 to 1815
Yawnghwe during his reign covered a large territory

Sao Pya          Naw Mong          Nang Hseng Pu.
                 1818 to 1821      m. Sao Hkun Hseng Hong,
                                   Hsenwi Saohpa 1746

SAO HSE U                          Hkun Shwe, in charge of Lawksawk
(1) 1815 to 1818
(2) 1821 to 1852

Sao Hsu Dewa    Sao Shwe Hom    Sao Shwe Le          SAO NAW HPA    Sao Nang Shwe Ein
Assassinated                    m. Lawksawk daughter  1858 to 1864   a consort of Pagan Min
m. Sao Nang Khin

SAO CHIT SU
Usurper
1852 to 1858

SAO MAWNG           SAO ON          Sao Chon       Sao U    Sao Kye    Sao Mya Yit    Sao Chok
Adopted by MINDON   1887 to 1897    Myosa of Indein                   Myosa of
(1) 1864 to 1885                    m.                                Hsikip/Hsahtung
(2) 1897 to 1926                    (1) Nang Hse

                                    (2) Nang Sa

Sao Nang Mya Nyunt    SAO SHWE THAIKE    Sao Shwe Tin    Sao Myat Htu    Sao Nang Mya Sit
                      1927 to 1959

## *YAWNGHWE FAMILY TREE*

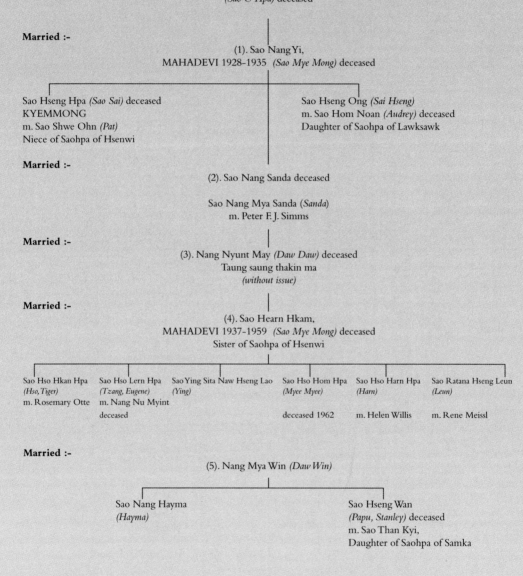

SAOHPA OF YAWNGHWE 1927-1959
SAO SHWE THAIKE 1896-1962
*(Sao U Hpa)* deceased

**Married :-**

(1). Sao Nang Yi,
MAHADEVI 1928-1935  *(Sao Mye Mong)* deceased

Sao Hseng Hpa *(Sao Sai)* deceased
KYEMMONG
m. Sao Shwe Ohn *(Pat)*
Niece of Saohpa of Hsenwi

Sao Hseng Ong *(Sai Hseng)*
m. Sao Hom Noan *(Audrey)* deceased
Daughter of Saohpa of Lawksawk

**Married :-**

(2). Sao Nang Sanda deceased

Sao Nang Mya Sanda *(Sanda)*
m. Peter F. J. Simms

**Married :-**

(3). Nang Nyunt May *(Daw Daw)* deceased
Taung saung thakin ma
*(without issue)*

**Married :-**

(4). Sao Hearn Hkam,
MAHADEVI 1937-1959  *(Sao Mye Mong)* deceased
Sister of Saohpa of Hsenwi

Sao Hso Hkan Hpa
*(Hso, Tiger)*
m. Rosemary Otte

Sao Hso Lern Hpa
*(Tzang, Eugene)*
m. Nang Nu Myint
deceased

Sao Ying Sita Naw Hseng Lao
*(Ying)*

Sao Hso Hom Hpa
*(Myee Myee)*

deceased 1962

Sao Hso Harn Hpa
*(Harn)*
m. Helen Willis

Sao Ratana Hseng Leun
*(Leun)*
m. Rene Meissl

**Married :-**

(5). Nang Mya Win *(Daw Win)*

Sao Nang Hayma
*(Hayma)*

Sao Hseng Wan
*(Papu, Stanley)* deceased
m. Sao Than Kyi,
Daughter of Saohpa of Samka

# Index

Numbers in bold refer to illustrations